The Philosophy of
Rich

A True Story About Brothers and Resurrection

Ted Courtemanche

Iterim
Publishing

Greensboro, North Carolina

THE PHILOSOPHY OF RICH

Iterim Publishing
P.O. Box 39778
Greensboro, NC 27438

This is a book of nonfiction. Some embellishments have been made by the author in describing specific details in certain scenes and events within the book, but the stories themselves are based on actual occurrences. Several names were invented in cases where the original name was unknown or forgotten by the author. Some names have been changed to protect the identities of individuals, businesses and institutions involved herein.

ISBN-13: 978-0-9798942-9-9
ISBN-10: 0-9798942-9-8

First Iterim Publishing Edition 2007

Printed in the United States of America

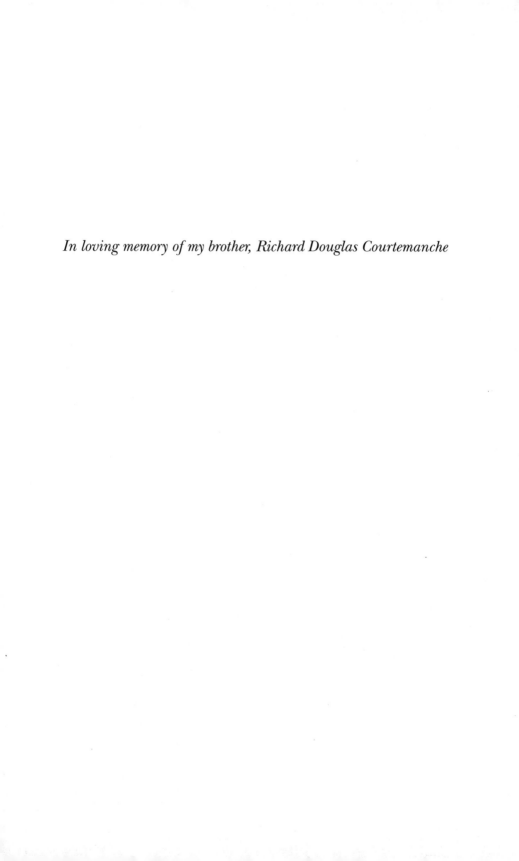

In loving memory of my brother, Richard Douglas Courtemanche

❧ CONTENTS ❧

❧ AUTHOR'S NOTE ❧

As soon as Rich's funeral service was over in November of 2005, I started writing *The Philosophy of Rich*. Each time I wrote, I healed a little bit. I had no idea what the book would be like when I began. My goal was simple: I wanted everyone to know my brother, Rich, as I'd known him.

In a funny way, stories aren't so much created as discovered, emerging from wherever they do onto the temporary permanence of the printed page. In the early stages, the stories that made me feel best were the ones that made me laugh: Rich delivering gifts in a rented black Cadillac to his godchildren, getting stuck in a stairwell before a job interview or being hauled against his will to a country music festival by Mom and Dad.

As the book started to crawl, I added in philosophy. I wasn't looking to make sense of Rich's death but rather for a way to accept it. Bertrand Russell wrote, "To teach how to live without certainty, and yet without being paralyzed by hesitation, is perhaps the chief thing that philosophy, in our age, can still do for those who study it." Philosophical writing can be hard to crack—it's in the "aha" behind the words that the solace lies. I wanted to put into everyday language the concepts that helped me most.

From philosophy, I moved on to science and theology. I was searching. What does science have to say about death? What does religion have to say about death? Once you get past the dogma, is there any underlying consensus on what happens after we die? Each question I asked brought more questions.

The information started to pile up. To help keep track of different subjects and ideas within the book, I separated what I was writing into two basic sections. In one area, I had stories about Rich. In another, I had facts—philosophy facts, science facts, history facts. The divisions began to show signs of permanence. As they did, I realized it was time to make a change. I didn't want to write a book that read like a novel in one place and a textbook in another. Before there was written history, people learned through oral storytelling. I gathered pieces from the story side and pieces from the fact side and started fitting them together. The idea was to allow philosophy and science to breathe, to keep them connected to the scenery that gives them life in the first place.

Rich had bipolar disorder. I wish I'd learned more about it while he was here in his physical form. This book offers some of what I found out about mental illness, particularly bipolar disorder and major depression. What are the signs? What are the triggers? What are the standard treatments? Are the treatments the same from culture to culture? Rich died from suicide. I wrestle with the topic. I wrestle with how it is designated a mortal sin. I go to the sources, to the people who initiated the designation from the start. Beliefs don't have to rest on truth—most recipes don't even call for it.

Does life simply not matter for people who complete suicide? Research indicates the truth couldn't be further removed. For Rich, all of it mattered—that was the paradox. He was right there on the front lines, engulfed in it, and couldn't back away. Aristotle said the purpose of tragedy as art is to purge hurtful emotions. The final two months of Rich's life were tragic, filled with sensationalism beyond the realm of fiction. They weren't easy to write about, nor do I think they will make easy reading. Getting it out in the open, seeing the chaos from different perspectives, helped me process my grief.

As I wrote, one question kept nagging me: What was I missing when I missed Rich? It seemed so obvious at first—I was missing *Rich*, of course. Sometimes what seems obvious turns out to be anything but. As I kept mulling the question over, Rich began to take on an elusive quality. I couldn't wrap my mind around what exactly I was missing. What in Rich survived the changes that time inevitably wrought on him, the changes as he progressed from child to teenager to adult? Descartes, Hume, Kant—they all pondered the same basic question, prodding it from different angles. Until you engage them, the force of some questions stays hidden, and so it is with this one.

Once I compiled somewhere around four hundred pages of material, I left my job—I pulled a Rich. I set up a little office in the room above the garage and sat down to type every morning. I've never looked forward to work as much. I cobbled the book together, sometimes in spurts but mostly in gradual increments. Writing a book is a lot like pottery: First you get the shape, and then you add the details.

If I had to boil down the book into neat categories, I'd say there are four storylines that ultimately lead to the same center. One is about the last two months of Rich's life, particularly the chaos surrounding his final day. Another follows Rich's career as a futures trader, sometimes making or losing $300,000 in an afternoon. The third lightens the book. It's about Courtemanche family vacations: bee stings in Maine, monsoon fishing in Massachusetts and all the times we left our structured world behind. And the fourth storyline is an inquiry into what people miss when someone dies. Supported by work from philosophy of mind as well as from the latest research in cognitive neuroscience, the fourth is more of a winding river.

Life didn't happen to Rich: He took it on. He was the complete package, saint and sinner—just the way Jung described it. I've gotten to know Rich in a new way by tapping out words here at my desk. I get the feeling he's smiling within these pages as he always could.

Rich and I liked listening to ocean waves. One follows another in a symphony of here-then-gone, here-then-gone. From life comes death and from death, life. May reading *The Philosophy of Rich* bring you the same renewal that writing it has brought me.

Ted Courtemanche
August 2007

THE PHILOSOPHY OF RICH

❧ CHAPTER ONE ❧

And slow howe'er my marches be
I shall at last sit down by thee.
—Henry King

RICH'S OBITUARY

Rich was my only brother, two years younger than me. I've changed a few names and omitted addresses, but other than that, his obituary is presented intact.

AUSTIN, TX – Richard Douglas Courtemanche, 36, died on November 5, 2005, of a gunshot wound, self-inflicted at the Barton Creek greenbelt in Austin, Texas. He was the beloved son of Betty Courtemanche and Bob Courtemanche.

Richard was larger than life, fatally flawed and could light up a room with his smile. He received an MBA from the Sloan School of Management at MIT, a BA from Babson College, and prior to that, served in the United States Marine Corps, earning an honorable discharge.

He worked primarily in the investment business, beginning at Putnam Investments in Boston, later at the Anlage Bank in London and finally as a self-employed futures trader. During his short life, Richard lived in Boston, Sicily, Okinawa, London, San Diego and Austin. Austin, he said, was the place he could be himself.

He was a masterful storyteller and one of those rare individuals people gravitate toward. He had bipolar disorder and alcoholism. His family will always remember him for the joy, comfort and solace he could bring to others despite his own excruciating inner turmoil.

Richard loved nature, his dogs, solving a problem and laughing with friends. He was surrounded by family and love when his life-support system was disconnected in the intensive care unit, and he passed.

Richard is survived by his loving parents; his brother, Ted Courtemanche, and Ted's wife, Deana; his fiancée, Sharon Masuda; his uncle, Edward Zaleckas, Jr.; and his boxers, Daisy and Zack, who will live with his mother.

There will be visiting hours on Saturday, November 12 from 4:00–5:00 pm at the John Stone and Sons Funeral Home. A service will immediately follow at 5:00 pm.

The funeral home director didn't think the newspapers would print an obituary with phrases like "self-inflicted" and "gunshot wound." They prefer "passed unexpectedly." Mom, Dad and I were adamant. We paid to have it published. It is what it is; Rich died from suicide—no need to hide from the fact.

The Austin papers and TV stations covered the story. It was headline news. I don't want to get into it—the SWAT team, the negotiations, the phone calls, the hospital—not yet. Looking back, it shouldn't have been a surprise how crazy it got.

The best I can say right now is that when you look at Rich's life from a different angle, the way he died is really just a small part of the story.

FAMILY TRIPS AND COUNTRY MUSIC

Rich and I were twelve and fourteen, respectively, trying to enjoy our 1982 summer vacation from school. We'd been dreading this day, Saturday, all week. We lived in eastern Massachusetts, and Mom had found a country music festival in the western part of the state that sounded like fun to her. Mom required that the Courtemanches go on one family outing each month.

"Come on, boys. Time to go," Mom said.

"Where is this thing?" either Rich or I asked—individual identity not important because Rich spoke for me on the concert issue, and in case he missed anything, I spoke for him, too.

"It's in Lenox," Mom answered.

"How far is that?"

"About an hour and a half."

"An hour and a half?"

"Yes, an hour and a half. We won't have forever to take trips together. As long as you're in this house, we're going to enjoy family trips."

"Mom, an hour and a half? We don't even like country music."

"You'll survive. This is what we do as a family."

"Mom, we eat dinner together every night. We see each other every day. Why do we have to go two hours to Lenox to hear a concert that none of us likes?"

"It's not just a concert. It's a spring festival. You don't know if you'll like it or not. You've never been to a festival."

"Come on, Mom! We're driving two and a half hours to go to a country music concert? We're too old for this."

"It's an hour and a half, Richard and Theodore. And you're never too old to enjoy time with the family, *never*."

"God, Mom. God."

Dad was silent as Rich and I ranted. Mom wasn't changing her mind; we knew that. Mom dug in her heels on some issues, and this was one of them. What we were hoping is that even though our logic was addressed to Mom, Dad would be the one to *hear* it—and hearing it, he'd grant us a last-second reprieve.

"Richard and Theodore," Dad finally said, "enough. We're going to the concert." With no other option, Rich and I took our positions in the backseat of the Volkswagen Rabbit. We were stuck.

About half an hour outside our hometown of Sherborn, Massachusetts, Mom started in with comments like, "Look, boys, the scenery is different as you get into the western part of the state," and "It's certainly turning into a beautiful day." After each one, Rich and I looked at each other and rolled our eyes. Here we were driving out to Lenox on a Saturday to see a country music concert with our parents—it was outrageous.

It's not all one fluid scene in my memory; I see snippets. We go by small farms. We see short trees with lots of branches, probably fruit trees, but Rich and I don't recognize them as such—they're just trees to us. It's in an orange haze; I guess that's the film that develops over old memories. There's tall grass in fields. A breeze is nudging leaves on the side of the road. When I look through the back window, the leaves gently explode into the air and float back to the ground.

When Rich isn't looking out the window, he's fidgeting. He's kicking his feet on the floor mats. He's playing with the zipper on his sweatshirt. Every once in a while, I smack him and he punches me back.

"How much longer?" Rich and I asked occasionally. If timed out long enough, we'd get something like, "About forty-five minutes" or "About thirty minutes, boys." If asked too close together, we wouldn't get a response from the front seat.

Shortly after a "fifteen minutes" update, a group of Harley-Davidsons drove by us in the opposite direction. The bikes were about as big as the Rabbit, and the car seats vibrated from the roar of the engines. The relationship between Dad and minibikes in the neighborhood at home was strained. The problem with minibikes for Dad was twofold. First, they were noisy—the kids riding them tended to buzz by our house late at night, when they should have been home instead. Second, and more infuriating, riders used to cut across part of our lawn (our house was on a corner lot). If the lawn was wet, the minibike tires made gashes in it—long, narrow puddles with clusters of uprooted grass blades floating on top.

We'd lived in Sherborn ever since I was four. Over the years, neighbors had occasionally spotted Dad as he jumped out from concealed positions in the brush and trees on the edge of our property. His target? Minibikes. By staying hidden, he could first catch and next reprimand riders cutting across our lawn. Today, I applaud Dad for his vigilance. I almost tried a similar approach when I found empty beer bottles in my backyard last summer: You have to be crafty to have a realistic shot of catching the little bandits in the act. Back in Sherborn, though, I wasn't so sure; cutting across the Courtemanche lawn in the late 1970s became a badge of courage among the neighborhood minibikers.

On the ride out to Lenox, I didn't like the feel of the Harley riders going by; their motorcycles were really just dinosaur-sized versions of minibikes. Dad tensed his jaw a bit and kept driving.

When I look at pictures of Rich and me from our early teen years, I can hardly recognize us. Our bony knees, mine in particular, stick out from our shorts. Short-sleeved shirts are too short or too long. If we're in long-sleeved shirts, they've almost always got a T-shirt underneath to add bulk to our limbs, themselves outgrowing the rest of our bodies. Our hair, which we battled to keep long—Dad preferred "off the ears" haircuts—is somewhere between half-way and almost all the way over our ears. It's as if we're using our hair to desperately cover the rest of us.

Once we got to the festival, we parked in a field—the only option available. The field was filled with pickup trucks, people wearing cowboy boots and cowboy hats, and more bikers. Harley engines were popping and gurgling from different sections of the makeshift lot. We exited the Rabbit silently and headed to the entrance.

The image I remember most clearly is that of a music stage, surrounded by trees, one big tree in particular, and a sparsely populated grandstand. I also recall seeing beer cans, cigarettes and men with hair much longer than Rich's and mine. Rich and I stuck close together, attempting to distance ourselves from Mom and Dad. We stayed at the festival for about thirty minutes.

No complaining was needed on the ride home. If Rich and I thought the family didn't fit in with the festival crowd, Dad felt it more strongly. Shortly after we left the parking lot, the issue of future family trips was opened for discussion. Mom gave in; the country music festival was the last family trip we were ever required to go on.

When he died, Rich owned two motorcycles, including a Harley-Davidson. He told me he sometimes gunned the engine in the neighborhood where he'd lived in Del Mar, California. Mom used to have a picture of his Harley hanging on a corkboard by her refrigerator. Rich purchased the bike with earnings from his trading and money the family had loaned to him. He also owned a black pickup truck with tires so big that you needed to climb up to get into the cab. Free of the confines of childhood, Rich fit in well with just about any crowd. He wouldn't mix well at a Gatsby summer party, but with Gatsby himself? Good friends.

AFTER THE WEDDING

Hey, everyone, shut up and get over here, I was thinking. My brother is talking.

Deana and I got married in August of 2005. About a month before the wedding, I asked Rich if he'd do the traditional best-man toast. Deana and I weren't having groomsmen or bridesmaids, and I'm not a detail person, so the toast slipped through the cracks. Rich emailed back, "i would be honored to give a toast. thanks."

I said I'm not a detail person; I'm not a micromanager either. Rich and I exchanged emails in the month before the wedding. We covered topics such as when he was going to be arriving, what he should wear, where he should stay—tactical issues. We didn't talk about the toast.

The Friday before the wedding, Rich and Sharon flew into Greensboro, North Carolina, where Deana and I lived. That same night, Deana and I had a wedding rehearsal. We were getting married on the roof of the Kress Terrace building in downtown Greensboro. Built in the 1930s, the building has an art deco feel to it. From the top, you can see all of Greensboro. What we liked most about the space is that half is inside and half is outside. We were having the ceremony on the outside space, but if it rained, we could all move inside.

There wasn't much to rehearse. I was going to seat the mothers; I'd get some friends to seat everyone else. Deana would walk down the aisle with her dad, and we'd get married. Then we'd walk back down the aisle in the other direction, and the party would start.

As I was waiting for the rehearsal to get going, I noticed that at 6:00 pm it was hot and sunny on the roof. That meant two problems: I'd be sweating during the ceremony—making things uncomfortable most of the night—plus, the sun would be in my eyes as Deana and I looked at the pastor. It was too late to get an awning, and I wasn't about to ask that the wedding ceremony be moved inside for my personal comfort. I hoped for clouds.

Right after the rehearsal, everyone went over to Natty Greene's, where Deana and I had rented a private room on the third floor for a combination rehearsal dinner and pre-wedding party. We were expecting about sixty guests. It was the first time our parents had met, the first time our two groups of friends had met and the first time either one of us had been married: We were ready for a few drinks.

Rich and Sharon arrived right after I'd gotten my first plate of food. Most of the guests were there by that time. He was wearing a white cotton shirt—the kind you might see someone wearing on vacation, with short sleeves, marbleized buttons and patterned fabric. He also wore jeans, sandals and a matching tan. You couldn't miss him. He was the biggest guy in the place.

I was caught up talking with someone when he first arrived. It had been ten years since I'd seen some of the people at the party. It took me a while to get over and see Rich. When I did, I shook his hand, and we hugged.

I forget who told me that Rich hadn't written the toast yet. A short list of suspects: Mom or Rich himself. Under more normal circumstances, I would have been concerned. Not finished yet? Come on. That was the Rich who would take the last piece of meat without asking if anyone else wanted it, who'd drink the last drop of milk, who thought about one guy and one guy only: Richard Douglas Courtemanche.

On this night, having had a few drinks and surrounded by friends, I wasn't bothered. The Rich who showed up for the rehearsal dinner was the Rich everyone wanted to be near. The Rich who got asked for autographs when he went to Las Vegas because he looked like he had to be famous. The charming Rich who made you a better person simply because you were standing next to him.

The space where we had the rehearsal dinner was like a gigantic game room in a log cabin, with leather couches, TVs, a long picnic table, dartboards and a pool table. Rich and I shot a game of pool. To describe Rich as "competitive" wouldn't be nearly strong enough. With Rich, Ping-Pong could turn into a workout. One time when Rich went to his friend Matt's house for Christmas, he and Matt stayed up half the night playing with the kids' games. The two of them cleared out the living room for a miniature golf match, and they were the only two who played—Matt's kids watched from the couch. On the rehearsal night, Rich and I didn't have much interest in who won the pool game. The outcome just didn't seem important.

Some memories are more vivid, more poignant than others. "Rich, want anything to drink?" I asked.

"Sure, what are you getting?"

"Bookers," I said.

"Yeah, sounds good."

I sat at the bar and ordered the bourbons. Around me, the party was at the point right before it tips and starts to slow down. Rich left his conversation with Sharon, Mom and a half-dozen others by the vegetable and pretzel trays. He sat to my right. From where we were seated, we could see other buildings across the street through the oversized wooden windows. Greensboro is a small city with quite a few refurbished brick buildings like the one we were in that night. The ceiling in the room was high and had lamps hanging down from powder-black fixtures. The wall behind the bar was brick, with bottles of alcohol lining the shelves. Around us, people were talking, shooting pool, playing darts—they were moving around and standing still. The whole scene was mixing together. The only person I saw in focus was Rich.

The memory that sticks is more of a feeling. What is it? It's the same feeling I'd get when we were little and slept in the same bed: total comfort. With Rich, I was part of something bigger than me, and the feeling has a certain lightness about it. I wasn't aware of anything but the flowing oneness of it all. The warmth of the bourbon kept the edges soft and undefined.

During the first part of the wedding the next day, Rich was on his best behavior. We have pictures of him laughing and posing with my friends. There's one of Rich, Sharon, Deana and me all smiling like the moment will last forever. The wedding started at 7:00 pm.

Earlier in the day, some of the relatives brought their pit bull to see Deana and me. They'd arrived at their hotel room the night before with their dog in a luggage bag (the hotel didn't allow pets). When the room needed to be cleaned, they decided to bring the dog to the house. I'd been out looking for handkerchiefs, just in case it was hot and sunny at the ceremony, and arrived home to a group of people walking out the front door. They had a pit bull in tow—short one tooth, I'd later learn, after fighting with Rocky, our dog. After introducing herself, Deana's cousin told me, "Deana's inside crying; there was just a fight." At the time, I had no idea it was a dog fight. When I told Rich about it on his cell phone, he did one of his high-pitched chuckles.

Deana and I lucked out at the wedding. It was cloudy and cool while we said our vows, and then the clouds broke up and went away. After Deana and I finished the first dance (prepared for diligently with six dancing lessons), there were the usual father-daughter, mother-son dances. The whole thing went by so fast. Deana and I had just gotten our first drinks as a married couple, cosmopolitans served from tabletop fountains filled with the drink, when Rich tapped on the microphone.

When he starts speaking, he's standing where the band is going to play, in a blue shirt and gold tie. Deana and I stand right before him. Even though most people are talking and drinking next to the bar or by the doors that lead to the inside area, Rich keeps going—classic Rich. He doesn't care if people are ready or not, if they're listening or not; he started his talk, and he's going to finish. It bothers me for a second that people aren't paying attention, but as word spreads that he's speaking, a swell moves closer to him. By the time he's through, he is the only one saying a word.

I had a lump in my throat when he was done. I know me saying his toast was great is like new parents showing you their kid's picture. I wasn't the only one, though. People came up to me, one by one, to say how good the toast was. From the speech, you could tell he could have been a public speaker. When things were going well with his investment trading, Rich would tell me he was thinking about teaching some of his techniques at a local college. Would it have happened—the teaching? Maybe, maybe not, but he had it in him.

The essence of the wedding toast was this: Rich said he was known as Ted's brother when he was growing up, and as he was reacquainted with old friends and introduced to new ones at the wedding, he was again proud to be known as Ted's brother. He had created the speech in his hotel room earlier in the day. The irony is that I thought about myself as Rich's brother. He was a guy who said "screw it" to convention and followed his heart. He'd lived all over the world. I was in awe of the way he could do his own thing no matter the consequences, no matter what anyone else thought.

Once the reception really got going, I jumped from person to person. It's not like I didn't talk to Rich, but the conversations I had with him were short ones—maybe pose for a picture here, enjoy a toast there. Somewhere around 11:00 pm, as the band packed up to leave, I sat down next to Rich. He was sitting on a folding table where the bar had been. He was trashed; he was swaying and couldn't hold his drink straight, spilling it all over his tie. Before the bartenders left, he'd convinced them to leave him a 1.75 liter bottle of rum. He made me a rum and Coke, and it was almost pure rum. You had to be as drunk as Rich was to be able to communicate at that stage. The only reason I felt okay leaving him at the end of the night was that he was with Mom, Dad and Sharon.

The next day, around lunchtime, Rich arrived at the house with my parents and Sharon. "T," he said, "my head is killing me. Got any beer?" He started to perk up a little after the first one. Sharon told everyone how he'd ordered three pizzas from their room when they got in after the wedding.

"Richard was sleeping before the first pizza arrived," she said. Everyone laughed.

Rich drank a few more beers and sat at the kitchen table with his back to the outside. He patted Rocky and Jack, our dogs, and talked with the relatives. After an hour, he went upstairs and took a nap with Sharon. He looked a lot better when he headed to the airport for the flight back to Austin.

After Deana and I got back from our honeymoon, Rich sent me the following email:

From: Richard Courtemanche
Sent: Wednesday, September 14, 2005
To: Ted Courtemanche
Subject:

i went to your wedding with the idea that i would commit suicide the day i came back because i knew my life would never see a day as happy as i was the day you got married. and its true. it was the happiest day of my life. and i came home and have cut myself relentlessly every day since. i dont understand myself T. but you gave me the most wonderful day i will ever know.

mom and dad are lost about me. i am too. i dont think i will make it much longer T. i have scars all over my body and i am tired.

your brother, Richard

It wasn't the first time I'd gotten an email like that. I hadn't seen one in a while, but it was not new. In the past two years, Rich had started sending out group emails to Mom, Dad and me. A lot of times, they'd have really depressing updates on how he was doing. Hours before this latest email, he'd sent me a happy birthday email. It was belated because he'd forgotten my birthday, which was the day before.

That's the way Rich's depressions went. They'd come out of the blue and hit hard. Then, like any wave, they'd recede. The question now was how long his latest depression would last.

A Primer on Bipolar Disorder

Bipolar literally means "two poles." On one end is a high, the mania; on the other is a low, the depression. Rich would tell me, "T, no one understands what I've done; no one can help." According to the National Institute of Mental Health (NIMH), "Children with mania are more likely to be irritable and prone to destructive tantrums."

One of my earliest memories is cranking a swing that rocked baby Rich back and forth in the kitchen. The kitchen seems cramped; it's wintertime, and the scene is close to black and white. My image of myself and Rich is influenced by pictures I've seen of us when we were small. If I stop cranking the swing, if I turn it too fast or too slow, and sometimes for no reason at all, he cries.

Rich cried uncontrollably in traffic jams as a kid. At the first sign, even just a few cars lining up at a red light, Rich would start to suffer. I can see his face, completely red, nose creased at the bridge, eyes projecting terror and tears flowing uncontrollably. Some experts believe that the tantrums of children with bipolar disorder are caused by seizures occurring deep inside the brain.

It's not unusual for someone with bipolar disorder to think he or she is untreatable. According to the NIMH, "Often people with bipolar disorder do not realize how impaired they are, or they blame their problems on some cause other than mental illness." Rich knew he had problems but didn't think he was treatable. He refused to stay on medication because it blunted his senses. Among other addictions, Rich was addicted to adrenaline—to the highs he got from his investment trading. He could make thousands of dollars in the course of a few minutes. When he was on medication, he couldn't feel the rush.

I sometimes see bipolar disorder in terms of switches and levees. When most people get slighted or have a bad thought, they can manage it. The bad thought might pop through one levee and perhaps another before the switch is flipped and they catch and stop it. Their spirits pick up, and they realize at some level that the negative thought was just that: a negative thought.

A person with bipolar disorder has faulty levees and switches. A negative thought sinks to the lowest possible level. In his last year or two, Rich got into the habit of apologizing for being a bad brother when we spoke, not all the time but enough to be noticeable. He'd say it during his depressions, usually after recounting something he was ashamed of doing—which with the levee system Rich had, could be just about anything. It's as if he preferred to think of himself in a bad light, somehow craving the abuse he gave himself.

I always expected the situation to improve. Rich would call me, drunk out of his mind, telling me he was useless. "No, you're not," I would tell him. "You have everything going for you." I thought it would make him feel good, but a person with bipolar disorder in the middle of a depression doesn't see it that way. Rich took a comment like that as more evidence that he was useless. He would think, "I have everything going for me, yet I'm no good." It's like the positive comment slipped through a levee, going down a channel it wasn't supposed to go through, wasn't even intended for, and came out as another put-down, another weight sinking him into self-loathing and depression.

It's not just the person with bipolar disorder who suffers. After Rich's obituary ran, people would call or write, telling me they had a family member with major depression or bipolar disorder. One friend wrote about depression turning a "vibrant young man into a recluse."

After Rich's service, a guy who worked at the funeral home pulled Mom aside. He was a big, rugged guy, the kind of guy who at least from the outside looked like the world couldn't touch him. He told Mom he had a brother with bipolar disorder. His brother would call his mother and him, telling them he was going to commit suicide in some awful way. As he talked to Mom, tears started welling up in his eyes. He'd asked his brother not to burden his mother with the phone calls anymore. She was seventy-two and just couldn't take it anymore.

By almost all accounts, depression and bipolar disorder are growing health concerns. It sounds odd to lead the last sentence with "By almost all accounts," but it's a challenge to understand if a disease or health problem really is a growing problem or not. Health care data are notoriously difficult to work with, and any time data are interpreted, not everyone is going to agree.

One indicator of the problem depression poses has been generated by the Global Burden of Disease project. The project is financed by the World Health Organization and is intended to provide bias-free (or as close as it can get) insight into world health issues. In 2002, unipolar depressive disorders (major depressions) were the third leading cause of disability in the world. The two leading causes were lower respiratory infections and HIV/AIDS. Bipolar disorder was the number thirty-two cause of disability. By 2030, unipolar depressive disorders are expected to be the second leading cause of disability, after HIV/AIDS. Bipolar disorder is expected to jump seven places to number twenty-five—ahead of falls, wars, fires and breast cancer.

Rich's friend Matt said at the service, "If Richard had died from cancer, we wouldn't be sitting here wondering why. Bipolar disorder is a disease; that's what killed him." It's a disease that includes many accompanying addictions. According to the NIMH, "Bipolar disorder may appear to be a problem other than mental illness—for instance, alcohol or drug abuse. . . . Such problems in fact may be signs of an underlying mood disorder." In this sense, addictions to alcohol, drugs, adrenaline, gambling, sex and a host of others are co-morbidities that make the consequences of the underlying disorder that much more disabling. The addictions, if you will, allow the bipolar disorder to fully blossom, to manifest itself as wholly and inextricably in the person as it can.

It's like cancer taking over a host cell and, gathering steam, overcoming other cells until there's no turning back—that person is going to die from cancer. But with bipolar disorder, the person can look completely normal. The lack of outward, physical manifestations is one of the many insidious features of psychiatric disorders. Our society typically isn't very tolerant of a problem we can't put our finger on, can't say, "My God, he looks sick."

"Just pull yourself together" is a comment I sometimes hear in reference to people with depression, as if battling depression is simply a matter of willpower. The fact is that a person with depression cannot just start thinking positive thoughts. The hallmarks of depression are guilt and negative thoughts.

Paul Ekman, an authority on the subject of emotion, wrote in *Emotions Revealed*, "People who are depressed not only feel helpless to change their lives, they feel hopeless. They do not believe it will ever get better." The brain structure of people with a predisposition to depression emphasizes the bad. That's how it is. They basically suffer excruciating agony in obscurity—thoughts racing around in their heads, breaking through levees they were never intended to go through, solidifying for them that they are people with no value to themselves, to society, to anyone or anything.

Bipolar disorder combines the worst of depression with varying forms of mania, swinging the individual from one extreme to another. The tragic consequence of all that agony is that people with bipolar disorder die from suicide at significantly higher rates than the general population. If substance abuse problems like alcoholism are added to bipolar disorder, the risk for suicide grows. The potential for suicide is greatest in those individuals who have bipolar disorder, substance abuse issues and *no consistent treatment plan*—who, in effect, rely on "pulling themselves together."

WHAT'S IN THE TRUNK?

As low as Rich could go in his moods, he'd circle back to the other extreme. You wanted to be around him when he did.

One time in the middle of July (I'm guessing the year was 1994), Rich decided his godchildren needed squirt guns; he was the godfather to all three of Matt's boys. He drove over to Matt's house in his black Mustang and revved the engine once he got there. Matt and his three boys came marching out. After Rich distributed the squirt guns, the boys ran inside with them. As soon as the kitchen door closed, it opened again. Three redheaded commandos tore down the steps, and in a matter of seconds, Rich was soaked.

The next year, around the same time, a car pulled into Matt's driveway. It was a black Cadillac, and no one in Matt's family knew anyone who owned a black Caddy. No one could see through the windshield or the windows because they were tinted, and the sun was glaring off them. Matt saw the car and walked out the front door, cautiously. His wife and three boys stayed inside and watched from the kitchen window.

Loud music was blaring from the car. As Matt slowly approached the window on the driver's side, Rich purposefully stayed inside for a little while. When he stepped out, he was dressed in black jeans, a black T-shirt, black boots and black sunglasses. He stretched his 6'3", 220-pound frame and closed the door of the Cadillac he'd rented specially for the occasion. The boys quickly filed out the kitchen door. Rich presented an empty pump squirt gun to each of them, like the year before.

"Hold on," he said, and they waited before filling them.

He went back to the trunk, moving slowly, a kind of strut he sometimes did. The kids expected good things, so they followed him closely. When Rich popped the trunk, the boys' eyes got bigger. From it, he pulled the bazooka of squirt guns—a monster you could use to wash a car. It was fully loaded, and there was only one. Brian, Matt's oldest, was the first to start running when he realized what was about to happen. It made no difference. Unarmed, all three boys got soaked.

If you were a kid, you'd want Rich as your godfather. He visited Matt's boys only when he was feeling good. Brian cried uncontrollably at Rich's service. To him, Rich always seemed so happy: Why would he want to die? It just didn't make sense that Rich wouldn't be around anymore.

Nietzsche wrote, "What is great in man is that he is a bridge and not an end." Brian and his brothers got the best of Rich—but they only saw part of the bridge. It's the same for all of us. We experience only parts of other bridges, parts of our own, moving from wherever we are to wherever we're going. Maybe someday when he's ready, Brian will read through these pages and meet more of Rich. Clouds don't ruin a sunset; as long as there's some blue sky, they expand the radiance.

GARBAGE, TRASH AND GO-CARTS

Rich and I mowed lawns, fed dogs, raked yards, shoveled snow and did other odd jobs when we were growing up. Our standard daily chores came down to two: Rich took out the garbage (which included anything you could put into a compost pile), and I took out the trash.

On most nights, you could hear either Rich or me mumbling about the crappiness of it all as we took care of our assigned duties. Rich grew to be a huge fan of the garbage disposal. Into it he'd drop bananas, coffee grounds, chicken bones and anything else that might otherwise find its way into a small plastic garbage bag.

We both liked going to the dump. In Sherborn, you could drive your trash over to the town dump if you missed trash day. The dump almost guaranteed excitement. As soon as you went through the gates, you'd see fire burning on top of a mound of trash. In another area, there might be a bulldozer pushing trash from one place to the next. No one could get Rich out of the dump if the bulldozer was going. As if fire and a bulldozer weren't enough, there were also pigs. They ate garbage in the pig area. The only thing that kept Rich from forcing all the garbage secretly down the disposal is that the pigs might not get enough food.

The town dump was a great place to look for parts—maybe if you were building a go-cart or something like that. The dump manager tried to keep things structured. Old furniture was kept in one area, pure trash in another, old machinery in still another. Rich and I could march around the dump, test out something that looked like it might be useful for a project, and if it wasn't, we could throw it as far up onto the pile as we liked and not get in any trouble at all.

Even though different kinds of trash might *look* different, much of that trash is made from the same basic stuff. For example, in any dump, you might see a milk carton made from cardboard sitting next to a discarded shoebox also made of cardboard. There is lots of plastic in dumps: cups, plates, toys. If you surveyed the dump back in Sherborn, you might have seen an old lawnmower made of metal, rubber and plastic next to a discarded rake made of metal and wood. If circumstances had been a little different, some of the metal that was in the lawnmower might have instead been in the tongs of the rake. That the materials constituting the lawnmower or rake somehow found their way into one or the other involved chance. In a way, it came down to being in the right place at the right time.

Rich and I couldn't abate the steady flow of trash and garbage in the Courtemanche house. We might not know exactly what individual items would be in the trash or garbage, but we could be sure that, in the aggregate, there would be a bag of trash and a bag of garbage waiting to be removed from the house each night.

Like the metal that could go into either a lawnmower or a rake, the particles that make up human beings are not distinct to human beings. Within each of us, there are oxygen, carbon, hydrogen, nitrogen, calcium, phosphorus and lots of other elements and compounds. Oxygen is not unique to humans. Carbon is not unique to humans. Hydrogen and nitrogen? Not unique to humans. There is not a single chemical element in humans that is unique to us. We're made from the same stuff that countless other organic and inorganic things are made from.

When we're born, we're like a thought that arises from nowhere. At an early stage, we're simply two cells combined into one. Through some divine or mechanical process, that cell initiates a progression of cell division and generation that, with some luck, leads to us. Practically speaking, Rich's dividing cells took whatever chemicals were available and built him, adding on and adding on. He continued to evolve, never exactly the same group of cells from one moment to the next. In a very real sense, he, like all of us, was made from scraps.

I mentioned a go-cart a little earlier. The go-cart was one of greatest projects Rich and I worked on in our early years. We took wood that was stored in the basement, rope that was tucked away in the corner of the garage, nails from the workbench, screws from the same workbench and—critically—tires and axles from a baby carriage at the dump. We hammered and drilled and assembled the parts until we had a go-cart. The steering system didn't work out exactly as we planned; we'd pictured a carlike steering wheel, possibly made from another tire at the dump. We abandoned the steering wheel for a simple rope.

We had big plans for the go-cart. Eventually, we were going to add an engine. How the engine would drive the rear axle was something neither of us had figured out, but finding a working lawnmower engine at the dump remained high on our priority list.

Once the go-cart was done, we took test runs in the driveway by pushing each other in it. With the steering system less than 100 percent reliable, we decided to add a brake. We sawed a piece of wood, drilled a hole in it and then attached it with a screw to the side of the seat. From the seat, we could pull back on the piece of wood, it would press against the tire, and voilà, the tire would stop—a working brake.

Rich was the driver on the go-cart's inaugural run down the hill on McGregor Drive. Four or five other neighborhood kids also brought their newly built racers. The way we'd planned it, everyone would introduce their carts at the same time. The route started at the top of the hill where we waited for the bus on school days. Rich took off, along with a few other kids, as the rest of us howled about the excitement of it all. About halfway down the hill, the steering system in our cart failed, or Rich didn't use it right, and the go-cart turned into the

Fitzgeralds' lawn. Once on the lawn, it rolled once or twice; Rich fell out, and then the go-cart came to a stop. Rich had grass stains all over his T-shirt and shorts, and his knee and elbow were bleeding a little. I ran down to the crash site and retrieved both Rich and the go-cart.

At the top of the hill, we inspected the cart and concluded that except for the seat, which was now loose, it was still roadworthy. The kids who hadn't ridden yet were a little wary of testing their own go-carts after seeing the punishment Rich had just endured. I considered passing on my turn—the thought crossed my mind—but I knew I had to ride, too. That's what brothers are for. On the plus side, Rich had proven that an accident was easily survivable. I tested the brake a few times. It seemed to work. Rich gave me a push, and I was off.

One thing became clear quickly: The steering system was almost completely useless. A few seconds later, I realized that the brake worked only on flat surfaces. Having generated some speed, I used my feet to help control the cart. Twenty yards into the run, I put my foot down a little too hard on the left side and lost control. Instead of going onto the Fitzgeralds' lawn, I shot toward the curb on the other side, behind which was a sidewalk and then woods. The go-cart stopped immediately as it hit the curb, and I kept going. I went over the curb and landed knees and palms first on the sidewalk, skidding a little before entering the woods.

Rich came running down the hill. Shaken and bleeding, I walked over and kicked the seat. Pulling our battered go-cart back up the hill, Rich and I told the other kids that we needed to do some more work on it, and then took it home. Mom repaired our cuts, and the next day, we repaired the cart. We removed the sides of the seat, the ones damaged by my kicking, and resecured the axles. We also wrapped tape around the brake to make it work better.

Rich and I took the go-cart out to a smaller hill and tried again. A few engineering insights later, and we realized our feet were better brakes than the piece of wood with tape wrapped around it. Our sneakers became important parts in the overall working of the go-cart—not good news from a cost-of-goods perspective as far as Dad was concerned. For one summer, Rich and I rode the go-cart made from old spare parts down the biggest hills in the neighborhood. We had more crashes, with more parts needing to be modified, repaired or replaced both on the go-cart and on Rich and me.

We didn't ask a single nail or piece of wood or sneaker if it wanted to be involved in the endeavor. Our bodies, likewise, didn't check with Rich or me to see if we were okay with the new cells that were added. As far as I know, none of the new cells were consulted before being used for repairs. The go-cart and Rich and I were made and repaired from spare parts that happened to be available at the time. They were used for a purpose that they had no say in or knowledge about.

To refer to a person is, in some sense, to refer to a go-cart: a system made from parts that never knew they were going to be used for that person in the first place. And they're not unique parts—they're the same parts we'll find in

14

every other person. Like it or not, we're all made from the equivalent of non-consenting, universal junk.

When the go-cart summer was over, Rich and I never rode it again. We used most of the go-cart parts, except the nails we couldn't straighten, for other projects. After we dropped the bent nails into the trashcan, the trash truck took them to the dump. The dump has since been turned into game fields on which kids play soccer and baseball. The dirt the fields are made of, probably ten or so feet beneath the surface, surely contains pieces of the nails that were in Rich's and my go-cart—the nails now rusted and decayed beyond recognition.

With all the parts gone, that seems to be it for the go-cart. Or is it? I wonder if it's accurate to say that the go-cart is gone. At present, at least an image of it appears to be safely stored away—available for use anytime I like.

❖ ❖ ❖

When we were teenagers, Rich and I played one-on-one basketball games in the driveway in Sherborn. In our later teen years, Rich was just about the same size as me. Sometimes I would win; sometimes Rich would win, but the outcome wasn't something we took lightly. Whoever lost usually took out his anger by kicking the ball into the woods. If the winner wanted to play again, he retrieved the ball. Sometimes we'd play for hours, flipping on the outside light when it got dark.

When we played, the goal always seemed so obvious: win. Yet like the nails in our go-cart, ideas and opinions have a way of transforming over time. I'm no longer as clear on the goal of our basketball games. From where I view it now, it seems a worthier goal would have been learning to lose with dignity. Or maybe that's not it either; perhaps the real goal all along should have been playing in a way that would someday give me good memories when I thought back on them?

I suppose this book is going to play out in the same manner. We'll experience stories about Rich, each of us forming opinions as we go. Perhaps those opinions will change once or twice as we learn about bipolar disorder and major depression, examine suicide more closely or get a firmer handle on what in us survives the progression of time. In the end, we surely won't be done sorting out all of our opinions. With a little luck, though, we'll still be able to take away a few worthy memories, memories that we can access even as the book itself sits on a shelf.

❧ Chapter Two ❧

I am moved by fancies that are curled
Around these images, and cling:
The notion of some infinitely gentle
Infinitely suffering thing.
—T. S. Eliot

An Oak Tree

In the email Rich sent to me on September 14, 2005, he wrote that he wasn't sure he was going to make it much longer, and that since getting home, he'd cut himself every day. One of the ways Rich dealt with his torment was by deliberately cutting himself. The first time he told me about it was in a July 2003 email (a few weeks after a trading incident that I'll describe in Chapter Seven):

From: Richard Courtemanche
Sent: Sunday, July 27, 2003
To: Ted Courtemanche
Subject:

one thing. not sure if you can help me with this. i will be talking with doc about it, still need to find the right psychologists. please dont share with mom or dad, it would simply cause worry.

i sent you guys an email, 2:15 my time i think. was feeling pretty level. and then... well here goes, and this has happened before. i can quote it all by memory now i think of and watch it so often.

i put on apocalypse now. i watch two scenes, the first one is where martin sheen [who plays Captain Willard] meets the general and harrison ford. the general makes the comment (and some spelling is off i know but bear with me):

"you see Willard, there's a conflict in every human heart, between the rational and the irrational, between good and evil. and good does not always triumph. sometimes the dark side overtakes what maslov called the better angels of our nature... every man has a breaking point, you and i have a breaking point. walt kurtz has reached his, and quite obviously he has gone insane."

and then the last scene, when willard is talking to kurtz, and kurtz relays the story of the arms of children being hacked off by viet cong troops and says

16

"and then it hit me, like i was shot with a diamond, a diamond bullet in the center of my forehead. and i realized, they were stronger then we were."*

anyways, i watch these scenes, and i take a knife, piece of broken glass whatever (and this isnt suicidal stuff, not at all) and i cut myself, sometimes to bleed, sometimes just deep scratches. sometimes while watching this movie, sometimes for no reason at all. and i have trouble understanding it. the pain is strangely satisfying. reminds me of the albino in the da vinci code [who practiced corporeal mortification] (although nothing close to that degree). but i was wondering if you have any thoughts on it. i mean its not completely unnatural, lots of times people lift weights not just for the body building effect but the pain, somehow being cathartic.

and now, 90 minutes later, i am fine. my back is red with marks, and i know they will be somewhat permanent, as the ones on my arms and chest are. eventually they become just fine lines that only i see. but they are there. sorry if this is a little much to handle on a sunday eve... just wanted to ask. tks, r

Presently in the United States, millions of people deliberately cut or burn themselves each year. In her book *A Bright Red Scream*, Marilee Strong estimated the number to be close to eight million, with the vast majority going unreported.

Why do people cut themselves? The experts are agreed: It's not to antagonize other people, and it's not for attention. Karl Menninger, one of the pioneers in the analysis of self-destructive behavior, wrote in *Man Against Himself*, "Self-mutilation is actually a compromise formation to avert total annihilation. . . . It represents a victory, even though sometimes a costly one, of the life-instinct over the death-instinct." It's a sacrifice of one part of the body for the benefit of the whole.

If this is difficult to digest, think about what happens when you are in physical pain. For example, you've just hit your thumb with a hammer. Can you think of anything else? Is your world suddenly polarized into a single, albeit, painful focus? Cutting is a coping mechanism, one that takes the cutter's mind off whatever he or she was worried about the second before. It's not a healthy coping mechanism as Menninger points out, but it is a coping mechanism.

The account Rich gave will not differ dramatically from that of other self-injurers: "The pain is strangely satisfying." The pain is absorbed, and in the

---

* If you're not familiar with *Apocalypse Now*, the second scene Rich is referring to is one of the movie's most famous. According to the fictional character, Colonel Kurtz, he was one of a group of American soldiers inoculating Vietnamese children for polio during the Vietnam War. In the incident he told Willard about, the soldiers returned to a village they had just left and found that the Vietcong had cut the inoculated arms off the children. In trying to understand the unspeakable brutality, Kurtz theorized that the Vietcong who committed the atrocity were themselves moral people. He reasoned that they had families and understood the viciousness of what they'd done. For Kurtz, their act was therefore one of strength (the insight that struck him like a "diamond bullet")— they had managed to break from the grips of their own moral convictions.

17

absorption, the individual experiences a kind of transcendence. The blood is an outward representation of the inward pain being released. To the cutter, the whole experience is sheer release—freedom. Experts are torn as to whether cutting is a disorder like bipolar disorder or an addiction like alcoholism. It's not uncommon for people with bipolar disorder to engage in self-injurious behavior, and it's not about suicide as Rich related; it's about escape.

Rich's cutting was, in a way, easy for me to overlook. I'm not saying I could ignore the fact that he cut, but I didn't feel an emotional connection to it. It was a sterile subject. I responded to it the same way native Floridians might respond to being told the temperature was 10 below zero in Bangor, Maine, the night before last. Without a framework to make sense of it, a person who's never experienced that kind of cold can't associate with what it feels like. For me, Rich's cutting was simply an occurrence that I heard about every so often in emails, where it remained a lifeless fact.

When Rich told me he had been planning to end his life after the wedding, I sent an email back to him the same day—September 14, 2005—telling him about "finding his state of mind," that life is about finding a pleasing state of mind. I told Rich there are multiple paths that can take him to the state of mind that is right for him, and only he can figure them out. When I wrote to him, I made the same kind of mistake many people make when they communicate with other people: I assumed that the window through which Rich viewed the world was just like mine. I assumed that he thought and reacted just like I did. Had I researched his condition more, I might have taken a different tact. At least I would have had more insights into what he was going through.

At the wedding, I talked to him about his trading. I'd long suspected the ups and downs of his trading were creating major problems and told him so. He said, "T, the depression comes with or without trading these days." In the later stages of bipolar disorder, researchers have identified an effect known as "kindling." In his book *Bipolar Disorder: A Guide for Patients and Families*, psychiatrist Francis Mondimore wrote, "There may be a 'point of no return' where the illness has been sufficiently 'kindled' that stress management no longer has much of an impact." In the beginning, a depression may be caused by an external event, something outside the person. Once a person has enough depressions, though, they can happen spontaneously, with no outside influences necessary. Just as wooden kindling causes a log to burn on its own, the person eventually self-generates the manic depressive states that destroy him or her from the inside out.

In the first line of the September 14 email I sent to Rich, I quoted a Bob Dylan song ("Meet Me in the Morning"): "They say the darkest hour is right before the dawn." I ended the email by digging back into the whole trading issue again, complete with a biblical quote:

My own thought is that it would be worth your while re-examining trading to see if bad states follow bad trading days.

18

Here's a biblical quote I think is relevant (Matthew 4: 5-7): Then the devil took him to the holy city and had him stand on the highest point of the temple. "If you are the Son of God," he said, "throw yourself down. For it is written: 'He will command his angels concerning you, and they will lift you up in their hands, so that you will not strike your foot against a stone.'" Jesus answered him, "It is also written: 'Do not put the Lord your God to the test.'"

What this has always meant to me is, "don't put yourself to the test." Don't hang out with alcoholics if you're an alcoholic; don't hang out with drug addicts if you're a drug addict. It boils down to: don't put yourself in a situation that you know you're not ready to handle.

In anyone's life, that means evaluating those things that cause known but avoidable grief (even if they may occasionally result in pleasure) and cutting them out. It's an art, absolutely. But the simple rule of thumb is to change those things that can reasonably be changed and whose change will remove a major source of ongoing and debilitating grief.

Find your state of mind.

Peace,
T

Rich replied just a few hours later.

From: Richard Courtemanche
Sent: Wednesday, September 14, 2005 3:56 PM
To: Ted Courtemanche
Subject: Re:

my only peace is when i am bleeding. ashley [a "New Age" therapist Rich talked to about his problems] once told me the pain stops with me. as i cut, i feel not only does it stop with me, it culminates with me. i am so lost. i used to just rely on alcohol to ease my pain. now its cutting. and the only time i dont cut is when i am drinking. i wake up in the morning and cut.

feeling the blood is more important than my coffee. i tried prozac again, it was ok. then one day, just before your wedding, i finally cut after two weeks. and it was vicious. prozac didnt stop it, just made it pent up. after everyone told me how good my toast was, i wanted only one thing... to cut. when bad things happen, i cut to release the pain/anxiety (ie trading). when good things happen, i cut 10 times worse (after the wedding). feel unworthy, undeserving. i sat in the mirror, recalled dylan telling me it was best toast he had heard, and i cut until i couldnt stand it any more.

i dont believe in god or the devil. i dont believe in heaven or hell. the only thing i believe in is the love of people here on earth. i know my family loves me. i know sharon loves me. it has sustained me for some time. but it cant sustain me forever. and in my head, every cut i make is like an axe swinging at an oak tree. i am an oak tree. and i am dying. and i am ready to fall down.

thank you for writing. i wish i could have been a better brother

Rich had been in the throes of one of his worst depressions at the wedding. No one knew. Though his email had shock value, I'd been shocked before. I figured he'd settle down, just like he'd done every time in the past. I wrote the following back to him as soon as I got his reply.

From: Ted Courtemanche
Sent: Wednesday, September 14, 2005 4:06 PM
To: Richard Courtemanche
Subject: Re:

I'm carrying my cell. Call me before you make any decisions.

Love,
T

OF GROUT AND BIPOLAR DISORDER

Nietzsche wrote, "It is by invisible hands that we are bent and tortured worst." What does it feel like to have bipolar disorder? You'd have to have bipolar disorder to know exactly what it feels like, and then you'd only know, for sure, how it feels for you. Nevertheless, one of the distinguishing characteristics of bipolar disorder is that it can lock those who have it into a single state of mind. It's certainly possible for people who don't have bipolar disorder to get a sense of what it's like to be locked into a single mind-set that seems inescapable. We've all had that, haven't we? When we lapse into a state of frustration or some other state, and we're impervious to suggestions that things might not be as frustrating as they appear to be.

A few years ago, I played in a men's ice hockey league. It's not really relevant to this story, except in the following way. I came home from a game one night, around 11:30 pm, and was getting ready to take a shower. I noticed one of the tiles at the base of the shower was loose. I looked at it closely from a standing position. I got down on my knees and looked closer, putting my face right up next to the loose tile. I pushed it in slightly, softly. It was very pliable. Next, I pulled on the edge of the tile—softer then firmer. "There's nothing holding this tile," my brain told me. I pulled it right out, and the surface was wet underneath. I followed the same process with an adjoining tile, and before I knew it, I'd pulled off five or six tiles.

The shower tiles began for me an odyssey that lasted more than four months. I'm cheap when it comes to home repair; I will not pay someone to fix something that I should be able to fix myself. I've been soaked by faucets; I've had toilet water drain onto my forehead, and my arm still has a scar from a hot iron I used to steam wallpaper off a bathroom wall. In the case of the tiles, I tried to fix them myself first. I bought a trowel, grout and everything I thought I'd need to do the job.

I started by removing the outside tiles and, still seeing wetness, continued into the shower itself. I asked the crew that did maintenance for the townhouse complex I lived in to give me a quote on fixing the problem. I was curious about the cost, but ultimately, I think I just wanted to learn more about how to fix the tiles. One of the guys (maybe sensing my intentions) told me, "You can never really be sure where the leak is, so you need to regrout the whole shower."

I searched the Internet for instructions on grout removal. I burned out a friend's Dremel tool (requiring the purchase of a new one) removing grout. I cursed and screamed as tiny grout removal drill bits broke after five minutes of use. I purchased a special power tool from Germany, uniquely designed to remove grout from showers. I watched in horror as $80 diamond-tipped blades lost their diamond coating after only two or three rows of tiles. The master bedroom adjacent to the shower was covered with grout dust on multiple occasions.

I didn't work on the project all the time, though it might seem so based on what I've written thus far. Still, it's safe to say that it was in the top ten list of things I thought about each day.

The low point came about two months into the project when I was just about done removing grout from the shower. The majority of the tiles were still on the wall, with no grout between them. With the tiles still on the wall, I wouldn't have to do much in the way of laying tile; I'd just put new grout between the tiles. My hair white with grout dust, as it always was, I was de-grouting away with the German tool when, all of a sudden, every tile on the far shower wall fell off. I'd somehow removed a critical piece of grout that had been keeping the tiles together, and when that came off, they fell to the shower floor like icicles from a gutter. Some broke, some remained whole, and I saw that the whole wall was damp. I sat down among the tiles: filthy, tired and utterly out of my mind. I took a hammer to some of the unbroken tiles, cursing them. After the tantrum, I sat there feeling nothing for about half an hour.

From there, I brought in a low-cost maintenance person to fix the shower. His heart just didn't seem to be into his work—the finished grout he applied looked like it had air bubbles in it. So I redid what he'd done, creating more work in the process, and had a second tantrum on the shower floor. Finally, I hired experienced help to do the job.

The relevance of the grout story is that while I was caught up in the project, it was the only perspective I knew. I was going to fix that shower, and that was it. No amount of friends telling me, "Ted, have you thought of getting a contractor to do it?" made a difference.

"I'm not crazy," was my position. "You're crazy for not wanting to fix something like this yourself. You're crazy and irresponsible." I could get there pretty easily; anyone who would not want to take on a job like this was both crazy and irresponsible.

The thought process behind my regrouting episode underlies a big part of the mental health problem. When someone is in the state I was in or in the states Rich used to be in, there is only a single option from that person's perspective. In a calmer, less obsessed state of mind, I know and everyone else knows there are many other options. For the person caught up, these options don't exist. Mere mention of another option might be met with open hostility. "No, dammit. I'm fixing the shower!"

When a person with bipolar disorder is down, it's next to impossible to reach him or her. The best chance to connect, in a way that your words might help, is during the "normal" times or as close to normal as that person can get. Sometimes, normal is not a feeling they have. Their perspective—I'm worthless and nothing can change it—is the only reality they can access. Anything you try to say to them will not reach them; the only way a message will find its way into their mental state is when it has been twisted to support their reality.

Remember when I described removing one piece of critical grout that seemingly held the whole wall together? That example underscores another oddity. In some things, we have unlimited opportunities. We can swing for the fence as many times as we like. All that matters is the one swing that connects. In other situations, we seem to have only one chance. Not only is it hard to tell which are the one-chance opportunities, but we also don't always have control over the decision to swing.

In addition to causing strokes and other health problems, sickle cell anemia causes unbearably painful episodes for people who live with it. In these episodes, red blood cells clump together, creating pressure that leads to pain. Sickle cell anemia is caused by one faulty gene—just one. People with the disease have a whole different set of problems than others without the disease, all because of one gene. You can't see it with your naked eye; it's such a tiny imperfection. In terms of sickle cell anemia, either you have the faulty gene or you don't—one chance, and you have no input in the matter.

Unlike sickle cell anemia, no one knows exactly what causes bipolar disorder. There isn't a single test that can be used to diagnose it. Mondimore wrote, "The reason for this sorry state of affairs is that the biological and chemical basis of bipolar disorder remains nearly a complete mystery; no one knows what to test for." It's possible that one doctor may conclude a person has bipolar disorder, and another won't. For the same person, there are multiple symptoms that may, or may not, lead a physician to conclude that the individual has bipolar disorder.

There are two basic types of bipolar disorder. Bipolar I is marked by full-fledged mania and major depression. In full-fledged mania, people think they can fly, or they think they're the second coming of Christ. They might get six hours of sleep in a week. In this manic phase, people feel like they're supercharged, connected directly to an ever-flowing energy source. They'll talk and talk, thrilled about whatever they're discussing and oblivious to the fact that it might not be so intriguing to someone else. People in the manic phase can appear to be delusional, but despite the outrageousness of their behavior, they have a hard time recognizing it. The NIMH says denial that anything is wrong is one of the symptoms typical of a manic person.

Bipolar II is the kind of bipolar disorder Rich had. In bipolar II, the mania is referred to as "hypomania," and it's not as high as in Bipolar I. To get a sense of it, imagine being pleasantly wired on caffeine, with the addition of a shot or two of your favorite spirit. Or think about the feeling you'd get if you won the lottery. Anything is possible. The world is yours for the taking. You're not delusional—though as bipolar II progresses, you may start to become so. You're just feeling magnificent. The feeling of hypomania is the main reason people with bipolar II stop taking their medications. Who wouldn't want to feel super-good?

The hypomania comes with a price. People with bipolar II tend to experience more episodes of depression—lows during which the person can't get out of bed, can't talk on the phone and can't interact with anyone. Rich could be on top of the world—funny, exuberant and capable of controlling a room—and then turn utterly despondent, sometimes days, sometimes only hours later. No one would hear from him while he was depressed. If someone in the family tried to call him, he wouldn't return our calls. If we tried emailing him, we wouldn't get a response. When he was in that state, nothing felt good because it was all veiled in melancholy.

The bipolar spectrum doesn't stop at bipolar I and II. There's cyclothymia, a condition characterized by relatively rapid movements between states of elation and depression, in neither case being as high nor low as those in bipolar II. There's also a milder form of bipolar disorder called "bipolar III," marked by high energy levels (but not hypomania) and recurrent periods of depression.

When does bipolar I become bipolar II or bipolar III? According to Mondimore, "[Emil] Kraepelin [who was *the* pioneer in the diagnosis and treatment of bipolar disorder] noted that 'it is fundamentally and practically impossible to keep apart in any way' the various forms of bipolar disorder, and that 'everywhere there are transitions.'"

Bipolar disorder and major depression are called "relapsing remitting diseases." They can go dormant and then resurface, perhaps days, months or even years later. Lacking observable physical manifestations, depression and mania can engulf a person without him or her knowing what's happened. You feel depressed, and that's all there is. Your mind won't say, "Here we go, depressed again." That is, you can't view yourself from a distance. Depression overpowers you, and you're stuck in the current. Life for the depressed person isn't hopeless because of how he or she is interpreting it through the filters of the brain. It's not recognizably hopeless because of how their brain is working—it's hopeless because life *itself* is hopeless.

There's another type of bipolar disorder, first identified by Kraepelin. Some experts believe it's not so much a "type" as a "state" experienced by certain people with advanced bipolar disorder. In today's vernacular, it's called "dysphoric or mixed state mania." So far, we've been discussing manic episodes and depressions happening separately: On one side is mania and on the other is depression. In dysphoric mania, they occur at the same time. Typically, the mania melds into the depression. People with dysphoric mania do not feel on top of the world. Instead, they just want to rip themselves from their state. Kraepelin called it "anxious mania."

Can you imagine being alert as can be but trapped in a hole of stifling depression? You can't do anything but wilt under the weight of your own suffering. What would you do if this was your norm? What if every day you felt like you'd just lost whatever was most precious to you, and you'd lost it in the most agonizing of ways? You couldn't escape in sleep. You couldn't escape through willpower. You'd be stuck. An outside observer wouldn't be able to look at you and see that you have dysphoric mania. Worse, you wouldn't be able to see you have it yourself. You'd be trapped in an invisible prison.

Getting back to the shower in my townhouse, it was never completely right. I described hammering vagabond tiles that fell from the wall when I tried to repair the shower myself. Within the tile manufacturing industry, it's normal to phase out tiles from year to year. The original tiles used in my shower were no longer available, so I mulled over my options. I could either let go and accept a multitiled shower, start all over and replace the tiles with a plastic enclosure (an option that I was told would require new plumbing) or completely redo the whole shower with a different kind of tile. The passage of time and reassurances of friends allowed me to ease into choice number one. The repairman fixed it with the closest match he could find. For a few weeks after the repair work was done, each time I went into the shower, I could see the damned thing was patched together. I purposefully wouldn't look at the tiles, hoping if I avoided eye contact, they'd lose their separateness.

When I finally sold the townhouse, the couple that bought it loved the tiled shower. I think the wife called it "playful."

RIVER RAFTING OUT WEST

In 1981, I started seventh grade and I had a lot of teachers. I liked having a lot of teachers because if you did not like one teacher, you weren't with that teacher all day. That year for vacation my family and I and my Uncle went out West. We flew to Las Vegas then we drove to the Grand Canyon. After that we drove to go on a river rafting trip on the Colorado River. Finally we drove to Yellow Stone National Park and then to Salt Lake City.

Richard Courtemanche
School Writing Assignment, September 20, 1982

The 1981 river rafting trip had ended earlier in the day, and as far as Rich was concerned, there was no justice. Not in this family. I'd been allowed to drive when I was his age. When I was eleven, I'd gotten to drive Stan-the-Van down the tiny street that connected Woodland Avenue and Mill Street more than once. Now, here we were, somewhere in Utah, on a highway as long and straight as could be, and instead of letting Rich take over, Dad was driving the rented station wagon. There wasn't another car in sight. The situation was intolerable. Rich needed to be in the driver's seat, foot on the accelerator, running the show. When was he ever going to learn how to drive?

The logic resonated with the adults: Mom, Dad and Uncle Ed. I didn't see it entirely his way, but he had a majority and the big influencers. Dad pulled over to the side of the highway. As the sun beat down on U.S. 89, with nothing but rocks and desert around, Rich climbed into the front seat and drove.

There we are: Rich is in the driver's seat, Mom is in the passenger seat and Dad, Uncle Ed and I are in the backseat. The car is climbing from thirty to forty to fifty miles per hour, and Rich is smiling. I focus on the horizon; it seems like it stretches out for infinity.

"This is big sky country," Mom says.

The only things that interrupt the horizon are huge, orange rocks. They look like they're made from chalk; I've never seen anything like them before. I wonder what it would be like to climb on rocks that big in the middle of a desert; maybe build a little fort right underneath them and live out there for a while.

When we'd landed in Las Vegas seven days earlier, the first thing Rich did when he got off the plane was run straight toward one of the slot machines in the airport. As he dropped a quarter into it, a security guard charged up to him and said he needed to be eighteen to gamble.

"Where are your parents?" the guard asked.

Rich pointed to Mom and Dad, as they were heading down the walkway, and next said he wanted his quarter back. Mom, Dad and Uncle Ed saw what was happening and hurried over to the slot machine. Everyone was talking at once until Uncle Ed took the lead. To the security guard's approval, Ed pulled the slot machine lever as Rich stood next to him. Different pictures came up on all three windows. No coins dropped into the coin tray. The outcome wasn't satisfactory for Rich. Uncle Ed told him that's how it goes. It still didn't sit right. If Rich had been the one to pull the lever, it might have been okay.

Mom and Dad walked forward because we needed to get to the baggage claim area. Rich and Uncle Ed hung back. I saw what was going on, spotted the secrecy, and hung back, too. Very quickly, Uncle Ed dropped another quarter into the slot machine. Very quickly, Rich pulled the lever. Before anyone could see that an eleven-year-old was gambling, two coins plunked into the coin tray. Rich got them both. Uncle Ed took another risk. I dropped in a quarter, pulled the lever and . . . nothing. The quarter was gone. We caught up with Mom and Dad and got our suitcases.

We stayed at the Grand Canyon for three nights. After that, we went on the river rafting portion of the vacation, which lasted three nights and four days. The Courtemanches weren't a "camping" family. We liked a permanent roof over our heads and access to bathrooms with real toilets. The river-raft trip was a break from the norm—none of us were sure how it was going to play out. Over-all, there were fourteen people on the raft: the five of us, a guy with big calves and his son, two women, a mother and father, one lady in her forties who'd always wanted to river raft and the two guides. The guy with the big calves was having problems with his wife that he talked about with the adults.

At the end of the first day of rafting, the guides established a campsite on the river's edge. A few minutes later, they set up what looked like a canvas phone booth away from the camp. "That's the porta-potty," Mom said. Dad asked if they'd be providing magazines—everyone chuckled except the kids (who hadn't yet developed an association between bathroom breaks and reading). Rich and I had no plans for taking a number two in the porta-potty. We could make it four days. If it was number one, we'd just go off on our own. Number two, we'd hold it.

Each night, we would set up our cots after dinner—which, on the first night, happened to be Dinty Moore beef stew with canned fruits. Rich and I loved it because we loved almost any meal that came from a can. The second night, Rich and I set up on a small sandbar. Shrubs and rocks surrounded us, and we could see a giant canyon wall on the other side of the river. We cleaned up with the biodegradable soap Mom bought for the trip and then went to bed. It got cold at night, but our sleeping bags were thick. I woke in the middle of the night and looked over at Rich.

"Rich, you awake?" I asked.

"Yeah," he said.

"Can't believe how many stars are out."

"I know."

"They're so bright."

"Wonder how many of them there are."

"Don't know. Lots—maybe a million."

"This is neat sleeping outside," Rich said. "We should do it at home."

"Yeah, we should."

The river murmured in the background, and the moonlight cast everything in black and white. We named a few of the star patterns glowing overhead. Slowly, I eased back to sleep.

Early in the third night, both Rich and I realized we had to go number two. The third day was a big rapid day, and all the bumping around shook up our insides. I didn't want anyone to know that I had to go number two. A fart in mixed company was bad enough. I sneaked into the porta-potty when I thought no one else was looking. Rich wasn't as trusting of the porta-potty setup as I was. He needed support—someone guarding the potty entrance.

As for my qualifications to guard the entrance, they weren't great. I was good for playing games and watching stars with, but I'd proven myself to be less than 100 percent reliable when it came to Rich's welfare. Rich captured the formative incident in a story called "My Most Embarrassing Moment" that he wrote for school when he was ten.

It was about seven years ago. My brother was with me. It was late and we were in our room. My brother was telling me there was a bear in the hallway. Then I started to scream and cry. My mother came in and told me to stop crying, and I didn't know what to say. After I heard it was a lie I was very mad. Since then we have played tricks on each other.

Rich didn't explain how he learned there wasn't a bear in the hallway: Uncle Ed ratted me out. He heard our conversation from the hallway. When Mom told Rich to quiet down, Uncle Ed told Mom the whole incident was my fault.

So on the third rafting night, Rich asked Mom—Rich's old reliable—to stand guard outside the porta-potty.

After the river raft trip was done, the next item on the itinerary was to fly in a little plane back to the landing strip where we'd left our car. At the time, Rich wanted to be a pilot. He and I were looking forward to the flight almost as much as the river rafting trip itself. Neither of us had flown on a plane powered by a propeller. Once we got on board, Rich sat right behind the cockpit, and the pilot was happy to explain some of the plane's instrumentation.

As we flew, we looked over the canyons we'd rafted through during the last four days, miles and miles of canyons carved and chiseled over millions of years. The flight in the little plane was much more turbulent than the one on the jet we flew to Las Vegas. At about the halfway point of the flight back to our car, Rich got pale, puking into a barf bag a few minutes later as Mom stroked his head.

Once we got the car from the parking lot after the plane ride, Rich was miserable—his chances of being a pilot didn't look very good if he vomited on dinky propeller flights. He stayed like that until the possibility of his driving came up. He initiated the idea. Somehow, it popped into his head, and he took it from there. When he got into the driver's seat, he was a bundle of happiness. Even though he was taking driving time that might have been mine, I couldn't help but appreciate how the process squashed the bad memories of the flight. Now that he was behind the wheel, the puking could easily have never happened. When Dad took over again fifteen minutes later, all Rich could talk about was the next time he would get to drive.

After the rafting trip, we went to Yellowstone National Park. Seven years after the Courtemanche out-West trip, wildfires charred Yellowstone. The park had engaged in over a hundred years of fire suppression policy. With all the branches and leaves and dried fuel that had built up, the fires burned uncontrollably once they started. Some people thought Yellowstone would be destroyed, but it thrived instead. Old forests were replaced with grassy fields and wildflowers. New trees grew, and the park regenerated itself.

When the Courtemanches were in Yellowstone, we mostly toured by car. At night, we stayed in little park cabins. On the second night in Yellowstone, as Rich and I played catch with a tennis ball in front of our cabin, two girls walked up from an adjacent cabin and started talking to us. I didn't know what to do.

I had no idea how to make conversation with a strange girl. What do you say? I hoped Mom and Dad couldn't see what was happening.

"Where are you guys from?" the older girl asked.

I threw the ball and, trying to contain myself, said, "Massachusetts."

"How did you get here?"

"We flew." Rich tossed the ball back and I caught it.

"Where have you been?"

I threw the ball. "The Grand Canyon."

"We went river rafting, and I drove the car in Utah," Rich added.

"Really?" the younger girl asked.

"Yup."

Rich tossed the ball, and I caught it. I bounced the ball against the pavement, bounced it again and then threw it to Rich.

"Are you two brothers?"

"Yup."

The girls asked a lot of questions, and I gave more one-line answers, most of them one or two words. Every once in a while, Rich would add color commentary, at one point offering advice on washing eating utensils when on a river rafting trip. We continued like that for about ten minutes.

"We're going inside now," the older girl finally said.

"Okay. Bye," I said. *Thank God!* I thought to myself. To make clear to the girls how calm and relaxed I was, I continued tossing the ball with Rich as they walked away. I swallowed hard when it was time for Rich and me to go in. That was the first time a girl who didn't go to my school had said more than a few sentences to me. Rich had given the longest and most exciting answers to the two girls' questions, but here I was, smitten. I hoped and hoped I'd see the older girl the next morning, but I didn't. I felt sick for almost a day.

As Rich stated in his 1982 school writing assignment at the beginning of this section, the out-West trip ended in Salt Lake City. We went to the Great Salt Lake just after we got into town. Like the Dead Sea, the Great Salt Lake is salty because it doesn't have any outlets. Tributaries flow into it, and the small amounts of salt they bring have nowhere to go, so they accumulate as the water that brought them evaporates.

The Great Salt Lake is about seventy-five miles long and thirty-five miles wide, and there are many ways of getting to it. We accessed it via a parking lot in a state park. The parking lot was roughly two hundred yards long, a tiny section out of hundreds of miles of shoreline. It just so happened that some older kids were hanging out there, smoking cigarettes.

At home in Sherborn, the Carters' had a tree fort in their backyard. Mrs. Carter let the neighborhood kids play in it. I'd gone up there one time with Marty Ledwell and some of his friends, when I was about eleven. Marty was an older kid and the toughest guy in the neighborhood. For whatever reason, he liked me. He was the one who got me involved in the neighborhood street hockey games, which eventually led me to play ice hockey. When we were in the tree fort, Marty asked, "Hey, Teddy, you want to see something?"

I had no idea what it was but wasn't about to say no.

Marty ordered one of the other kids to get whatever he was going to show me. The kid removed a piece of paneling from the wall of the tree fort, took a rolled up poster from the hiding spot and gave it to Marty. Marty placed the rolled up poster on the floor in front of me. Holding down the top edge, he slowly started unrolling it. There were four rows of pictures in all. In each progressively lower row, an old lady appeared to be getting madder and madder, as if someone behind the camera said something that got her angry. When he got to the last row, Marty covered the last frame—to nods of approval from the other older kids. Based on the first two pictures in the row, the old lady was more furious than ever. When he finally took his hand off, the old lady had gone berserk: She was giving the picture-taker the middle finger.

Giving someone the middle finger, I'd been told, was the equivalent of shouting all the swear words combined at them. Swear words were bad; all the swear words combined were really bad, horrible. And an old lady giving the middle finger in a poster removed from a secret wall panel? It was pure evil.

I laughed sheepishly. "Great poster, Marty." I was hoping the older kids wouldn't see that I was floored by it, practically devastated by the vile scene. Later that day, I told Rich about it—how Marty slowly unrolled the poster, and then there was a picture of an old lady raising her middle finger. Rich wanted to see it.

The next weekend, we did the unthinkable. We biked to the Carters' house, safely stowed our bikes in the woods and then sneaked back to the tree fort. After I checked a few times to make sure no one was watching, we climbed the ladder into the fort. We pulled back the paneling where the poster had been hidden, but it wasn't there. It had been moved—or maybe God Himself had incinerated it. Rich wanted to find the poster, but I didn't want to risk being caught turning the fort upside down, so we left.

The relevance of the middle-finger story to our visit to the Great Salt Lake is this: I knew that you couldn't be sure what older kids might do; they could be bad. So when I saw the ones at the Great Salt Lake, smoking and drinking beer right there in the parking lot, I slinked down a little in my seat in the rented station wagon.

As to the lake itself, Mom said we could lie on top of it and just float because it was so salty. No one tried it. The Courtemanches got a bad feeling in that parking lot. Up the shore only fifty yards or so, away from the parking lot, we probably would have seen a completely different picture. We almost certainly would have jumped into the water; Uncle Ed, Rich and I were three of the biggest fans of saltwater you could meet. Instead, we left the Great Salt Lake with the following impression: It's flat, kind of boring and dirty—cigarette butts and beer cans littering the ground. Plus, it's overrun with long-haired teenagers who should be doing something better with themselves.

The last night we were in Salt Lake City, we went to hear the Mormon Tabernacle Choir. Dad liked listening to classical music, but neither Rich nor I did. As far as we were concerned, a choir sang classical music, so this night was sure to be awful. When we got to the Tabernacle, we were greeted with good news: The Choir was not singing that night. So instead, we toured the Tabernacle and then went to a little park nearby. The night got better when Rich spotted an ice cream stand next to the park. We ended our out-West vacation by sitting on park benches and eating ice cream cones to the sounds of running water from a park fountain.

The next day, it took a little over four hours to fly from Salt Lake City to Philadelphia. We'd originally flown out of Philadelphia to begin the trip because we left Tiffany, our English mastiff, with Granny and Gramps. They lived in Feasterville, Pennsylvania, just outside of Philadelphia, and Uncle Ed lived with them, too. Once we got back, we stayed the night at Granny and Gramps's, and then drove to Sherborn the following day with Tiffany.

What happened next requires a brief history. I was the only one in the family who recognized that the flying ants that showed up each spring in the corner of the family room were trouble. They'd emerge in late May, hundreds of them. No one took them seriously. I'd spray them with Raid, and the next day they'd be swarming again. I couldn't stand insects. We lived in the woods, and insects were everywhere.

We hadn't been back in the Sherborn house for more than two minutes—the out-West trip now a memory—when I noticed small dark things on my socks. When I looked closely, I could see them moving. They were some kind of insect. If I tried to grab one, it'd hop, and I couldn't find it again. Rich wasn't bothered by them, but I was, deeply. "I must have brought them in from outside" was my first thought. "A bath will fix the problem" was my next.

As soon as I was out of the bathtub and dressed, the insects were on my socks again. I took another bath and scrubbed extra hard. It didn't matter; the insects got on my socks again, the third pair that day. My first year in college, when Rich was the only child left in the house, Mom sent me a letter telling me that the insects I'd seen each spring were actually termites. Most of the woodwork on the porch had to be replaced.

As to the insects that were on my socks, they were fleas. I'd been savaged by fleas when I got into the house. Mom and Dad agreed to hire an exterminator after the fleas attacked them as well. Since we'd been out of the house, the fleas hadn't had any dogs to jump on, so they jumped on the first thing that walked through the door—which was me.

For Rich, the fleas weren't a big deal. As soon as he walked into the house, tiny, blood-sucking parasites on his socks or not, he dropped his slot machine winnings—two quarters—into the jar he kept at his desk. He'd buy something with them later.

SUICIDE AND AUGUSTINE

Who have I become? I alternate between feelings of happiness and sorrow. At this moment, I seem to be in the grip of sorrow again. Tears well up in my eyes and fall silently against my skin. I am not sure why I am writing this. Perhaps simply for those who cared about me to have a glimpse into my existence. I long for sleep. More tears. A constant reminder of sadness. Tears when I sleep, tears when I rise. Does depression know a bottom? . . . Maybe tomorrow will be different. A flood of tears as I write that last line, perhaps my mind already knows that the sadness will not leave so easily. I believe in the Lord and I ask for forgiveness. May all forgive me.

Richard Courtemanche
Journal Entry, August 26, 1999

From a religious perspective, suicide carries the stigma of mortal sin. It wasn't always that way. Early Christians didn't have a clear-cut opinion on suicide. Part of the reason is that the Bible doesn't specifically mention suicide—there's no call, one way or the other. The notion of sin and its role in who goes to heaven and who doesn't led some early Christians to take their own lives to avoid the temptation of sin in the first place. They chose to bypass Earth in the hope of going directly to heaven.

According to the Old Testament, Samson died by collapsing temple pillars onto himself. His final words were, "Let me die with the Philistines!" (Judges 16:30). Samson took his own life and, in the process, also took with him the entire Philistine leadership. Almost all early Christians had good words for Samson and the way he died.

It's important to understand that early Christians were a downtrodden group. They were largely poor and persecuted, and they realized little protection from the ruling groups. Stories abound of Christians being mauled for sport. To early Christians, this world was filled with anguish, and all accounts of the next world indicated it was not. There was also a prevalent belief that the end was near. Judgment Day was not a faraway concept, thousands of years in the future—it was right around the corner. If you took your life, it wouldn't be long before you were resurrected for eternity.

Around the fifth century A.D., the situation changed. Christian leadership moved to a position of total vilification of suicide. From the early Middle Ages up to the 1800s, the bodies of suicide victims were regularly dragged through the streets, mauled and then hung from trees at intersections until the bodies decomposed. The earthly possessions of people completing suicide were confiscated by the state, and their families were brutalized. All of this happened with the support of the church.

What led to the extraordinary change of opinion? How could suicide become a sin that required punishment of the surviving family members? The change appears to have been heavily influenced by one man: St. Augustine. In A.D. 413, he began penning his seminal work, *The City of God*, itself comprising twenty-two books totaling nearly nine hundred pages. It takes a reader only a page or two to realize that the work is not easy to read or follow. In the introduction to one of the book's translations, Thomas Merton described Augustine's writing style as "extraordinarily unhurried." Within the same introduction, Merton asked, "How many Americans will have the patience to follow him through all of this?"

Augustine wrote *The City of God* as a rebuttal to Roman claims that Christianity was the cause of the fall of Rome to the Goths. Augustine referred to the Roman gods as "conquered gods," one of the ways he tried to create separation between the Roman gods and his God. Merton did not consider the first ten books of *The City of God* to be Augustine's most important work. According to Merton, "The saint does not settle down to treat the real theme of his work until he reaches Book Eleven." Augustine addressed the topic of suicide in Book One. Unfathomable atrocities have been exacted on the families of suicide victims throughout the ages in large part due to the influence of Augustine, and he was really just warming up when he broached the subject.

In the same section that he covers suicide, Book One, Augustine wrote of the rape of Christian virgins by the Goths during their siege of Rome. Augustine's position on rape was not what you might think. He believed that the rape victims were either proud and contemptuous to begin with—thus, their rape was a good thing—or they were on the road to becoming proud and contemptuous—and again, their rape was a good thing. They didn't lose their chastity, according to Augustine, "but rather gained humility." Augustine's position on the rape of virgins didn't hold the same staying power as his take on suicide.

Part of Augustine's motive in tackling the topic of suicide is that he wanted to keep church membership up. As John Hewett pointed out in *After Suicide,* voluntary self-killing was becoming epidemic among Christians. It appears that Augustine took aim at virgins because a growing number were being held as heroes when they took their own lives after being raped. To put it another way, at a time when church membership needed to grow, a handful of the leading role models were virgins completing suicide.

The commandment Augustine relied on to support his belief that suicide is wrong is "Thou shalt not kill." The Ten Commandments are presented in both Exodus and Deuteronomy, books within the Old Testament. Both books include additional commandments, rules and decrees beyond the first ten, many of which are extremely detailed. Here are a few examples.

Within Exodus, Christians are instructed on issues such as retribution for a stolen ox or sheep: "If a man shall steal an ox, or a sheep, and kill it, or sell it; he shall restore five oxen for an ox, and four sheep for a sheep" (Exodus 22:1). Precise dimensions are outlined for a table built so that God may commune with believers: "Thou shalt also make a table of shittim wood: two cubits shall be the length thereof, and a cubit the breadth thereof, and a cubit and a half the height thereof" (Exodus 25:23).

Several decrees within Deuteronomy address farming techniques, including this: "Thou shalt not plow with an ox and an ass together" (Deuteronomy

22:10). As well, penalties—very specific penalties—are outlined for wives who improperly break up fights between their husbands and other men: "When men strive together one with another, and the wife of the one draweth near for to deliver her husband out of the hand of him that smiteth him, and putteth forth her hand, and taketh him by the secrets: Then thou shalt cut off her hand, thine eye shall not pity her" (Deuteronomy 25:11–12).

The God of the Old Testament is generally acknowledged as a vengeful God, yet it is from the Old Testament that we get the Ten Commandments. In one of the same books in which the Ten Commandments are presented, we find God wholly endorsing the slaughter of beaten armies (Deuteronomy 2 and 3). What would we say today of an army that defeated and then slaughtered every last one of its enemy?

It's worth taking a brief pause. The purpose of this exercise is not to poke holes in the Bible; it's to get a better handle on how Augustine built his argument against suicide. We have just explored a small sampling of some of the codes of conduct within Exodus and Deuteronomy. We saw that rather than being vague, the instructions, at least those reviewed, tend to be well defined. Many more, not reviewed here, are equally well defined.

How about the commandment that Augustine used to build his case against suicide: "Thou shalt not kill?" The problem is that it doesn't specifically say, "Thou shalt not kill *oneself*." Although that might seem like nit-picking, as we've seen, the details within other decrees leave little margin for error. The omission of a reference about who should not be killed within "Thou shalt not kill" opens the door to interpretation. It was an issue Augustine recognized and sought to rectify.

The way Augustine extended "Thou shalt not kill" to include a reference to oneself was by advocating a universal interpretation of the commandment. That is, he believed it meant that no one could be killed. He said that the case against suicide was particularly strong precisely because a reference to "thy neighbour" was not included in "Thou shalt not kill." Augustine asked his readers to consider the commandment "Thou shalt not bear false witness against thy neighbour," which specifically references "thy neighbour." His point was that there's no doubt as to the reference: It's your neighbor. Before he continued, though, he warned his readers not to take what he'd just written and conclude that it's okay to bear false witness against yourself—it's not. For Augustine, all one had to do is go to the decree "Thou shalt love thy neighbour as thyself" (Romans 13:9) and cross-reference it with "Thou shalt not bear false witness against thy neighbour" to understand that it is not acceptable to bear false witness against yourself. With that bit of potential confusion cleared up, Augustine returned to the issue of suicide.

Before he could wrap up his argument, he needed to tackle one more problem: "Thou shalt not kill" is not written in a way that limits it to humans. To adhere to the letter of the commandment, one would need to refrain from killing anything. Addressing the issue was an exercise in absurdity from Augustine's perspective. He asked, "Are we thus insanely to countenance" the notion that "Thou shalt not kill" could possibly extend beyond humans? Insofar as creatures like dogs, cats or other "irrational animals" were concerned, Augustine wrote that they are "subjected to us to kill or keep alive for our own uses"—as simple as that. He ended his argument on suicide by writing that "Thou shalt not kill" really means "Thou shalt not kill man" (italics added). In doing so, he edited the Bible.

If you were even a little confused by his logic, you're not alone. Following it is like watching a rock bounce to the bottom of a ravine. In the end, you can see the rock is at the bottom, but it's anybody's guess as to how exactly it got there. Augustine pulled one idea from here, another from there, and lastly just dropped the whole thing and wrote, "Thou shalt not kill man." The key is that it's not the Bible that said, "Thou shalt not kill oneself": It was Augustine.

On the next page of his book, we realize there's more to his position than he first lets on. In Augustine's opinion, "Thou shalt not kill man" is not an absolute. For example, soldiers are justified in killing others if the killing has been ordered by the state. In fact, anyone is justified in killing if he or she does so according to "a just law that applies generally."

Even with wiggle room like "a just law that applies generally," Augustine still had a dilemma—he was stuck with the Samson issue. Samson had unquestionably taken his life without being compelled to do so by any just laws. In response, Augustine offered the following: A person can take his or her own life if provided "special intimation from God." Samson was justified, in Augustine's opinion, because he had received a secret instruction directly from God—a whisper heard only by Samson and recognized long after by Augustine. The catch-all exception for any suicide was, thus, "secret instructions" from God. Of course, the trouble the rest of us are left with is how exactly we verify the secret instructions.

It's reasonable at this point to take another pause. Knowing what we now know about Augustine's argument, we might think there would be some acquiescence in terms of how the church dealt with survivors of suicide: something like, "Yes, the logic of Augustine's argument is shaky at best, and there really isn't anything specific on the subject in the Bible. Though our stand is one of condemnation, we're going to work to help you through this devastating time." What really happened? After viewing the body of their loved one hanging from a tree, families could be forced to leave their homes, give up their possessions and wander as vagabonds—with approval from the church. How is this possible? How can an institution that purported to help people create this kind of misery?

The answer lies in a distinction Augustine made, a distinction hinging on an *us-versus-them* thought process. For Augustine, people could be divided into two categories: the virtuous and the sinners. People completing suicide were sinners; they were "thems." The church accepted and endorsed his view on suicide because the church as an organization needed membership. That's neither a statement on the overall ideology of the church nor a statement on today's church; it's a recognition that there are certain prerequisites any organization needs—and one of those is membership. Augustine's stance afforded the church a practical means of maintaining membership. Whatever you might think of the Bible, the foundation of Christian theology, it offers no opinion on suicide. The church's position at the time of Augustine was based on a reaction to a problem, formulated not by a deity but by a man.

Augustine admired Plato. Among Plato's many theories and philosophies was the concept of the "Royal Lie." It was a lie that he suggested could be taught to rulers and citizens within his Utopia. The lie goes something like this. God has created three kinds of people. There are those made from gold who should rule. There is a second class made of silver; these people are between the rulers and those being ruled, a class of liaisons. And finally, there are common people made of brass and iron.

Within Plato's Utopia, commoners would accept their lot in life and, having accepted it, move on with the process of living. This is not unlike what happened in medieval times with serfs, royalty and kings. Serfs simply accepted their role in life, not having any inkling of becoming royalty because they had no framework for such a thought—they were serfs. Plato's insight was that the first generation to whom the Royal Lie was introduced would not believe it. However, if the lie was repeated to each successive generation, it would become more and more real. At some point, it would cease to be a lie and instead be viewed as the way life is: reality.

For early Christians, the morality of suicide was not clear-cut. Augustine changed all that. Georges Minois pointed out in his book *History of Suicide* that despite Augustine's stated beliefs in *The City of God*, in *De bono conjugali* he wrote, "it is better to die of hunger than eat food sacrificed to idols"—thus, endorsing suicide in any instance in which the only available food was not sacrificed to the right god. This, too, was not unusual. Minois wrote that ecclesiastical suicides were often hidden from the public, that the church had a double standard. Just as priests known to be pedophiles were moved from parish to parish in the twentieth century by authorities within the Catholic Church, suicides within the medieval Christian church were also covered up.

Outside church walls, though, Augustine's doctrine on suicide gained increasingly solid footing. Eventually, it was effectively forgotten that the Bible contains no official judgment on suicide. Enough generations were told that suicide is a sin that the label stood. Even today, the Vatican will not endorse the provision of last rites or funeral services to people who die from suicide.

Augustine's solution to suicide underscores the bedrock of human oppression. If you want to encourage people to abuse other people, there's an easy way to do it: create an *us-versus-them* paradigm. Make people see others, the "them" in us-versus-them, as "its." You can do anything you want to an "it." Christian martyrs who killed Philistines were heroic precisely because Philistines were "its." Islamic extremists view suicide bombers as heroic because they see infidels as "its." People denigrate, torture, maim and kill *its*.

The situation today has changed in terms of suicide: Most Christians take a compassionate approach to survivors of suicide. Nonetheless, the vestiges of the Augustinian position remain—both in the Vatican's current stance and in the secrecy and shame still associated with contemporary suicides and suicide attempts.

THE EASTER BUNNY HALLOWEEN

Mom made our clothes when we were small. She has hundreds of pictures of Rich and me in one-of-a-kind outfits. I think it started with Mom sewing a shirt for Dad at Christmas; the next thing Rich and I knew, we were in the loop, too. In some of our grade school pictures, we're in 100 percent original Courtemanche clothing. What the whole Mom-making-your-clothes thing lacked in terms of fitting in, it made up for on Halloween. We had some of the best costumes in town.

One Halloween, Rich was the Easter Bunny. It's one of those happy, satisfied-with-life memories. Rich liked the concept of the Easter Bunny: a big rabbit that brings candy to kids. The Easter Bunny didn't get the same attention as Santa Claus but accomplished as big a miracle. Hopping with no reindeer from house to house, bringing kids Easter baskets and candy, and finding time to hide eggs in the yard—that's a lot of work.

The year Rich was a rabbit, we regularly played "Here Comes Peter Cottontail" in the bedroom we shared. Once the song was over, either Rich or I would move the arm on our little-kid record player to the beginning, and "Here Comes Peter Cottontail" started all over again. While the song played, Rich hopped around in his costume with the rabbit ears bouncing up and down, eating a carrot. If it went on long enough, Dad would yell, "Richard and Theodore, quiet down." During this phase, the refrigerator had to be well stocked with carrots because Rich could easily go through half a bag in a day.

When Rich was a bunny, I was Count Dracula.

Images of childhood: I'm sitting in a third-grade classroom on October 31, listening to a Halloween story, wondering when the day is going to end. I get home from school, toss a football with Rich in our front yard and watch as the sun sets above and then below the trees in the backyard. The last tinge of orange drains from the horizon clouds. Evening turns to dusk and trees sway as forms instead of details. It's darkest in the bushes and brush under the trees. There's substance to the deepening shadows. The story I heard at school mixes with the images reflected in my head. I get a sense that I could lie down in the brush and darkness, safe.

Inside the house, Rich and I can't eat our dinners because we're too geared up. The wait for full darkness outside is excruciating. Mom puts a pink nose and whiskers on Rich as the final part of his costume. Our first attempt at trick or treating ends when we see a group of older kids down McGregor Drive, at the outer limits of the streetlight. We're partway down the street, roughly at the tree where the neighborhood kids—including Rich and me—like to climb. We first walk quickly and then run back to our house to avoid possible confrontation until more kids are out. It's not Rich's idea to turn around. In my little mind, more trick-or-treaters mean more targets and less chances of Rich and me being the ones to get egged.

My memory fast-forwards and now we're standing outside the door at Denny Sciabbar-rasi's house. Rich is hopping up and down, and I'm crying because my Dracula teeth fell out. There's surprise on Denny's face when he sees me bawling. He drops candy into Rich's bag and mine. I try to pull myself together but the damn Dracula teeth! They torment me the whole night. Everyone loves the hopping Easter Bunny. I spend most of the night a victim of my own costume.

The teeth disaster is largely forgotten when Rich and I get home and spread our candy in piles on the floor. After we eat a few Reeses peanut butter cups, we eat a couple of Snickers bars. Then some other favorites—including a handful of Pez candy after we load them into the dispenser. I take my costume off, including the white makeup on my face. Rich keeps his whole costume on and goes to sleep in it.

I don't always get ahas from what I write. Sometimes, I just get memories, stories of my childhood with Rich—like the two of us marching around the neighborhood, with Rich up and me down. While I remember them, they're the present moment for me. I'm lost, unaware as I'm captured, of the room where I sit typing.

GAMBLING AT BATES

On an early January day in 1988, I drove Rich back to his second semester at Bates College in Lewiston, Maine. We were both on winter break, and Rich had to be back to school a few days earlier than I did. We drove in the Courteman-che family's newest car, a blue Oldsmobile.

Two or three years later, I got into an accident in the Oldsmobile at the busiest intersection in Sherborn. Another car ran a stop sign and crashed into the Olds as I sat in the driver's seat. I wasn't hurt, but the front of the car was crumpled. I didn't know what to do after the accident. I pulled the car off to the side of the road so that it wouldn't impede traffic—a definite "do not do" according to the police. Leaning against the car, I watched the passing traffic and hoped no one would recognize me in my predicament. I saw a friend's mother driving by. Thanks to at least one car being cleared from the scene, she drove by quickly. I waved to her, and when she caught sight of me, her eyes opened up wide. Something about her look suggested that I really didn't need to be wondering if any of the passersby might recognize me; the damaged hood I was leaning against was trouble enough.

On that January day I drove Rich to Bates, the Olds was still in pristine condition. I liked driving with Rich. We'd go for long stretches without saying a word, yet it felt relaxing, especially in the isolation of the car interior. The drive up I-95 from Sherborn to Lewiston is basically one road all the way. Rich and I left at about 3:00 in the afternoon for the three-hour drive.

In the winter, rocks on the side of the road in the Northeast are covered with ice. It's not really accurate to call them rocks. They're more like boulders, blasted in half so that the road could cut through. Water from melting snow trickles down the face of the natural holding walls, making it look like easy waterfalls were stopped in mid-flow. If you look closely, you can see detail; there are usually greens, blues and grays in the ice as well as a few huge hanging icicles. The scene is suspended momentarily in time until spring when it melts away.

When Rich and I get to Bates, it's dark. We go into his dorm room. It's sterile and white, and there's an unmade metal bed. The fluorescent lights add to the artificial feel. Rich's friends come pouring into the room when they realize he's back. I say goodbye and in less than fifteen minutes, I'm back on the road again. It's the only time I ever visit Rich at Bates.

The Bates football coach recruited Rich to play football there. I eked my way onto the Tufts football team in college; no one got cut. I received no phone calls from coaches, no invitations to play. The only playing time I consistently got was on the "skull" team. The skull team is the one that gets the starters ready to play. You go to all the meetings, practice three hours every day and then watch from the sidelines on game day. I started playing during my sophomore year and hated it from the first week on. I played for two seasons because I worried that after college, potential employers might find out I quit, call the coach and I'd get a crappy reference. I'm not kidding—that's why I stayed with it.

Rich, meanwhile, quit the Bates team after three weeks of practice. He wanted to relax, hang out with his friends and get away from the three-hour daily football grind. So he did. The coach, from what I heard, was furious.

Instead of playing football, Rich gambled on football at Bates. I gambled, too. I had a bookie; I felt important having one. Gambling is an addiction like alcoholism and drug abuse. When a person gambles, he or she can transcend all kinds of worn-out euphemisms. You don't need to work hard; you definitely don't need to be thrifty. When you win, it's so obvious. Of course the quarterback was going to fumble in the fourth quarter to preserve the point spread! When you win, the feeling is intoxicating: Winning literally makes you high. If you're not careful, you can ascribe to yourself mystical powers. Not only are you good at gambling, but you're also good at life.

The gambling gods never let me win much. I'd win for maybe one or two weeks, but then I'd lose every pick on a Sunday afternoon. By the end of that Sunday, I'd be an emotional wreck. I stopped gambling once my losses totaled somewhere around $400, the equivalent to a week's worth of painting houses (my summer job). Rich never had to face the reality of losing from what I know. The teams he thought were going to win won by what they were supposed to win by. He had a knack for picking the right teams—he won thousands of dollars.

In the March-April 2006 issue of *Harvard Magazine*, Harvard professor Sendhil Mullainathan said, "We think big things drive big behaviors; if people don't go to school, we think they don't like school. Instead, most behavior is driven by the moment." Traditional economic theory holds that "economic man" makes the best choice possible at any given time, and the choice is respectful of short, medium and long-term time frames. To the contrary, Mullainathan holds that most decisions "aren't purposeful, thoughtful choices." Instead, what's happening in the current moment will "disproportionately influence" your thinking. Little things can drive big decisions; that Rich won when he bet gave him confidence when it came to chance.

I don't know much about what went on with Rich at Bates. We talked every few weeks or so, but that time in his life is sketchy to me. I look back on those years for young Ted Courtemanche and shake my head. I drank a lot because that's the way I thought I could fit in. Rich drank, of that much I'm positive. There was a tradition at Bates called Newman's Day. You have to drink twenty-four beers in a twenty-four-hour period. Rich happily reported to me that he finished his beers and then helped friends finish theirs.

When he was home on the winter break in 1988, Rich showed me a switch-blade. I was fascinated. To me, switchblades were part of a whole different world. I assumed that Rich had the same intellectual curiosity about the knife as I did. A few years later when he was in the marines, he told me he'd pulled the switch-blade on someone in Lewiston, while he was going to Bates, and robbed them at knifepoint. His story didn't floor me the way it should have. I wouldn't have even thought it a possibility. When Rich told me the story, he did so completely levelheaded—that delivery took the edge off the reality of what happened.

Poor emotion control is a standard feature of bipolar disorder, anger particularly so in bipolar II. Rich's brain was wired for all kinds of problems: for episodes of hypomania that inevitably roller coastered to depression, for recklessness, for a belief in his own inescapable worthlessness. It was designed for addictions, and he gravitated toward activities like drinking that would cut him off from the predispositions in his brain. It doesn't excuse things, but it gives them perspective.

There was a force or forces within Rich that he listened to. One of the great challenges for anyone is recognizing the trusted voice. Which *you* is telling you the right thing? When are we regrouting showers that we shouldn't be messing with? When are we caught up in a foreign current, and when are we being ourselves? More subtly or perhaps more to the point, who is the *you* within you? When manias get too high or depressions too low, a person with bipolar disorder can experience psychosis. The "which voice" challenge becomes practically unsolvable.

At some point at Bates, Rich added things up. Maybe it was after a hangover or a series of hangovers or after the knife incident. He took stock of what he was doing and decided he needed discipline. As Rich mulled over what he should do, the voice that told him he needed discipline started to lobby for the marines. He believed the voice was a good one, a voice that was on his side. So against the advice of the whole family, Rich dropped out of school and joined the marines.

❧ Chapter Three ❧

I heard a thousand blended notes,
While in a grove I sate reclined.
—William Wordsworth

The Marines: Ruminations from I-93

Addressed to Mom and Dad, the formal letter from the marines arrived in early September 1990. It said Rich answered the meritorious promotion board's questions in "a clear, confident, correct and concise manner." Among other things, the evaluators felt Rich "did especially well with the oral board portion." The letter pointed out that Rich had competed against five other "well-deserving Marines." It ended, "I'm proud to announce and honored to be able to promote your son, Richard, to Corporal meritoriously on 2 September 1990. He will continue to be an invaluable asset to our Company, Corps and Country."

A handwritten note accompanied the formal letter:

Mr. and Mrs. Courtemanche,

As the senior board member, I was thoroughly impressed with your son's professionalism, knowledge and personal pride. He's clearly an outstanding Marine.

D.R. Jones
Capt USMC

The letter arrived around the same time that a policeman was blowing a whistle in the middle of a two-lane highway, motioning me to pull over. A second before, I'd been admiring the greenery and mountain air as I drove in my Buick Century up I-93 in New Hampshire.

I was dressed in a short-sleeved, button-down shirt with a tie. Add fifty more pounds, and I was Ralph Kramden getting ready to drive the bus. There were steel factoid papers all over the backseat. I was a specialty steel salesperson at the time. What is specialty steel? That's a question I used to hear often. Here's the answer I'd give: "You know how a telephone is built from plastic? The plastic has to be dropped into a die made from steel. That steel is specialty steel." Then I'd add, "You can also use it to make punches for electric circuit boards."

As I pulled over, the policeman looked at me in my short-sleeved shirt and tie. He saw the papers all over the inside of the car, saw the big dent from where I'd backed into the trashcans behind my apartment and maybe saw the "I Support State Troopers" sticker, which I got after donating $10 to the local chapter of the Massachusetts state trooper society. The New Hampshire state trooper saw all that and took mercy.

"Pull over up there. Just go to the front of the line and wait. I'm not going to give you a ticket," the trooper said. I didn't really trust that I heard him right and thus waited at the front of the line with my driver's license and registration ready for his review. He'd pulled over a group of cars.

As I waited, it gave me time to think about what I was doing. I was in New Hampshire looking for tool and die shops to which I could sell specialty steel. I lived in eastern Massachusetts and covered a territory that included western Massachusetts, Vermont, New Hampshire and Maine. I commuted about four hours every day to peddle steel, traveling from my apartment in Natick, Massachusetts, to locations all over the Northeast. The average person would not know that the shops that needed my products even existed. I developed a special sense, as do all specialty salespeople, that allowed me to recognize which tin building in an industrial park of twenty tin buildings housed a shop that could use specialty steel.

My boss had a system for figuring out commissions that neither the other guy he hired at the same time as me nor I could decipher. From month to month, our paychecks could vary wildly through no observable logic. We just accepted a big paycheck or a small paycheck as acts of providence.

Anyway, I was now miserable and pretty sure I was going to get a ticket. At times like these, Rich grew larger in my eyes. He left Bates, a school where he was recruited to play football—meaning, they wanted him to go there!—with no regrets; he simply wanted a change. I could never pull a stunt like that. In the marines, he was seeing things and going places that I'd never go. Rich was out there plucking life from the tree. Here I was in a career I hated, dressed in what could have passed for a Halloween costume.

The only stories I had from selling steel involved me in some jackass situation—like the first time I made a sales call on my own. It was at a gun manufacturer in New Hampshire. The company bought a lot of specialty stainless steel for gun barrels; I think it was 400 series (a kind of steel that has more chromium and less carbon). As I sat before the buyer, I knew that I was supposed to small talk but wasn't good at it. I repeated the fact that the company I worked for sold 400 series at each break in the conversation. My brain said, "Here we go again," as the words "we have 400 series in stock" rolled from my mouth, with me unable to stop them. My face was bright red when the purchasing manager said he had another appointment and that I needed to leave.

One of Rich's favorite stories from the marines was about mealtime. Rich liked keeping an eye on the drill sergeants when he was in basic training at Parris Island. He told me how he watched them peeking out from behind the doors of the drill instructor barracks to see how other drill sergeants were berating recruits.

Rich said recruits could be broken into three different groups at mealtime: those who were thin, those who were heavy and those who were in-between.

The mealtime story he liked was about two recruits named Harris and Akers. He always started the story by imitating a drill sergeant: "All right, fat bodies on the near side of table one. Beanpoles on the far side, facing the fat bodies. Now!"

Heavy, thin and in-between recruits started hurrying to tables. As they did, a drill sergeant yelled, "Harris! Are you trying to insult me? Are you laughing at me? Is this some kind of a joke kids play in Alabama? You get your big fat, Southern ass, and you sit on the near side of table one."

"Sir, yes, sir."

"Sir, yes, sir, what?"

"Sir, yes, sir. I'll sit my big fat, Southern ass on the near side of table one," with which the drill sergeant nodded in approval.

Once the recruits were seated, half of the drill sergeants descended on the divided tables—the ones with heavy and thin kids facing each other—while the rest kept an eye on the in-between kids, looking for any signs they were outwardly enjoying the proceedings.

The drill sergeant who went to table one, like the drill sergeants at the other divided tables, instructed each recruit as to what he could eat. He said to Harris, "Recruit, you can eat that pea and that bean. Separate them out, recruit."

"Sir, yes, sir."

"Well, recruit?"

"Sir, well what, sir?"

"You insolent son of a bitch, recruit. Do you know what 'insolent' means?"

"Sir, no, sir."

"Insolent means disrespectful. Are you trying to be disrespectful?"

"Sir, no, sir."

"You better not be, recruit. You better not be."

"Sir, no, sir."

"Good. Well, what are you going to name your pea and bean?"

"Sir, I don't know, sir."

"You insolent son of a bitch, recruit. Are you being insolent?! Do I need to define insolent for you again?"

"Sir, no, sir."

"Well, recruit, what are their names? Don't make me ask again."

"Um, that there's Pea Number One and that there's Bean Number One, sir."

"In the name of Jesus our God, recruit. In the name of Jesus our God. How would you like to be named Pea Number One? How would you like it? Do you think Pea Number One likes his name? Is Bean Number One a name any vegetable could feel good about?"

"Sir, I'm not sure, sir."

"Not sure, recruit? Well, let me straighten things out for you. No God fearing vegetable would ever want to be named Pea Number One or Bean Number One."

To the thin kids, the order was a little different. A drill sergeant said, "Akers, hold up your arms and wave them so I can see where you're at."

42

Hearing the command, Akers held up his arms and waved them.

"Oh, Christ Jesus, recruit, you wave those arms too much, there'll be nothing left. Stop the goddang arm waving."

"Sir, yes, sir," Akers responded, positioning his arms by his side.

As Akers looked wide-eyed at him, the drill sergeant issued another command: "Recruit, go up to that mess line and bring back two plates of potatoes and another plate of hamburger."

"Sir, yes, sir"—whereupon Akers hurried to the mess line and brought back the required food, waiting for further commands once seated.

As soon as each heavy recruit and each thin one had received eating instructions, the meal began. The heavy recruits were restricted to only their selected vegetables while the thin ones had to finish every plate of their food. It didn't take long for the heavy recruits to finish. They had to sit and watch while directly opposite them, a thin recruit struggled to eat two or three plates of food.

Inevitably, one of the heavy recruits would try to sneak a piece of food. As soon as Harris did on this day, the drill sergeant screamed, "Harris, you greedy son of a bitch! Now I know you're being insolent! Or is it you think I'm stupid? Do you think I'm stupid, recruit?"

"Sir, no, sir."

"Recruit, you come with me. I'm going to get that French fry back! That's my French fry. Mine! And I will get it back," after which Harris did push-ups and other conditioning drills in the outside exercise area (the pit) until the French fry was returned.

While the divided table chronicles were going on, the other drill sergeants mitered out penalties to anyone in the in-between group caught laughing. A handful of in-between recruits always wound up at the pit, too, doing push-ups next to a nauseous heavy one. When I heard Rich tell the story, I was of the opinion that it was a story with distinction. You'd seen some things, you'd lived life, if you could tell that kind of a story.

One of the bonuses of making it through basic training is that full-fledged marines occasionally get weekend passes, allowing them to leave the base. For Rich and his friends, the weekends consisted of renting a hotel room, getting falling-down drunk, ripping the hotel room apart and looking for girls or fights, whichever happened to be available at the time.

Mom, Dad and I visited Rich and his friends at Virginia Beach shortly after he graduated from basic training. No sooner did these guys get into the hotel room then they began making phone calls to girls out on their decks. I couldn't believe how brazen they were. "See the girl over there? What do you think the room number is? Maybe 317? Okay, call her."

The guys bought a keg and hit it often. The Saturday night we were at Virginia Beach, Rich, his friends and I went out on the town. It's one of those blurry nights. The night before Rich left to go to basic training, Rich, some of his high school buddies and I drank in the refurbished attic in the house in Sherborn. We had beers and Jack Daniels, and I managed to fall asleep on a weight bench. In Sherborn, the night was contained—we never left the attic. The night in Virginia Beach was not contained. I felt like I had to impress Rich and his buddies, show them that while I may not have been in the marines, I could nevertheless get drunk and rowdy. One of the memories that has seeped back into my head is of sitting in a bar.

There's laughter and music; I see a guy with a beard and his girlfriend or wife. There's a haze of people behind the couple, and there's a bar and bartender off to the side. Next, I see me hitting glasses of beer on the empty table behind me with my elbow. It's not an accident; it just feels like the right thing to do. I see beer spilling into the air, and it's all moving in slow motion.

After my antics, we leave the bar and head onto the street. I start pulling antennas and mirrors off of cars. Rich is behind me, but his friends are nowhere in sight. He's watching what I'm doing. The night is warm; streetlights are shining yellow-white, and I'm belligerently stumbling along. Rich asks me why I'm doing it. I pull the mirror off a BMW, and I tell him it's because the mirrors should be ripped off BMWs.

As I look back now, I can see an outline of Rich in the darkness and yellow-white lights: In the destruction, there's a softness—my brother is following me. When we were together, that's all I needed. It didn't matter where we were; that was home. He accepts my explanation—"that mirrors should be ripped off BMWs"—and the memory fades. After the trip, I didn't see Rich again for three years. He went to Okinawa and then to Sicily.

We kept in touch via letters. While Rich was in high school, he had his nose broken on two different occasions by friends. He didn't fight back in either case. One time, he was playing cards with his friends in the basement—I guess they were freshmen. Rich kept doing pull-ups over one guy each time the guy lost, telling him to try harder. The guy finally punched Rich in the nose. Rich just looked at him as if to say, "What took you so long?" and that was it.

The other time, Rich and a friend were playing pool. Rich was winning every game. He'd put his pool cue right under his friend's nose and say things like, "Mr. Pool Cue wants you to hit the next shot, but he doesn't know if you can." The guy kept telling him to stop. He continued missing shots, so Rich kept it up. Finally, the guy punched him in the nose, too. As with the first punch, Rich didn't fight back. Rich's nose was twisted after the second blow. He needed plastic surgery to fix it. Before that punch, he'd always had a little hook in his nose. After the surgery, his nose was completely straight. He began to develop the facial features of a lead actor more and more after that surgery. His cheeks filled in; his jaw filled in.

In her book *Bipolar Disorders: A Guide to Helping Children and Adolescents*, Mitzi Waltz wrote, "Statistically, males with bipolar disorder are more likely to get involved in potentially criminal, aggressive, assaultive or risky behavior than females."

Each platoon within the marines has one person who is the designated leader, the toughest guy in the unit. He gets that distinction by beating up anyone in his platoon who wants to fight. Rich was that guy in his unit. The toughest guys from different platoons inevitably fought. Rich told me about a fight he had with another guy considered to be the toughest marine on the base. The guys from his platoon convinced him to fight.

I can see it: There are about fifty marines standing in a circle, Rich and the other guy in the middle. There's cheering and yelling and two guys stalking each other. In a letter he wrote to me, Rich told me he thought about me as he fought. I never really understood why Rich was so taken of an image he had of me. It occurs to me now that during the fight, he stepped into his rage place—the place where only he could go. Rich said the fight was quick, and he had to be pulled off the guy by both platoons. If he hadn't been pulled off, he said he would have kept going. In a twisted way, it made me proud. I welled up inside thinking of the power he'd conducted. I'm sure it would have been different to be there but to hear about it in the third person, it became more of an intellectual pursuit that I savored like fine scotch. The problem with morality is that it's directly proportionate to proximity.

There was another story Rich told about his time in the marines. Not quite as good as the Harris and Akers story in my opinion, but I'm one person whose opinion is most directly relevant to one person. As with mealtime, bathroom requests engendered creativity on the part of the drill sergeants. During one of their usual training routines, Rich observed a recruit go up to a drill sergeant and say, "Sir, this recruit is in need of an emergency head call, sir."

The drill sergeant, as explained to me by Rich, responded, "An emergency head call, recruit?"

And the same young man said, "Sir, yes, sir. An emergency head call, sir."

"Recruit, so I understand what you want, explain to me what exactly an emergency head call is."

"Sir, yes, sir. An emergency head call means I got to go to the bathroom real bad, sir."

"Is that right, recruit? Anything else I should know?"

"Sir, no, sir."

"The important thing is that you are now in need of an emergency head call?"

"Sir, yes, sir. An emergency head call, sir."

They were doing an exercise that involved the kind of orange pylons used to mark construction zones on highways. The drill sergeant said, "Recruit, put this pylon on your head and run around the compound and make a siren sound like an ambulance. You let everyone know you need to make an emergency head call." The recruit ran around the compound whirring like an ambulance with an orange pylon on his head. If anyone laughed, they were punished, just like at mealtime.

I thought of the second story as the state trooper made his way to my car at the front of the line on I-93 in New Hampshire. "You're free to move along," the trooper said. When he did, I drove off, late for my sales call but happy—much happier than I would have been without meeting the trooper.

As to the letter described in the beginning of this section, Rich enlisted in the marines because he wanted to be one of the "grunts." The marine who recruited him encouraged Rich to go the officer training route; Rich wouldn't do it. Had the marines been aware of his bipolar disorder—no one in our family, including Rich, knew he had it at the time—he would have been barred from serving in the military.

THE MOTORCYCLE ACCIDENT

During our honeymoon in Maui, Deana and I went to a little town called Hana. I'd never heard of it before and Deana hadn't either. It's on the east coast of Maui. Some of the websites we visited cautioned that the east side of Maui can be rainy. The websites also said the natural beauty of Hana is stunning. We took a chance, drove out from the west side and spent a couple nights in Hana. When we first got there, the grounds of the place where we were staying looked like a campground. All the buildings were stained a brownish green. My first reaction was: We're spending *how much* for this? When we got to the main lobby, one of the employees gave us iced towels with essential oils in them. I placed one of the towels on my forehead, and in a few seconds, all the voices in my head settled.

We stayed in a cabin, and it overlooked a field where horses grazed among flowing grasses. Beyond the grasses, lava rocks lined the shoreline where they were kneaded by breaking waves from the Pacific. In the distance, a solitary island rose from the ocean, a knot of palm trees growing from its center. The view was humbling, one of the most beautiful I've ever seen. All three days we were in Hana, it rained at night and was sunny during the day. The locals told us that it rained night and day the month before we arrived.

I still had the image of Hana in my head when I got the second email from Rich on September 14, 2005, telling me that he now cut himself every day and that he wasn't sure he would make it much longer. Rich also sent a similar email to Mom and Dad. As I think back to Rich's downturns, what strikes me is how draining they were. They were fire drills the whole family threw ourselves into. There wasn't much research, just reaction. None of us knew what to do, yet at a certain level, we each thought our gut would guide us correctly.

My pattern was to craft email after email. I never sent most of them. I'd write some that had a "pull yourself out of it" bent and others that had a "get yourself into a psychiatrist" bent and still others in which I quoted things—mainly philosophy. In the emails I typically sent, I tried to get Rich to see that the way he felt, all the pain of the depressions, wasn't permanent. To Rich, how could the emails be anything other than hand waving in a downpour? When he was raging, the chemicals churning in the circuitry of his brain filtered everything he saw. But as surely as he raged, his moods would clear.

As a teenager, I happened on Rich once when he was having a breakdown in the backseat of the Rabbit in the garage. His face was bright red.

"What's wrong, Rich?"

"I suck."

"Rich, no you don't. My God."

"I FUCKING suck."

He clutched the back of his head with his hands and rocked himself. Something clicked in my head, and I said, "Rich, we can get help. There are doctors that can help."

"No one knows what I'm like," he said, and then he broke down even more—totally unreachable. He curled over on himself in the backseat of the car, his body and face contorted. He got red, just so deeply red.

I watched him. Other times, I might try to find Mom, or I might try to put my hand on his shoulder. He'd keep going. On this day, I told him that I'd leave him alone, and I walked away from the garage. At dinnertime, Rich was back to normal. We never talked about the incident again.

I thought my first September 14 email response—the one with the Bob Dylan quote—would be therapeutic for Rich, that it would somehow get him to stop trading and help him to carry on. When I got the next email, in which Rich said his self-inflicted cuts were like axe swings against his own body and that he was dying, I realized my first message hadn't helped. I took it personally in a way: I was *failing* in my attempts to reach Rich. "If I just write better emails, I'll get through." It's a standard phenomenon for people to believe that they have the power to make other people, who are depressed, feel good again. Realizing that I wasn't helping, I began to feel stuck. With stuckness came frustration and irritation, intermingling together. I think it was irritation, rather than compassion, that drove me onto the Internet to look for inpatient resources for Rich.

Having someone committed to a psychiatric facility is not easy. (If it was easy, can you imagine how many psychiatric hospitals would be needed? How many family fights would end with someone in the psych ward?) At the time in California, a family member and one other person both had to witness before a judge, presenting evidence as to why the person in question should be committed. The judge would weigh the evidence and then either sign or not sign an order committing the person to a hospital. The catch was that the hospital could only keep the person as long as he or she exhibited behavior that warranted the stay. I knew it wouldn't take Rich more than a day or two before he talked himself out. Even though it wouldn't be easy to get him committed, and he probably wouldn't stay long, I couldn't think of any other option.

"These emails just need to stop," I told Mom during a phone call. "We all keep doing the same things every time Rich sends one out. It's time to rethink our approaches." Mom was considering flying out to San Diego to see Rich. I said to her, "You can't just fly out to San Diego without some kind of a plan, Mom. I know it's hard, but we have to think about inpatient treatment for Rich."

Right after I lobbied for inpatient treatment, Mom said, "Rich is completely broke." In fact, he was beyond broke. He was in debt for about $100,000. Wild spending sprees are not unusual for people with bipolar disorder. For Rich, the debt was from his trading. Hearing about his financial situation stopped me.

"Jesus, that's a lot of money," I said.

"I want to see what it's like out there," Mom said. "I can't get a sense of it over the phone."

I thought about the debt as we talked. It occurred to me that bankruptcy might be exactly what Rich needed. He'd declare bankruptcy, and then he'd be out of the trading business all together. (Futures trading is basically a cash business, with accounts always settled at the end of the business day. For that reason, you need to have a good credit history—so that the company you trade through can be confident you'll pay up if you lose.) Mom and I talked some more. Then I circled back to the inpatient facility.

"Mom, this is even more reason to get him into a facility. He just needs to cool out. They can give him sedatives. His brain just needs to be stopped."

"Okay," Mom said. "I'm going to talk to Sharon about it." When we talked the next day, Mom told me that she and Sharon were going to have Rich committed.

A few months before my wedding, I ruptured my Achilles tendon playing softball. I spent five hours in an emergency room waiting for a diagnosis. When I got it, there was no second guessing. I went in for surgery a couple of days later, and within three months, I was walking again.

You can't stitch up bipolar disorder or major depression and wait for it to heal. There's not just one approach. A doctor can't say, "Take two of these," and have confidence the medication will do the trick. It's like the great wilderness, and almost anyone can run in with treatment suggestions blazing—such as me wanting Rich to be admitted to a psychiatric hospital. Mental disorder is a raving menace that shifts and dives and disappears and reappears. And when it reappears, it's almost always a surprise. "Rich is thinking about suicide again? I thought that phase was over." Many experts believe that the majority of bipolar disorder cases can be controlled with the right treatment; usually the treatment is medication.

There are some, however, who question this view, especially in regards to medication. In an article titled "The Latest Mania: Selling Bipolar Disorder," psychiatrist David Healy wrote, "There is . . . much less evidence than many might think to support these claims for the prophylactic drug treatment of manic-depressive illness (bipolar I). And there is almost no evidence to support such claims in the case of whatever community disorders (bipolar II, bipolar NOS, cyclothymia) are now being pulled into the manic-depressive net." As might be expected for a condition with no known cause, there's a lot of confusion.

Mom emailed Deana and me the day before she left to see Rich.

From: Betty Courtemanche
Sent: Tuesday, September 20, 2005
To: Ted and Deana Courtemanche
Subject:

Hi Deana & Ted,

Wanted to let you know that I am going to San Diego tomorrow morning and will be home Saturday night. I'm not sure what will happen while I am out there. True to the pattern, Rich is now talking rationally and refusing treatment options. He has agreed to go with me on Thursday to see Ashley. I've talked with her and am hoping that she will help him form a treatment plan. She feels strongly that he needs medication.

I am available by cell phone and will call you on Sunday.

Love from Mom

Ashley didn't have any specific counseling degrees that I knew about, yet she was Rich's primary source of therapy (Rich didn't like the counseling provided by psychiatrists or psychologists). For Christ's sake, I thought. Of course Rich should be on medication. As soon as Mom got out to San Diego, the plan changed. Rich and Mom talked about him going into a facility, but one of Rich's biggest fears was being locked up. When Mom returned to Boston, Rich was still living at Sharon's condo in San Diego. Nothing had changed except for the fact that he was now in more debt than he'd ever been in his life. Mom said he was officially considering filing for bankruptcy—how I wished he'd do it.

Almost a week after Mom got back, Rich sent me an update.

From: Richard Courtemanche
Sent: Thursday, September 29, 2005
To: Ted Courtemanche
Subject:

hi T. i am doing better. ashley told me i am not addicted to cutting. i am addicted to feeling bad. thats why i cut and tell people. it makes me feel even worse. it may seem small, but a light went off in my head when she said it. like i can at least identify what my addiction/demon is. i havent cut for two weeks. i hope you guys are doing well and happy on your (as of tuesday) one month anniversary.

A huge wave of relief went through me. I reread it. Something had gotten through.

A few hours later, he sent me another email chronicling his moving fiasco. Prior to the wedding, Austin was Rich's primary residence. When Mom went to visit him, he'd just moved back to San Diego and was waiting for his belongings to be delivered by a moving company. Rich told me that the moving truck had arrived in San Diego at 11:00 pm on a Saturday night, after the movers first said

49

they'd arrive on Friday afternoon. He was at a barbecue with Sharon's parents, and he had to leave to meet the movers. The first item out of the truck was a metal desk, mauled in the transit. The next was a concrete ottoman that had somehow been split in half. Rich picked the moving company precisely because they specialized in moving motorcycles. He had two at the time, a Harley-Davidson and an MV Augusta, that he liked to ride in Texas without a helmet. Both were damaged during the move.

In one part of a letter Rich was going to send to the moving company, he described asking the driver for a ramp to get his bikes out of the truck.

> He told me there was no ramp. At this point, I would have thought nothing could surprise me. However, not having a ramp to get a 400lb bike and a 600lb bike off the truck was, in fact, surprising. I asked the driver why they had no ramp. He responded that he'd told the people at the loading dock he would need one but they didn't give it to him. I am not sure what his plan was. By this time, it was 12:30 am on Sunday morning. The driver insisted that he and his partner could lift the bike down and gently place it on the street. I forbid them to do this. I suggested that we put my mattress from the move (a mattress I SLEEP on) under the truck and try to lift the bikes down to the mattress. At this point we had four people (my fiancée helped as well) and even with four of us, the bikes made it down but only after falling and bouncing on the mattress. Luckily there was no further damage to the bikes, but I am now sleeping on a mattress with grease stains which I am not charging you for.

The letter was a good sign. Rich was getting his sense of humor back. As I read through the two emails he'd sent, I decided that maybe Rich hadn't needed an inpatient stay.

Five hours after Rich sent the moving letter, he sent another email. He'd gone into Mom's email account—my guess is that she'd inadvertently left a link to her account on his computer while she was visiting. Maybe she'd clicked the "Remember Me Next Time" button. Anyway, he got into her account and read email exchanges between Mom and Dad, exchanges regarding Rich's financial situation. Mom and Dad had been divorced for about fifteen years, but they kept in close contact. No one ever really knew Rich's exact financial situation at any given time. Rich hadn't been able to buy a wedding gift for Deana and me. Added to his $100,000 debt, he also needed surgery on his hand (damaged by punching through a TV the year before) plus an operation for Daisy (one of his dogs).

Emil Kraepelin wrote that for people with bipolar disorder, "Trifling external occasions may bring about extreme outbursts of rage." The email between Mom and Dad hit on the biggest issue we struggled with as a family. When do you cross over the line and start enabling? The point Dad made in the email that set Rich off is that Rich needed to start taking accountability for his finances. Everyone in the family had loaned Rich money at one time or another.

Rich sent an email to me that he was prepared to send to Dad, and in it, he seethed. He wrote things like, "Try sleeping on a bed that is covered in blood stains in the shape of crosses," and "Try watching Sharon's face fall apart when the movers brought that mattress in, and she saw all the blood I had shed while I was alone." He said Dad belittled him in the email exchange with Mom. When I read what Dad had written (Rich sent me the email that offended him), I couldn't find belittling in it.

Rich's states tended to change quickly, especially toward the end, an effect know as "rapid cycling." People with bipolar disorder who rapid cycle are notoriously difficult to treat. As I look back on it, my guess is that at the time Rich read the email exchange, he was switching back and forth between depression and mania, and the two were probably mixing. Not only was he rapid cycling, but he also likely had dysphoric mania. From what I later found out, he'd probably had it for at least a year. I had no idea his bipolar disorder had progressed so far, and, regretfully (*forever regretfully*), had no idea it got worse over time.

I talked with Mom the day after she returned from San Diego. Both Dad and I thought Rich should get a regular job, something outside futures trading. "A nine-to-five job isn't possible right now," Mom said. "He's just too emotional."

I couldn't relate to it. "No, he just needs to stop trading," I said. "He needs to take some time off and start sending out resumes."

Mom told me that Rich *had* sent a resume to an investment company in San Diego but hadn't heard anything back. He took that as rejection, and it was towering. He learned about the job on Monster. "Mom," I said. "I've applied for jobs on Monster, jobs I'm overqualified for on paper, and haven't heard anything back. That's the way it goes. Sometimes you hear back on the ones you don't think you have any shot on. That's the way it was for me back when I was job hopping, and it hasn't changed."

There can be single, double and triple guessing in families dealing with bipolar disorder, as well as side-taking, secret conversations and worry about how people are going to react. "Walking on eggshells," is how some experts describe it. There are also invisible mental lines that can't be crossed. Mom said there was no way Rich could get a job. I took her comment as simply being overprotective of Rich.

Why didn't I just call Rich myself and say to him directly, "Get a different job?" The answer is complicated. Rich always told me that I was the one who had faith in his trading. And I did. The problem was backing off, treating it like a business. It was because of what he'd told me that telling him to stop outright seemed like a betrayal. From where I viewed things, I worried that telling Rich directly would be too much for him. As I write this, I'm struck by the hollowness of it. Why didn't I just call him? The best I can offer is that patterns that seem obvious and easily surmountable from the outside can be violent, impassible rapids on the inside.

When Rich forwarded the email he was planning to send to Dad, I didn't respond, and he ultimately never sent it. A few days later, I sent Rich an email, a short one telling him that some analysts were downgrading their rating of Harley-Davidson's stock. For about ten days, I didn't hear anything from Rich.

On October 8, I checked my email.

> From: Richard Courtemanche
> Sent: Saturday, October 08, 2005 3:01 AM
> To: T Home
> Subject:
>
> hey T. just so u know. on this thurs i am leaving for a four week stay at an inpatient facility for those with psychiatric problems.
>
> i had 6 beers the other nite, went for a ride, took off my helmet, and launched my bike into a tree. at last second i lost control or i would be dead. instead, i ripped off the skin on the right side of my body and after spending nite in hospital, i was discharged.
>
> dad is paying for my month stay which is very generous of him. i am not allowed contact with anyone sans 30 mins a day with sharon... cant even see my dogs.
>
> u dont have to say anything, just didnt want u to hear it from mom or dad and not me.
>
> best. R

The email I sent back had only one line, "Be honest with them. Good luck. Love, T."

MONSOON FISHING

In 1980, I had Mr. Franklin as my sixth grade teacher. That year, I mainly did math. We went to the New Jersey shore for vacation. That was fun because their were big waves in the ocean and the water was warm.

Richard Courtemanche
School Writing Assignment, September 20, 1982

Rich and I were about ten and twelve, on our way to Long Beach on the New Jersey shore for the Courtemanche family vacation of 1980. The traffic was stopped, the morning sun was shining down and Rich and I were sitting in our family's van, which we called Stan-the-Van. Everything seemed flat, and the brilliance of the sunlight reflected off the asphalt and the windows around us. Cars edged forward, then stopped and edged forward again. In the back of Stan, the beach supplies shifted a little with each acceleration.

We'd been to Camden, Maine, the last three years in a row. We wanted to try something different vacation-wise. This was our first trip to the New Jersey shore. There were so many cars. Once we got up to the lake cabin in Camden, we always had plenty of room to relax in solitude. At the New Jersey shore, your car alone was one among what seemed like millions.

The rental house where we stayed in New Jersey was a row back from the beach. A path between our rented house and the next one over led to the shore. Our house was surrounded by many other houses, some one story, some two, some on stilts, some not. All built with the idea that they were the only house on the beach, with no real notion of having to fit in.

On the first night, Rich and I were sleeping in the same room when we noticed what smelled like rotten eggs wafting in through the window. It was a smoke bomb.

"Hey, would you mind out there? That stinks!" Dad yelled from the other bedroom.

I looked out the window. Two kids and an adult were standing around the smoke bomb, a family happily lighting off fireworks together. The father said, "It's the sulfur," thinking all Dad wanted was an explanation for the stench.

"Yeah, it stinks. Go somewhere else," Dad said, unimpressed with the details.

Shuffling feet followed, and the smell of the smoke bombs drifted away.

Mom, Dad and Uncle Ed were planning on staying one week at the beach. That week was their summer vacation. Afterward, both sets of grandparents were coming at different times the following week to stay with Rich and me.

Rich loved building sand castles. At the end of a beach day, Rich usually was covered with sand. I'd get disgusted. "How could someone care so little about what other people think?" I'd ask myself.

Rich, Uncle Ed and I built a monstrous sand castle on Sunday, the day after we got to the beach. The beach was packed, and Rich had a crazy, red beach hat on his head—one with a two-inch floppy brim all around. As usual, he and Uncle Ed were caked with sand.

I got involved in the sand castle after the foundation was set. Beach walkers gave us a wide berth; it probably had something to do with Uncle Ed's size (6'7") and the fact that both Uncle Ed and Rich showed little regard for anyone passing by—every now and then, Rich would get a burst of energy and dig like a dog searching for a bone. As the day wore on, some of the incoming waves started creating problems, the larger ones hitting the base of the sand castle and eroding it a little bit. To remedy the problem, we dug a moat around the castle.

We kept an eye on other castle builders, looking for any strategies they might be employing to create a superior sand castle. We saw one group picking up sand, mixing it with water in buckets and dribbling it on the towers of their sand castle. We liked the effect, so we did the same thing. Instead of a bucket, we used water and sand from our moat.

As the tide came in, we built a wall in front of the moat as extra protection. At first, only the biggest waves jumped the wall, plowed through the moat and crashed into the castle itself. As the tide kept coming in, the situation got worse. Even the tiniest waves delivered a wallop. Around 5:00 pm, all that was left of the castle was a mound of sand. As a final salute, Rich took a big jump onto the mound after we came in from the day's last swim. Then we all jumped around on it. The obliteration was almost as much fun as the building. That night, Mom and Dad listened to nonstop sand castle talk during dinner.

During the first week at the beach, we got a steady dose of miniature golf. As Rich alluded to at the beginning of this section, he was good at math. He kept score during the miniature golf games, games that could easily lead to tantrums.

No Courtemanche has ever been a good golfer, not even an acceptable golfer. Miniature golf was different. Had there been a professional miniature golf tour, both Rich and I would have felt qualified to join. Long Beach had several miniature golf courses. Rich and I preferred the one that had a giant windmill. One particular game during the New Jersey vacation ended in a draw—Rich and I had the same score.

Mom, who couldn't care less whether she won or lost (and yet still managed to win some games, to the fury of the Courtemanche males) was in fourth place. Uncle Ed, to the delight of Rich and me, was a distant fifth. When Uncle Ed got an eight on the second hole, we peppered him with advice on how to play better. At the end, Dad, the closest competitor, was two strokes off the lead. A Courtemanche miniature golf game could not end in a tie. There had to be a clear-cut winner—at least that is what Rich and I argued. Caving to our demands, Dad purchased another round for Rich and me when the eighteenth hole was done.

The twist was that the match had to be sudden death—meaning that the first person to win a hole won the match—because everyone wanted to get to the ice cream stand. Rich and I tied on the first hole and tied again on the second hole. The third hole was the one with the giant windmill. It was Rich's turn to go first. He studied the movement of the windmill, studied a little more, drew back his putter and putted. Yes! His ball bounced right off the bottom of one of the spinning windmill arms and came back at us. He banged his club on the ground and prepared to watch me shoot. I stepped up to the line and took a few practice putts, swinging the putter into an imaginary ball—just like I saw golfers do on TV. When I actually putted, I delivered what would be my calling card in pressure sporting situations—I hit the ball straight off the bottom of a windmill arm, and like Rich's, the ball bounced backward.

On his next shot, Rich made it by the windmill arms and somehow landed his shot in the hole. I stepped up again. I'd taken three practice strokes on my previous shot; clearly three strokes was bad luck. I took two practice strokes and hit away. My arms felt weak as I did. I tapped the ball so lightly that it nearly got hit twice by windmill arms. The ball rolled inside the windmill, and as I watched for it to come out the other side (hoping it would head straight for the hole), it rolled back out the front of the windmill. I stomped my foot on the ground at the unfairness of the situation. Rich congratulated me and tallied our scores. We already knew who won, but the game wasn't official until the scores were penciled in.

On the car ride to the ice cream stand, I snatched the scorecard from Rich, ripped it up, swallowed a piece and threw the rest out the window. I learned the swallowing trick from Rich—he'd ripped up a miniature golf scorecard before and tossed it on the floor, only to have me tape it back together.

Later in the first week at Long Beach, a hurricane passed by, way out in the Atlantic. We got hard rain and had to spend a day inside. This was before every vacation house had VCRs. No one wanted to go shopping, and there are only so many games of cribbage you can play in one day.

When Rich and I asked, "Can we go to the beach?" it was a question completely outside the realm of possibility at the beginning of the day.

"Boys, it's pouring rain outside; tomorrow will be a good beach day," one of the adults would say.

Hearing it fifty times or more either makes you deaf to it or weakens your will. "Can we go to the beach?" changed from an actual question to background noise for Mom, Dad and Uncle Ed somewhere between 12:00 and 3:00 pm. By 5:00 pm, though, the rain had slowed, no longer a complete downpour. At 5:00 pm, "Can we go to the beach?" became a question again—and made sense.

The response was, "Why not? Let's take a walk down there."

The surf was the roughest it had been. Rich and I loved bodysurfing, and these definitely were bodysurfing waves. It started to pour again, but what's pouring rain if you're already soaking wet? We bodysurfed and played in the crashing waves until we were too tired to play anymore.

I see clouds and foam from the waves. I hear big crashes. Rich is laughing. Ride one wave, get another—each different from the one before. I look out from the beach. Off in the distance are whitecaps; they look orderly. Right in front of me, the individual waves keep crashing and crashing. The order and structure of the distant waves dissolves to chaos as the individual ones crash to shore. Instead of sand castles, that night we talk about waves.

The following Saturday, Granny and Gramps came up from Philadelphia. They weren't avid miniature golfers, and the miniature golf games lost some of their luster because the grandparents were too easy to beat. Without Uncle Ed, building sand castles wasn't the same either. If it weren't for the deep-sea fishing trip, the vacation might have fallen apart.

The fishing idea was hatched during home movie time on the Friday before we went to the shore. One movie showed Gramps pulling in a fish while surf fishing. Surf fishing? Rich and I had never thought about it before. We'd used thread and a hook to fish off the little dock in Camden in the years before. But seeing Gramps hauling in a fish—*wow*—surf fishing looked too good to be true. The first two nights Granny and Gramps were there, we surf fished. It lost its appeal when we didn't catch a single thing.

In general, Rich spent more time with the grandparents. I was at the age when I was getting interested in girls. I couldn't very well watch girls from the corner of my eye with Granny and Gramps around. It would be too embarrassing if I got caught—by either the girls or the grandparents. We settled into a routine: Each time Granny and Gramps came down to the beach with Rich, I went back to the house. My estrangement from the grandparents ended when Gramps suggested we go deep-sea fishing.

"Deep-sea fishing?" Rich and I asked, eager for details.

"We'll go down to the docks and go out on a boat. Whoo boy, there'll be fish out there," Gramps said in a way that made the words sound extra good.

That fishing trip was the highlight of the New Jersey vacation. Rich and I caught at least fifteen fish each. The sky was pure blue, with no more than one or two clouds the whole day. The sea was calm, and everywhere the boat stopped, we pulled up fish—Rich especially. I have a picture in my mind of Rich during the trip: He's wearing the red vacation hat as he pulls up a fish, biting his lip and hunching his shoulders from the weight of his catch. He was the first one on the boat to catch a fish and usually the first or second to pull up a fish when we switched locations. Some of the adults drank beer, but Rich and I got a full supply of Coca-Cola, which we enjoyed as the boat gently rocked, the sea rising into the air.

When we got back to shore, Granny and Gramps wanted to cook the fish fresh for dinner. Rich and I wanted fried shrimp from a roadside stand. We ended up eating fried shrimp. What a day!

Our other grandparents, Mommom and Poppop (Dad's parents), took us out fishing later the same week. We rented a little motorboat and headed out into the bay. Someone told us there'd be plenty of flounder out there. We caught a few fish, but not nearly as many as we'd caught with Granny and Gramps. Still, the weather was great, and being closer to the water, we could really get a sense of the little bay waves lapping against the side of the boat. And Rich wore his red hat again. The hat was the same one that Granny and Gramps would later use to identify their car in a parking lot. "Our car is the only car with a red hat in the rear window," Granny would tell everyone.

After the second week at the shore, Rich and I came back to Massachusetts full of fishing stories—flounder this; sea bass that. Photographs, rolls of them, showed us during the trips with Granny and Gramps and Mommom and Poppop.

A few weeks after we were home, Dad agreed to take Rich and me deep-sea fishing. We went to Gloucester, and during the early morning drive, it became clear that we weren't going to get much sun that day. We didn't so much drive as tiptoe to Gloucester, hoping the rain would hold off. Why didn't we just not go? We'd already made up our minds: *Today was the day!*

When we got there, we saw that the fishing boat was about the same size as the one we went on with Granny and Gramps—a good sign. But we needed jackets to keep the morning chill from affecting our psyches. The wind and the screeching of seagulls made the cold air get into us a little deeper. Even with the cold, Rich and I were excited; soon we'd be dropping our lines. We knew what that meant: Fish would bite, we'd haul them up and the helpful boat attendant would net them. We might even take a stab at pulling the hook out like we did with the grandparents.

About forty-five minutes out to sea, the captain cut the engines and the boat stopped. He told everyone that he'd found a school of fish. The people on the boat weren't as helpful or as interested in Rich and me as they'd been in New Jersey. In New Jersey, Granny and Gramps made us the show. Here, we were just two kids fishing with everyone else. When the boat stopped, everyone dropped in their lines. Twenty minutes later, two things happened. It started to rain, and someone at the back of the boat caught the first fish of the day. It was a shark and would be the only fish caught that day.

Shortly after an attendant pulled the little sand shark up on deck, removed the hook and then tossed it back to sea, a hard rain started to fall. The waves, which were small whitecaps on the ride out, grew larger. The boat began rocking—we rolled up one wave and down another. Any thought of fishing ended when the captain announced we were headed for shore. Waves were pouring through portholes on the sides of the boat as we made our way back. All the travelers huddled on a small platform in the middle of the deck. Every so often, a huge wave would crash over the side of the boat, drenching everyone on the platform. Rich and I sat on either side of Dad and tried to keep warm. If only time moved as slowly in the good times as it did on that boat ride back, life would be better. The day of deep-sea fishing with Dad and Rich was about as cold as I've ever been.

Our clothes stayed damp the whole ride back from Gloucester. When we finally got home, all three of us stripped off our soggy, freezing clothes and ran straight upstairs to change into sweatpants and sweatshirts. Dad lit a fire, and Rich and I drank hot chocolate. We called the grandparents that night to tell them what happened.

Whenever I used to think about deep-sea fishing, I thought about Rich and the first trip with Granny and Gramps. It wasn't until I sat down to write this story that I remembered the trips with Mommom and Poppop and then Dad. That's the way memory works. One thing leads to another and leads to another. We can't always tell which thought will take us where. In the case of deep-sea fishing, now I keep all three trips together.

TREE FORTS AND INTERDEPENDENCY

When Rich and I were kids in grade school, one of the ways you could establish popularity was by being invited to a friend's house. Every other Wednesday, the students at Pine Hill Elementary School, where Rich and I went, had a half-day from school. If you were going to be invited to a friend's house, it was usually on a Wednesday half-day.

Rich and I weren't particularly popular in grade school. We usually played in our own backyard by ourselves or somewhere in the neighborhood with a few friends. Playing with neighborhood kids didn't do much for your popularity. If all you did was play with local kids, you were a small-timer. You really needed to go to different neighborhoods, ride on a different school bus than your own, to boost your personal profile.

One Wednesday afternoon, my friend Paul invited me to his house. For me, being on a different bus than my own was a little nerve-wracking. At least on my own bus, I knew which kids were to be avoided—the ones who would zap you with spitballs if you sat too close. Once we got to Paul's house and had lunch, we went into his backyard. I forget what we did at first. As a boy, you don't have to worry much about making conversation once you're at your friend's house. "You like salamanders? Wow, me too. Let's go turn over some rocks!" Two hours later, it's time to go home.

At some point, and I think it was early in the afternoon, we went to Paul's tree fort. For an eight-year-old, the experience was jaw-dropping. The tree fort was actually a miniature house, perched in a tree. It looked like a real house! It was white, had shutters and a swing ladder that you climbed to get into the fort. Paul had all kinds of stuff up there—baseball cards, hockey cards and football cards, plus *Mad* magazines and *Sports Illustrated* swimsuit issues. When I got home, I told Rich about it right away.

Rich had a friend with a tree fort, too! Once you decide to get a new car, you start to see the brand you're considering everywhere you go. So it was with tree forts. When Rich and I thought about it, we were just about the only family that didn't have a tree fort. Rich and I considered ourselves pretty handy. For example, Rich built toy models. It wasn't unusual for Rich to smash one to pieces if it didn't match the picture on the box, but the point was that he knew how to put stuff together. I once tried to build an engine from wire, wood and a battery, in a design bearing no resemblance to an engine. I have no idea why I thought it would work, but I was upset when I touched the end of the wire—which I'd carefully wrapped around a wooden spool—to a battery and nothing happened. Here again, though, the actual result of the project wasn't important; the point was that I, too, could put stuff together.

The day after I went to Paul's house, Rich and I went down to our cellar, pulled a hammer, some nails and a saw off the wall, and got to work. We started cutting wood and hammering the pieces together. The first few building sessions were not productive from an end-product perspective—a tree fort was a bigger project than we were prepared to handle at our then-current building skill (the go-cart I described in Chapter One was also still a few years in the future). They were ideal, though, from an enjoyment perspective. In the next few weeks, we pulled out whatever wood we could find from all the crevices in the basement and the garage. We cut up different shapes and built battleships—single sections of 2 x 4s with smaller blocks nailed to them. There were lots of nails lying around, so the battleships would be fully loaded with canons. We sailed the ships in the rain puddle that formed in our driveway, and we threw rocks at them to simulate battle conditions.

Though we might lose sight of it at times, Rich and I never entirely forgot that the ultimate goal of our building sessions was a tree fort. After enough pestering, Mom and Dad said we could have one. Our first job was to designate a spot for it. We wanted it in the trees in the front yard—where the whole neighborhood could see it. When Mom and Dad resisted, we agreed to a location in the woods behind the house. Uncle Ed was the building expert in the family, and so we consulted him. He flew up from Feasterville and became the lynchpin for the project, even negotiating a more visible spot for the fort—in the woods that were on the side of the house, near the driveway. He was almost as excited about the tree fort as Rich and I.

The day Uncle Ed began construction was a happy day. Rich and I sat at the kitchen table as Uncle Ed drew up plans. We went to the hardware store with him and followed him around the building site. We held boards, sorted nails and hammered where we could. Once the fort was done, I rode my bike around the neighborhood, a victory lap like racecar drivers do after they win a race. Both Rich and I realized our fort was not like Paul's. It was a brown box about ten feet off the ground, completely open to the elements (meaning no glass windows or even screens) and had no furniture inside. Plus, it had a permanent wood ladder. We couldn't pull it up like a rope ladder. Mom was the architect of the wood ladder—fearing we might go up there, pull up the rope ladder and hide, maybe for hours. Uncle Ed did create one secretive perk: peep holes on all the walls. Thanks to them, Rich and I could see if someone was approaching the fort.

All in all, the tree fort probably had over 500 nails in it and maybe 100 different pieces of wood. The tree fort remained a fixture at the Courtemanche house long after Rich and I stopped playing in it. You could always recognize the brown box when you pulled into the driveway. Like all things, as the years rolled by, it started to look decrepit. One day in a winter snowstorm, it fell down. We hauled the wood to the dump, and the broken tree in which the fort had stood was all that remained.

❖ ❖ ❖

In order to miss something, we have to know what we're missing, don't we? We refer to ourselves as "I" or "me" or by some variant of our names. What was I referring to when I said, "There's Richard Courtemanche"? It's simple to say that I was referring to the physical person I could point at. In the same way I pointed at the tree fort and said, "There's our tree fort," I could point at Rich and say, "There's my brother, Rich." That, though, seems to imply that Rich was simply a physical object.

The tree fort contained a lot of parts. Human beings contain an unfathomable number of parts. We're all composed of cells. The human body has over ten quadrillion cells. From a cellular perspective, not one of us—not one—is the same person we were five years ago, one year ago or even one day ago. Cells die and new cells are created. In an article titled "Retrospective Birth Dating of Cells in Humans," published in the journal *Cell* in 2005, Kirsty Spalding and her colleagues concluded that most of our cells are under seventeen years old. Our body is a collection of new and old and in-between.

There's a philosophical paradox concerning time travel. If to travel in time, you needed to go through a time machine that would vaporize your parts and then re-create them at another point in time, would you be the same person? That is, if all your cells were wiped out and then were reassembled somewhere else, would you be the same person or would it be more accurate to say that you had died and been re-created (or reborn)? Regardless of your answer, that is what happens to us here on Earth.

Living on and among the ten quadrillion cells of our bodies are quadrillions more bacteria cells. In *A Short History of Nearly Everything*, Bill Bryson wrote of the bacteria cells: "We couldn't survive a day without them." Bacteria dispose of wastes in our bodies, change what we eat into useful sugars, manufacture vitamins in our intestines and "go to war on alien microbes that slip down our gullet." We are a lot more interdependent than we first appear. What looks like us is not *all* us by a long shot.

Not only are our physical bodies made from scraps, but they're actually amorphous collections of countless different cells, many of which aren't even our own. The bacterial parts on and inside of us have their own agendas. They're not here to serve us. On the contrary, we are here to serve them.

When I pointed at Rich's body, I was pointing to an ever-changing collection of parts, some of which were Rich's—at least for the time being—and others that were not. I asked if we need to know what we're missing in order to miss something. What you or I or anyone else actually *is* starts to get tricky. At first glance, it seems like what we miss when someone dies is the physical person, the one we could reach out and hold. A person's physical body, though, is ending and beginning, again and again, every day. When the seventeen-year mark hits, and almost all of our cells have died and been replaced by new cells, somehow we—whatever *we* are—live on.

As to what we miss when we miss a person, I have to say I'm not all that sure. At this stage, I'm really only hammering nails and experimenting, just like Rich and I did when we were small.

Wrestling Jet Skis

Sometimes when I think about Rich, I see a two-word subtitle: "Irrational Complexities." Most people living in the presence of bipolar disorder see the same thing. Nietzsche said, "One must still have chaos in oneself to be able to give birth to a dancing star." When Rich was feeling good, he had an energy you just wanted to tap into. It's not unusual for people with bipolar disorder to be larger than life. Rich always had a crew of friends. No matter where I visited him, there would be a group of people who seemed like they'd do just about anything for him.

Once at Martha's Vineyard (after Rich was out of the marines), he asked his high school friend Tommy if he could use his Jet Ski. He had a way of asking that was really a way of telling Tommy he was going to use it, so that Tommy knew.

"Gee, Rich, we've had a couple beers. I don't know about that."

"Tommy, I've got my life vest here; the Jet Ski is in good hands."

"I don't know; the water's choppy today."

Rich and Tommy bantered a minute or two before Tommy's wife, Stephanie, said, "Come on, Tommy, let him use the Jet Ski."

"Rich, do me a favor, take a cell phone," Tommy said.

"Got it, Tommy."

Rich went into the house and came back with Tommy's cell phone in a Ziploc bag; Rich's phone remained in the house. He waved his arm without looking back and dragged the Jet Ski into the surf. His friends watched as Rich took a few laps in front of the house. Tommy, I'm sure, could hear the Jet Ski straining under Rich's weight. Once he finished his laps, he gunned the motor, and they all watched as Rich became half his size, a quarter his size, an eighth until finally he was gone, somewhere way down the beach.

Rich kept the throttle at full speed. He couldn't see the house anymore when he looked back. He was having a great time: The ocean was there for his enjoyment. He started doing laps. He was farther out than he'd been back at the house. Rich never played it safe. If there's one point of stability for Rich, it's that he never played it safe.

At the far end of one of his loops, the farthest he'd been from the shore, he took a tight turn and flipped the ski. On most falls, the ski stays right side up and does little turns so that you can swim back and get on it. The way Rich had turned, the ski flipped, the engine gurgled, some blue smoke came out and it came to a stop, seat facing down. Rich swam over to the ski and tried to right it. The weather was windy, and the waves were higher than normal. Rich says he tried to flip it over for at least an hour, maybe two. It seems like a long time, but his friends tell me that he was definitely gone for at least three hours. They tried calling him but couldn't get through. They did what we were all forced to do with Rich: sit and wait and hope for the best.

At some point, Rich started swimming with the Jet Ski to shore, pulling it as he went. The process didn't go very quickly. According to Rich, after he swallowed enough salt water, he took a break. He held on to the bottom of the Jet Ski (which was facing up) and just floated for a little bit. He noticed during the quiet time that he could use the motion of the waves to help him right the ski. He finally flipped it. He climbed back on and tried to start it, but it was completely dead. He sat on the ski for a while, still a decent way from shore, and then jumped back into the water. With the ski righted, he started pushing it from behind.

Don't get the sense during all this that Rich was out in the water on his own. On Martha's Vineyard, there are always boats somewhere in view. Each time someone asked him if he wanted help, Rich just waved them on. One boat kept an eye on him. The driver was cruising up and down the beach, probably enjoying the same sensation Rich had. Rich said he saw the driver pass him about ten times. On the eleventh pass, the driver had finally seen enough. He said, "Here's a rope; let me pull you in."

Rich answered, "Okay," climbed on the Jet Ski and took hold of the rope.

"Where are you going?" the guy asked as he pulled Rich to shore.

"Just up the beach a little bit."

"I'll tow you there."

"Don't worry about it," Rich answered. Once they got to shallow water, Rich said, "This will be fine. I could use the exercise." As the other boater drove off, Rich walked until the water was up to his waist and then started dragging the Jet Ski the eighth or quarter mile back to the house. That's just the way Rich was; there's not really a logical explanation as to why he wouldn't accept a tow all the way back.

His friends were sitting on the porch when they first noticed the dot on the horizon. It got closer and closer until they saw it was Rich, dragging a waterlogged Jet Ski. When he finally got back, he pulled the Jet Ski up on the beach and approached the house. With his friends waiting for an explanation, he took the Ziploc bag out of his pocket and handed it to Tommy.

"Sorry about the phone," he said, and Tommy emptied the water from the Ziploc bag.

Rich went into the house, grabbed a beer, flipped on the TV and sat on the couch. Eventually, his friends followed him in to find out what happened. According to Stephanie, that night Rich complained when one of his friends spilled barbecue sauce and a little got on his shirt.

No matter what he did, Rich had a way of striking each note as forcefully as it could be played. When he was the captain of the Dover-Sherborn high school football team in 1986, the team didn't win any games. After they lost the season finale on Thanksgiving Day, Rich walked home like he normally did, a walk of about ten miles. When he got home, he was drunk. One of his friends told me that Rich walked home with a bottle after every game. At Rich's service, a father of one of the younger players from the 1986 team said that Rich was the reason his son kept playing football. His son thought of quitting, but Rich always talked him out of it. Rich treated him like a little brother, and he went on to be captain of a later team.

In the marines, Rich tutored the guys who were having a hard time with the classroom portion of basic training. He'd teach them basic math and English. He did it on his own time, the time when recruits could write letters or just relax from the chaos for a few hours. There was no reward, no medal—just a few guys passing basic training who otherwise would not have.

A few months before his four-year enlistment was set to expire, Rich finished a tour in Okinawa. While there, he applied to colleges back in the States. He got into Babson College in Wellesley, Massachusetts, a short drive from Mom's house in Natick. His commanding officer let him out of the marines early so Rich could start school right away. The discharge process wasn't as smooth as my description makes it sound. There was lots of paperwork and hand-wringing as Rich's request moved up the chain of command, but he ultimately got what he asked for: an honorable discharge.

Rich had been searching for discipline when he went into the marines, and he definitely found some. When he first got out, he kept every hanger in his closet exactly one inch from the one before. All the clothes in his bureau looked like squares of cardboard, neatly stacked on top of each other. He said "Yes, ma'am" and "Sir" and wondered why people in the civilian world didn't just listen to direction like the marines. But as you can probably tell from the Jet Ski story, his wild streak remained firmly in tact: if anything, cultivated during his enlistment.

Another of Rich's traits fostered in the marines was a kind of single-mindedness, an ability to focus on a subject to the exclusion of everything else. Once discharged, the first task he set for himself was graduating from college. His goal wasn't simply to graduate; he looked at an undergraduate degree as a stepping stone for something much bigger. He was determined to get into a business school like Stanford or the Massachusetts Institute of Technology, where he would study investing.

Rich's life was one of extremes. What better extreme than to have been both an enlisted marine and then a graduate from an elite business school? Earning a degree that would facilitate the kind of material wealth that stood in glaring contrast to the image of a marine grunt.

❧ CHAPTER FOUR ❧

And bread I broke with you was more than bread.
—Conrad Aiken

DINING IN NATICK

In early August 1994, I moved from Natick, Massachusetts, to North Carolina so that I could attend the University of North Carolina at Chapel Hill. At the time, I drove an early 80's Oldsmobile Cutlass that a friend's dad had sold to me for $100. The paint was faded; the seats didn't move too well, and the side window didn't roll all the way up. When I left from Natick, no one was sure the car was going to make it all the way down to Chapel Hill. Rich was the last person to see me off.

There I am in Mom's driveway, sitting in the Cutlass with the driver side window rolled down. I'm getting ready to say goodbye to Rich. He's in school himself, at Babson College, saving money like I was by living with Mom. It's a sunny, blue-sky day. Inside the car, heat is radiating off the crimson seats. Outside, the air temperature is just right; either long or short pants are comfortable. Rich is in shorts and a ripped T-shirt, heading over to shake my hand.

A week or two before I left, Rich and I played a game of "H-O-R-S-E" on a Saturday afternoon. Rich had just hit a left-handed shot while standing behind the hoop. We each had special shots—shots that the other wasn't going to make. We could only do those shots once, but they were practically a guaranteed letter for the other guy. I took a drink of beer after my shot clanked off the bottom of the backboard. Rich grabbed the ball before it rolled down the driveway (Mom's house sits on a hill). Next, he did a one-handed set shot.

"No arms, just wrist, only net," he said, which meant the only parts of my body I could move to take the shot were my wrist and fingers, and the ball could touch only the net—no part of the rim and definitely not the backboard. I missed again and took another drink.

"Warren and I have finalized the company tagline," Rich told me. "Results are guaranteed." Then he said, "On the fine print, we're going to put, 'Direction of results may or may not match individual investor expectations.'" When he said the part about "individual investor expectations," he changed his voice and speeded it up to match one of the investment videos he and his friend Warren watched. Warren went to Babson as well, and the two of them had investor books lying all over Mom's house.

In terms of investments, Rich liked complicated ones. Trading individual stocks was not enough. When he was at Babson, he talked about derivatives.

64

The value of a derivative is *derived* from some other vehicle—maybe a bond or a stock or currency. Futures contracts, the specialty on which Rich ultimately focused, are a subset of the broader derivatives market. Derivatives offer more leverage than ordinary stocks and bonds, meaning you can make or lose a much higher percentage of your total investment. You command more capital.

The only way you can lose your whole investment when you purchase stock directly is if the price of the stock drops to zero. If instead you buy a derivative like a call option on a stock, you're purchasing a contract that is linked to the price of the stock but is not the stock itself. With a derivative like an option, you can lose the entire amount of your investment without the stock dropping to zero. And you can double or triple your investment without the price of the stock doubling or tripling. That's leverage. I couldn't keep up with Rich and his derivative theories. When he and Warren talked trading, they were talking a different language.

Once he was out of the marines, Rich moved into Mom's house, about a year before I moved down to North Carolina. "Cheap" is a good description of Rich's communal buying habits. I knew he'd saved money in the marines. He had a black Mustang 5.0 that looked like an undercover highway patrol car. The car got special gas, special parking (in the garage while the Olds stayed outside) and special love—he used to clean parts of the engine with a toothbrush. But Rich's money got very tight when it came to food and bath products.

A bar of soap didn't stand much of a chance with Rich. I'd get a new bar, put it in the shower on Sunday, and by Thursday, it would be a tiny sliver. I've never seen soap dissolve so quickly. Rich used Gillette Sensor razors, like me. The razor blades at the time cost something like $0.60 a pop. Rich switched the blades out every other day, and he never purchased a single blade that I can recall.

He had a voracious appetite. When I bought a gallon of milk, it would be half gone four hours later. Rich took what you gave him from a grocery perspective without a shred of remorse. If I complained enough, he'd get a token bag of groceries. Then as soon as Mom was within earshot, he'd say something like, "T, groceries are in the fridge—had to cut into my school money to buy them, but the good of the family's worth it." That would always buy him a month or two of soap, razor and milk free rides.

Mood disorders like depression lock a person into a single state of mind. The only possibility is the one you're in now. A kind of tunnel vision evolves that can make it almost impossible for the person to see things from another perspective. A natural by-product is for the depressed person to see things as being all about them. If you can't escape your moods, if you have no way out, then you stay there, mired in the muck.

One time, Rich decided he wanted to go see his girlfriend, Kelley, at her parent's house on Cape Cod. He convinced Peter (an old friend) and me to go with him. It didn't take much convincing—a night out on the Cape in the summer beat sitting around in Natick. The three of us drove two and a half hours to Cape Cod. When we got there, Kelley and Rich talked for two more.

Then Rich decided he didn't want to stay, and the three of us drove back that night. Peter and I had a total of seven hours of being towed around by Rich.

"Rich," I said when we got home after dropping Peter off, "you can't drag your friends to the Cape and then turn around and come home when we were expecting to go out."

"Okay," is all he said. He said it from some other space, a space he stepped out of for a second to answer my question. He wasn't arguing. The way he responded, I just let it drop.

There's a difference between moods and emotions. In general, emotions are short-lived. You're excited, and then you come back down. You're distraught, then you come back up. Mood disorders aren't one-time events. The way I think about them is that they're like stage music. They're not a note, and they're not a single song: They're a score. The curtain goes up, and then you don't even notice the music because it's been playing all along. Moods are ongoing symphonies that accompany us as we move through life.

Before Rich moved into Mom's house, I had no social life. I'd moved into Mom's house because I was unemployed, having quit my job selling steel before first getting another. All my high school friends were married. I'd hang out with them once in a while, but too much time with them just reminded me that my career aspirations weren't moving ahead as I'd hoped they would and that I was single. An exciting Saturday night back then was buying a six-pack of beer and watching cable TV by myself.

About two months after Rich got home from the marines, he organized a Monday night dinner club. Both he and I went to the same gym. We worked out around the same time every night, and Rich knew almost everyone there. That's where he met Kelley. For Monday night dinners, we'd invite our friends from the gym.

"Peter, that's ridiculous," Granny said at one of the dinners. Granny and Gramps, Peter, Kelley, Warren and a few other friends were there. Peter's eyes went wide. He didn't yet have a college degree but was explaining how he was going to start working in an investment firm, securing a position typically reserved for newly minted MBAs. According to Peter, he'd gone on several interviews already, each interviewer more impressed with him than the one before.

Peter was as loyal a friend as anyone could have, but everyone knew he stretched things. Few people doubted him directly. That's where Granny came in. She had no filters. Rich, myself and the whole table laughed out loud when she confronted Peter. He defended his story as the rest of us munched away on a pasta and meat sauce dinner.

"Oh, for goodness sakes," Granny said again.

Peter, cornered, tried to fire back, insisting that at least one company had offered to pay for both his college degree and an MBA—the only condition being that he work full time; his insights were needed immediately. Granny just sighed. Peter responded again, and then people jumped in to support him and support Granny. That was the spirit of the dinners: There was always a lot of laughter. The dinners wouldn't have happened without Rich. When Rich was up, life was livelier for everyone around.

I heard an interview on the radio the other day, a musician talking about how important it is to have balance in life. As he was getting increasingly more famous, the musician kept reminding himself to get away from his work. That's effective for some people. Others need intensity of purpose; the more they drive themselves, the better. Rich prospered on intensity of purpose.

As I was doing odd jobs to earn some money and filtering in and out of the house, I'd run across Rich studying in the room attached to the garage. He'd lock in on his books. If you went into the room when he was studying, he might not even acknowledge you; you knew you should turn around and get out. That steadfastness of purpose motivated me to get my act together.

I'd always been interested in health care. At one point, I thought I wanted to be a physical therapist—that changed as soon as I volunteered for a single day in a physical therapy office. I realized I had no interest in the "hands on" side of health care, instead wanting to be on the business side. The easiest way to do so, I concluded, was to go back to school to get a degree in health care administration.

I studied the same way as Rich did when I was preparing for the Graduate Record Examinations. I kept an egg timer on my desk to pace myself on practice exams. The first few times I took a practice test, the egg timer would go off before I was half done. By the time I sat for the actual test, though, I knew instinctively how long I had for each section and knew every kind of question that might be asked. The only surprises were the actual questions; I'd drilled the structure and subject matter of the test indelibly into my head. It was as if with the preparation I'd done, I had no choice but to score well. Rich's work ethic gave me the example I needed to go back to school.

When I shook his hand through the Cutlass's window on the day I moved down to Chapel Hill, it occurred to both of us, me for sure, that I was leaving something unique. It had to end at some point—we couldn't live in Mom's house indefinitely, but while it lasted, it was a special time. With me leaving, we wouldn't have the spontaneous little day-to-day diversions like shooting baskets in the driveway anymore. We wouldn't sit on either side of the couch and watch sports. We wouldn't be woven into the fabric of each other's life on a daily basis as we'd been the past year. I guess we both realized all that in the form of a feeling.

As I pull out of the driveway, we both cry. I have to look away; tears are streaming so hard. There is my little brother—my number-one fan—and we're both starting on new life chapters.

DOGS, CULTURE AND MENTAL ILLNESS

Researchers have debated nature versus nurture ever since they realized that both impact behavior. Identical twins of people with bipolar disorder, major depression, schizophrenia and other psychiatric disorders have only a 50 percent chance of developing the same disorder. Wherever you stand on nature versus nurture, it's clear that how we're wired is part of the issue but not the whole issue.

In a world of cat and dog people, the Courtemanches were dog people. We owned or cohabitated with large dogs. There were Winston and Tiffany, both English mastiffs who weighed 210 and 180 pounds, respectively, and Chester, a bull mastiff, at 160 pounds. There was also Olie, a German shepherd and the original Courtemanche big dog, who weighed close to 130 pounds.

From the time Rich entered the Courtemanche household to the time he left for Bates, there were dogs. If Winston or Olie or any of them wanted to get on a bed, all they had to do was climb up there. They had free rein. Dogs were part of the Courtemanche culture.

Culture can be specific to a family or friends or it can extend to a city or state or country. If it's a group, it has a culture. The Courtemanches liked sweatshirts, the *Bob Newhart Show* and sitting on the porch on a Friday night listening to crickets while drinking lemonade (Courtemanches under twenty-one) or mixed drinks (Courtemanches over twenty-one). We weren't big fans of social get-togethers, were appalled by dress codes and liked to keep our issues in-house. Courtemanche adults forbade the watching of floozy TV shows like the *Love Boat*, but Courtemanche children understood that watching the *Love Boat* was perfectly acceptable on nights when Mom and Dad went out.

Culture is created by individuals but belongs to the group. In the book *The Psychosocial Aspects of Depression,* Janis Jenkins and her colleagues wrote, "culture is of profound importance to the experience of depression." The authors argue that culture plays a role in all aspects of depression, from how it is defined and treated to the course of the disease and its eventual outcome. Culture, they say, is critical to "the very constitution of depressive illness."

What is the attitude in the United States regarding mental illness? Our puritan forefathers required that people with mental illness be kept out of sight. Mental illness was to be hidden. Today, the situation has changed, or so it appears. Television commercials describe the signs and symptoms of depression for millions of viewers. As a culture, not only do we talk about mental illness, or at least depression, but we also seem to *care* about people who have it, holding their best interests at heart.

Before we get too comfortable with that impression, remember that commercials are some of the most widely viewed sources of information about mental illness treatment options. The role of commercials is to help consumers recognize their unmet needs. As marketing professionals know, a tried and proven way to help people recognize a need is to *create* it, by instilling insecurity.

On television, on the Internet, in magazines and on billboards, we're told that if we had this or that good, we'd be part of an "in" group—the group of luxury car owners or American beer drinkers or people who like to save money on car insurance. On the same mediums we're bombarded with commercials about our inferiority—and how that inferiority can be remedied if we just bought the product being advertised—we also watch commercials that encourage us to talk with our doctors about medications for depression.

The TV commercials usually show an unhappy person, perhaps lying in bed, who suddenly starts smiling once he or she consumes the depression medication being advertised. The medication could be replaced by Viagra, and most of the ads would still flow. Is there any limit to the amount of happiness we can reasonably buy? You wouldn't know it if you spend a lot of time being entertained by television or movies. Dream big, and best if your dreams include fancy cars and big houses because those things grease the wheels for the rest of us. The United States now has more consumer debt than at any other time in our history. Inventions like credit cards have made debt convenient. We can get interest-only loans in which we don't have to make any payments toward what we actually borrowed.

In a society in which we dispense pills—our treatment of choice—for depression, we have an economy that's both strengthened by individual insecurity and encourages debt. We can all see the bar up high. Few of the messages we hear say, "Don't jump for it." Most scream, "Jump!"—and even if you miss, go ahead and buy something so that it looks like you made it. All that buying creates financial stress, which, as it so happens, is a trigger for depression—a primary trigger.

I asked us not to get comfortable with the notion that we, as a society, hold the depressed person's best interests at heart. William Blake said, "Thy friendship oft has made my heart to ache; do be my enemy—for friendship's sake." If you're a company that manufactures or sells pills for depression, it's good for your bottom line if your potential customers are burdened with financial stress and insecurity. Some experts believe the increased incidence of depression in the United States is due wholly to advertising, that we've been sold the idea we're depressed. David Healy suggests the same thing is happening with bipolar disorder (in his article "The Latest Mania: Selling Bipolar Disorder").

No matter the reason for the climbing rates of depression and bipolar disorder, my goal is not to suggest that pills do not work. They don't work for everyone, but for those that they do, they're life changing. Selective serotonin reuptake inhibitors (SSRIs) helped me to stop the part of my mind that told me I should reevaluate each conversation I had with a boss at work. When I was a teenager, I put an odometer on my bike. I thought it would be fun to see how far I rode each day. The fun was replaced with a compulsion to return the bike to the garage on whole numbers only. I'd ride, get back to the garage, and if the 2.0 mile marker slide to 2.1, I'd go out riding again until I could garage the bike at 3.0. If the same thing happened the next time, with the odometer sliding to

3.1, I'd go off riding once more. Sometimes, I'd just carry the bike home. SSRIs helped me to break the grip my compulsions held over me. When Rich was being treated with medications, I thought he was better off.

Pills don't treat circumstances, though; they treat symptoms. Feeling anxious? Some SSRIs and medications like Valium or Xanax can eliminate the anxiousness. The symptom is considered a foe to be conquered. Importantly, the symptom is not a message but noise. Like a scene from a bizarre science-fiction movie, pills can help us to live in circumstances that would otherwise mire us in depressions, on one hand, or drive total mental breakdowns, on the other.

Does it have to be that way? Can a culture embrace mental disorder rather than just aiming to eliminate (or profit from) the symptoms? Julian Silverman authored a paper titled "Shamans and Acute Schizophrenia" while he worked at the National Institute of Mental Health in 1967. The essence of the paper is that the psychological characteristics of what Silverman called the "essential schizophrenic" are similar to those of a shaman in a so-called primitive culture. When Silverman wrote the article, an "essential schizophrenic" was defined as a person who had lost touch with the outside world—for example, a person who mumbled to imaginary acquaintances on street corners. In modern culture, the prognosis for the equivalent of an essential schizophrenic is poor.

Silverman concluded that the main outcomes differentiator for people realizing essential schizophrenic characteristics in any culture is the degree to which the individuals and their characteristics are accepted by the culture. Shamans, for example, hold a revered status in some primitive cultures. Silverman wrote that when a potential shaman first experiences a schizophrenic-like ordeal, the person is helped by an established shaman, someone who has experienced the same symptoms and come out of the ordeal stronger. The resolution is a metaphorical rebirth of the individual. It's as if the apprentice shamans begin to understand the messages being sent by what Jung would refer to as their unconscious, and in the process, they develop a better understanding of their potentialities. At no point in the process are they made to feel flawed: They are *embraced* by their society.

For an essential schizophrenic in a modern culture, there is no resolution, no understanding and no expanded consciousness. Instead, he or she spirals progressively inward until there is no escape; the person is lost within a chaotic, ever-morphing internal psychosis. At best, the person becomes a drain on society.

In his book *Recovery from Schizophrenia: Psychiatry and Political Economy*, Richard Warner wrote that the treatment outcomes for psychosis in third-world countries often exceed those of the Western world. Warner described a 1978 World Health Organization (WHO) funded study in which 63 percent of people seeking treatment in third-world countries for psychosis experienced improvement in their condition versus only 37 percent in developed countries. Third-world treatments included traditional and religious healers, and non-medicinally based therapies like yoga. The difference in outcomes, Warner noted, was not due to diagnostic criteria, and the results did not dissipate over time. A follow-up study in 2000 found that the third-world participants in the 1978 WHO study were still faring better than their developed-world counterparts.

As would be expected, the success of third-world approaches is not uniform. Warner described the attitudes of two primitive tribes for whom individuals with psychosis "should be tied up forever, allowed to starve, driven away to die or killed outright." The keys to successful third-world treatment are conflict resolution and social reintegration. Like Silverman, Warner wrote, "In the West, a psychotic episode is likely to lead to increased alienation."

The concepts of *acceptance* and *alienation* recur over and over—the distinction driving the difference between "therapy helped" and "therapy failed." Instead of labeling outcomes based on socioeconomic designations like "third world" and "developed," the "us-versus-them" vernacular we used in investigating Augustine and his attitude toward suicide is another option. Successful treatment of psychosis is, in this way, a function of feeling like an "us."

When he died in 1987, Joseph Campbell was considered the world's leading authority on myths. He believed that ancient myths provided psychological road maps for modern people, offering solutions to age-old problems. His position toward psychosis was as follows: embrace not only the individual but the psychotic experience itself; make the episode an *us*. Campbell wrote in his book *Myths to Live By*, "The whole problem . . . is somehow to go through [the psychosis], even time and again, without shipwreck." For Campbell, the answer was not in preventing the individual from experiencing the symptoms, "but that one should [be] taught something already of the scenery to be entered and the powers to be met, given a formula of some kind by which to recognize, subdue them and incorporate their energies." Campbell's observation is a variant of Silverman's shaman model. Psychosis, for these authors, is not something to be avoided but rather something to be experienced and journeyed through.

It sounds so foreign to consider treating the symptoms of psychosis this way—to embrace them? The person is hearing voices! You just need to stop the voices, and everything will be okay. With bipolar disorder, instead of relying primarily on lithium or Depakote to level out moods, the person would learn from someone who has successfully lived with bipolar disorder. The treatment wouldn't mean no medication. It would mean enduring the lows and the highs in the presence of someone who's been there, too, in the expectation that the experienced person with bipolar disorder could help the novice navigate the territory. At a minimum, it would mean opening the gates, talking about the meaning of the symptoms rather than extinguishing them while coals still burn underneath.

The question is whether it's possible. Can the shamanistic "learn from one who's had it" or the "third-world social reintegration" treatment model work for bipolar disorder? If they were drugs, there would certainly be studies to investigate them. In the absence of studies, we can fall back on some time-tested observations: The role a good teacher has on a student and that culture has on guiding, molding and defining the individual is undeniable. Successful treatment is not about us-versus-them; it doesn't have to be pharmaceuticals *or* social reintegration. There's room for anything that helps. Psychiatrist Kevin Turnquist wrote in his article "Are We Becoming a Nation of Depressives?" that in the future, "Therapies aimed at improved relationships or at decreasing our eternal preoccupation with striving for status may become as respected as medications—especially if [they're found] to evoke similar changes in brain functioning."

Chapter Two mentioned sickle cell anemia. The faulty gene that causes the disease also affords a potential benefit: It can protect those who carry it from malaria. Nature tends to produce yings with yangs. Francis Mondimore wrote, "The prevalence of bipolar disorder is simply much higher in groups of accomplished artists than in the general population." According to Emil Kraepelin, "The volitional excitement which accompanies the disease may . . . set free powers which are otherwise constrained by all kind of inhibition." The secret behind Sigmund Freud's psychoanalytic technique was a freeing of the individual from the usual inhibitions of his or her own conscious mind.

Rich's decision to get into the investment business was, no doubt, influenced by many things: Courtemanche family culture (Dad was in the investment business), Western culture and materialism, Rich's skill in math, his good fortune in betting, his belief in his own natural ability and possibly an awareness that the trading business would be tolerant toward his extremes in mood. More, he could lose himself in it, forever examining nuances in the markets, occupying his mind—and perhaps short-circuiting its penchant for turning against him. He threw himself into the business with a passion you really had to see to appreciate. For a time, each market report, each book on trading and each investment article Rich read were a mixing of paints that he shortly applied to his own canvas. His approach was like, I suppose, Winston Churchill to politics—or maybe to painting.

OUT OF THE HOSPITAL

Karl Menninger wrote of inpatient stays at psychiatric hospitals, "To encourage relatives or patients to believe that a few weeks or months are likely to bring about a fundamental change is only to disappoint them with certain failure."

When Rich sent me the email about going into the psychiatric hospital—the email in which he wanted to make sure that he told me about it instead of me hearing it from Mom or Dad—I sent him a short email back: "Be honest with them. Good luck. Love, T."

Instead of worrying about Rich, I was relieved. *Finally!* I thought. Finally, his long history of suicide contemplation would be out of the closet. It wouldn't just be family dealing with it, with Mom, or both Mom and Dad, flying out to see Rich after a suicidal downturn. He was going to get the intensive psychiatric help he needed. As to his physical wounds from the motorcycle accident, he was tough. I knew he could handle them.

I didn't actually hear the details on the hospital visit until about three weeks later, when Dad told me. The psychiatric stay was going to cost $30,000. Rich had asked Dad to send $30,000 in the form of a check made out to Sharon. Dad was aggravated that he hadn't heard anything from Rich or Sharon after sending the check. The more that Dad and I talked, the odder it started to sound: Rich telling him to send the check direct to Sharon, in her name. Strange things can have an air of normalcy in a strange situation.

Psychiatrist David Janowsky, in his famous paper titled "Playing the Manic Game," described the manipulative or "gamey" behavior that can be employed by people with bipolar disorder in the midst of a manic state. Once removed from the mania, once the episode settles down, the person is wracked by guilt.

I talked to Mom and said we needed to learn more about where Rich was. Afterward, Mom sent an email to Sharon asking how Rich was doing—and if he was still in the hospital. Sharon sent back an email saying Rich was doing okay and "of course" he was in the hospital. In the same email she asked, "why would you question it?"

A day or two later, Mom found out that Rich was no longer in the hospital. Rich had called her—sticking to his usual pattern of reaching out to Mom at some point in a depression. He typically called her at one of the lowest stages, sometimes calling her multiple times, spread out over a few days. Once he called Mom, it tended to mean that the depression would shortly begin to lift.

When Mom told me that he was out, I was stunned. Rich had never done anything like this before: taking advantage of Dad's willingness to send him money—$30,000!—and then leaving the hospital without telling Dad he was no longer there. In my mind, Rich was scraping rock bottom. What was he thinking? I assumed as I always did that he was rational, aware of what he was doing. And I did what I normally did when I heard bad news about Rich; I composed an email that I would never send.

November 3, 2005

Rich, Hope you're doing well. I've given this a lot of thought, and you should tell Dad you're out of the hospital. I know I can't get you to do it and it's not an order - not that I could make you do anything anyway. But I don't think there's even a question about it. Eventually, all this will come out - inevitable. So much better to get it out now.

Love,
T

Why didn't I send the email? The answer is straightforward: I figured I'd sit on it and see if Rich ended up telling Dad on his own. He usually made the right decision.

A few days later, we found out that he'd crafted Sharon's email response himself and that he never went to the hospital at all. He used the $30,000 in a last-ditch effort to cure his financial problems, opening a trading account in Sharon's name. Throughout his trading career, Rich had demonstrated an uncanny ability to parlay similar sums into huge trading windfalls.

THE STAIRWELL INTERVIEW

Shortly before Rich graduated from Babson, he had a job interview at an investment company in Boston. He was taking summer classes at the time and needed four more credits to graduate early. Rich arrived for the interview in his best suit. He took the elevator up to just about the top floor of what I would guess was about a forty-story building.

The receptionist smiled and said, "How can I help you, sir?"

"Hi, Richard Courtemanche, I'm here for an interview with David Hill."

"Yes, Mr. Courtemanche. Let me phone Mr. Hill." The receptionist then had a brief conversation with David.

"Mr. Courtemanche, Mr. Hill isn't ready to see you yet. He says it will be about ten to fifteen minutes."

"Okay, thanks. Is there a bathroom around?"

"Yes, the easiest one to get to is one floor down, right off the elevator."

Rich glanced at the elevator, saw a group standing there and looked for an alternate route. He noticed a sign that said "Exit" above a door and reasoned it must be the stairs. The temperature that day was hot. Rich opened the door, saw the stairs and started walking down them. The door behind him closed and clicked shut as he did. He went down one flight of stairs and approached the entry door. He tried turning the doorknob, but it didn't move. He tried it again, and one more time. The doorknob was not turning.

As Rich explained it, the first pang of panic went through him. He walked at a faster pace down to the next floor and tried the door there. Like the one before, it was locked. The stairwell didn't have air-conditioning, and he started to sweat. He jogged up two flights of stairs and tried the door where he'd originally exited, locked. He considered pounding on the door but decided that wasn't the impression he wanted to create for his potential employer.

He quick-stepped down three flights of stairs and tried the next door, nothing. Running to the next door, he tried it: locked. Full-fledged panic set in. He'd spent what seemed like five minutes in the stairwell and knew each minute he stayed brought him closer to being late for the meeting.

He started sprinting—knees-pumping, tie-flapping, shirt-coming-untucked sprinting. Was there a door somewhere between the top floor and the lobby that was unlocked? My guess is yes, but I can't know for sure. He didn't bother checking the doors. He was jumping down the stairs three at a time. When he got to the first floor, he burst through an emergency exit and onto the street. He ran on the sidewalk, around the corner, avoiding the lunchtime crowds, and into the lobby. He was sweating heavily and rode the elevator back up to the fortieth floor. The receptionist acknowledged him and did a double take.

"Oh, hello, Mr. Courtemanche. Mr. Hill is ready to see you now."

Rich went into David's office. The resumes he brought in his leather notebook remained dry, and he presented one to David. Just like at the wedding, Rich did one of his magic tricks: He pulled himself together. He sat there in front of David and started on the interview as if nothing was wrong. Very shortly, they got into why the hell he was covered with sweat.

I don't remember which company Rich had the elevator interview with (the dots don't always connect as nicely as I'd like). It could have been Putnam Investments. Whoever it was with, he ultimately started working with Putnam after Babson. Rich kept living with Mom to save money.

CLIFF DIVING IN CAMDEN

In 1977, we got our second dog. We already had a German Sheppard. The dog we got was a mastiff, and we named her Tiffany. She got very big very fast. Now she weighs about one hundred and eighty pounds. My family and I went to Camden, Maine that year and we stayed at a little cottage on a lake. It was really nice their because we had our own boat and dock and a little beach. My Uncle came with us on that vacation and he has been on all our vacations since then.

Richard Courtemanche
School Writing Assignment, September 20, 1982

The Courtemanche family vacation of 1977 started the way most of our family vacations did: a fairly long car ride during which at least one dog barked most of the trip. The trip from Sherborn to Camden, Maine, took about four hours, and we traveled with our two dogs in Bessie, the family station wagon. Olie, the German shepherd, was the one doing all the barking. Tiffany, the mastiff, mostly lay in the back.

Once in Camden, the directions the rental agency gave us said to look for the second big tree after Chinook Street. We saw the tree as we were driving past it; wooden boards tacked to it named the cottages. We turned around and started down the dirt road behind the tree. The summer sun shined through the clouds, creating streams of light. Rich and I commented on them. Mom said, "Those light beams are called 'Jacob's Ladders.'"

"What are they?" Rich asked.

"Those are the light beams angels use to get to heaven."

Both Rich and I knew heaven was a place where good people went when they died. The thought of death frightened me. When I was six, Dad's aunt had died at age eighty—that seemed to be a fairly standard age for death. I got panicked when I realized I'd be that age in only seventy-four years. Mom, Dad and I had to have a talk about it.

"Don't worry, Theo, eighty is a long, long way away," Dad had said. He also held out the possibility that I might live to be a hundred.

That kind of eased my fears, and although I wasn't as scared during the drive down the dirt road as I was when I was six, the concept of "here on Earth and then gone" really spooked me. It was best if I just ignored death. Thank God for heaven, and now, thank God for Jacob's Ladders. Before we could get going on more questions about Jacob's Ladders, Dad said, "There's the cabin."

Immediately, we redirected our attention to the brown wood building in front of us. The cabin was a little different from what I'd pictured in my mind, and the real thing was better. This was going to be great: a whole week in a log cabin on a lake. The orange pine needles that covered the ground, the tall trees, the uncharted woods, the cabin—it was the perfect environment for exploration. Dad drove the car into a parking space near the cabin, and we got ready to unpack.

I feel a sharp pain on my cheek and then another. I drop my suitcase. I feel another pain on my arm, like a needle stuck me. Something is wrong! I scream.

Luggage stored, we were now sitting on the big rock that jutted into the water about two hundred feet downhill from the cabin. A wooden sign nailed to a tree on the rock read "Big Ledge." Big Ledge was like an extension of the hill, only instead of being dirt, it was gray, porous rock. It looked like gray lava.

By then, I had white meat tenderizer caked on my face, four different places on my arm and one place on my leg. Rich had meat tenderizer on his face because he liked the way it looked. I'd stepped on a tree root that had a hornet's nest under it as I was carrying my suitcase into the cabin. One of my friends had gotten stung so badly when he was small that he became allergic to bees. A whole hive attacked him—he escaped only by jumping into the neighbor's pool. Luckily for me, the whole hornet's nest didn't come out, just enough to get me away from the nest. Mom and Dad both scrambled to help me.

"Christ, the owners should do something about this," Dad said. "As soon as I get inside, I'm calling them up." That's right, I thought. For Christ's sake, they should do something about it. It felt good to get angry at the owners.

Mom found the meat tenderizer in the first kitchen cabinet where she looked, and Dad hurried me to a chair at the kitchen table. Rich sat next to me. The meat tenderizer looked like icing after it was prepared. Rich tasted a little and spit it out. Once Mom finished with the application, a good portion of my visible skin was covered with meat tenderizer, and it didn't take long before it began to itch. As we sat on Big Ledge, Rich noticed the dried meat tenderizer on his face was itchy, too.

"Can we go in the water?" we asked Mom.

As soon as we finished our question, we heard Dad say, "Boys."

We looked to our left and saw a group of trees, and between them, a dock. Dad was on the dock, and just to the right of the dock was a motorboat. That's right, I remembered: The place has a motorboat! All thoughts of itchiness disappeared. As Mom sat on Big Ledge with Olie and Tiffany, Rich and I ran back into the woods and followed the short trail to the dock. Uncle Ed, who joined us on the vacation, was not far behind.

By 5:00 pm, the four of us—Dad, Uncle Ed, Rich and I—were sitting in the motorboat. Dad started it to a cloud of gray smoke. The water under the engine gurgled and bubbled. As the sun slowly set behind the cabin, we drove around the lake in the motorboat. I got special treatment because of the hornet stings and was the first out of Rich and me to drive the boat.

I pressed forward on the throttle with my hand. The water in back of the boat bubbled, and we moved ahead. From Big Ledge, if you looked straight and a little to the right, you could see a mountain—not a big one, more of a hill-mountain. Forest separated it from the lake. Near the top of the hill-mountain was a white cross that begged for explanation.

"Dad, what's the cross there for?" I asked, suspecting it had something to do with death.

"That's probably to mark where someone fell."

"Someone fell?"

"People put crosses like that to remember where someone had a bad accident." Dad surely knew he was in shaky territory.

"Do you think the person died?" Rich asked.

"Yes, Richard, I think the person probably did."

"Do you think they're in heaven?"

"Oh, yes, they're in heaven."

"Maybe they got up there on a Jacob's Ladder?" I added.

"Maybe, Theo, or maybe the person just went straight up."

"So crosses don't just have to be in graveyards?" Rich asked.

"No. They can be just like that cross. Just to remember."

If I hadn't been driving the boat, the discussion might have kept me up the first night. Fortunately, my mind was almost completely preoccupied with driving the motorboat. The words didn't have a chance to seep in, take hold and completely unsettle me. I pushed the throttle forward after the conversation, and the thoughts remained lifeless facts, not having a chance to trigger any feelings.

When it was Rich's turn to drive, he gassed the engine. Our heads snapped a little as he got us going. Dad told him to lighten up a little. Rich loved boats. At age four, he got Chris-Craft boat catalogues sent to the house. He'd analyze them, looking for ones that suited his tastes—tastes that tended toward big boats. The catalogues would be delivered to "Mr. Richard Douglas Courtemanche."

To get Rich to settle down a little, Dad suggested we explore some of the inlets. Rich was a good captain. He carefully took us inland as Uncle Ed and I kept a lookout for rocks. There weren't many stretches of straight shoreline along the lake; almost all of it was jagged. The little inlets were like presents.

They were best if the shore looked straight from a distance but when you got close, a cove opened up. We had no idea what we were going to find. Everything was new.

Rich had a cowlick on the right side of his head that he'd sometimes flatten with spit. As he was driving the boat, his cowlick shot straight up in the air. The last area Rich drove us by was on the other side of the lake from the cabin. It was a cliff that went nearly straight up from the shore. Uncle Ed thought it was about four stories high. Even a foot from the cliff, the water was so deep we couldn't see the bottom. Rich and I admired the cliff for a minute or two. Pine trees grew out of it. In some places, the trees grew straight up from one of the rocks jutting out. In other places, they grew out of the cliff itself and then curled up to the sky.

When we got back to the cabin, we told Mom all about our motorboat trip. We told her about the inlets, the cliff and that we'd found some really good fishing spots we'd get to later.

At night in Camden, Rich and I slept in the same room, on the lower floor. From the front, the cabin looked like it had only one story, but once you got inside, you could go downstairs to another set of bedrooms. Uncle Ed also got one of the rooms downstairs. Mom and Dad got the upstairs bedroom near the kitchen.

What was a typical day in Camden like? We'd get up and have breakfast. Mom, Dad and Uncle Ed might have eggs, but Rich and I would have sugar cereal. After breakfast, Rich and I would explore while Mom and Dad had more coffee. Then we'd all go down to Big Ledge where Rich and I would comment that the water was chilly, and then jump in. Mom bought Rich and me a raft specially for the trip; it was red and had a Red Baron logo on the back. There was something exciting about gliding on top of water that was over our heads. If we rowed too hard in the Red Baron, water would come in over the sides.

For lunch, we'd either eat at the cabin or go into town for a hamburger. After that, Rich and I might have a water fight with Uncle Ed. We'd gang up and splash him like monkeys attacking a gorilla. Mom would swim laps between Big Ledge and the tip of land on the other side of the dock, and Dad would usually read in a lounge chair under one of the pine trees. His favorites were horror books. Rich liked hearing about them, but I didn't. I read through a few pages of *The Shining* and had to make sure Olie and Tiffany were near me for the next couple of hours after I did.

At dinnertime, we usually grilled out behind the cabin. After dinner, we'd go into town for ice cream. There's a harbor in Camden where yachts dock. You can walk up and down the pier, read the names of the boats and see where they're from. We'd sit at a picnic table where we could take in the whole harbor and eat our ice cream.

I can feel it—the air is comfortable as we sit at our table on the harbor pier. Ice cream melts over the sides of the cones. The evening sun is glowing orange behind us, and boats are slowly bobbing in the harbor. Rich is telling us he's going to have a big yacht someday. It will have a bedroom and a kitchen, and he'll be able to drive it wherever he wants to go. He says he'll keep a motorized raft on it that he'll use to get to shore. When we finish our ice cream, we listen to waves lapping against the pier and occasional catcalls from seagulls overhead. Then we walk back to the car.

We stayed at the cabin three years in a row. Typically, when the Courtemanche family found something good, we stuck with it—as long as it wasn't outrageously priced.

In the late afternoons, older kids would jump off the cliff we'd investigated on the other side of the lake. From Big Ledge, we'd first see them splash in the water and then hear the splash. Rich and I jumped off Big Ledge after being inspired by them; there was one place where we could jump about five feet into the water.

The big cliff across the lake had two basic ledges that the older kids jumped from. The first was somewhere in the middle of the cliff; the second and more exciting one was at the very top. It wasn't unusual to see a kid stand at the top of the cliff and peek over a few times. The longer he stayed up there, the less likely he'd actually jump.

Rich and I talked about the cliff frequently. We'd strategize about the best way to jump (feet first), how far out you'd need to leap (as far as you could) and what it would feel like on the way down (a roller coaster was a good bet, we both thought). After enough talking, Rich and I decided to approach Mom and Dad with an idea: We wanted to jump off the cliff. I don't think we formally requested it until the third year we were in Camden—we didn't seriously consider jumping until the second year. We badgered Mom and Dad enough so that they agreed we could try. We all drove over to the cliff one afternoon in the motorboat. Rich and I knew the older kids didn't get there until late, so we went in the early afternoon; there was no sense creating the kind of pressure a group setting could generate.

From Big Ledge, the cliff looked manageable. It still looked manageable as we first approached it in the motorboat. The question in both Rich's and my mind was not whether we'd jump but whether we'd jump off the top ledge. It took less than a second to hit the water, so it couldn't be that high. As we drove nearer, the cliff kept getting taller and taller. By the time we got there, we had to tilt our heads all the way back to see the top—and then we couldn't *see* the top; we could just see where the top started. Immediately, the plan ran into logistical issues. From the water, I couldn't tell how to get up to the top. Even if we were going to jump from the middle ledge—and no one was saying that's what Rich and I were going to do—how did we get to it? It looked like sheer rock.

"Richard and Theodore, you'll need to go around the cliff to go up," Uncle Ed said. We drove to where the cliff ended and the pine trees started, and we got out of the boat. I got scratched by branches as I walked into the forest and onto a worn trail. Dad stayed with the boat while Uncle Ed and Mom walked with us. When we finally came to a clearing at the top of the trail, we were at the highest point on the cliff—the top ledge. My knees started shaking, and my head got woozy. I didn't even need to contemplate it: I was not jumping off from that height. Even if Rich, Uncle Ed or even Mom jumped, I wasn't going to do it. Rich agreed with my assessment, and we went back into the woods, looking for a trail that led to the middle ledge.

More scratches and a few false starts later, we found the trail for the middle ledge. It looked so much higher from up there than from ground level, across the lake. My head got woozy again. Even thinking about walking along the narrow path that led to the middle cliff was disturbing. Too high, I thought; much too high. And what if you didn't jump out far enough? We hadn't seen one kid fail to jump out far enough, but it was a possibility. What if you simply fell walking out to the middle cliff? The path was narrow with pine needles *and* moss on it! I put one foot on the path and leaned my entire body, front first, into the cliff wall, and then I inched out sideways. As I did, Rich and Mom walked out onto the middle ledge. I went forward, or sideways, a step or two after them but couldn't go any farther. I was almost frozen. We were probably twenty-five feet in the air. My stomach was churning like a washing machine. It was pure relief when I eased my way off the ledge and back onto the trail.

Fortunately, Rich decided he didn't want to jump off the middle cliff either. It wouldn't have been easy if Rich had gone ahead and jumped—the transition of brotherly power would have happened right then. Uncle Ed never even went onto the path to get to the middle ledge because of his knees (he'd hurt them playing basketball when he was younger). Happy to be done with the whole poorly conceived idea, I was almost at ground level when I heard noise. Rich was shrieking—his excited shriek. I looked beyond a crag in the cliff and saw that Rich had made his way out to a ledge about twelve feet off the water. Then, my God, he jumped! Everyone cheered. I raced back to the woods, scurried through pine branches and climbed onto the same ledge. Even this one seemed high. I swallowed, then jumped out as far as I could. The experience was sheer thrill. My mind, if it could have, would have exploded on the spot.

Rich and I climbed onto that twelve-foot ledge and jumped off it until Dad had enough. Rich and I reveled in the satisfaction of it all when we got back to Big Ledge, where we enjoyed ice cream sandwiches.

The last year we went to Camden, I spent an hour one afternoon petting Olie. He was old then, almost thirteen. I didn't spend much time with Olie anymore. First there was Tiffany and then Winston, our second mastiff. Rich and I would wrestle with Winston and Tiffany, but Olie never was the wrestling type, and now he was too old. When I was a baby, Mom said I could climb all over Olie and pull his ears, and he wouldn't do a thing. He closed his eyes and licked his lips every now and then as I petted him that afternoon in Camden.

Outside, the sun shined through the clouds and the pine trees. Later in the fall, Olie needed to be put to sleep.

When he was ten, Rich was asked to describe the saddest thing that ever happened to him, as part of a school writing assignment. This is what he wrote.

> *It was about four months ago. My brother and I were at our house. My mother and father went to the vet to put our old dog to sleep. His name was Olie. He was almost thirteen years old. He was put to sleep because he had a disease in his back legs and he could hardly walk. My brother and I were very sad after he was put to sleep.*

The worst part for me about Olie's death is that I'd known Mom and Dad were taking him to the vet, but I chose to sleep in. When I realized I hadn't been there with Olie at the end, I felt sick. I was lazy not to go, and now I'd never see him again. Mom and Dad said he died peacefully. His body was cremated and buried behind the house in Sherborn. His grave was marked by a slate stone. Mom painted on it, "Olie / 1966 to 1979 / A good old friend."

Olie didn't get much attention in Camden except for when he was swimming up to someone in the lake—all it took was one scratch from his paws, and you knew he was there. I wished I'd spent more time with him; Rich did, too. Now, he was gone. We had a special ceremony for Olie in the backyard in Sherborn. Mom, Dad, Rich and I attended, as did Winston and Tiffany. At the end of the ceremony, Mom and Dad reminded us to think of Olie as "a good old friend" whom we'd someday see again.

BODIES, BRAINS AND FEYNMAN

At the kitchen table, I watched a candle burning today. From my seat, I could see the flame as it danced to the backdrop of a window framing trees outside. Above the flame, heat flowed into the air, a bunch of excited molecules undulating feverishly to the movement of the flame. Though invisible, the heat noticeably changed the air into which it flowed—like a translucent river.

In the mind-versus-matter debate, some people believe that we are simply physical beings, nothing more. *Materialists* say a person is a body: a body that contains skin, bones, veins, arteries, cells and all the other things that constitute a body—including a brain—and that's it. *Dualists*, on the other hand, say, "Yes, humans have bodies, but we have minds that are separate from our bodies." For dualists, a person is not a body but is, instead, a mind; sometimes the mind is equated to a soul. If you believe in an afterlife in which you continue on, minus your body, you are a dualist.

Rich and I liked sweets when we were small. We liked candy bars, ice cream, pie, pudding and just about anything with sugar in it. One afternoon when Rich and I were home alone, we made a cake.

I see myself pulling down a Betty Crocker cake mix box from a shelf in the laundry room. Rich and I put the box ingredients together in the bowl Mom uses when she makes cakes. We take out milk and butter from the refrigerator. At the end of the counter closest to the kitchen table, we get the sugar that's stored in a dull yellow container. We mix the ingredients together using an electric beater that is stored under the sink and pour the batter into a cake pan. Our two dogs at the time, Olie and Tiffany, supervise the project, licking up whatever drops on the floor. While the cake is baking, the batter burns to the pan because we didn't grease it. We pry the finished cake from the pan and leave the burned part alone. We put on pre-packaged icing and take our first bites. It's terrible. The salt we used instead of sugar causes instant mouth watering; we spit the cake out and rinse our mouths.

Scientists, philosophers and theologians alike have all speculated on what it is about humans that makes us human. As far as DNA is concerned, we're almost identical to chimps. John Pickrell, in an article for the *National Geographic News*, wrote, "[Morris] Goodman and colleagues used computer methods to analyze the amount of similarity between 97 important human and chimp genes." The results? "Humans and chimps share 99.4 percent identity."

Ninety-nine point four percent identity?! As with the single faulty gene in sickle cell anemia, that 0.6 percent difference is a big one. What makes us who we are? What makes us "us," capable of being aware of being aware? Are materialists right—are we just *bodies* that include brains?

One of the ways you might recognize a friend, one way I recognized Rich, was his physical body. That's usually how we recognize people every day, isn't it? I'm the guy I see in the mirror. As we saw in earlier chapters, though, that body is an ever changing collection of parts. It can change shape, too. Not only have most of my cells died and been reborn since I was a kid, but the actual appearance of my body has also changed. For practical purposes, it's not the same body. To take it to an extreme, someday in the future, it might be possible to transplant our brains into new bodies, and we would be *us* even though we'd have new bodies.

Does that mean we are our brains? As draconian or exciting as this may sound, it's actually an old philosophical paradox popularized by René Descartes, who wondered about the same thing. Philosophers have historically referred to it as the brain-in-a-vat paradox. The modern version goes like this: Is it possible that we are just brains in vats being stimulated and prodded by a scientist (the scientist is usually a mad scientist) such that we are having conscious experiences?

Something like this can actually be done by neurosurgeons. Various areas of the brain can be stimulated, thus generating emotional responses and bringing back memories. The only "outside" in this case is the neurosurgeon and the tool being used to stimulate the brain. What does this imply? Does it mean that it's possible nothing we're seeing is real?

The brain-in-a-vat paradox is a strange, kind of morbid thought, but one with a very important offshoot: No one has been able to adequately resolve the conundrum. That is to say, no one has built a definitive argument demonstrating that we are not simply brains in vats (though some have tried valiantly). All of our experiences could as easily, and more important, *logically*, be the result of a scientist toying with our brains—as crazy and unintuitive as it might sound.

Philosopher Nick Bostrom built on the brain-in-a-vat scenario. He proposed the possibility that we are living within a computer simulation. All that we see and feel could be the result of computer code. His argument goes something like this: Given the increasing power of computers, someday it will be possible for our descendants to produce lifelike simulations (consider how realistic some computer games are today). The simulations won't just be life*like;* the beings created will be computer-generated sentient beings. The descendants with such powerful computing power will be part of what Bostrom calls a "posthuman civilization." In order for Bostrom's computer simulation scenario to be realized, he holds that two "ifs" must transpire. First, humans must make it to the posthuman stage, and second, the number of descendants interested in running what he refers to as "ancestor simulations" cannot be close to 0 percent. Provided these two conditions are met, Bostrom concludes that it is certain we are now living in a computer simulation.

If he is right, we wouldn't even need the kind of brain we appear to have today. Our brain would instead be a software program running on some kind of supercomputer. Our mind would be "substrate independent."

In his book *Surely You're Joking Mr. Feynman*, renowned physicist Richard Feynman described an experiment in which he tried to observe the exact time he fell asleep at night. In trying to figure it out, he started to carefully examine his dreams. He wrote, "One night, while I was having a dream, I realized I was observing myself in the dream. I had gotten all the way down, into the sleep itself!" He said that as he observed himself, he noticed that waking up could be a "fearful" time. He described feeling "rigid and tied down" when he started to wake up. "It's hard to explain, but there's a moment when you get the feeling you can't get out."

Feynman stated, "You might like to know how this process of observing my dreams stopped." He had a dream in which he was sleeping with his head on a brass rod. He felt the rod with his hands. Then he felt the back of his head; it felt soft. The dream was vivid: He was convinced he was actually sleeping on a brass rod. When he woke up, there was no brass rod, just his pillow. Why did this dream stop his experiment? Feynman explained, "Somehow I had become tired of making these observations, and my brain had invented some false reasons as to why I shouldn't do it anymore."

The brain, whatever its substance, is not always as accurate as we might hope, nor is our interpretation of what it's telling us. A simple example is a mirage on the highway. Once you get to it, you realize it's not a pool of shimmering water. And our brain is not always as "on demand" as we might like. Consider the process of trying to remember a fact. You leave it for a while, and once you've diverted your attention, the fact then reappears (or does not appear)—your efforts seeming to play little role in the process. Lastly, our brain is not always as discerning as we would hope. You can get stuck regrouting a shower, oblivious to any other possibilities.

If the brain is ultimately *us*, it has some issues that make it hard to pin down as the core of an "unchanging us," which others are able to recognize. Aside from snags involving accuracy, personal control and discernment, isn't the brain afflicted by some of the same problems as a body? Let's stick to the belief that our brains are made of neurons and chemicals, the kind of brains that scientists tell us we have. Is the brain you have right now the same one you had a year ago? There is some debate as to how many cells turn over in the brain. Some studies suggest that even in the neocortex, the area believed most directly responsible for rational thought, cells turn over during the course of our lives. Whether new brain cells are born or not, cells in the brain definitely die. To look at your brain and say that's what you are is to look at a collection of cells that changes from one day to the next. The brain that was there last week had a different collection of live cells than the one this week.

Focusing on the brain as a whole, no neuron actually touches another neuron. Thoughts are triggered via electrical impulses that must be communicated to the next neuron by means of chemicals floating between the neurons. The area the impulse is ferried across via chemicals is the synaptic cleft. Getting back to equating you to your brain, from one moment to the next, electrical impulses are constantly being generated, signals bathed in a changing sea of chemicals. Even if all the cells remained the same, the structure of the whole thing is constantly changing as the chemicals wash from one neuron shore to the next. Saying your brain is you would be like standing above this sea of change and saying, "Stop there, exactly as it is right now—that's me." No sooner would you shout the words than the whole thing would have changed. Over time, the same electrical impulses won't be ferried the same way or with the same chemicals. An obvious example is Alzheimer's disease. More sublime is maturity, responding to the same stimuli differently. When you were younger, you might have reacted differently to a problem than you do now. When Rich was small, he cried in traffic jams; he didn't cry in them as an adult.

Even in the brain-in-a-vat paradox, there's another twist, or more information we have to consider. The brain must be fed, and there must be something stimulating the brain; an environment (even just an electrical stimulus) must interact with the brain. A brain without any energy being delivered to it via blood or otherwise, a brain further without stimulation—something with which to interact—well, that brain would simply be a collection of cells. Without an energy source and without stimulus, there is no *functioning* brain. The brain doesn't work if it's there all alone.

We're made from scraps; we have quadrillions of foreign bacteria cells living rent-free within us, and our physical brain changes from second to second. I'm searching for what I miss when I miss Rich, but it's getting confusing. I'll do what Rich and I used to do—leave it for a little while and maybe search around the garage for other things to entertain myself with.

MIT, Parking Spaces and Glass

All Rich's studying at Babson and his work at Putnam paid off. He got into the MBA program at the Massachusetts Institute of Technology—the Sloan School of Management, class of 1999. Rich applied to Stanford, the University of Chicago, MIT and a few others. Most of the schools required as essay. He wrote one about his challenges with alcoholism—how it had impacted his life, and how he'd worked to overcome it. He planned to include the essay in each application that required one.

Shortly after I left for UNC, Rich was arrested for drunk driving in Rhode Island. One of his friends told him about a lawyer in Rhode Island who handled drunk driving cases. Dad hired the lawyer, and the charges against Rich were dropped. On his lawyer's advice, Rich wore his marines dress uniform to the hearing.

The arrest was a wake-up call for Rich. He stopped drinking for a while. Karl Menninger wrote:

> Alcohol addiction can be thought of not as a disease, but as a suicidal flight from disease, a disastrous attempt at the self-cure of an unseen inner conflict, aggravated but not caused (as many think) by external conflict. It is literally true that the alcoholic, as he himself says, does not know why he drinks.

Not one of the colleges to which Rich sent the essay on alcoholism accepted him, including the one he applied to for an early decision on his application. He wrote another more mainstream essay and got into every school where he sent that essay.

While he was getting his MBA at MIT, Rich lived in an off-campus apartment, a row house that had been broken up into apartments. His had a kitchen, a bedroom, a hallway and a little room in the front where he put a TV and a reclining chair. From the TV room, you could climb out the window and stand on a small roof that was actually the overhang for a bay window in the apartment below. There were probably six apartments in the whole building. Not another student lived in his building. Rich lived with the locals, people who'd lived in Cambridge most of their lives; the same people who were prone to disliking the hoards of students that attend the Boston colleges.

I once watched a Patriots game in his apartment before a flight back to North Carolina. The same weekend, we'd gone to a bar in Boston on Friday night and got fairly liquored up. Sitting together at the bar, Rich and I agreed that life held out a lot of possibility for us—what with him being in business school and me fresh out of graduate school at UNC. One of the girls at the bar, after learning we were brothers, couldn't stop commenting on it the whole night. "Brothers, that's a special thing," she'd say. Have another, I thought each time she said it. On Sunday afternoon, Rich and I watched the Pats game together.

As the game plays on the TV in the corner, we sit in his tiny family room, Rich in the recliner and me on a beanbag. We don't say much. Maybe Rich is down or maybe this is one of those times that I know I won't get enough of in life—a time that's good when it's happening but has some underlying sadness to it. At halftime, Rich opens the window in his family room, and we stand on the roof of the apartment below, surveying the neighborhood from atop the bay window.

Anyone who's lived in Boston or any snowy city knows that parking becomes a major commodity after a snowstorm. In Boston, the streets are narrow and the only street parking is *earned* by people who dig out a space. During Rich's first year at MIT, there was a major snowstorm. When it was over, the city streets were covered by about thirty-two inches of snow. For anyone not familiar with city snow-plowing protocol, slow plow trucks push the snow to the side of the road, where it piles up. By the time they finally clear the roads, you might have to dig through more than five feet of crusty, dense snow to make a space for your car.

At the time, Rich drove a Ford Bronco given to him by Uncle Ed. In the marines, Rich did a lot of running with heavy backpacks—ever since he got out, he had problems with his back. By the time he went to MIT, he'd had two surgeries on his lower back. After the first one, his high school friends brought his bed into the family room at Mom's house, and that's where Rich stayed for the week. At MIT, Rich couldn't drive the Mustang anymore because his back hurt too much when he stooped down to get into the car. He gave the Mustang to me when I was living in Chapel Hill.

When he started at MIT, the Mustang was the only car Rich had ever treated well. He was the last person to drive Stan-the-Van before it was towed to the dump. Rich beat Stan mercilessly. He managed to rip off the front and back bumpers, tear out the bench seat in back and seemingly gnaw the buttons off the radio. To the Bronco, he added bending the ignition so that only he could get the key out and—how do I describe what he did to the transmission?—punishing it so that your best bet was to leave it in drive and just move forward.

On the day after the storm, Rich spent about two hours digging a parking spot for the Bronco. Shoveling plowed snow is ferociously hard work. It could be minus 10 degrees Fahrenheit, and chances are good you'll be sweating when you're done. When he was finished, he drove off and did whatever he needed to do. While he was gone, a neighbor started to dig a spot right in front of where Rich dug; probably reasoning that it would give him (or her) a head start. The neighbor quickly tired and from what Rich could tell, decided to annex his spot. The neighbor reserved the space with a long beach chair.

When Rich got back, he saw the spot he'd dug out and saw the beach chair. He edged the Bronco up to the snowy unshoveled space right before his own. Twisting his head so that he could see out the back, he shifted the Bronco into reverse (he was the only one who could) and revved the engine. Releasing his foot from the brake, he backed over the beach chair. I never heard whether the other person looked for the beach chair or not.

During the next winter and on an especially cold night, Rich was cooking hamburgers in his apartment. Being the impatient guy that he was, Rich cooked everything on high. He left the room for a while, probably checking CNBC or talking on his cell phone. He smelled smoke and then noticed it wafting into his bedroom. When he went back to the kitchen, his burgers were on fire. He opened the second-story window and threw the pan and the burning burgers out. By the time he did, it was too late. The smoke alarm went off. All the residents had to go outside and wait for the fire department to check the building before they could reenter.

At MIT, Rich focused his studies on investing. Between his first and second years, he got an internship at Greene Foster in New York City. During that summer, he lived in an apartment at one of the state universities in the city. Greene Foster was *the* internship for someone who wanted to work in investments. Rich was particularly interested in working with the traders— the guys who bought and sold stocks, bonds, currency and derivatives. The marines were good training for Rich's time with Greene Foster. Interns were at the beck and call of the traders. Some traders liked torturing the interns, making jokes about anything. If they saw it got to you, they'd hit it even harder. Rich did well. All summer long, he worked and saved. He ate breakfast, lunch and dinner for free at the Greene Foster dining room. As long as he worked later than 7:00 pm, the company would pay a car service to take him back to his apartment.

I heard Rich tell the following story a few times to his friends. About a week before his internship was set to end, Rich and a friend went out to get some beers after work—sounds like a standard beginning to a lot of after-work stories. There's a part Rich usually kept to himself. To include it is to reveal one of those private crosses we all try to keep secret. On the same day, one of the traders at Greene Foster noticed Rich had had plastic surgery: hair transplants. The first procedure didn't turn out very natural-looking; he eventually had many. His girlfriends, platonic and otherwise, who met him after all the operations were done thought he was a guy with naturally full hair.

On the day Rich went out with his buddy for beers, the same trader who noticed the plastic surgery sent out an email Rich wasn't supposed to see. Someone printed it off, and of course Rich read it. Basically, it trashed his early stage transplants. What do you say to someone who gives you crap about something like that? Yeah, I had them, I'm learning to live with them, but in the meantime, bear with me. Right now, I'm working through the fact that I don't measure up to the standard Hollywood image.

Comments like that, comments that submarined Rich's self-esteem, always cut deep—as they cut deep with many people. So as Rich and his friend headed out, Rich had coals charring beneath the surface. Rich and his friend first got a few beers at a local bar. I don't know what they talked about—likely the whole Greene Foster experience, what they were going to do back in school and what they wanted to do after school. Rich and his friend were feeling pretty good after they left the bar, and as they were walking to dinner, they went by Scores, a strip club.

Scores looked inviting, so they went in, sat down, had a few more beers and observed. I'm sure it started to get dreamlike. They started talking to the dancers and started tipping better and better. One asked if they'd like to go into a back room for a private party. This is common practice: The dancers try to get big spenders to go into a back room where they can focus more attention on them, creating an environment conducive to optimal spending. At their entertainers' suggestions, Rich and his friend graduated to hard liquor in the back room (the girls make a percentage on the drinks). After an hour or two—it's hard to keep track of time in a dream—Rich ran out of cash and used his debit card to get additional cash at the bank machines any self-respecting strip club has.

The night got wild. Rich and his friend paid for single lap dances, dual and triple lap dances, and who knows what other activities. Touching wasn't allowed from what I was told but everything else, short of touching, was. Eventually, Rich started using his credit card alone. By the time the night was over at 4:00 or 5:00 in the morning, Rich had spent his entire summer bonus. The total bill for Rich and his married friend was around $5,000.

As they were leaving the club, the owner stopped Rich and gave him fifty free passes, valued at $25 each, encouraging him to come back the next time he was in town. A few weeks before, Rich had started living with a girl he met in the city. He spent most nights at her place. After Scores, Rich decided to go to his girlfriend's apartment. When he got there, his suit was covered with candle wax, the result of some kind of "members only" dance in the back room. His girlfriend, seeing the state he was in, simultaneously broke up with him and kicked him out of the apartment. He spent his three final weeks in New York City back at his own apartment, dating one of the girls who'd danced for him at Scores.

It's not uncommon for people with bipolar disorder to fly off the handle at a slight. The NIMH describes reckless behavior like spending sprees, binge drinking, sexual promiscuity and, of course, impaired judgment as some of the ramifications of bipolar disorder. When Rich was small and Granny and Gramps visited, Gramps would sometimes tell him that he'd borrowed a few quarters from Rich's piggy bank. Rich would immediately run upstairs and start counting. It took about twenty-five years, an asshole, lots of alcohol and the unnoticed progression of bipolar disorder (at least unnoticed to his family) before Rich arrived at a point where he could blow $5,000 in a single night.

About four weeks after the Scores incident, when Rich was back in school, he sent an email to the guy who made the comment about his transplants. The email started something like, "You fat, useless piece of shit," and went downhill from there.

In his second year at MIT, Rich accepted a job with the Anlage Bank in London. He was hired to trade securities for them—just what he wanted to do. This wasn't unusual for Rich; he could burn bridges, and new ones would open up. Before he moved to London, Rich had one last fireworks show at his Cambridge apartment. In the same building where he'd forced everyone out in the street in the middle of the winter, Rich had a meltdown.

He broke every piece of glass in his apartment, every one. He started with drinking glasses, then went to pictures and then went to the television screen. Rich's body was an energy processor, like a hurricane passing over warm water. He was spinning and spinning, pulling in energy from wherever it was. Break a glass: energy. Break another: more energy. His face, I'm sure, was grimacing, his muscles engorged. He had a look when he got that way; it was otherworldly. Wherever he was when he went there, you couldn't reach him.

Change is notoriously difficult for people with bipolar disorder. Rich's meltdown was precipitated by his impending move to London and by all kinds of hormones and chemicals roaring around in his head. I'd guess he had at least half a liter of gin loosening his resolve, too. What stopped him? Maybe he was like any hurricane that spins and spins; it doesn't go on forever. It hits cold water; it hits land and as quickly as it starts, it ends. Rich got whatever he needed out, out. Police cars with flashing lights woke up the whole building. As police exited their cars, some of the building residents opened their windows; others stood around outside the front door, and Rich sat on the sidewalk.

One of the cops walked up to Rich and asked him what had happened. Rich's hands were still bleeding, and his clothes were covered with shards of glass.

"What a mess," he said to the cop. "Final exams; guess I got stressed out," and then he laughed. The cop started laughing, too. The police let him back into the apartment. Rich slept that night amidst the wreckage and a few weeks later, left—off to London for a new beginning.

❧ CHAPTER FIVE ❧

The dust of the traveled road
Shall touch my hands and face.
—Carl Sandburg

TRAVELING TO LONDON

Rich sent me a story three months before I visited him in London.

From: Richard Courtemanche
Sent: Wednesday, September 27, 2000
To: Ted Courtemanche
Subject: short story

so last night i'm on late shift, didnt leave til 745... long day. get to tube, train was delayed 12 minutes, tonz of people waiting. i cram myself on to the end of the car, wedged in, have my back to the door. we go a couple stops, no one can get on cause train is so jammed. we get to one stop (one of em that has the big gap - "mind the gap" - between train and platform). my back still facing platform, just waiting for the hellish journey to end. all of a sudden, as the doors are closing, my left leg gets knocked with something from behind. i turn around. a guy has thrown his suitcase on to stop the doors from closing (big suitcase) and he tries to squeeze in (he had thrown the suitcase into my leg). i turn around and give him the "what in god's name are you doing" look. his suitcase starts to fall out as the doors open back up. he grabs the suitcase again (he is still on platform) as the doors fully open. he then proceeds to throw it on again, doors closing. same situation, except this time, i kick his suitcase off, it falls "into the gap" between train and platform. doors close. he gives me evil look like he wants me dead. i wave to him. people in the car start to cheer for me as the train pulls off.

❖ ❖ ❖

I'd just climbed 530 stairs taking me to the Golden Gallery and the top of St. Paul's Cathedral. I was in London visiting Rich, a few days after New Year's 2001. It's cold on the gallery; from the railed deck, I can see the whole city. I watch a barge chugging slowly along the River Thames. Rich said that on the Fourth of July, there was a fireworks show that included part of the Thames being set on fire.

Inasmuch as an inorganic object can be a survivor, St. Paul's Cathedral is one. The Nazis targeted it during the Blitz of London. Bombs blasted it in 1940 and 1941. About 230 years before the bombings, St. Paul's was rebuilt by Christopher Wren—a work completed in 1708. Before 1708, St. Paul's was rebuilt three times—variously burned, sacked by Vikings and subjected to the wreckages of time. It's a testament to perseverance. Rich told me I should check it out.

I have to steady myself to the wind. I'd walked to the cathedral from Rich's flat. The sun peeked out during my walk, but now it's another misty London day. It isn't raining, just a constant pelting of tiny water droplets that can't bring themselves to form full-fledged raindrops.

The day I arrived in London, two days before New Year's Eve, Rich and I went to a nightclub. His girlfriend, Zatta; his roommate, Brendan; and a few others went, too. Zatta actually lived in Los Angeles. She was visiting Rich, for about three weeks, in London. The two of them had met while on vacation in Mexico.

In the nightclubs in London, you can buy full bottles of alcohol. One of Rich's co-workers bought a bottle of Grey Goose; it must have cost a hundred bucks. "He drops money like that all the time," Rich said. "He doesn't have anything else to spend it on."

What a foreign concept—enough disposable income and a positive enough disposition toward the future, or utter neglect, that you could burn money. Both Rich and Brendan were in the investment business, working for different companies. Rich worked at the Anlage Bank.

As soon as Rich got to London, he had an attack of what was diagnosed as psoriatic arthritis. Like rheumatoid arthritis, the biggest problem with psoriatic arthritis is that it can cause crippling pain. In the weeks after the first attack, Rich had to use a cane to get out of bed because his knees were so sore. The connection between chronic disease and depression is well documented; it's an empirical fact lacking a causal link. Researchers have looked for the link. At this time, the best they can say is that diseases like rheumatoid arthritis and psoriatic arthritis have a correlation or an association with depression. The psoriatic arthritis only seemed to flare when Rich was under a lot of stress.

Psoriatic arthritis is a "real" illness—that's the way I saw it back then; it's not just in your head. It causes the same skin problems as psoriasis, and it can make the skin at your joints crack and your nails fall out. It can disfigure you, and the pain can shut you down. I figured that with psoriatic arthritis, there would be no more weightlifting for Rich, no more physical activity. About one million people in the United States have the disease. The reason Rich hadn't gone on the walk to St. Paul's was partly because of the arthritis.

On New Year's Eve, Rich and Brendan invited a few friends over for a pre-New Year's Eve party. They'd gotten tickets to a nightclub for later in the evening. There were six of us in total, three guys and three girls. One of the girls was Zatta.

Rich took center stage once our little party got going. Before he officially moved to London, Rich was required to attend the Anlage company orientation in Germany. During the orientations, employees heard from key executives and other experts in the company. One of Richard's favorite stories was about a high-level executive who spent about thirty minutes with the new employees. In a thick German accent, he began his address with, "Good morning. I vant to velcome everyone to da Anlage Bank. Anlage, as I am sure you are avare, has a very proud history."

As he spoke, the new employees sat straight up, their eyes following him at the head of the table where he stood. Near the end of his presentation, the executive said, "Let us talk a little bit about our cultoor. Vee value diversity. You can be sure vee do." This was nothing new from a standard talk on company culture. What company doesn't value diversity verbally? The executive went on to say, "Look, as a matter of a fact, around dis table. You can tell vee are committed to diversity. For example, see der are tree vimen here today. And look at da end of da table. Der is a black man and a Chinese man. You see, dis is our cultoor. Vee are a company vorking togeddar. Vee have vimen, blacks, Chinese and all kinds of ovars working in our proud company."

Rich described and visually represented the expressions of astonishment from the group. He told how the women looked at each other, their eyes wide; how the whole group knew the guy who was labeled "black" was actually Indian, and the Chinese man was actually Vietnamese. Rich loved the way the executive thought he was embracing the new employees.

The nightclub on New Year's Eve was a total letdown. My buzz from our pre-party started to wear off. As it did, the volume of the music seemed to go up. I would rather have stayed at the flat, talking and listening to stories. All in all, we were at the club for about two hours. We considered going out to a late-night eatery afterward, but Rich didn't want to go—so everyone headed home. When we got back to the flat, Rich flipped burgers for himself and me. Once we finished eating, New Year's 2001 was over.

I chuckle to myself thinking about Rich's work story as I stand atop St. Paul's. The barge I'd been watching keeps traveling up the Thames, getting smaller at it goes. I steady myself on the Golden Gallery deck and take a deep breath. The sting of the cold air is good for me.

Before I'd climbed the steps to the Golden Gallery, I'd gone into the crypt beneath St. Paul's. There are more than 200 memorials in the crypt. Some are for famous people, like Admiral Nelson, and others are not. The famous and not-so-famous are distinguished now only by their stories.

On the gallery, a gust of wind hits my face and snaps me back to the present moment. The mist keeps falling, making the air feel colder. My mind jumps to thoughts about how I haven't yet adjusted to the time change in coming to London.

As my flight from Philadelphia was getting ready to leave for Gatwick Airport, I took a sleeping pill, an Ambien. My vision was me sleeping the entire flight— waking up refreshed and ready to start my vacation as the wheels touched down in London. Half an hour into it, I was still as awake as I was when I'd gotten on the plane, maybe a little more so. I reached into my backpack, pulled out my vitamin holder, and took another Ambien. An hour later, still with no signs of sleep, I considered taking another half of an Ambien. A friend once told me a story about how a guy he knew took two Ambiens and had to be carried off the plane in a stretcher after the flight was canceled. I decided against another half pill and was still awake four and a half hours into the flight. All around me, passengers slept soundly. Finally, I dozed off for forty-five minutes. Orange light was cresting through the windows when I woke up.

Once in London, I took a taxi from the airport to Rich's four-story flat. The "four-story" description makes it sound bigger than it was; the flat was more like a two-story townhouse that had been split in half, with the two halves then piled on top of each other. Rich's flat was near Notting Hill. The streets are narrow in London; parking is nearly impossible. It's not practical to own a car there, and neither Rich nor Brendan had one. As I climbed the stairs to the second-story front door of Rich's flat, I wasn't sure what to expect before seeing him. I didn't know if he'd have any of the outward manifestations of psoriatic arthritis. As he opened the door, he looked like the same old Rich—no visible signs of the disease. After I shook his hand, I met Brendan and Zatta, went up to the room where I would be staying, and slept until 3:00 pm. I didn't recover from jet lag the rest of the trip; the only day I got up any earlier than 11:30 am was the last day, and then just to catch my flight.

I went out to dinner with Brendan one night. Brendan seemed like a calming influence. Rich told me a few years later that Brendan had bipolar disorder. He'd taken lithium as a kid. Some experts believe that medication can be discontinued once children with bipolar disorder stabilize. After ten years or so, Brendan stopped taking lithium and focused on meditation. Brendan and I didn't talk about bipolar disorder that night; we talked about trading strategies.

"Rich is a cowboy," Brendan said. "We've talked about it before. He believes in big risks for big instant payoffs. It's a kind of impatience to me. You're setting yourself up for problems, but Rich doesn't see it that way. I couldn't live with that kind of uncertainty. You can make as much money as you need without the mental pain. My theory is, 'Wait on it.' Look at Warren Buffett. There's a way to get a reasonable return without exposing yourself or your investors to too much risk. You just have to be patient."

We talked about how Buffett made billions slowly and methodically by finding underpriced stocks, snapping them up and turning them later for a profit—"value investing." We talked about how in futures trading, you might risk your total investment or at least a huge chunk every day.

Brendan told me a story from *The Sopranos*, a story meant to underscore the importance of patience. In it, two bulls, a father and son, are watching a herd of cows from the top of a hill. The son, who is entering bull puberty, gets excited and tells his dad they should run down the hill, find two cows, and have intercourse with them. The dad tells the son that instead of running and scaring the cows, they should walk down the hill and "[screw] them all."

I told Brendan how I worked with numbers—I ran an analytics department at a health care company named Synchronic in Greensboro. "Over the long haul, numbers tend to display patterns," I said. "Over the short run, anything can happen." In the short term, unquestionably you can find good bets from a trading perspective, we agreed, but it requires either insider information or luck that they'll work out the way you want on any single occasion. We both knew the logic behind the numbers didn't matter to Rich. The fact remained that he was going to be a futures trader.

As daylight fades from the sky, I decide to leave the top of St. Paul's. The barge I'd watched when I first arrived on the gallery is now nowhere in sight. I walk through a doorway to the stairs, leaving the mist and chill of the Golden Gallery behind. The steps down are narrow; I focus on them as my mind wanders around, jumping from Greensboro to London and back. About halfway down the stairs, my thoughts drift again to the crypt.

In a book edited by Hiroshi Obayashi titled *Death and the Afterlife: Perspectives of World Religions*, George Bond wrote that some primitive cultures afford little significance to thoughts of life after death: "Death is taken as a matter of course, the burial rites are simple, and beliefs of an afterlife are almost nonexistent." No matter your thoughts on an afterlife, in the cathedral crypt where crowds walk every day, where life is everywhere, there is the constant reminder of death. You basically look eye-to-casket at the tombs; it's not something that can be avoided.

It was dark outside when I got to the bottom of the cathedral stairs. A church service was about to begin. I considered staying, but time was getting tight. I was meeting Rich and his friends from Anlage at a bar in an hour, so I walked around the cathedral. Climbing a set of stairs to a second-floor balcony, I observed. As people arrived for the service, locals loosening their scarves and jackets, the tourist crowd thinned. I was standing behind a wooden railing, leaning my forearms on the top of the beam. The scene was simple, just long shadows mingling with candlelight. Every once in a while, the candle flames would flicker from a draft, and darkness and light would briefly trade places.

The walk to the bar from St. Paul's was cold. When I got inside, my hands were freezing. The bar area, beneath a restaurant on the street level, was smoky and crowded. I saw Rich standing near the bar; he looked taller than usual because the ceiling was low. I waved; he waved, and I joined his friends and him. We all ordered beers, and one of Rich's friends, Martin, told a story about Rich.

According to Martin, shortly after Rich joined Anlage, the company started a "business casual" dress policy. Rich took clothing seriously. He knew all the name brands, wore cologne and had lots of shoes. He always looked good. One day, he was sitting at his desk wearing a button-down, collarless shirt as he analyzed whatever commodities he was supposed to be analyzing. As his boss was walking around the floor, he did a double take when he saw Rich.

He stopped at Rich's desk and quietly said, "Richard, I'm afraid you're not in compliance with the Anlage dress policy. The policy requires that you wear a button-down shirt with a collar. It can't be collarless. It's okay for today, but please keep that in mind in the future."

Rich looked at him, and as soon as his boss finished speaking, Rich nodded and looked back at his computer screen. At lunch, Rich went to a men's clothing store, searching for a good shirt. He returned to his desk at Anlage in a button-down, short-sleeved dress shirt with a collar—size: medium. The shirt just barely covered his belly button; he worked the rest of the day in it.

We all clanked glasses after Martin finished his story. More stories and more toasts followed. I chatted with Martin. He seemed a little different from the rest, easier for me to talk with. After the night was done, Rich told me that Martin had joined Anlage before trading was fashionable. He was an entrepreneur and didn't have a college education, let alone an MBA from a top-tier school. He lived with his wife and kids on a country farm in the same town where they'd both grown up. In the mornings, he left the farm and traveled an hour and a half by train to the office.

"He has more money than he knows what to do with," Rich told me.

Martin said he'd been in the right place at the right time with Anlage—that was it. Six months after I visited, Martin left Anlage and became a missionary.

One of the constants during the London trip was a card game that Rich and Brendan called "eights" (short for "crazy eights"). When Brendan, Rich and I played, Rich did his usual trash talking. As we sat at the kitchen table, he'd try to hurry us into playing the wrong card. During the games, Rich was a bundle of energy—tapping his feet, playing his cards, sipping beer, giving Brendan crap about the cards he played, frowning at the cards I tossed or how I slowed the game.

The object of eights is to get rid of all your cards. If you can't play a card, you have to pick from the unused card pile until you can play one. When Brendan or I had to pick from the pile, Rich would start counting, "And one and two and three and four and, wow, that's a lot of cards, six and seven . . ." He especially liked it if Brendan or I had to draw more than ten cards.

In eights, as in most card games, the better you can remember what's been played, the better are your odds of winning. Even though there's a large luck component, Rich told everyone it was skill—remembering old plays—that made him good. Of course, the game was luck if he lost. I got shellacked in eights.

My last night in London was the best. After a game of eights, we decided to have spaghetti for dinner. My job was to go to the corner market to get Stella Artois beer—a task I completed to the letter. Brendan made spaghetti sauce, Zatta set the table, and Rich drank beers and put a roll of paper towels on the table, to be used for napkins. The dinner cost about ten bucks (less the beer). We all sat around and talked.

Rich spent quite a bit of time in his room with Zatta when I was in London. I think he was going through a down spell. The last night, he seemed to be moving to an up spell. After dinner, we went downstairs to watch a movie. Rich told me I had to see *Dumb and Dumber*. I'd never seen it, and we almost always liked the same movies. The downstairs heater was broken, and we all got under covers—Brendan in one seat, Rich and Zatta on the sofa and me on the recliner.

There was nothing expensive or particularly special about the last night, just dinner and a funny movie, but we all hung out together. Those were the times I liked most with Rich.

I left London the next morning. The whole flight back was under the light of day and went faster than the flight out. Once I got home, I fell right back into my East Coast sleep schedule.

WEIGHTLIFTING AND DEPRESSION

It's hard to pinpoint exactly the incident that pushed me over the edge to start lifting weights. There are a few leading candidates:

- Being told by Granny, "You need to put some meat on your bones."
- Being told by a girlfriend (platonic) that my arms made me look like I was starving.
- Having a friend tell classmates the reason my arms were so skinny was that I didn't use them.
- Hanging on to (hugging, really) a bench, itself drilled into the locker room concrete, as my gym classmates tried to pull me from it so that my head could be dunked into a toilet bowl.

The main motivators for lifting weights, then, were body image and personal security. Unfortunately, I'd read articles about kids having their growth stunted by weightlifting. I was stuck in the middle of a frustrating paradox in grades six through nine. I was skinny to the point of being picked on (another incident was having my shorts pulled down as I walked into the locker room, again in gym class) but couldn't do anything about it for fear I'd stunt my growth.

Finally, in the summer between ninth and tenth grade, I got a weight set. I was almost six feet tall at that point and willing to risk being stuck there forever. Rich, Mom and I drove to K-Mart and purchased a weight bench and weights. As a family, we were always mindful that you never knew when the money might run out, so the bench I bought was the cheapest one we could find. It was brown and had two thin arms that served as holders for the weight bar. The bench wobbled, but I didn't know enough to expect that it shouldn't.

I set up the bench in the cellar under one of the few light bulbs down there. No one in the family had ever lifted weights. As a guide, I used the instruction book that came with the weight set. It described how to do a bench press, a military press, shoulder pullovers and three or four other exercises. It didn't say how much weight to use on each one, so I just assumed you should use the same weight. Using the same weight on every exercise makes some easier than others.

If I concentrate enough, I can smell the summer humidity in the Sherborn cellar. It was my own space—just the bench, the weights and the rug I put the bench on (to cushion the weights in case they hit the floor). I did my weightlifting routine the same way each time. The only real variable was the frame of mind I'd start with. Sometimes, I would be perfectly happy heading down the cellar steps to start my exercises. Other times, I'd be in a state about something, maybe some kind of injustice done to me during the day. Once I got down there, I did my first set of bench press. I lay on the bench, raised the bar above my chest, lowered it, raised it and repeated. Every once in a while, I'd have to roll the bar off myself because I couldn't lift it anymore. Whatever my state of mind when I first sat on the bench, lifting weights evened me out. As I lifted, endorphins were released into my body—that's part of what contributed to the calm. The other part was a kind of liberation from my mind. I only had to focus on this one simple thing: pushing or pulling weights from one place to another. The struggle of pushing and pulling kept my mind occupied.

Researchers are in agreement that physical activity can play a role in relieving depression. A minority believe physical activity is as effective as pharmacology. Rich started weightlifting about a year after I did. As far as I know, Rich wasn't picked on by his classmates for being skinny; he wasn't skinny. He was picked on—we shared that—but it was for other reasons. Rich had a temper. Kids would provoke him, and then he'd lose it; when we were small (third grade or so and younger), he might start crying. Once you're tagged as a kid, it takes a lot of effort to remove that tag. Weightlifting helped in the reversal I needed, and it helped in Rich's, too.

We became passionate. We'd ingest huge quantities of protein and weight-gain powder. You could see giant guys on the protein powder labels, guys that had clearly benefited from the same products we were ingesting. The most common side effect of the nutritional products was gas. In high school, not only were we either bigger than our classmates or at least not pick-on skinny (in my case), but we always had an available reservoir of gas. Young men revere other young men who can fart on demand. If someone else let go a little toot, Rich and I could explode a bomb that would put the little toot to shame. Don't get the sense that we farted all the time: We didn't. But when necessary, we could call on our gaseous reserves to let go a whooper. For Rich and me, weightlifting became a shared bond.

Change didn't happen quickly when I was weightlifting. I stayed thin for a while, but as I kept it up, my body started to morph. Hippocrates explained the principle behind weight training when he wrote, "That which is used develops, and that which is not used wastes away"—kind of like what my grade school friend had said (only nicer).

To grow stronger and definitely to get bigger, you have to eat. Rich's favorite eating aid was the blender. He'd drop oatmeal, protein powder, yogurt, milk and maybe some cinnamon into the blender, flip it on and then drink the shake. He called it an oatmeal shake. Rich experimented with all kinds of food in the blender, the goal being not so much taste as convenience and speed. Rich could do other things if he was drinking a turkey sandwich shake—things besides sitting at a table and chewing away—while still getting the carbohydrates and protein of the sandwich, all in less than two minutes. To get the turkey sandwich shake to blend, it was a good idea to let it stand in milk for a little bit. The same thing worked with Cheerios. I survived my first year in graduate school on oatmeal shakes.

When you're weightlifting, it's just you and the weights. You, individually, are pushing or pulling a weight, and by stressing whichever muscles are doing the pushing or pulling, you're making them stronger. That's it. I started lifting for body image and security—pretty standard for a young guy. The older a person gets, the more likely it is that health benefits play a role. Whatever the reasons, chances are the weightlifter forgets about them when he or she is in the process of doing an exercise.

The reality of the "weightlifting is individual" observation similarly can be lost. If you don't remind yourself that it's just you and the weights, you can get caught up in external considerations, such as comparing yourself to other people. The easiest benchmark is how much weight a person can lift. It's hard, especially for a young guy, not to get caught up in the "who can lift the most weight" syndrome at some gyms. As you're sitting at your machine or bench, some guy—or, worse (for a young guy), some girl—gets on the machine next to you and does more weight. That's when your form falls apart. You start arching your back on the bench press or bouncing the weight off your chest so that you can do a little more.

In the last section, I wrote about my trip to see Rich in London. Once I got home from London, Rich and I went back to our regular communication routines: phone calls every few weeks and emails in between. In April, Rich sent me an email about Finaplix.

From: Richard Courtemanche
Sent: Monday, April 23, 2001
To: Ted Courtemanche
Subject:

hey T, been reading a lot of good stuff on finaplix, lots of chat rooms about it... cheap and effective. going to supplement w/dandelion, milk thistle combo along with a cranberry [supplement] as i read cranberry juice very effective at helping kidneys from avoiding damage. later, r

Rich had told me about Finaplix before. It's sold legally to veterinarians for cattle. The active component is trenbolone acetate, which is an anabolic steroid used to increase the rate of weight gain in cows. Weightlifters and bodybuilders (who use steroids) like it because it's powerful and gets out of their systems quickly. I wasn't sure what to think of Rich's plan to take steroids. It didn't surprise me—the bodybuilding magazines we read were basically full-color endorsements—yet I wasn't sure he'd actually start. I searched the Internet for information on Finaplix and sent him an email on what I'd found.

From: Ted Courtemanche
Sent: April 25, 2001 10:14 AM
To: Richard Courtemanche
Subject: info

<<Link to site with information about steroids>>

Hey Rich, thought you might find this link interesting. Apparently, decadurabolin is one of the safest available - safer than finaplix. This site gives a summary on just about every one on the market. According to these guys, finaplix is one of the most toxic you can take.

Later,
T

Rich responded a short while later.

From: Richard Courtemanche
Sent: April 25, 2001 11:31 AM
To: Ted Courtemanche
Subject: Re: info

hey T, thanks for the info. i have been on a ton of sites about fina. I have read about the toxicity before, but all the users seem to think thats overblown. especially with the topical method of delivery [putting it on your skin instead of injecting or swallowing it]. i would try deca but dont know where to find it. i actually belong to a site over here that lists suppliers, maybe i will try it. will let u know either way.

A month went by as Rich and I exchanged emails. He'd give me updates on what he'd read and learned about steroids. In June, his first shipment arrived.

From: Richard Courtemanche
Sent: June 06, 2001
To: Ted Courtemanche
Subject:

got my "paperstrol." what is this, u wonder... well, its winstrol [a steroid], but in "paper" form. its wild, T. they take the winny, basically crush it into fine bits, put it in between two pieces of thick paper and its divided into squares. basically, u get a 3x3 inch piece of cardboard lookin thing which u cut up on premarked lines. u take the square, unfold it, place under your tongue and then swallow after a few minutes. ya, u swallow a tiny piece of paper, not really an issue in my book. not all products available this way, people claim (users that is) that its more powerful than regular pill form. will see. will keep u posted. r

Many anabolic steroids are derived from the male hormone testosterone. A study done at Harvard Medical School's McLean Hospital showed that some clinically depressed men with low testosterone levels who had not previously responded to treatment showed dramatic improvement when given a combination of testosterone and antidepressants (the results were published in the *American Journal of Psychiatry* in January 2003 under the title "Testosterone Gel Supplementation for Men with Refractory Depression: A Randomized, Placebo-Controlled Trial"). The study's finding wouldn't surprise steroid users. The first thing a lot of users notice is a feeling of euphoria.

If you have any doubts as to the addictive quality of anabolic steroids, all you need to do is take a quick look on the Web. Anabolic steroids make people bigger and stronger than they could be without them. When a person stops, the effect goes away. George Bernard Shaw said, "I tell you that as long as I can conceive something better than myself, I cannot be easy unless I am striving to bring it into existence." If people who want to be bigger and stronger get bigger and stronger and then see it starting to slip away, odds are good they'll want to get bigger and stronger again. First-time users think they can do one or two cycles of steroids and then be done. The main reason people with bipolar disorder quit their medications is the euphoric feeling of hypomania—they want it back. People with addictive personalities who access the euphoria plus the physical gains of anabolic steroids will find it hard to stop.

It's an inevitable fact of nature that lacking breaks, the speed that we go up is the speed we come down. The euphoria doesn't come cheaply. Harrison Pope, Jr., and David Katz authored one of the most widely cited articles on the psychological effects of steroids: "Psychiatric and Medical Effects of Anabolic-Androgenic Steroid Use." In it, they wrote that 23 percent of anabolic steroid users "reported major mood syndromes—mania, hypomania, or major depression—in association with steroid use."

"Depression" is a word that describes a state of mind. For anyone who's experienced it, it's a strangling black fog; and once it sets in, there's little memory of another time. The fog is unshakable. It governs everything you do. Anything that grants freedom, even just a taste, is welcome—even if the freedom comes at a heavy price. Physical activity like weightlifting can help in treating depression, but prone to extremes and short-term escapes as he was, Rich jumped into steroids. He was seeking happiness: That's the way I see it when I get outside the words. The only time he was as excited about a new venture is when he started futures trading on his own.

STAN-THE-VAN AND MIND BOUNDARIES

Stan-the-Van wasn't mobile in snow. He couldn't fit in the garage, either. If you were entering the Courtemanche driveway in Sherborn from the road, you'd drive straight for about one hundred feet and then turn right to get to the garage. Stan's parking spot was at the point you'd take a right. He had off-road parking under a pine tree. The tree fort Uncle Ed built, until it collapsed, was about thirty feet in front of Stan.

One particular winter day, Stan was parked in his usual place. The temperature was slightly above freezing, and snow and ice were melting and mixing with the dirt and mud underneath. Rich and I were getting ready to drive Stan somewhere. As I tried to back up, Stan's back right tire broke through the thinned ice on top of a shallow puddle. He stopped going backward. I put him in drive, and he didn't go forward. I put him in reverse, and the tires started spinning. I shifted to drive, then reverse and then back to drive, trying to create a rocking effect. It didn't work. Stan wasn't moving. I shifted him to reverse and put the accelerator all the way down—nothing. I got out to survey the situation. Rich did, too.

No doubt about it, Stan was stuck. The back bumper was covered with mud. Either Rich or I had to try pushing Stan forward to free him. We'd gotten other cars out of similar situations the same way. Pushing Stan in the mud was a lousy job, and we both knew it. I lost whatever method we used to make the decision and got behind Stan; on a count of three, Rich shifted him into drive and hit the accelerator. The only part of Stan that moved was the back rear tire. With more water and mud in the puddle than I'd expected, my pants got covered.

"Stop," I said. "STOP!" Rich stopped.

Rich got out of the car. He laughed a little at my pants and then said, "What do you want to do?" We'd never been in a situation where Stan was just plain stuck. We didn't have any preconceived notions, so we just started freewheeling.

"Let's try putting a board underneath there," I said.

We went to the garage and found a board. We walked back to Stan and put the board under the back tire—as close to *under* as we could get it. I got in the driver's seat, and Rich watched from a safe distance. I tried to accelerate with Stan in reverse. The board went flying out, and then Stan's rear tire started spinning in the mud, the smell of burning rubber filling the air. Whatever Rich and I had been planning on doing would have to wait.

We got out shovels from the garage and started to dig the ice, snow and mud from behind Stan's rear wheels. We got two more pieces of wood from the garage and put them both under the stuck tire. We used a sledgehammer to really bang the wood under it. I got in the driver's seat, put Stan in reverse and tried to accelerate. The extra wood didn't help. It just meant more wood flying out from Stan's tires.

Rich and I went back to the garage. We saw old woodchips in a bag, and next to them, a bag of sand. That's when it hit us. We carried the sand over to Stan and poured it into the muddiest hole. I climbed into the driver's seat, put Stan in reverse and drove him right out of the parking spot.

It took trial and error to find the right method to free Stan. In the future, Rich and I made sure to keep sand around in case Stan got stuck. Sand for us became associated with freeing cars from snow. In the right setting, something might click in my head, and I'd remember how sand can be used to free cars. The trigger could be the sight of a car stuck in snow or just the sight of sand and snow together.

Memory triggers come in many shapes and forms. We'll hear a song or smell a scent and an old memory will flash. Memory triggers can initiate a cascade of old memories. When I think about Stan, more thoughts of him jump from my archives.

Rich and I are waxing Stan in the driveway in Sherborn. It's the middle of summer, and the sun is blazing through a mix of pine and oak trees. As we rub wax off the roof, we keep towels under our knees because Stan's metallic-brown color absorbs the sunlight and radiates it out as heat. . . . Mom is driving Rich and me to Hopkinton State Park, which is about thirty minutes from Sherborn. We have a canoe in Stan's cargo area. Rich and I both like canoeing to the small islands scattered across the park's reservoir. . . . I'm driving Rich and myself to school. The weekend before, Mom and Dad told us we could use Stan anytime we wanted—as long as they didn't need him that day. We see other kids getting off their buses as we pull into the Dover-Sherborn High School parking lot, and we soak up our new freedom.

From the drive-to-school memory, I can go onto other memories, most of which have nothing to do with Stan.

In this book, we've been exploring what we miss when we miss anyone. The purpose is to help us break through the natural tendency to think that what we miss is the physical person. One of our earliest findings, in the go-cart story, is that what we miss is not unique to the material we're made from. We're made from universal scraps. We've seen that we're actually collections of homegrown and foreign cells. Well over half of the cells in our body are foreign bacteria (estimates put the number of human cells in our bodies at 10 quadrillion, and foreign bacteria at 100 quadrillion). It's nothing more that an out-and-out illusion to look at another person and think, "There stands an independent being." People have all sorts of living things inside them that are not them, but without which they couldn't survive.

In the "Bodies, Brains and Feynman" section in Chapter Four, we concluded that a brain cannot operate properly without nourishment and stimulus. The standard definition of a working or functioning brain is a *mind*—a mind is a brain in action. In his book *The Problem of the Soul*, philosopher and neurobiologist Owen Flanagan wrote, "The brain working in concert with the rest of the nervous system is our *res cogitans*—our thinking stuff." This takes us to next area of exploration regarding what we miss when we miss anyone— the mind. Is what we actually miss the person's mind? Before we tackle that question, or attempt to, let's first explore a peculiarity of our minds, which has to do with how self-contained they actually are.

In 1998, philosophers Andy Clark and David Chalmers published a paper called, "The Extended Mind." In it, they argued for *active externalism*, a view that holds that the process of thinking, cognition, expands beyond the confines of our heads. Their theory may seem odd at first but consider the case of Stan-the-Van getting stuck, with sand—an external object—triggering memories in my head. Every day, we rely on things outside of us to trigger not just memories, random or otherwise, but to aid us in the process of thinking. We create lists on paper or in our computers so that we'll know what we want to get done during the day. We'll reference a calendar to see what we're planning on doing in the future, or what we did at some point in the past. We store thoughts, perhaps jotting them in a notebook or, again, in our computers, so that we won't forget something we just learned or were thinking about. Those lists, dates and notes are, in fact, part of our cognition process. We use them in concert with information stored in our brains, and as such, they're every bit as influential on our cognition as the neurons and synapses and chemicals in our heads. For this reason, Clark and Chalmers argue that those external objects are part of our minds.

Daniel Dennett wrote in *Kinds of Minds: Toward an Understanding of Consciousness*, "[Human] brains are modestly larger than the brains of our nearest relatives . . . but this is almost certainly not the source of our greater intelligence." He believes the main source is "our habit of offloading as much as possible of our cognitive tasks into the environment itself."

Sometimes the process of offloading information is conscious, as in the case of "to do" lists or thoughts we write in notebooks. The offloading can also be unconscious, as in the case of sand and Stan-the-Van. Dennett described the problem some seniors experience when they are removed from their homes and put in a hospital or a nursing home. They can appear demented. They can't feed, wash or clothe themselves. If they're put back in their homes, they function normally again. What's happening is that their actual homes are filled with what Dennett calls "ultrafamiliar" landmarks. These landmarks are memory triggers that drive routine life processes for the seniors. See the kitchen table in the regular place? The routine known as "eating breakfast" is triggered. According to Dennett, "Taking [seniors] out of their homes is literally separating them from large parts of their minds—potentially just as devastating a development as undergoing brain surgery."

The unconscious transferal of information to the environment is common. You or I might see our toothbrush in the morning and begin the process of brushing our teeth. Or we'll see an empty coffee pot in the kitchen and proceed to remove the coffee from wherever it's stored, get a filter, put coffee grounds into the filter, add water to the coffee maker and hit the start button—without thinking consciously about how to do any of the steps. We just do them, and seeing the empty coffee pot, an object external to us, triggered the process.

"The mind," as Clark and Chalmers wrote, "extends into the world." Whether you agree or not with philosophers like Clark, Chalmers and Dennett that those external objects are part of our minds, there's no doubting a toned down version: We owe our mind's ability to function in this world to external objects such as notebooks, computers, cell phones and sticky notes—anything it can employ in the process of being *us*. Whether we choose to believe in Darwinian evolution or not, it's happening right now. Instead of more brain cells, we're adding on hard drives, RAM and microprocessors so that we're capable of more than we'd be without them.

The people we miss wouldn't have been able to be who they were, or appeared to us, without the external objects to which they off-loaded cognitive tasks. This is to say, the line between "foreign objects" and "person we miss" is hazy, not just from the inside out, but from the outside in—we're not only dependent on things like bacteria to be who we are, but our minds are dependent on external objects.

In the chapters that follow, we'll be investigating many of the things our minds *do*, in the hopes of getting a better handle on what that person we're missing actually was. But for now, the key takeaway is that our minds rely on more than just the gray matter inside our heads.

THE PHONE CALL AT WORK

On the morning of Thursday, November 3, 2005, I'd learned that Rich wasn't in the psychiatric hospital that he said he was going to be in. I responded by crafting an email that I didn't send. That Thursday afternoon, while I was at work, I received a phone call from Rosalyn at the front desk. She told me that she had Rich on the line. Rich hadn't called me at work in years. "Hi, Rosalyn. Yeah, go ahead and put him through," I said, waiting a few seconds before saying, "Rich?"

"Hey, T," he answered.

"Hey, Rich, how's it going?" I asked. I forget what we talked about for the first thirty seconds or so. I could tell Rich wasn't really into it, that his mind was somewhere else.

Once we hit the first lull in the conversation, Rich said, "T, this is the last time you'll ever hear from me. I wanted to say goodbye."

My head started to tingle. "Rich, what are you talking about?"

"T, this is the last time you're going to hear from me. I've had enough. I have a shot gun in my truck, and I wanted to say goodbye."

The situation felt so totally out of my control that I just gave up on the spot. I couldn't reach into the phone; I couldn't transport myself to wherever Rich was. I shattered, just a collection of pieces held together by force of habit.

"Rich," I said, "I don't know what to say. Do Mom and Dad know?"

"I sent an email to everyone, T. It should be in your inbox."

"What happened with the hospital?" I asked.

"T, don't try to get me to change my mind. I'm doing it."

"Okay, Rich. Okay," I said. Worried that he might hang up, I scanned my brain for things to say, anything just to keep him on the phone. I said the following without thinking—the words just came out: "Are you going to do it in a beautiful place?"

"Yes," he answered. "It's going to be beautiful," and I could hear him start to cry.

I don't remember any other parts of the conversation after that. It didn't last long. I know he didn't tell me where he was. Whatever words were shared, perhaps they're somewhere in the recording tape of my head, or maybe they were erased as soon as they were spoken.

Rich hung up, and I sat in my chair, still tingling and dazed. When I played football, I'd sometimes slam helmets with another guy, maybe when I was blocking him, and then I'd see dots moving like shooting stars across my field of vision. It's hard to describe, but after the stars, I sometimes felt like I'd drifted outside my body, a kind of high that lasted only a second or two. That's what it felt like after Rich called: the high following a blow to the head. I walked into the hall, and I stumbled, almost banging into one of the cubicles outside my office.

Synchronic, where I worked, employed over one hundred nurses in our call center. We had a standard process in case one of our nurses got a call from a suicidal patient. I couldn't bring myself to get anyone else involved. I thought about doing so while I was talking to Rich, but it didn't seem worth the risk— Rich could have hung up while I was in the process of trying to get someone else on the line. After we hung up, I considered talking with one of the people who'd developed the company suicide-call policy. But then I thought about Rich's history: how he'd go up, and then come down, and then go back up again. What if this was just one more in a long line of lows? What if I did get someone else involved, and then Rich emerged from his depression shortly afterward? I'd have to deal with this other person or people every day—after they'd seen a slice of my life I didn't want them to see. It's not unusual for families living in the shadow of bipolar disorder to share a self-imposed isolation.

I called a national suicide prevention line. Better to seek anonymous help, I thought.

"How did he sound?" the girl who answered the phone asked.

"Like he's going to shoot himself," I said.

"Has he talked about it before?"

"For twenty years."

She asked me to hold. I guess so she could check in with a supervisor. She got back on the line.

"Does he have a plan?"

"He told me he's going to shoot himself today in a beautiful place." Rich had called from his cell phone; it showed up on the work caller ID system. "I have his cell phone number. Can we track him?"

After she put me on hold again and then clicked back in, she said, "You can't track cell phones." She talked about exactly why you can't. After she was done, neither of us had anything more to say.

"Okay, I'm going to hang up now," I told her.

"I'm sorry," she said.

Once I hung up, I checked my email. I saw the one that Rich had sent.

From: Richard Courtemanche
Sent: Thursday, November 03, 2005 2:58 PM
To: Betty Courtemanche; Bob Courtemanche; T Home
Subject: hi

hi all. just sending u an email. i have left san diego. my treatment was ok. but in the end i am out of here and its happening now.

first... Sharon is confused. i told her i was going back to boston. i told mom i was going back to TX. neither is true. i am somewhere else... where i am at peace to die. i will send a final email with location of dogs. they are ok. they have plenty of food and water. but they need to be picked up. if any of u cant take them, pls contact diane [the breeder from whom Rich got his dogs]. mom has number. they always have a home there.

there is nothing left to say. i might drift for a while trying to find peace. but i am done. u all tried ur best. thank u.

dont be sad. i have waited 36 yrs for this. its here. and i am happy. my phone will be shut off. i will no longer have contact with any of u.

and my only wish is that u dont try to figure out what was wrong with me. it would take all your remaining yrs and you wouldnt find an answer

god bless u

richard

After I read Rich's email, I looked out the window at the trees across the street. I just sat there for a while. I called Mom, and she was losing it. The world was breaking apart. It had broken apart before. If Mom could have stopped time and scoured the world for Rich, she would have done it. I called Deana and Dad. I felt completely helpless; that's the best I can describe it, helpless.

I had a project that needed to get done at work. It's easy for me to get lost in numbers, so I went back to crunching them. When I tired of that, I started writing out thoughts on my computer—a relaxation technique that's always served me well. The day passed and the second email, the one that was supposed to tell us where his body was, where the dogs were, never arrived.

Shortly before I left work, Deana called and said she'd been talking to Mom. Rich had called Mom and told her he was someplace in Ohio. This is the way the pattern always went. Rich would have a breakdown during which he'd say he was considering ending his life, and then he'd pull himself back together and move on. He'd never written the kind of note he'd written today, but with Rich contacting Mom, I thought things would soon be in the clear. He might make a few more upsetting calls to Mom, but overall, he'd find his way out. I was glad I hadn't gotten anyone from work involved.

When I got home at the end of the day, Deana was talking to Mom again. Rich had told Mom that he was checking himself into a hospital for the night.

A huge relief went through me. He'd be safe in the hospital. I'd had the insides sucked out of me, and now I could start the reconstruction. I knew the drill. What mattered most was that Rich was going to be all right.

SUICIDE AND AQUINAS

When we were in grade school, Dad sometimes got Boston Bruins tickets from his company. He'd usually get only two, and take either Rich or me. In 1977, he got tickets to the fourth game of the Stanley Cup, Bruins versus the Montreal Canadians. The Stanley Cup! And it was Rich's turn to go.

"Come on, Rich! Can't I go?" I asked.

"I want to see the game," Rich answered as he fit together the roof of a Lincoln Log house.

"You don't even know who plays for the Canadians."

"Yes, I do," Rich said, and he went to our hockey card collection. He showed me who played for the Canadians. "See, Steve Shutt and Guy Lafleur."

Rich pronounced "Lafleur" wrong. He didn't care about the game, and both he and I knew it. He went back to the Lincoln Logs. I continued to argue my case, but he was ignoring me. He icily put one of the flat Lincoln Logs onto the roof of the house he was building. I took the Lincoln Log container.

"Last time, Richard, let me go."

"Theodore, give 'em back," he said.

I held the container out of his reach. "Can I go to the game?"

"Give 'em back," he said.

We fell into a "Can I go?" then "Give 'em back!" routine.

"Mom!" Rich yelled. Mom wasn't around.

"Richard, can I go to the game?"

"Give me back the Lincoln Logs!" Rich screamed. He was furious. Good, I thought to myself. I had him right where I wanted him.

We scrapped, and I struggled to get him pinned. Tears flowed; bitterness mounted, and we both got a few rug burns. When Mom got home, she was quickly brought up to speed on what had happened. Dad was apprised of the situation when he got in from work, too. Rich and I were both scolded for fighting: That was issue number one. The wrongness of fighting clear, Rich, Mom and Dad went off on their own and negotiated a deal whereby I got to go to the game. In return for letting me go, Rich got a bunch of lunches at McDonalds (his favorite restaurant), an undisclosed amount of cash and a day of his choice to see the fishing boats in Gloucester. As if those things weren't enough, he also got a full box of baseball cards. You could only get a full box one town over in Ashland—the bubble gum alone made it valuable.

In my opinion, Rich got all this stuff because of the baseless assumption that he liked hockey. He didn't was my point: He only liked going to the games because he got to eat hot dogs and drink Cokes. Sometimes, he'd just ask for the money in place of the food. "So what?" was the look Rich gave me as he sorted through his new Red Sox baseball cards. Months after the Bruins lost 2-1 to the Canadians in overtime, Rich was still working through the gum. Whatever Rich's argument to Mom and Dad, he made it persuasively.

❖ ❖ ❖

St. Thomas Aquinas is considered by many to be the church's greatest theologian. Among his writings, he argued persuasively on the topics of God, the Trinity and the nature of Jesus Christ. True knowledge of God, he maintained, is only possible through the "confluence" of faith and reason. After Augustine, Aquinas is the other Christian thinker most influential on the Church's position on suicide. He argued in *Summa Theologica* that suicide is a mortal sin for three reasons:

- First, "suicide is contrary to the inclination of nature, and to charity whereby every man should love himself."
- Second, by completing suicide, a person "injures his community."
- And third, "because life is God's gift to man, and is subject to His power, Who kills and makes to live. Hence whoever takes his own life, sins against God."

Aquinas' stance has been attacked on many fronts. The philosopher David Hume chose not to publish a rebuttal contained in his paper "On Suicide"— the decision a testament to the power of the Church. Copies of Hume's paper were discovered after his death and published posthumously. In delving into Aquinas' arguments, the question is whether they're any more solid than Augustine's. The reason suicide is considered a mortal sin is due in large part to Aquinas' arguments.

The "inclination of nature" is an important part of Aquinas' first argument against suicide. What is such an inclination? Karl Menninger wrote, "Conscious motives cannot be relied upon to explain human behavior. There are too many instances where motives cannot be confessed, cannot be interpreted, and most pertinent of all, are not to the slightest degree recognized by the person himself." In an article titled "Cell Suicide in Health and Disease," Richard Duke and his colleagues wrote, "Burgeoning research indicates that the health of all multicellular organisms, including humans, depends not only on the body's ability to produce new cells but on the ability of individual cells to self-destruct when they become superfluous or disordered."

This is to say that the inclination of nature, whether human or cellular, is far from obvious. As Duke points out, it appears that suicide is necessary for the survival of the whole on the cellular level. Even if we accept Aquinas' position that suicide is not natural, his conclusion that suicide is therefore wrong doesn't follow. Challenging "the way things are," striving to reach a goal and achieving it against the odds, is the hallmark of human courage. Because things are not natural—whatever *natural* really is—it does not follow that pursuing them is wrong.

Regarding Aquinas' other justification in his first argument—namely that suicide is wrong because it is contrary to charity—he offers as support the notion that "every man should love himself." His position here is even less solid than the "inclination of nature" reasoning. Anytime the word "should" is used, it's a red flag for "Here comes an opinion." There is nothing contradictory in a person loving something *and* ending its life. The most straightforward example is a pet owner who, loving his or her pet, chooses to end the pet's suffering—it's done *because* of love. Disregarding the validity or invalidity of Aquinas' claim that every man naturally loves himself, it's possible that charity is one of the reasons a person takes his or her own life.

As to Aquinas' second argument that suicide injures the community, the claim just doesn't stand on its own. The list of actions that injure a community, but aren't considered mortal sins, is long: littering; smoking (second-hand smoke); driving cars (releasing carbon dioxide into the atmosphere); even placing unsightly lawn ornaments in your yard. Consider, too, that moving from one community to another has largely the same effect on the former community as someone who ends his or her life via suicide. The person who moves—unless circumstances keep him or her tied to the last place of residence—is no longer able to benefit the prior community. Another major problem with Aquinas' second argument is that it's not always true. A soldier who jumps on a grenade thrown among his or her platoon saves lives, and so does a potential mass murderer who takes his or her life instead of killing others. Aquinas' second argument against suicide is no more valid than his first.

In his third argument, Aquinas postulates that our Creator should be the one to decide whether we live or die. In other words, God created us, and He alone has the right to take our lives. From the outset, Aquinas' third argument assumes that we were created by God. That assumption is a sinkhole: We could argue back and forth on it and never get anywhere. What if we just accept the idea that we were created by God? Hume took just such a position. In "On Suicide," Hume wrote, "Were the disposal of human life so much reserved as the peculiar province of the Almighty, that it were an encroachment on his right, for men to dispose of their own lives; it would be equally criminal to act for the preservation of life as for its destruction."

Hume gave the example of someone who avoids a falling stone. For Hume, if we hold, as Aquinas does, that it is an affront to take our own lives, the converse must be true as well. If we save our lives by avoiding stones that otherwise would kill us, through medical procedures, leading a "safe" life or by any other means, we are going against God's will in the same way as someone who completes suicide. Hume catches Aquinas in a pretty standard theological sleight of hand.

The problem with Aquinas' third argument, as Hume makes clear, is that Aquinas can't have it both ways. Daniel Dennett wrote in his book *Darwin's Dangerous Idea*, "The philosopher Ronald de Sousa once memorably described philosophical theology as 'intellectual tennis without a net.'" De Sousa's observation is particularly relevant in the case of Aquinas. Aquinas was one of the great thinkers of his time (as was Augustine). He used logic powerfully in his writings. In his third argument against suicide, Aquinas opted to forgo logic and instead rely on a kind of literal, but one side only, interpretation of a passage within the Bible. For de Sousa, the logic net is up if it's your turn to discuss suicide with Aquinas, and down when it's his turn.

Despite theological sleights of hand, I've found myself partial to Aquinas' second argument, that the person who completes suicide injures his or her community. The quality that attracts me is this: It talks to utility. For me, it says we have a role here on Earth, a *purpose* that we're here to complete. The world at large seems to offer support. I'll use mosquitoes as an example. I think it's safe to say that most people would consider mosquitoes a scourge. The world would be better off without them, wouldn't it?

The problem is that while mosquitoes may be a scourge to humans, they add utility to the planet. Mosquitoes pollinate flowers. Their larvae are a critical food source for fish and frogs, and adult mosquitoes are staple food items for bats and birds. Mosquitoes have a purpose, even if that purpose is simply being an appetizer for a bird. I don't mean to get caught up on the topic of mosquitoes other than to say that the world at large appears to support the utility perspective. If nothing else, bacteria, plants, insects and animals are all part of a food chain or integral to the proper functioning of a food chain.

To me, Aquinas' strongest argument against suicide is as follows: that in taking their own lives, people remove themselves from the utility chain, and they can no longer realize their purposes. There's a problem, though. Even if you agree with me, even if we proclaim, "Yes, every human has a purpose and therefore should not take his or her own life," there's another issue: How can we be sure that we're right? Further, even if we were somehow able to prove that all of us do have purposes, how would we know for sure what they are? As much as I might like to believe we are put here for a purpose, that God, as Einstein said, "does not roll the dice," I'm struck by how confusing, how malleable and how downright indefinable that purpose can appear to be.

We are not provided at birth with a document that handily specifies what we've been set here to do. Not only do we have to figure it out on our own, but our purpose (assuming we have one) is an issue that's open to interpretation. If you are good at math, you don't *just* have to be a math teacher; you could do lots of things with good math skills. Our search for a purpose can also be impacted by what we're being told our purpose is, making its identification even more difficult. Humans, as we know, are an incredibly suggestive lot. That's why we get pummeled by advertisers.

Given the trouble we have identifying our own callings, how can anyone ever know what someone else's purpose is—especially when we're mired in the mud of day-to-day living? I know I'm not privy to God's master plan. Unless someone out there is, determining another person's purpose is a question whose answer is outside of our reach. Hamlet said, "There are more things in heaven and earth, Horatio, than are dreamt of in your philosophy."

I got onto this string of thought by investigating Aquinas' arguments against suicide. I was checking whether they were any better than Augustine's. No matter the invalidity of Aquinas' arguments, his conclusion has influenced thinking by Christians and non-Christians to the present day.

Even though both Augustine and Aquinas secured their positions on marshland, the idea they've left us with—suicide is a mortal sin—has served to create misery and agony: That's fact. What was an intellectual exercise for the two men has driven unimaginable suffering. If they'd extended their intellectual prowess toward actively helping those contemplating suicide or to those living in the aftermath, perhaps they would have come closer to their purpose. Or maybe they nailed their purposes exactly. Who can say?

TRADING FULL TIME

Rich and I went through phases when we wouldn't email for weeks and then go on a run in which we'd send messages every day. We went on one of our runs right after Rich started his first steroid cycle in June of 2001. In his emails, he got outside himself. He wanted to know how I was doing. Did I have a girlfriend? How was work? Was I still playing hockey? Knowing what I now do about bipolar disorder, I suspect that Rich was going through a hypomanic state—it can happen without any outside stimulus, but steroids can kick one off.

As we were bantering back and forth, I told him about how a few people at Synchronic had looked out a third-story window in our office building and saw a man leaning against the base of a billboard near the highway. The billboard was about two hundred yards from the building. He first leaned against the base and then slumped down it, descending in slow motion with his back to the highway. Everyone looked closer and realized it was one of our medical directors. He just sat there for about twenty minutes, occasionally shaking his head. Around the office, most people could tell he was stressed out, snapping in meetings or complaining loudly about his new boss, but no one realized how stressed out he actually was. The same medical director went into the CEO's office the following Monday and quit. He said he just didn't want to work at Synchronic anymore and then walked out of the building—no goodbyes to anyone.

From the billboard story, Rich and I started talking about work-related stresses, and from there, the benefits of running your own business—we both agreed that with your own business, you at least have a better shot at controlling your destiny. In one email, Rich told me he was seriously thinking of quitting Anlage and trading on his own. He said if he quit by the end of the summer, he could be back in the U.S. in time for football season. He wanted to live in San Diego if he came to the States—San Diego has everything that London doesn't. There are sandy beaches. It's sunny and warm, and there is plenty of daylight for outdoor activities.

Aside from business, Rich told me that he was eating a lot, a sweet potato before and after every workout. He wanted to gain fifteen pounds of muscle and was doing a lot of cardiovascular exercises to keep his body fat down. Rich was a whirlwind of good news and big plans. I responded to his emails as soon as they came in because the whole process made me feel good. In the fall, he was planning to go to Miami with his friends for a short vacation and wanted to know if I'd like to join them. I told him that October would be a good time to visit Miami. After I did, he sent me an email about his short-term plans.

From: Richard Courtemanche
Sent: Thursday, June 21, 2001
To: Ted Courtemanche
Subject: Re:

that would be great if u came to florida. would be awesome i am sure. ok, i think i have my life figured for the moment... gonna stay in london til march 31 02 (bonus paid). then i will have extra cash, buy a car. move to san diego. i am gonna do two cycles in that time. one for bulk, one to cut up. figure i will take advantage cuz so much harder to get stuff in u.s. those are my short term goals anyway. will see. have a couple weeks vaca left this year, will definitely do miami in oct if thats better for u. man i am fired up already!!! would be great to see u. always is. hope work day is ok. hope day is good.

Shortly after he told me about Miami, our email wave crested. Three months later, on September 11, Rich lost about $100,000 in one day. We usually didn't talk about the trading account he kept on the side. When he told me about the loss, I couldn't believe how much he'd made *or* how much he'd lost. Shortly after the market closed on 9/11, he told me that he wasn't sure he was going to be solvent the next day. It was the family's first taste of the violent downturns of futures trading.

After 9/11, we steered clear of discussions about trading—other than him letting me know that he was still solvent. Plans for the Miami trip fizzled and disappeared, and after September, we went our own ways for a few months, hardly communicating at all. I figured that with his trading losses, his plans to leave London in March and trade on his own were off. We didn't talk business again until January 2002. By that time, his trading was back on track. In February, almost six months after he'd lost just about everything in his trading account, he sent me his career news.

From: Richard Courtemanche
Sent: Wednesday, February 27, 2002
To: Ted Courtemanche
Subject:

hey T... it is today. i resigned this a.m. although have to go in monday to officially hand it in, as my boss not in this week. and although i am nervous and its a big step, i havent felt this happy in years. i am here for 3 more weeks, lifting, trading and just chillin out. zatta prob coming for my last week which will be nice. then off to LA before moving in july to boston or s.d. i am really excited for it, and thanks again for all the confidence you have given me. r

Rich's plan was to get an apartment near Zatta's in Los Angeles. She was in the process of applying to law schools in San Diego and Boston. Depending on where she got into school, Rich and Zatta would move to that city next.

On bad days for me, days when I was off presenting to clients and getting chewed apart by questions about an analysis, I'd say to myself, "I have the same genes as Rich and a lot of the same talents. I should be trading, too." I'd think about the conversation with Brendan over dinner, talking about the risks of futures trading. For Rich, the proof was in his bank account.

From where I stood, he was pushing forward, no chains, only possibility.

CHAPTER SIX

Fly, envious Time, till thou run out thy race.
—John Milton

THE FIRST TRIP TO SAN DIEGO

As I boarded a plane bound for San Diego at the Greensboro airport, I was sweating and had blood on my pants. Sometimes it's not easy to pinpoint exactly when a situation changed or what circumstance ushered you down the path to your current mental state—not on my way to visit Rich in late July 2002. About an hour before boarding the plane, I stopped to get my parking ticket at the entrance to the airport long-term parking lot. As I did, I accidentally lowered my car's back window instead of the driver window. I was rushing and just hit the wrong button by mistake.

Once inside the lot, I tried to raise the back window. I pressed what I thought was the up button, but instead hit the down button again. The window dropped a little, but glass was still showing. I hit up next and nothing happened. One more time I pressed up and again, nothing. I pressed down and it went lower. Immediately, I took my finger off the button. I tried up, and the window still didn't move. This was a problem.

I was going to be away until Sunday, and it was now Wednesday afternoon. I didn't have time to drop off the car at my house and take a taxi to the airport. This window needed to go up. I drove into a parking space and went to work. I gripped the window and started tugging. It didn't move. I tried harder—nothing.

A girl walked by towing a suitcase, and I asked her if she could do me a favor. We were the only two people in our football-field sized portion of the parking lot. She tried to pretend that she didn't hear me.

"Excuse me," I asked one or two more times. She stopped. "My rear window is broken," I said. "Could you just hit the up button on the driver side door? I'm going to pull the window up as you do."

She walked over and pressed the button before I was ready.

"Okay, one more time; just let me know when you're pressing it."

"I'm pressing it now," she said.

The damn window was slippery from my sweaty hands. I asked the girl to wait a second. As she watched, I walked over to a small sand pile near a drainage grate and rubbed some sand on my hands. With my improved grip, I grabbed the window as hard as I could. The girl pressed the button again. I tugged with all my might, using my legs to get more leverage, but the window still wouldn't budge. I thanked the girl for her help, and she walked off. I called the 1-800 number in the service booklet that I kept in the glove compartment.

"Roadside assistance?"

"Yes, I'm here at the airport, and my window won't go up."

The person on the other end was silent and then said, "Yes, sir, which airport are you at?"

"I'm at the Greensboro, North Carolina, airport."

"Okay, we can have someone out there within forty-five minutes."

"I can't wait forty-five minutes. I have a plane that leaves in forty-five minutes."

The person was silent again. "Let me connect you to the driver on call."

I waited and then went through the same story again with the driver.

"Why don't you try pulling the window up?" he asked.

I had a pretty good idea that the conversation was going nowhere. "I've tried, and it won't budge."

"Let's see, I'm about an hour away."

I thanked him and got off the phone.

After I hung up, I got a brainstorm. I called Greta, a friend at work, and asked her to meet me at the dealership where I bought the car. In my state, the plan seemed logical. The dealership was much closer than my house. Greta would pick me up and then drive me back to the airport. All in all, I'd arrive about ten minutes before my flight was scheduled to take off. While I passed cars on the right shoulder in rush-hour traffic, wind roared through the open back window, vibrating the car like a giant bass drum.

When I got to the dealership, Greta was waiting. I dropped off my car key at the service counter (I'd called them to say I was coming), and then Greta raced me back to the airport where her aunt, who worked at the airport, had organized a production line to get me on the plane. A security guard directed me through a special security check because the regular one was backed up for ten minutes. I ran down the airport corridor, and when I got to my flight's gate, an attendant was holding the door open to the walkway. Indebted to Greta and her aunt, I boarded the plane and quietly took my seat.

Joseph Campbell said that when you look back on your life, the pieces start to fit together like chapters in a book. The chaos surrounding my first trip out to San Diego was a fair reflection of the day-to-day operations of Rich's life once he became a professional futures trader.

I arrived in San Diego at about 9:00 pm. Rich was waiting for me at the airport, and when we greeted each other, we shook hands. Rich had an exaggerated way of shaking hands—using his arm like a giant pendulum, he'd swing it back and then forward, grabbing your hand at the end of the loop. As we walked out to his car, it was a little chilly. I'd brought almost all short pants and realized I'd be wearing my one pair of jeans every night. The only other pair of long pants I had were the ones I was presently wearing, soiled by the blood from my thumb—hurt on the rear window.

Rich paid for parking at an automated machine, and we approached his brand-new BMW 3 series. After Rich cautioned me to put my suitcase directly in the trunk and "not on the bumper," we hopped in and started for his apartment. The inside of his car was gray and spotless. He rented a garage for the car at his apartment complex. As a kid, he had a penchant for destroying things—model boats, garbage disposals, desks. As an adult, he was meticulous about his cars (except for the Bronco). I sat in the passenger seat, and we yakked on the way back to his apartment.

It's so close when I remember it; I'm there in the car with Rich, lights from other cars mixing with the dim, yellow light of the dashboard. It's just Rich and me and my expectations of San Diego.

The trip out to San Diego was part research. Rich told me, "T, you can come out and live with me. I have plenty of room." I'd always wanted to live in San Diego, ever since I was a kid. I didn't have a strong basis for wanting to live there; I just equated San Diego with sunshine and contentment—an unexamined childhood belief. The timing for moving there was right because rumors were going around at work that Synchronic was on the market (actively seeking to be purchased). If we were purchased, I figured I could take a year off and write a book. If nothing else, the book could be about a start-up company that gets bought out.

As Rich and I drank a few beers back at his apartment, Zatta came in. She lived in the apartment just above Rich's. Rich was the architect of the two-apartment setup. He had to have his own space, a space where he was guaranteed solitude when he needed time alone. Still, Zatta managed to spend most of her waking and sleeping hours in Rich's apartment. From Rich's balcony, I could see rolling sand hills sprinkled with brush, a few short trees and newly built houses. Between the complex and the hills were more apartments and one- and two-story buildings. I slept on the mattress in Rich's second bedroom.

The night after I arrived in San Diego, we went to a little restaurant on the water in La Jolla. "When it's clear," Rich said, "you can see the seals off the shore." We sat on an outside deck, looking off into the foggy water, an outline of cliffs, rocks and a smattering of lights visible near the shore. We ordered drinks and dinner. When we first got to the place, I was self-conscious about what I was wearing. "It's basically a tight T-shirt and jeans," I told myself, comparing my outfit to Rich's. He was wearing a silk, short-sleeved shirt with sandals and Polo jeans. Each successive drink lowered my standards for my outfit.

After we'd been talking for a while, Rich said, "My next door neighbor goes to work every morning at 7:30, and I wave to her from my desk in pajamas. Sometimes she just gives me an evil eye." Zatta added, "Everyone in the complex knows Rich." During the day, Rich sat in front of his computer for hours at a stretch doing his trading. When he took breaks, he'd sometimes check in on the girls who worked in the rental office, seeing what they were up to, maybe gossiping about residents. Rich once applied for a job as the complex security guard because he wanted to go to an interview in a T-shirt and shorts. The girls in the rental office recognized his name on the application and squelched his ploy.

After dinner, we had another drink or two, and then Zatta drove us back from the restaurant. As she did, I kept the rear window down. I'd driven almost the same route earlier in the day when Rich had let me borrow his car. While going up the hill we were now going down, I'd nearly stalled and ground the gears in the process. Fear of grinding them again led to at least two more grindings. Rich also had a black pickup truck with gigantic tires; I drove it whenever I needed to borrow a car for the rest of the trip.

With the window down, the cool San Diego night played off my face. Rich turned on one of his CDs. Whatever the latest musical trend might be, Rich knew about it. He was always popping in some new sound—and he did it so confidently. It typically takes me a while to decide if I like new music or not. I need to develop a relationship with it. Rich could blast a new song out his window whether he'd decided he liked it or not.

Rich wanted me to understand his business. I sat down with him the next day, Friday, and watched him doing his futures trading. He traded for himself—the money he made and lost was his to make or lose. He had two flat-screen computer monitors set up on either side of the desk in his San Diego apartment. The setup was wild, with charts and graphs and flashing lights, like a sophisticated computer game. Rich was forever communicating via email with other traders, checking message boards, watching his screens, picking up on rumors, catching rallies, predicting drop-offs, observing the market and—most importantly—digesting it all and making his trades.

The futures industry began in the mid-1800s as a way for farmers to reduce the risk and impact of price fluctuations when they sold their crops. Suppose you were selling wheat. You knew how much you'd spent to produce it. You also knew how much wheat was currently selling for and recognized that the price would earn you a good return on your investment. An enterprising farmer decided to sell his future crop to a buyer at the then-current price. The buyer took ownership of the wheat for delivery at a future date. In this scenario, a real commodity was bought and sold. Notably, the buyer actually wanted the wheat. Modern futures traders rarely want the actual product; they just want to profit from the price fluctuations.

When Rich showed me his trading setup and explained how he did his trades, he sensed that I wasn't understanding it. He said, "See how the New York Stock Exchange just went up two ticks," as we both looked at one of the two computer monitors on his desk; "I just made $5,000." I didn't see the change at first. On a nineteen-inch monitor, the increase was about a quarter-inch movement of a small dot on a graph—five thousand bucks.

The futures market is a paradise for anyone who wants or, more likely, *needs* to be busy all the time. The prices change constantly; you're guaranteed excitement. The room I stayed in opened to Rich's family room, where he kept his desk. I'd wake up in the middle of the night and see lights flashing under the door; they were from Rich trading the Tokyo markets. At 6:00 am Pacific Time, he'd start trading the U.S. Exchanges. Structure is important for anyone with bipolar disorder trying to regulate his or her mood. Structure helps to prevent the mind from jumping around, erroneously triggering a negative thought or emotion in the process. The only consistency to Rich's structure was that just about anything went.

Rich's sleep schedule in San Diego was anarchic. It had been that way ever since he got out of the marines. He could go to bed one night at 9:00 pm, get up at 3:00 am, and the next night, go to bed at 2:00 am. For reasons researchers don't yet understand, people with bipolar disorder tend to have faulty internal clocks. The errors start small and then accumulate. Mitzi Waltz wrote, "It's like a snowball rolling downhill: eventually the circadian rhythms are completely off track, resulting in extreme mood swings, and bringing on depression, mania or other abnormal states of mind." Exacerbating his own inconsistent sleep cycle, Rich chugged coffee all day long. He basically believed that sleep was a luxury.

On Friday afternoon, I took a walk. With a sunny, blue sky overhead, I followed a trail that wound through new apartment construction and down to a river that ran through the city. Rich didn't live in downtown San Diego. He lived, like most San Diegans, in a suburb. A few people were jogging on the trail, but for the most part, my walk was private. One step and then another; the rhythm was good for me. When I got back after having been gone for an hour or two, the whole mood of Rich's apartment had changed. I knew better than to ask him about it—the market had moved in the wrong direction. He was silent in front of his computer screens, and the energy he gave off was palpable. I went back outside to sit by the pool to get away from it.

What made Rich tick? It's hard to say. He was driven. When Rich traded, he was like a black hole, pulling all the energy in the room toward him. He had an intensity I've not seen in anyone but Rich. If you could have harnessed that energy and directed it toward some other purpose, some other goal, you'd have someone like, I suppose, a Martin Luther King or a Genghis Khan.

On Friday night, we went out to a bar in the Gaslight District of San Diego. This was one of the things I wanted to see: What's the nightlife like? We met one of Rich's friends, Don. He was at the bar smiling when we got there. He wouldn't let us buy a single drink; they were all on him.

"Crappy day today," Rich said to me, "but that's the way it goes. I've been reading books about traders. All of them say the single biggest thing you have to overcome is your attachment to the outcome. It's got to be like a slot machine. You put in your coin, pull the lever and go. Yeah, lose a coin, and you might lose $10,000, but you have to go at it without emotion."

"Sounds kind of Buddhist to me. I've been reading about it. There are four noble truths," I said, trying to recite something I'd read in Stephen Bachelor's book *Buddhism Without Beliefs*. "Life is suffering; the cause of suffering is attachment, and the key to ending suffering is letting go—which is a kind of knowledge." Fuzzy on the fourth truth but on a roll, I continued, "The fourth truth has to do with cultivating a path that relies on the first three. The path helps you free yourself from suffering. I might not have got them all exactly right, but the key is not being attached to things like outcomes."

Rich nodded and sipped from his drink.

"The cool thing about Bachelor," I said, "is that he doesn't say, 'There's only one way to be a Buddhist.' For him, Buddhism isn't a religion. It's a way of life. He says the Buddha wasn't a deity, just a regular guy that figured out how to end his suffering. The four truths aren't religious commandments, and they're not just intellectual concepts; they're more like ways of approaching the world. If you practice them, they can make you feel better."

I liked talking to Rich about philosophy and religion. The problem for me was knowing when I'd said enough, when I'd crossed the line to just blabbing away. Rich was like me in that he'd process things without saying anything. We stopped talking for about a minute.

Then Rich said, "How's the writing going?"

"So so, I guess; tapped out a few pages this morning."

"Given any thought to moving out here?"

"Yeah, I have," I said. "Synchronic is supposedly looking for a buyer. I don't know all the details. If it happens, I might take a year off, the one I always wished I'd taken between high school and college."

"I spent that year and three more in the marines," Rich said. We both cracked up.

Don, who'd been lavishing drinks on any girl who crossed his line of vision, kept buying Rich and me drinks as well. We had two full gin and tonics sitting in front of us. We drank down the first and by the time we got to the second, there was a third. Zatta was sitting quietly by Rich. The bar had three floors. We were on the top one, which was like a luxury bar, with granite countertops, leather chairs and couches. The middle floor was a regular upscale bar, with lots of wood, leather barstools and a big mirror that ran the length of the bar. The downstairs was below street level and served as a dance club. As we finished our second gin and tonic, we started talking again.

"T," he said, "I think I could make you some real money, trading for you. I wouldn't do this for anyone else."

I'd actually sent about $10,000 to Rich to invest earlier in the summer. He made me $2,000 in a month. I answered, "I have $30,000 in savings. I'm going to need it if I want to leave Synchronic."

"Things can go up and down in this business, but I know I can do it," Rich said. "You wouldn't need to invest all of it, but the bigger the trade, the more the return."

Now I had a moment of silence. "How would it work?" I asked. And Rich told me the details.

When he was done, we drank from our herd of gin and tonics. The night started to get blurry. I went downstairs to the dance floor and scoped out the scene. I was single, and my confidence was reinforced by all the alcohol. I'd go up the stairs, sit with Rich, Zatta or Don, and then go down the stairs again. It didn't take much to amuse me. When the bar was getting ready to close, Zatta drove Rich and me home. Don was still on the top floor when we left. Rich and I bought about $30 worth of Taco Bell food on the way home, and the floor in Rich's apartment was littered with wrappers the next morning.

The last night, Rich, Zatta and I stayed in and watched a movie. I think it was the *Green Mile*. The following morning, I flew back to Greensboro.

Rich wanted to give me the freedom to write, without me having to rely on my stock options getting liquid (most stock options issued by start-up companies aren't ever worth actual money). Since moving to San Diego, Rich had made over $400,000—more than I'd made in all my years of work. A few weeks before my visit, Rich had invited me to a New England Patriots versus San Diego Chargers football game at the end of September in San Diego, so I was planning on being out again in two months.

After I got home to Greensboro, I gave Rich $30,000 to trade—basically all of my savings. I believed he could do it for me, give me the chance to escape the everyday work world for a year. When I'd sent him the $10,000 earlier in the summer, he'd just mixed it in with his other accounts. We treated the $30,000 differently, keeping it in a separate trading account. First, it made paying taxes easier. Second, I'd have more straightforward access to the money, not needing Rich to cut me a check and send it along, a process that could lead to double taxation (the checks appearing to be gifts, subject to additional taxes).

There's something very different psychologically that happens when a person starts trading someone else's money. Rich told me he was more nervous about trading $1,000 of my money when it was in a separate account than he was with any amount of his own.

When Rich was trading and things were going well, he used to tell me, "It's like picking money off a tree." As I was scrambling to get an analysis out the door on a Friday afternoon or listening to an employee complain (from work-related issues to things like other employees crunching potato chips at their desk too loud), I'd look out the window and think about Rich working from home in his pajamas. As soon as the market closed, 1:00 pm San Diego time, Rich would go to the gym. After he was done with his workout, he might head to the beach. I thought Rich had found a way to beat the system.

BASEBALLS AND BELIEFS

On the plane flight to Philadelphia, Rich spilled his drink across the table where we were seated. I jumped out of my seat after getting hit by an ice cube that was leading the spill. We were seven and nine on our way to see the grandparents. The day before, we'd both thrown up in a parking lot, from sun poisoning. The day before our vomiting, we'd gone to Hampton Beach in New Hampshire.

Both sets of grandparents lived in or near Feasterville, Pennsylvania (about 30 minutes from Philadelphia). They were all waiting for us as soon as we stepped off the plane. We were burned so badly that any touch was painful. The grandmothers loaded us with ointments the first three days of the trip. After that, we started to blister. Rich and I also got the chicken pox another time we were at the grandparents' houses. We saved skin conditions for them.

During the trip, Gramps got us tickets to a Philadelphia Phillies baseball game. At the time, they had Mike Schmidt, Greg Luzinski, Larry Bowa and Steve Carlton: They were loaded. The day we went, the weather was sunny, with only a few wispy clouds in the sky. The field was made from artificial turf; it radiated vibrant green. We were seated up high on the first-base side. Rich and I wore Phillies caps and T-shirts, purchased by Gramps, and a thick layer of sunscreen on any piece of exposed skin.

Gramps was not a wealthy guy. Granny and Gramps lived in the same three-bedroom ranch Gramps bought when he got back from World War II. He worked his whole career as a safety officer at Uniroyal Tire. He gave Rich and me calendars with safety tips on them. One had a picture of a guy with an anvil on top of his foot. The guy didn't wear his steel-toed boots, and you could tell he was in pain. Message: "Wear your safety boots." Whenever we went out to get boots after that, Rich and I asked for boots with steel toes.

After the Phillies game, Gramps gave us two baseballs. Somehow, through some connection, he'd managed to have the whole Phillies team sign them. This was before the age of autographs for fees. The whole team signed the baseballs because that's one of the things ballplayers did: They smiled for kids and signed autographs. When we got home from Philadelphia, I put my baseball in a box and stored it away. A few weeks after returning, Rich and I had a game of catch in the front yard. I looked at the baseball we were tossing—it had ink smudges on it. Since getting back, Rich had been tossing his Phillies ball with his friends.

In order to want something, we must believe that it's valuable. It's really that simple. Rich believed, at the time, that the ball's value was best expressed in terms of utility. The names drawn on it meant little to him. From his perspective, it was good news that they didn't interfere with the flight of the ball.

Each time we left after visiting Granny and Gramps, Gramps would slip us each a bill, usually a $20. Dad didn't want him to give us money but he would, keeping the bill in the palm of his hand and shaking our hands, our secret handshake. We'd then slip the bills into our pockets.

Rich understood dollars and cents. He knew you could use them to buy candy and baseball cards. You couldn't do the same thing with a signed baseball. The earliest form of money was cattle, first traded for things around 9,000 B.C. Since then, people have used shells, whales teeth, metals and lots of other knickknacks as currency. In Roman times, people would actually cut the coins when they owed you change. What did it matter? The value of the coin resided in the metal itself. The money we use today in the United States is called *fiat money*. It's backed by belief, the belief that the government that underwrote it can make good on its debts.

After I moved to North Carolina, I'd go back to Massachusetts once or twice a year to visit Mom, Dad and Rich (before Rich moved to London). During one three-year stretch, Dad's neighborhood had one house (not Dad's) that was noticeably bigger than all the others. "Can you believe that thing?" Dad would say each time we passed it. Eventually, the owners of the modest house next door to the biggest house put up a "For Sale" sign, and someone bought their home. The new owners knocked down the modest house and replaced it with the twentieth-century equivalent to a castle. The former biggest house was still big but nothing like the castle. "Look what they've built," Dad said in reference to the owners of the now second biggest house in the neighborhood—it was a garage fit for eighteen-wheelers that effectively shielded them from the image of the castle.

In Chapter Five, I said we'd be investigating some of the things our minds do: one such thing is generating beliefs. The subject of belief crosses acres of cultural, religious, scientific, academic and rational and irrational grazing lands. The subject itself is contentious. Some question whether we can actually believe anything, whether we have free will—for them, everything is hardwired, and we can't change a thing. I am going to avoid the controversy and simply assume for the sake of this section that we do have beliefs. And what we believe plays a big role in the way we lead our lives.

The world at large seems to offer support. If I believe the car behind me is a police car, I'll stop at a yellow light. If not, there's a good chance that I won't. Beliefs are usually built on other beliefs. That the car behind me is a police car matters only if I believe the person riding in the car is a police officer. That the person in the car is a police officer matters only if I believe he has the authority to write a ticket. We can keep going back. Beliefs drive behavior, but they don't have to be provable, and we don't have to be conscious of them. As in the case of the police car, the hierarchy of my belief system does not reveal itself to me piece by piece. I just see the police car and stop at the yellow light.

There are subconscious beliefs that are vestiges from earlier times in our own lives. We've continued to carry them forward without ever contemplating them. The circuitry within our brains grows accustomed to generating certain responses to given stimuli. Kids who had good experiences with the family dog are apt to like dogs as they get older. Kids who had good experiences at baseball games will like ball games as adults. And kids raised in houses that hated blacks or hated whites will have a predisposition to the same.

There are also beliefs that we've taken the time to establish. We've contemplated them. We've sat back and asked ourselves why we're doing what we're doing—why we're striving for something, why we're upset about something. Even though we might logically understand something, that doesn't mean we're going to change. Both Rich and I liked the New England Patriots. Mom would ask if they gave us bonuses for being good fans or if the players sent us apology notes when the team lost. Yes, Rich and I understood that a Patriots win brought few tangible benefits for us. But we'd be miffed on Mondays if they lost.

Our beliefs are influenced by parents, teachers, friends and strangers. They're influenced by our own predispositions and personality traits as well as the culture in which we live. Our beliefs can also be driven by our experiences. A grandfather telling his grandkids that steel-toed boots are important can make the kids believe in the value of steel-toed boots. A society telling us that big houses and more things are better can make people believe that the absence of big houses filled with things is bad.

Anything that provides input to our brain is a potential belief influencer. What we pay attention to or what catches our attention is the leading source of sensory input. What do we pay attention to? When we're driving, it might be the road in front of us or the car behind us. At work, it might be a computer screen, co-workers or a boss. Much of the time, it's what's in front of our faces or blaring in our ears—television, magazines, newspapers and radio. When we put our feet on the floor each morning, it probably won't be long until we're barraged with some form of mass media.

"Greed," Gordon Gekko famously said in the movie *Wall Street*, "is good." Even if you can see right through Gekko's philosophy, do you still find yourself living it sometimes? Have you ever kept a job because you didn't think you could earn the same money in another? Maintained a failing relationship because you didn't think you could find a better one? If we believe that our worth as humans is linked to concerns like our appearance, social status or material possessions, our beliefs open us to suffering. We can feel poorly about ourselves if outcomes don't meet the expectations we've created in our heads.

That material things are desirable is one that's hard to escape. It might very well be an "instinct" type of belief wired into us from our ancestors. Economic historian Fritz Heichelheim wrote, "Palaeolithic man placed great importance on jewellery . . . the need for distinction and beauty, in addition to artistic magic, formed strong forces in the lives of our earliest ancestors, as they do still in our own." The Paleolithic age was at least 30,000 years ago.

How is a belief formed? Let's consider a good career. We learn what a good career is from our parents, siblings and teachers, as well as our experiences, what we pay attention to and a host of other factors. At the beginning, our sense of a good career is just a collection of observations. Like a juggler, we consciously or unconsciously toss career observations in the air. They bump, and fall, and fly this way and that. Eventually, they balance. With or without our willful consent, the observations join together. We might not know how in the world the career belief came to be, but there we are, juggling it in our head.

Even though our career belief is only in our head, it drives physical actions. New observations and new inputs are evaluated in reference to our existing belief. We might conclude: "I'm only going to consider careers that earn me X amount of dollars." When that happens, we limit ourselves. What could have been a good life pursuit for us is eliminated for reasons we might not fully comprehend. Whether known to us or not, an exchange occurred between the belief and us; an exchange we completed without receipt, in which we accepted the notion that more money is better. The belief that had to coalesce out of nothing, that balanced, became real and then disappeared—operating invisibly in the background—drove a real physical action on our part, as beliefs do every day. Oftentimes, we aren't even consciously aware of our beliefs, but we heed their direction anyway.

Alain de Botton wrote in *Status Anxiety*, "Being denied status . . . may be as painful for a modern Westerner as a loss of [honor] was for a member in a seemingly more hidebound society." If we believe life should be a certain way and it's not, real stress results. The line between bipolar I and II and III is amorphous. So is the line between anxiety and depression. Enough stress driving enough anxiety can, in turn, lead to real depression. What is the anguish based upon? In a lot of cases, it's our own internal evaluation process going on in the background, in which we compare our current state to how we believe the world should be. Bad beliefs cause real mental anguish.

Do beliefs drive all of our behavior? No. What we do also depends on many other things like moods, emotions, memories, sensations and, of course, the circuitry and chemical predispositions of our brains. Sometimes we just do things, but beliefs are a big part of how we act. It's not always easy to get at our own beliefs. We're "in here" with them. We have a career or a relationship or a life that's built on top of our beliefs. We're so closely intertwined with them that we can mistake an attack on our beliefs as an attack on us. It's not easy for people *without* mental disorders to recognize their beliefs.

What about people with mental disorders? What about people who feel shameful about themselves simply by virtue of the neural networks and neurochemicals erroneously driving messaging in their heads? Are they more or less likely to be pushed this way or that by flawed beliefs? In the absence of treatment, with the wrong treatment and even with adequate treatment, figuring out what normal is (assuming there is a normal) or what a good belief is can become an almost insurmountable challenge.

❖ ❖ ❖

When I noticed that Rich and I were tossing his Phillies baseball, I said, "Rich, do you know this baseball could be worth money someday?" The news startled him. The game of catch stopped, and we went inside and tried to retrace the signatures. We couldn't get the traced ones to curve the same way as the originals. The lines were scraggily, and the process started to get frustrating.

"How much money do you think it could be worth?" Rich asked.

"I don't know," I said.

"It's just baseball," he said.

"Yeah, it is," I agreed.

So we went back outside and started tossing it again because it was the best baseball we had.

IN THE GREENBELT

I keep a sticky note in a little wooden box on my desk. Rich included the note with a partial repayment he sent for money I'd loaned him. The note reads:

> *I should have the rest paid to you in next few months. Your faith in me sustained me through some tough times.*
>
> *Thank you,*
> *R*

Before I went home from work on November 3, 2005—the day Rich sent his email that said, "i am out of here and its happening now"—I sent an email back to him. I sent it before Mom told me that he had checked into a hospital for the night.

From: Ted Courtemanche
Sent: Thursday, November 03, 2005 4:28 PM
To: Richard Courtemanche
Subject: Re: hi

Hi Rich, assuming you wrote on a blackberry - maybe you'll pick this up. First, the dogs will be okay. Mom is going to pick them up. Second, got in touch with a suicide prevention counselor - really not much help. There's no way to track you down. I'd called them months ago and got the same impression then.

What do I say? I've been building a compost pile out back. It's made me think about life and death. All this stuff goes into the compost pile - grass, leaves, twigs. If it's yard waste, it's in there. It goes in as an individual ingredient and comes out as compost. It will then be put over the lawn or garden and turned into flowers, grass and some weeds, too, and the cycle will repeat itself.

You'll be turned into compost; I'll be turned into compost, and we'll all be recycled again. Maybe not the same parts but bits and pieces here and there. That's our physical self. The spirit - I can't help but believe we're put back into the same energy source we came from to be reinserted into another physical being at some point in the future - just like the compost, with other energy sources mixed with our own and dropped on in.

The fact that we're separate or ever were separate from any other energy source is the illusion. As you go back to the source, I hope it's peaceful. How can it be any other way? I'm guessing it will feel like it feels when I meditate and feel at one with everything. Rarely happens but when it does, there's no separation between me and anything else, no thought either. Simply a hum. It feels good.

I'm having a hard time. It brings up a lot of feelings to write this. Be strong on your journey. Think of me hugging you if it helps.

Peace and love,
T

I wrote the message for multiple reasons. In writing it, I felt a sense of connection to Rich; in a situation in which I had no control, it gave me just a tiny bit. I also hadn't felt like we'd gotten any closure during the phone call he made to me at work; my email provided me a semblance of closure. Most important, though, I hoped that he'd get my email, the reality of what he was thinking of doing would hit him, and he'd stop. Shortly after I sent it, I got the word from Mom that he'd checked into a hospital, and everything seemed to be on the upswing. Still, being prone to insomnia, I was surprised that I was able to fall asleep that night.

The next morning, Friday, at about 11:00 am I got a phone call at work from Dad. He was crying; my heart sank. I wanted to throw up because I knew what was coming.

"Did you see the email? It's done. Richard's gone," he said softly, crying.

Then Dad said, "Go home to Deana, and hold her."

I don't remember too much after Dad told me. I crumpled in the corner of my office, put my hands over my head and shook and cried. I looked out my office window at the vacant dirt lot across the street. Behind it, wind gently rocked trees back and forth. I went to my desk and sat in the chair. I walked back to the door. I paced. I just wanted to crawl away, to be engulfed into the walls, the trees, the sky—into everything. I sat at my desk and opened my personal email account. I saw the note from Rich.

From: Richard Courtemanche
Sent: Friday, November 04, 2005 11:31 AM
To: Betty Courtemanche; Bob Courtemanche; T Home
Subject: dogs

hi all. i am at peace. i am gone now. its ok... its ok

my dogs are at
[address deleted]
austin, tx

my friend heidi lives in this complex. she is taking care of them. pls call her as soon as possible at
[number deleted]

the last month of my life was a quick spiral down. and i am happy to be through this. the austin police will probably have contacted u by now.

please cremate my body and spread it where ever u wish. pls remember my happy times. the smiling. the laughter.

i am at peace. sleeping in peace.

i love you all. please again take care of my dogs. i live within each of them and each of u.

love richard

Rich was in *Austin*. Of course, I thought. He'd been there all along. I called the Austin police as soon as I read the note.

"Hello, my name is Ted Courtemanche, and I have reason to believe that my brother took his life and that you may know where his body is." I was passed along to a communications person, Athena. I repeated what I had just said.

"Yes, hold on just a second," Athena told me. "What did you say your name was again?"

"Ted Courtemanche." I waited for a little while—probably thirty seconds or so. I didn't know what was going on. I was numb.

"Ted, your brother is at the park right now. We've got a negotiating team speaking with him."

"He's alive?"

"Yes, he's alive. He hasn't shot himself."

Rich was in the Barton Park greenbelt in Austin, on a small island in the middle of a creek, surrounded by a SWAT team and members of the Austin police force. Trained hostage negotiators were there as well, trying to talk him out of shooting himself. Athena said that the negotiators might try to contact me so that I could talk with Rich.

"Would you be okay with that?" she asked.

"Yes, absolutely," I said.

Both Dad and Mom were under the impression that Rich was gone. When I hung up with Athena, I frantically made calls to them. Each call went directly to voicemail, which meant that they were on the phone. I assumed they were talking to each other. I called them both, about ten times, each time getting more frustrated and panicked.

RICH IS ALIVE!! I wanted to scream.

But I couldn't get through. I left a message for Dad. "Dad, this is Theo. Rich is alive. He's talking with SWAT team negotiators. You need to stay off your phone because he may try calling you."

I left a message on Mom's home phone and kept calling her cell, each time going straight to voicemail. Dammit, get off the phone! I tried breaking in on the line but couldn't navigate my way through the process of doing it from my cell phone. Finally, on what seemed like the thirtieth call, I got through.

Mom hadn't been on the phone with Dad. She'd been on the phone with Rich—for the last two hours. Somehow my call had gotten through and cut off her call with Rich. She told me that she was in the woods near her house, listening to what was happening with Rich. He was quoting *Apocalypse Now* to the negotiators. I knew exactly the lines he was saying.

Rich was having a meltdown, right there in the greenbelt. Mom and I hung up, and my thoughts turned to hoping—hoping with all my might—that she could reestablish a connection with Rich. As it turned out, Rich's phone battery had died, and that's why his call with Mom got caught off.

A few seconds after hanging up, I got another overwhelming sense of relief. I told myself that Rich would talk himself out and be taken in by the

127

Austin police. I knew very little about the laws in Texas, but I assumed he'd be sentenced to a psychiatric facility, and the time would be good for him. Maybe he'd be in there a year or five years; I didn't know—but whatever it took for this stage to pass and for him to find his footing again would be a good thing.

I called Deana and then journaled to pass the time. Both Mom and Athena told me they'd call if anything happened. When I left work at 4:30 pm, no one had called, and I sensed that their not calling was positive—the situation was under control.

On the ride home, I called Mom; she hadn't heard anything new. I hung up with Mom and then called Athena. She wasn't available, so I waited on hold. I went to Costco on Wendover Street to get gas. Friday traffic was moving in a constant, chaotic blur in both directions on Wendover. The trees on the other side of the street were swaying behind the barbecue joint and the strip club. Once I got back in the car, I hung up after having been on hold for fifteen minutes, assuming that I must have been forgotten.

I called Athena back and was again put on hold. I was pulling into the driveway when Athena picked up her line. She thought I was Dad. "No," I said, "this is Ted, Rich's brother."

She then told me the news: *Rich had been shot in the arm and had shot himself.* My heart sank; it sank just like it had sunk each time I got new, worse information in the last day. Now it was real. He had shot himself, for Christ's sake. Athena said he was in the intensive care unit in critical but stable condition. His wounds were "survivable." I got the name and the contact information of the hospital where Rich had been taken.

"The hospital can't release any information on your brother until the commanding officer arrives there and authorizes it," Athena said.

I took a deep breath after the conversation was over and then hung up. I had no idea where Rich had shot himself. My perspective was ratcheted in another direction. At least Rich was in the hospital. I rationalized that he'd get the scare he needed. He'd done damage all right, but it was "survivable"; he'd come out of this thing a new man.

I called Dad back with the information, and then I called Mom. Mom was the one who had been on the phone with Athena. She had gotten the same message as I did. Right after she hung up with Athena, Mom had called the hospital; they didn't have a record of a "Richard Courtemanche" being there. Athena said that might happen. *Jesus Chris! What is going on?* I thought to myself. Mom told me she was flying out on a 6:00 am flight from Boston on Saturday morning and would be in Austin by 11:00 am.

All we could do was sit tight and wait. I'd forgotten to bring home my journaling, so Deana and I drove back to the office to get it. My new security badge didn't work. From the front door of the building, I motioned Deana to go around to the back door. While she drove, I walked; the fresh air was good for me. The cleaning crew inside had left the back door open. Deana and I went in, and I saved my journaling to a disk.

I called Dad from a Chinese restaurant where Deana and I ordered takeout. I sat in the car while Deana went in. The next day, Dad was going to the hospital, too, and he told me he was rededicating himself to Rich. He was going to get Rich out of all the debts he'd incurred with his trading, and Rich would have a clean start.

When I got home, I called Mom. She hadn't heard from the hospital or Athena but had spoken with Rich's friend Heidi. Heidi had details on what had happened because she'd been required to file a police report—Heidi was the first one to call the police when she learned about Rich's plans. In filing the report, she talked to one of the officers about the situation. She confirmed that the Austin police had shot Rich in the arm. Rich had shot himself; she didn't know where, but the wound was clean. He was taken to the hospital, where they'd operated. She also confirmed that he was in critical but survivable condition.

Oddly, I felt good—exhausted but good. The pieces were coming together; Rich was going to live. I had some tea and thought about Rich, peaceful thoughts, before going to bed.

FERRYING TO NOVA SCOTIA

In 1975 I started first grade. My first grade teacher was Mrs. Bishop. That was the first year I started to have to write stories. That year I also started to learn math, adding and subtracting pretty well. I got reading and spelling books that year to. That year my family and I went to Nova Scotia for vacation. We drove are car to Portland Maine and than the car got loaded onto a ferry boat witch took us to Nova Scotia. Most of the time we were at the beach because the water was very warm. When we got home it was almost time for me to start school.

Richard Courtemanche
School Writing Assignment, September 20, 1982

Rich and I heard about the Nova Scotia vacation that Mom and Dad took; they went there for a late honeymoon. Mom said, "We sat in saltwater pools. When the tide goes out, it leaves water in the sandstone near the shore. They're like natural tubs."

Natural tubs sounded pretty good to Rich and me. We hadn't given any consideration to what we'd do when we got to the saltwater tubs, but come on! Saltwater tubs you can sit in? There would be plenty to do. For the Courtemanche family vacation of 1975, we went to Nova Scotia.

We stayed overnight on a ferry that carried us from Maine to Nova Scotia. A few years later, Rich would set his sights on being a pilot, but for now, he wanted to be a ship captain. Rich kind of yelped in excitement as the ship left the docks. By the time we went to bed that night, the situation had changed for Rich. He was practically gray. There was a tiny bathroom in the tiny room we shared with Mom and Dad.

Light is shining behind the closed bathroom door. Inside the bathroom, Mom is attending to Rich. All the other lights in the cabin are off. Dad makes a special point of telling me how safe boats are—even though I assumed that they were. When he tells me they're safe, I start to wonder: "How safe?" After the Dramamine Mom gives to Rich kicks in, he crawls into the bunk beneath mine and falls asleep. Wondering about how seaworthy the ferry actually is, it takes me a little longer to fall asleep.

Rich felt better the next morning. On the walk to breakfast, we went out on the ship deck with Mom and Dad. It was sunny and windy out there. After our meal, Rich and I found the jackpot. On the inside of the ferry, there was a recreation room. It had electronic games. Throughout the room, you could sit down to a table, put a quarter in a machine and play Pong!

As a family, we loved playing games. We had a table hockey game at home. Mom didn't play, but the three Courtemanche males did. When we played, we used an egg timer to time the games, three periods of five minutes each. Table hockey is a two-person game. Whoever wasn't playing would watch and wait for the game to be over—so he could play the winner. If you weren't playing, you could make almost any comment you wanted, as long as it didn't include a swear word. Maybe, "Theodore's players look sick today," or something like that.

The rest of the trip to Nova Scotia went by in a flash once we found Pong. Dad just kept pumping quarters into the machines. If you're not familiar with Pong, it basically started the video gaming industry. It was an electronic tennis game. On each side of the video screen, there was a little electric paddle that looked like a big dash mark; you controlled it with the equivalent of a radio dial. The object was to hit the little electric ball past the other person's paddle. We played game after game after game. We got lunch at the Pong tables so we could keep playing.

Once on land, we all noticed that the landscape had changed a little bit since Mom and Dad had been to Nova Scotia. The only saltwater tubs we could find were puddles. A few looked like we could sit in them, but no one could tell how long the water had been in there—plus they had barnacles on the sides. I wasn't about to take a crazy risk like sitting on a rock with barnacles. What if they jumped off the rock and started growing on you? Rich didn't think it was possible, but he was happier jumping around in the ocean anyway.

No Courtemanche vacation would be complete without some kind of unpredicted slight. We didn't stay near the shore the whole time we were in Nova Scotia; part of the reason for the trip was to *explore* Nova Scotia. One night, we stayed in a hotel next to a river. It stunk in the hotel, a stink that could get into your clothes, making you smell it days later. The slight was this: The travel agent had booked us for one night at a hotel next to a paper mill. Rich and I kept our hands over our noses and breathed through our mouths almost the whole time we were there—which wasn't long. We went to another hotel, and Rich and I got to enjoy the memory of the stink for the next few days.

Surrounded by seafood that he would later learn to love, Rich was in the middle of his McDonald's years in Nova Scotia. Every place we went to eat, we had to make sure it had burgers. For one whole week, I'm pretty sure Rich had burgers every night.

When the Nova Scotia vacation was over, we rode another ferry back to Maine. This time, we didn't take an overnight cruise. As soon as Rich and I got on board, we ran around looking for the Pong room, but only the overnight ferry had Pong tables. Instead of playing electronic games, we had to entertain ourselves. Most of the time, we stayed out on the deck and watched the ocean.

Around Christmastime in 1975, Atari introduced a home version of Pong. Rich and I pleaded with Mom and Dad for an Atari console. We probably wouldn't need another present ever again, we both agreed. Mom and Dad tried to find one, but supply was limited—Atari only produced about 150,000 consoles that Christmas, and Sears was the only store to sell it.

Instead of an Atari console, Rich and I got a brand-new table hockey game. This one had both an electronic scoreboard *and* a sensor that would indicate when one team had scored a goal; at least that's what it said on the box. We'd run into problems before determining whether goals had been scored or not, problems that could easily lead to tantrums. It didn't take us long to figure out that the goal sensor was solely a marketing gimmick. It only worked on the obvious goals, the ones that stayed in the net. It didn't help at all on the controversial goals that bounced out. The scoreboard was a different story. It added an extra layer of authenticity to our games. We didn't have to keep score on paper anymore; the scores of all the games were boldly displayed on an electric scoreboard with bright red numbers.

Mom and Dad didn't totally ignore the Pong issue; they also gave us a jar of quarters we could use to play Pong at the local arcade. After we went a few weekends in a row, though, Rich and I lost interest in Pong. Our eyes got weary watching the little electric ball bounce back and forth. Plus, once you played about a hundred games, Pong got boring. By the time we finally purchased an electronic game console a few years later, Pong was out of fashion, replaced by games like "Space Invaders" that basically afforded the same sense of excitement as Pong once did, just in a different package.

VISITING RICH IN NEW YORK CITY

In September 2002, I took a last-minute flight on a Saturday afternoon to New York City where Rich was meeting friends over the weekend. His broker had found him tickets to the New York Jets versus Patriots game in the Meadowlands (where the Jets play) that Sunday. After flying in from San Diego, Rich had arrived in New York City on Friday night.

By the time Rich was thirty-three—and he was thirty-three when he flew to New York for the Jets game—he'd had a third operation on his back. To alleviate the chronic pain, he usually had an ample supply of pain killers, especially when he traveled on long plane flights. Sitting for hours at a stretch in those small seats made his back throb.

I put my suitcase on the bed in the hotel room where I was staying and looked out the window. About fifty feet away, directly in front of me, was the back of a hotel. As I looked to the right, I saw the back of another hotel and to the left, also the back of a hotel. The hotels were all connected at the corners, creating a rectangular cube of gray. The buildings were tall enough so that little sunlight entered the cube.

I looked down. In the courtyard, four huge fans (part of the central heating and air systems) were pointing upward, the turning blades covered by metal bars. I swallowed. It looked like the end of the world at the bottom of that rectangular cube. For a second, I felt like I might fall out the window. I started to feel dizzy and closed the shades.

Before I flew up from Greensboro to join Rich for the weekend, I reviewed available hotels on the Internet. The hotel I'd selected (with the room that looked onto the fan pit) got reasonable reviews, but they didn't mention the vision just outside my closed window shades. I sat on the hotel bed and collected myself. Just knowing that I'd be returning to this room at the end of the night could spoil the whole trip. I splashed water on my face and went to the lobby to talk with someone at the front desk. The girl there transferred me to another room. The new room had a leak in the bathroom sink faucet, but it looked out onto the street, much better than where I'd just been.

Rich was staying at the Charles Hotel. I'd considered staying at the Charles. I'd gone onto Internet travel sites and almost hit the "reserve" button for a room at the Charles more than ten times. Each time, I stopped. I couldn't go through with it—the Charles was $50 more than my present hotel; each time I reneged on hitting the "reserve" button, the value of that $50 increased. By the time I finalized my plans, the Charles might as well have been a million dollars more. The bottom line was this: I'd gotten a better rate where I was staying and was only a few blocks from the Charles.

I left my hotel and walked over to meet Rich at the Charles.

I see taxis and limos zipping by the gates of Central Park during my walk. Sunlight peeks out from behind the thick clouds overhead, and as it does, the leaves on the trees inside the park brighten. The city is manageable: That's how it feels; I'm here with Rich. I turn on the street where the Charles is supposed to be. The street is practically empty, and I start to sweat.

I hadn't considered or valued the inconvenience factor when I made my reservations. I walked by the Charles lobby a few times, not recognizing it as I passed. The door that led to the lobby looked like an entrance to a private club. I finally recognized the door as the entrance that it was and opened it. Inside, I saw plants, wood beams and posh leather chairs. Jazz music was playing from a trendy bar. Good-looking women with shopping bags were getting ready to board the same elevator as me. The hotel where I was staying had none of this, just a fan pit and a leaky faucet. For only $50 more, I could have been staying at the Charles.

Before I went up to Rich's room, I checked with the reservationists at the front desk. The only room they could get me was a studio ("tiny and overpriced," a girl at the front desk told me), and it cost about $200 more than the room I saw online. They wouldn't give me the online rates. Dammit, why hadn't I just reserved the room online? I didn't have access to a computer. I was stuck at the other hotel.

Once inside Rich's room, I saw what the girl at the front desk had been talking about. It was a closet with a bed—no chairs, no desk. You could see into the bathroom because it was encased in glass walls. Rich was watching Notre Dame football on the room TV. As kids, we watched Notre Dame and Penn State football on TV with Dad. We liked Notre Dame because of the tradition and Penn State because they weren't flashy (they wore white helmets, blue shirts, white pants and black cleats—as humble-looking as it was possible for uniforms to be).

In his room at the Charles, Rich was lying on his bed. He seemed subdued. I didn't ask him how the trading was going, and I didn't ask him how my investment of $30,000 was working out. I just plunked down on the side of the bed and watched the game. Rich's mood seemed low, but seeing him in the hotel surroundings made me view him from a different perspective. I looked through his mood, and what I saw was my younger brother, cooler and richer than me, hanging out in a trendy New York hotel. When it started closing in on 5:00 pm, I went back to my hotel to get ready for the evening.

Rich's friend, Quinn, Quinn's wife and a few other of Rich's friends from MIT, now living in New York City, were meeting us out for dinner. These same friends said that the girl Rich had dated from Scores, in the weeks after his internship with Greene Foster, was the ideal match for him. No one drank much at dinner. I was expecting a wild group. Just the opposite, they were mostly new or expectant parents who had maybe a glass of wine each. They talked about what everyone was doing—the consulting, the investments—all like it was out of a Woody Allen movie.

When dinner was over, I asked if anyone wanted to get a few drinks back at the Charles. Quinn and his wife said they would like to, as did April, a girl who had quit her first two jobs and was now working on her third.

When we got back to the Charles, I bought the first round. The bartender said, "That will be $52," as he presented me with four Miller Lights and one cosmopolitan. I disliked him not only because he was gouging me mercilessly for the drinks but also because he didn't seem to care. He was more interested in flirting with girls than with giving me the attention I deserved for dropping an outrageous $52 on five lousy drinks.

"Come again?" I asked.

"Excuse me, sir," he said.

"How much are the drinks?"

"Fifty-two dollars."

Normally, I'm a 20 percent tipper. I dropped $52 on the bar. When I did, the bartender was engaged in conversation with two girls sitting a few seats down. I started to dislike the Charles. Rich, his friends and I sat down on stone benches in the bar's outside courtyard. My options were to seethe and drink my beer very slowly, sucking out every penny of the $9 it cost me, or to chug it quickly and quell the building resentment.

I drank my beer quickly and then bought another. I sucked it down, too. Then someone else bought a round, and I started to feel good again. Rich was so relaxed. He was sitting in this trendy bar in a T-shirt and looked like he fit in. I was dressed in a new multicolored shirt and felt completely out of place. Still, I was happy I wasn't wearing a button-down dress shirt like Quinn. Rich once told me how some of his friends had tried to get into New York City clubs in their work clothes, carrying laptops; the bouncers wouldn't let them in, making them wait in line until they gave up and left. Quinn was dressed the way I pictured those guys were, as they waited outside the clubs.

The night before, I'd made arrangements to meet one of my friends from UNC who now lived in New York City. As we sat on the stone benches, Rich told me that he didn't want to go out; he was going to head back to his room instead. The whole reason I'd gone up to New York was to hang around with Rich: I thought we'd have a big night. My enthusiasm was zapped, but Quinn, his wife and April all wanted to meet up with my friend from UNC, so we went. He took us to an office building that turned into a club at night. None of us had a problem getting in, not even Quinn. The music was so loud, we couldn't hear a thing anyone was saying. I tried talking to a girl, and it went disastrously. I retreated to a vacant chair, where I sat for the rest of the night and people watched. Around 2:00 am, we decided to leave.

Just before he went to his room, Rich had told me that he had an extra ticket for the Patriots game and that it would be available on Sunday if I wanted it. One of the guys had decided not to go. It was pouring rain when I got back to my hotel, and the chance of rain on Sunday was 100 percent. I didn't want to watch the game in a downpour and didn't want to spend any more money in New York City, especially not sitting alone in a sports bar watching the game. Instead, I got four hours of sleep and took an early flight home to Greensboro—I left a voice mail for Rich on his cell phone telling him what I'd done.

Later in the afternoon after I got home, Rich called to tell me he and his friends hadn't gone to the game after all because it had been raining too hard. They watched the game at a bar and drank. I kicked myself; I could have mustered a second wind if I'd known that's what they were going to do—it would have been money well spent. The Patriots ended up pounding the Jets. Rich had been down the night before, and today he seemed up. I was now the one who was down. After Rich and I hung up, I switched my focus to San Diego. I was looking forward to seeing him out there again in about two weeks.

WATCHES

Rich gave me an Omega watch during my first trip to San Diego; it's the same kind that Pierce Brosnan wore in all four of his James Bond movies. Rich had bought a Rolex and didn't wear the Omega anymore. Rich could forget my birthday, not send anything for Christmas, and then give me a $3,000 watch out of the blue.

Watches keep track of seconds, hours, minutes and, in some cases, days. Watches make it seem like time is real. Like a belief, though, we can't hold a second in our hands. In *The Psychology of Time*, Mary Sturt wrote, "Time is . . . a purely subjective condition of human perception, and in itself, or apart from the subject, it is nothing at all." Even though time might be a subjective condition of our mind, as Sturt suggests, we can't go back in time. If we could, death wouldn't be a problem. We could just reroll the tape and go back to when whomever we were missing was still here on Earth.

What is time? If we look at it closely, the kind of time that watches keep is relative to the movement of the Earth. A year is simply one rotation of the Earth around the Sun. A day is one rotation of the Earth on its axis. For purposes of discussion, I'll refer to the time that watches keep as "Time-Earth."

Time-Earth is what we use to plan meetings, doctor appointments and vacations. Time-Earth relies on the continued, constant motion of the Earth relative to the Sun. If the Earth suddenly sped up its movement around the Sun, we could choose to maintain the time that was based on the old velocity or create a new time in which years and days and so on would need to be redefined. Dependability is Time-Earth's hallmark. It marches inexorably forward, oblivious to death, war, peace and birth—it's a steady drumbeat heralding our own inevitable end.

Is Time-Earth absolute? It does have some quirks. It can vary based on the speed we're traveling. There's a famous physics thought experiment that involves putting one of two twin brothers on a spaceship traveling at close to the speed of light. One twin goes off for what seems like fifty years to his twin brother here on Earth. When the space-traveling twin returns to Earth, he's aged only two and a half years. If he was detailed enough and kept a calendar on the spaceship recording days via the hands on his watch, that calendar, too, would indicate only two and a half years had passed. In fact, if the Earthbound brother had been beamed onto the spaceship during the trip, his watch would begin to track time the same as his brother's.

The time it takes for a watch to move from one second to another, the time it takes for a cell to be born or die and the time it takes humans to age are all variables impacted by our frame of reference. Our bodies would age slower relative to an Earthbound relative if we were dropped into a spaceship flying at warp speed. To us, however, the slowed aging wouldn't be noticeable. A second would appear to take a second as it always does.

Time-Earth's quirks aren't theoretical only. Muons provide an example. They're tiny particles created by cosmic rays colliding with the Earth's atmosphere. Muons need to travel 150 miles once created to reach the Earth's surface. The problem is that they decay in two-millionths of a second—too little time for them to make it to Earth. Fortunately for muons, they travel at close to the speed of light. Thanks to the quirkiness of Time-Earth, muons make it to Earth's surface in regular abundance. If it weren't for the fact that their internal clocks slow relative to an Earth observer's clock, they'd never make it, decaying long before they got here.

It may not seem like it when we set our watches, but Time-Earth isn't the only kind of time. Consider time as it relates to recorded events—that is, memories. I'm going to refer to this time as "Time-Memory." Time-Memory is a lot more flexible than Time-Earth. We don't need to wait a year to pull up a memory that happened a year ago—it happens instantaneously. The memory of all past events, if we had the brain capacity to store *and* retrieve them all, would be available to us right now.

At its core, Time-Earth is a means of verifying movement. Imagine a card game. You're dealt a hand. You discard a few cards, draw a few more and then play what you have. Time-Earth forces an acknowledgment that the hand happened. You can't go back and play that hand over again, wiping out the old memory. You can play a new hand, creating a new memory, but not *that* hand.

Thanks to Time-Memory, we can revisit an old hand any time we like. If the hand brought us happiness, we can access that happiness thanks to Time-Memory. If it brought us pain, again, we can access the pain via Time-Memory. If we want to learn to deal better with future pain created by future cards, we can revisit old hands and figure out how to more appropriately cope with the same *kind* of hand or the same *kind* of situation in the future. Time-Earth just makes us live with our decisions. We can revisit, relive, re-respond, "re" just about anything, but we cannot *replay* the same hand.

Death isn't an issue for Time-Memory. Deceased loved ones are still living in our memories. When Time-Earth gets involved, that's when the problems start. Thinking that Time-Earth is unchanging, that it marches in only one direction, can cause us pain—especially in regard to death. Do we need to feel the pain? That is, how absolute is Time-Earth? We know it has quirks; it varies based on our frame of reference. Is part of the reason we view it as going forward, and only forward, simply because that's how we've been conditioned to see it? Is it possible that Time-Earth is like materialism—we've believed in and accepted the value of a $20 bill for so long that there's no other way, just like with seconds and hours and years?

Plato held that we can never know what reality *actually* is; we can only know what we perceive through our mind. To illustrate his point, he developed the Allegory of the Cave. According to Plato, we are like people in a cave, with only a small opening to the outside. What we see and hear and feel and taste, he reasoned, are simply shadows on a cave wall, created by things we can never access. We can only surmise what the rest of the world looks like, based on those shadows. We know there are problems in assuming that other people feel things the same way we do—people have different tastes, different ways of seeing the same scene. Plato's cave allegory goes beyond acknowledging that we can't know for sure how other people think or feel. Plato's cave allegory is meant to underscore that *everything* we observe is simply a personal representation of some underlying form. We can't say anything with certainty about the real world because all we're observing are shadows.

Consider Jung's view on the interpretation of dreams. From a Jungian perspective, dreams crop up from our unconscious and are represented to us by the closest approximations our conscious mind can generate. Dream images, in this way, are simply metaphors concocted by a conscious mind—itself hopelessly attempting to make sense of an unconscious emanation. We think that the image is real, but it's only an approximation of a different underlying actuality. It starts to sound like Plato's cave allegory.

Reflecting on this, we might ask, "Is Time-Earth simply one more shadow?" Is the time we use to schedule our lives simply a personal—or group— representation of an effect that we don't entirely understand? We know that when we explore our own bodies more closely, we find that they're made of scraps and include colossal amounts of foreign bacteria—that what we call "us" is not *just* us. Our minds, too, which seem self-contained, actually rely on external objects as part of the cognition process. As we peel back the layers of time within this book, is it possible that we'll find Time-Earth holds some secrets as well? That those seconds, minutes and hours we use to organize our lives are not quite as enduring as they first appear? For now, we know for sure that the watch that helps us arrive on schedule imposes no limitations when we remember the past.

The Second Trip to San Diego

I was lying down on a bed with two girls in a hotel room at about 4:00 am, Pacific Time. They'd been asleep for over an hour. There'd been no hanky-panky. I was fully clothed, as were they. Rich was outside on the balcony talking with a third girl. The girl Rich was talking to lived in San Diego, and the two girls sleeping in the bed with me had flown in from out of town for a conference. I'd arrived in San Diego about seven hours before, on my second trip to the West Coast to visit Rich in 2002.

If you'd told me at about 12:00 am that this was how the night was going to end, I'd have given you odds of less than 50 percent. The blonde was sending out all the buying signals they write about in men's magazines.

When Rich had first picked me up at the San Diego airport on Friday night, he rushed me back to his apartment so that I could change before we went out. I didn't see Zatta; Rich said that she wasn't going to be joining us. Disheveled from the six-hour flight from Greensboro to Charlotte to San Diego, I went into the spare bathroom.

"Rich, give me a few minutes to get ready," I said. Fiddling with my hair as it flopped unacceptably to one side, I noticed that I was white. I hadn't spent time in the sun in weeks. The whiteness made my now 1:30 am shadow (it was 10:30 pm Pacific Time) stand out unacceptably.

"T, what are you doing in there? I told Don we'd meet him at 10:00."

"Just a few more minutes," I said. I managed to nick myself while shaving. I came out of the bathroom with a small piece of tissue on my right cheek. The taxi was waiting outside.

At the bar, the same one we went to the last time in the Gaslight District, Don saw us coming. He was buying drinks for a girl whose outfit could not have been a single stitch tighter. Don waved, and Rich and I sat in basically the same seats as the time before. Rich had an urgency to him. He drank the first gin and tonic before I'd even settled into my seat.

"Rich and Ted, this is Sabrina," Don said.

"Hi," we both answered.

Rich said something and she laughed. I excused myself to go to the bathroom to make sure I wasn't bleeding from my cheek. When I got back, a girlfriend of Sabrina's had arrived, and she was talking to Rich. Two more gin and tonics were waiting for me.

When I was in college as an undergrad, I pledged a fraternity. As part of the process, the pledges would stand behind a bar at the fraternity house while the brothers asked us questions. With each incorrect answer, we'd have to take gulps from our beers. Within ten minutes or so, I'd have four or five beers in my stomach. The way the beers hit me was otherworldly. All of a sudden, like some kind of an alcohol drip, the intoxication would seep into my system. The walls of the fraternity, which a second before had been sharp and focused, suddenly became flowing. I'd melt into the scene. I'd realize that I was probably only feeling the effects of three beers, and more were waiting to be dripped in.

I finished the first three gin and tonics that Don bought and started slipping into the fraternity haze. It no longer mattered what I was wearing or if a trickle of blood was coming down my face (which the check in the bathroom indicated was not happening). I tried to buy a round of drinks, and Don refused to allow it.

Rich and I left Don, Sabrina and her friend, and went downstairs to the middle floor. Three girls were sitting at the bar, and we edged in between them to get a drink. Rich said something, and the girls laughed. We introduced ourselves, and one of the girls, Kayla (the blonde), and I hit it off. I bought a round of drinks for the group. Kayla was from Dallas. She had a boyfriend and another guy she saw on the side. As far as I was concerned, her dating habits were good news. "You need to make up your mind," one of the other girls said. Kayla laughed.

Rich started talking with one of the other girls, Stacey. Each time the group ordered drinks, the sexual references became more explicit. After one round, Kayla said she hoped I was ready—more good news. As the alcohol started to reach its maximum impact on me, I lost track of Kayla. After a while, Rich, Stacey and I were the only three of the original fivesome still sitting at the bar.

Kayla had gone outside with her other friend—who later reported back to us that Kayla had gotten sick.

At the end of the night, Rich offered to get the girls a ride home. When a cab pulled up, we all climbed in. We drove for what seemed like an hour through San Diego, looking for their hotel. I had a hard time focusing when we finally got there and went up the elevator to their room. Once in the room, Kayla was led into the bathroom by her friend, and Rich and Stacey went out onto the deck. When the bathroom door opened, Kayla and her friend went directly to bed—their intention being purely sleep.

After using the bathroom myself, I went outside and sat on a small chair in a corner of the deck. On the other side, about ten feet away, Rich and Stacey were talking. There was nothing sexual in their conversation. Rich was pouring out his problems, and she was listening to every one, a form of intimacy for Rich. By sharing his emotional pain, it was as if he was creating a bond, pulling some of Stacey's energy into him, draining her in a way.

I stared at the San Diego harbor to keep myself occupied. Lights were shimmering off the rippling waves. When I could barely keep my eyes open any longer, I went inside and lay down on the very outer portion of the bed where the two girls were sleeping. They didn't move. As I was settling into my spot on the bed, I heard the balcony door open; Rich was telling Stacey that I'd been up for over twenty-four hours. Mercifully, the night ended a few minutes later. Once we managed to hail a cab, Rich and I finally got back to his apartment at about 5:00 am. The first rays of sunlight were peeking over the horizon as I lay down on the mattress in the spare bedroom and drifted off to sleep.

I spent most of Saturday recovering, but by Sunday, Rich, Zatta and I were ready for the Patriots game. Don's cousin, Ben, came to the game with us. He ran a small painting business. Rich had helped him finance the startup of his company, buying ladders, drop cloths and other base painting products. Ben had addiction problems; I think it was prescription pain killers. Don talked with Rich about it, about how Ben would hit up the family for money. Before Ben came over, Rich said, "Five hundred bucks is all I gave him. I figure if I get it back, great. If I don't, well, lesson learned."

When the four of us boarded the public train to go to the game, the weather was warm and sunny, textbook San Diego. On the ride into Qualcomm (where the Chargers play), I was fully expecting a Patriots win. Once inside the stadium, we sat on the fifty yard line, about 100 rows back—some of the best seats I've ever had. As we enjoyed the sights and sounds, the Patriots remained flat almost the whole game. Walking out of Qualcomm after the Pats lost, we were surrounded by happy Chargers fans.

We rode the train back. Outside the windows, trees were changing colors, mainly muted browns and yellows. We got off at an early stop by accident and walked about a mile back to Rich's place, mostly complaining about the game. That night, we ordered takeout and watched TV. Early Monday morning at about 3:00 am, the light was on in the family room. I heard clicking; Rich was typing his trades on the computer. I rolled over, put my pillow over my head and went back to sleep.

I noticed a yellow sticky note on Rich's computer the next morning. On it, he wrote two words: "One million." During my second visit to San Diego, Rich was in the process of trying to increase the size of his standard trades. I didn't know what his standard trade was, but he could get movements of $25,000 in a day easily. By increasing the size of his average trade, Rich was hoping to earn a million dollars in the next year. Rich explained to me, "You've got to approach it the same way. It's just a trade. But it's hard to do."

I'd been thinking in the weeks leading up to my visit that maybe I could try my hand in trading, too. I worked with numbers for a career; it only made sense that I'd be good at trading like Rich.

My friend Dylan and I used to visit his sister at Dewey Beach in Delaware, when we were in our early twenties. Dewey Beach was a big melting pot; that was part of the fun in going there. There were old people, young people, career people and people who just wanted to lie in the sun. Once during the ride from Natick (where both Dylan and I lived at the time) to Delaware, we stopped at Atlantic City, arriving there at about 10:30 pm. Planning to complete the rest of the drive the next day, we drove around looking for a reasonably priced hotel to spend the night. We found one between two larger hotels. The room looked like something you might find in a reform school, or a prison, and had two single beds. I didn't feel safe sleeping on the sheets, but we were both happy with the $50-per-night price tag.

After checking in, Dylan and I went to the blackjack tables at one of the big hotels next door. On the drive down, I'd read part of a book about winning in blackjack. According to the book, first you have to find a good table, and then you need to have a system. The system the book described went something like this: once you start winning, bet bigger, because you go on streaks when you play blackjack.

It took me almost an hour to find a table. Not that tables weren't available, but I felt like I had to study them. What was the dealer like? What were the other players like? Were there any intangibles that made me feel good or bad? That's what the book advised. By the time I sat down at a table, it was about midnight. Dylan had lost all he wanted to lose, so he went to bed. About ten minutes after sitting down, I went on a streak. I started betting bigger and bigger. Having started with a $10 bet, I shortly had $500 of the house's money in front of me: That was almost a week's pay.

I see green felt from the table. A cloud of smoke layers the ceiling, and the scene gets darker at the edges of my vision. I place a $200 bet before me: I feel important doing it. The dealer starts dealing. She gives me a five and then a six. My eyes focus. A five and a six! I double down like the book told me I should do. The guy responsible for the blackjack tables, the pit boss, comes over to observe. I have the whole casino's attention—that's the way it feels. If the cards work out the way they're supposed to, I'll have $900 sitting in front of me. The dealer starts asking around the table if anyone wants more cards.

140

Before this hand, I'd been carefree, playing with a kind of arrogance; it didn't matter if I lost a bet because I was using the house's money. With a $400 bet on the table, though, I want to win. And more, I don't want to lose what I've won. That money means something to me; I've become attached to it.

The guy next to me is dealt a queen. Crap! The queen could have been my card. It's my turn. I sweep an index finger toward my cards indicating I want another. "Oh, come on," I silently plead, "Give me a ten, give me a ten." The dealer flips my card . . . it's a three. I feel the room sigh. The pit boss walks away. I have a fourteen and can't take another card because I've already doubled down. All I can do is hope that the dealer will bust. She has a seven showing. She flips her down card. It's a ten—the house rules dictate that she has to stick on seventeen. I lose $400. Within a few minutes, I'm down to zero. I tip the last chip and go to bed.

The next morning, after a buffet breakfast at one of the big hotels, I play blackjack again. This time, I stop as soon as I lose one hand and end up winning $120. A few of the nights in Dewey Beach end up being courtesy of Donald Trump.

The Tuesday after the Patriots game, I told Rich about one of my theories for making a fortune in futures trading. It utilized some of the same phenomenon I saw in Atlantic City years before, on the trip with Dylan, as well as statistical techniques I used on my job and investment strategies I'd read about. The theory hinged on the idea that at least one futures contract in a group of ten would realize large gains in any given day. By carefully watching all ten contracts (and using trading tools like stop-loss limits), we'd close out any that appeared to be going on negative runs, with the one or ones that didn't more than covering any losses. My assumption was that futures contracts behaved relatively consistently, not bouncing up wildly one minute and down the next.

When I first started explaining my plan, I had visions of Rich being impressed by the genius of it. Instead, Rich told me my plan would never work. The reason futures contracts are so difficult to trade, he said, was precisely because of their unpredictability. They can, and do, vary wildly from minute to minute, sometimes after hours of stagnancy. Rich tried to explain the best ways to mitigate risk in futures trading, but the explanation reminded me of when he and Warren used to talk about trading derivatives when we lived at Mom's house. I listened for a few minutes before I went outside to sit at the complex pool, where I read *Thus Spoke Zarathustra* by Nietzsche.

Rich believed there was a logic to futures trading, a logic that couldn't be explained in so many words but which existed nevertheless. Still, he could be a superstitious person when it came to his trades. He rarely talked about how he was doing, fearing he might jinx himself. Rich also had a rally ruler. He'd wave it at his computer screens when one of his trades started to move in the right direction. If the market moved the wrong way, Rich would break the ruler, sometimes along with the kitchen table behind his desk. He had a list of songs he played for the market conditions he wanted. Need the market to go down? Easy, pop in Bruce Springsteen's "Goin' Down." If he was sitting on a trade, meaning he was just waiting to see how the market was going to move (which could take hours), he had a library of *Saturday Night Live* skits and *Seinfeld* and *Simpsons* episodes saved on his computer.

Outside the Patriots, the biggest event from the second trip to San Diego was Rich getting his first dog. Daisy was an eight-week-old boxer puppy living in Tucson. While Rich drove to get Daisy from the breeder in Tucson, I went to see my friend Dylan who was now living with his wife in Phoenix. I rented a car and drove on I-8, which connects San Diego County and southern Arizona. The drive to Phoenix went by fast; the scenery was so different from what I was used to in North Carolina. Time-Earth has almost no meaning when you're interested in something; it holds none when you're enraptured. I stopped at an adobe rest area off I-8 and looked over the desert. Though the sun was pouring down, and the thermometer read 95 degrees Fahrenheit, the temperature felt comfortable. Not realizing I was doing it, I meditated looking over the prairie and brush and hills in front of me.

When I got to Phoenix, Dylan and I drank a beer or two and caught up. "How's Rich doing these days?" he asked.

I never really knew how to answer that question. "He's doing good. He trades for himself full time—futures trading."

"So what is that—like day trading?"

"Kind of, but it's a little more sophisticated," I answered, not exactly clear on what the difference was or if one existed. I tried to explain what Rich did as best I could. I never added that some days he would put his hand through walls, that we'd periodically get emails saying that he couldn't go on anymore, or that when you were at his apartment, he could stifle you with his intensity. "From what I can tell, he's doing okay," I said. I didn't mention his new BMW nor did Dylan ask about Rich's finances. We didn't pry that way.

Dylan; his wife, Sue; and I drank a bottle of wine I bought for them with dinner. After dinner, we started getting into what my plans were. I said that if Synchronic got sold, I might take some time off and write a book.

"What kind of book?" Dylan asked.

"About working in a start-up company in Greensboro, North Carolina," I said.

We laughed. Dylan gave me some unsolicited advice on how to develop characters after the second bottle of wine.

The next day, I drove back to San Diego on I-8. I passed through a dust storm just outside Gila Bend, Arizona. A man was walking outside; I had no idea how he could walk through the storm; bits of earth were whipping against him. I could feel the bits as they sprayed against the car, but the man kept going.

On I-8, there is so much territory. I'd see miles and miles of windmills, then nothing but prairie, then a small town, then more windmills, and then prairie but this time a little different—perhaps with redder sand or more tumbleweeds than the one before. When it's nothing but prairie, the landscape is raw. The winds blow incessantly. When I passed a truck traveling in the same direction as me, the car would jump. Sheltered by the truck's trailer, the rental car was safe from the wind. Once beyond, the car literally jumped a tiny bit. I'd have to grip the steering wheel when the wind belted the car again. I started to look forward to the sensation after it happened four or five times. But the first time I passed a truck, I got a full infusion of panic.

Rich got back to his apartment about the same time as I did. He drove ten hours to Tucson, picked up Daisy, and then turned around and drove straight back. Daisy was a complete monster. She barked and whined whenever Rich left the room.

Shortly after I got back, I went out onto Rich's deck as Daisy yelped inside. It had been a few days since I'd talked to anyone at Synchronic, and I called a guy from work about the takeover rumors that had been building over the past week or two. This guy usually had the inside scoop on anything happening at the office. The rumors weren't true, he said. Synchronic wasn't on the block anymore. As fast as the takeover rumors started, they ended. Now I needed Rich's trading to come through if I wanted to take a year off anytime soon.

The whole time I was in San Diego, Rich and I didn't discuss the money I'd invested. Rich didn't like to give regular updates on how things were going. I never knew if he was up $10,000 or down $10,000 with my account. Because the account I set up was in my name, I had the option to receive regular updates on how Rich was doing, but I never checked them. I suppose I was respecting Rich's preference.

As with the first trip out to San Diego, the second one just wasn't satisfying in terms of my time spent with Rich. He wasn't there mentally. I could feel the misery because he was losing money. It didn't bode well for my plans, but worse, it turned Rich into a black hole of bad feelings. I couldn't stay in the apartment for long stretches. There was no way I could write in the same apartment as Rich—I couldn't block him out even though he didn't say a word.

I was tempted to say that the best part of my second trip to San Diego was the drive on I-8, but that's not entirely true. Rich's complex had a Ping-Pong table right beside the pool. Rich and I played a few times in the early evening. We'd be surrounded by the red-orange glow of the setting sun—just him and me, bantering away. The matches were even, and the difference between winning and losing might be one effectively timed trash comment or a dinky spin serve. It gave me the same feeling I had when we played "H-O-R-S-E" in Mom's driveway in Natick.

The day after I was back in Greensboro, I got the following email from Rich.

From: Richard Courtemanche
Sent: Monday, October 07, 2002
To: Ted Courtemanche
Subject:

hey T. fucking horrible day again today. i will cut u a check for difference. i am gonna trade my way out of your account. you get your 30k, dont worry. thurs we had 35k in your account, today 20k. se la vie. let me trade it for a week or so. i owe you whatever the difference is. dont write back pls, i am pretty fuckin ripped about how things have been going.

This is what I'd been dreading. I wanted to close the account right away. What Rich was doing—trying to make up $10,000 in the course of a week—just wasn't sensible. The pressure of trying to do that is brutal. Against my better judgment, I agreed to Rich's plan. I wanted to check my account every day that week but I didn't. On Friday, I got the following email from Rich.

From: Richard Courtemanche
Sent: Friday, October 11, 2002 2:06 PM
To: Ted Courtemanche
Subject:

hey T... i am going to stop trading your account today. dont worry, its not down big. we got back to 30k, currently around 28k. whatever the diff is, i will send u a check. i have had a lot of problems lately, and i realized the pressure of trading yours as well as mine is something i just cant deal with. i am happy at least that i brought yours back from 20 to 28... or where ever we end today. i have been crushed personally, down 150k. i am really sorry. part of me feels like a failure again, and frankly all that has gotten me through this week is pain pills, for the mind, not the body. i struggle T. more then i let on to anyone. i am so sorry bro. r

I replied with the following.

From: Ted Courtemanche
Sent: Friday, October 11, 2002 2:51 PM
To: Richard Courtemanche
Subject: Re:

Rich, please don't worry about the 2K. In a way, it was a relief to get your email [on Monday]. I realized when I was out there the pressure you're under. You'll be back again. As I was flying home, it occurred to me that trading the 30K has interfered with you and me; it seems to be there in the background all the time. Let's wait about five more years and give it a go again. In the meantime, let's enjoy each other's company and start sending funny emails again. Peace, T

When he officially stopped trading my account, the balance stood at $30,354. Rich had made the whole thing up; he'd covered every loss and even eked out a little profit. As to the money he lost for himself, I felt a certain responsibility for it. His fortunes seemed to change right when he started trading my $30,000. I'd had reservations about him trading for me on a big scale (and the $30K was big to me), but I didn't listen to myself. Besides, I could never tell if the cautious voices in my head were just reverberations from my own anxieties or not. Now that Rich didn't have to worry about earning me money anymore, I hoped that he'd get back on track with his trading. Based on the material possessions that soon began to pile up in Rich's life, it sure looked like he did.

✽ CHAPTER SEVEN ✽

Along the sea-sands damp and brown
The traveller hastens toward the town
And the tide rises, the tide falls.
—Henry Wadsworth Longfellow

ICE STORMS

On a day in late March 2003, I was sitting three feet from my fireplace in a beach chair. The power was out in Greensboro. Outside, the trees were contorting under the weight of mounting ice. For the past thirty or so hours, a steady mist had floated down from the sky. The ice kept building up, ever so slowly. I watched it from the window. The mist seemed so innocuous—how could something so light be a problem? A little over a day's worth of mist combined with a temperature of almost exactly 32 degrees Fahrenheit, and tree branches started to snap.

From inside my townhouse, the buildup of ice was imperceptible. The only sign a branch had reached its limit was when it broke and crashed to the ground. Outside, the buildup was more noticeable. You could hear branches starting to creak. Maybe they'd lower a little, and ice would go flying off. Maybe they'd crack and then stabilize, and then bend or crack some more. What seemed like a spontaneous event from inside was more measured from the outside.

Sitting in front of the fireplace, I watched the flames flicker and pop. My townhouse was at a dividing line. If I went to the front door, everything outside was pitch black; the only light came from an occasional car on the street. Out the back window, I could see houses with full electricity a short walk away. I set up my chair in front of the fireplace so that the houses with electricity weren't visible.

Over the course of the three days the power was out, my thoughts narrowed to one: electricity—about how much I wanted the electricity back on. I'd think of how nice it would be to have heat and hot water and a working stove. All the hotels in town were full; not that I would have spent money on one, but it felt a little suffocating knowing they weren't available. Work had electricity, so I spent a lot of time there. I would have slept at work, but the thought of employees possibly seeing me sleeping on the floor was a hurdle I couldn't get over.

The Saturday the power came back on, I was just about to pack up and leave. I was thinking about going to a hotel on the coast, where I'd take a nice hot shower and then walk on the beach. As I sat in my heated car in front of the townhouse, I started to mentally go through the things I'd need to do to make the trip a reality. Right as I had my plan in order, the lights popped on in the house. I happily trotted to the front door, unlocked the deadbolt and sat on the sofa as heat filled my home. Once the power was back, I sent out an all-family email, letting everyone know I was okay.

Rich was still trading in San Diego. It seemed like he was a world away. We hadn't been talking on the phone much lately. We'd shoot each other occasional emails, but in terms of being woven into the fabric of each other's lives, we weren't close. I never knew exactly how things were going for him. On one side were emails like the one he sent a month before the ice storm.

From: Richard Courtemanche
Sent: Wednesday, February 19, 2003
To: Ted Courtemanche; Mom; Dad
Subject:

hi all. just wanted to apologize for my lack of communication recently. the fact is, i am in worst trading period of my life... and i am really struggling. i tell you this not to elicit sympathy, just to let you know. the fact is, given what i do, when it goes wrong there is not a soul on the planet that can help me. i hope all of you are well, and i will let you know when i am better. thanks for the understanding. love, r

On the other side was his growing stockpile of material possessions. About a week before the ice storm, he told me about his brand-new BMW M5. The car probably cost around $75,000. As I huddled in front of my fireplace during the ice storm, it's a good bet I had visions of Rich accelerating along the California coast. At the time, the M5 was the fastest four-door sedan in the world. It went from zero to sixty miles per hour in about four seconds. Rich bought all kinds of special cleaning utilities for it. He had soaps, wheel brushes, a pressure washer and a blow dryer—he said using regular towels might scratch the finish, which was bright fire-engine red. He had the "M5" tag removed so that there would be some mystery about the car; other drivers wouldn't know what they were dealing with when they saw him on the road.

My own perspective on Rich's trading tended to vacillate with his financial fortunes. If the news was good, as in the case of the M5, futures trading seemed like a career avenue worth exploring. I'd read more about it on the Internet or at the bookstore. If bad, it made me feel better about having a stable job.

Rich had moved out of his apartment in San Diego at the end of 2002 and was now living in a rented house in Del Mar (an expensive San Diego suburb on the coast). Zatta was officially living with him. While she went to school, Rich did his trading from home. When he told me he'd moved to Del Mar, I imagined him living in a little bungalow. Then I saw the pictures: His house was in a gated community, and it had a pool and a hot tub in the back. The house was about half a mile from the beach. He parked his M5 in the garage and the black pickup truck with the big tires in the driveway.

Rich's family had grown by one since I visited him. He purchased another boxer named Zack, who was about ninety pounds. Zack was bought primarily to be a companion for Daisy. She liked to chew on him and get him in trouble.

Rich would send pictures of the two dogs on walks, sitting on the couch or sleeping in the backyard. Here's a partial list of the things I know for sure the two of them destroyed:

- Rich's backyard in Del Mar—it required resodding on multiple occasions.
- Pillows—both down and polyester; they preferred down.
- Clothing Mom left in her suitcase when she visited Rich.
- Bedspreads.
- Assorted furniture—usually from chewing it, occasionally from pulling it apart in a game of tug-of-war.
- A window in Richard's truck—the result of an uncontrollable desire to climb into the bed area.

Both dogs were under a year old and semi potty-trained when Rich moved to Del Mar. He used a heavy-duty mop to clean up their mistakes. They loved the mop. They'd bite at it as he teased them with it. He'd run it across the floor just out of their reach. If one of them caught it, he lifted them into the air as they held on with their mouths. After Rich's trading day was done, Zatta said the mop playing could go on for hours. When it was over, Rich, Daisy and Zack would all lie on the floor and pant.

Courtemanches tend to like investigating other places to live. Rich was no different. The problem with California for Rich was state taxes. He and Zatta were looking at cities like Tahoe, Miami, Dallas and Austin—places with no state taxes. Just after the ice storm, I'd taken a trip to Tampa, and the weather there was hot. I told Rich if he moved to Florida, he'd need to get industrial-sized fans if he wanted to spend time outside in the summer.

States taxes or not, Rich's life in California looked good from my vantage point in Greensboro. By June of 2003, the only negative I'd heard the whole year, outside his February trading email, was that the psoriatic arthritis had returned after being dormant for a while. To treat it, he started taking methotrexate in April and was going to start a new biologic drug called Remicade in June. Shortly before his first Remicade infusion, he sent me the following:

From: Richard Courtemanche
Sent: Thursday, June 12, 2003
To: Ted Courtemanche
Subject:

question... what do u know about effexor for depression? i need some help, struggling a bit, and from what i have read it works without so much of the "sedated" feeling that you can get (at least i did) with prozac and the other ssri's. tks

I sent Rich an email telling him I didn't know anything about Effexor. I found on the Web that you're not supposed to discontinue it quickly and sent

him a note telling him as much. Two weeks after the Effexor email, he told the
family about his accident.

> From: Richard Courtemanche
> Sent: Wednesday, June 25, 2003
> To: Ted Courtemanche; Mom; Dad
> Subject: such is life...
>
> well, first, i am fine. everyone is fine... now the bad news, my car is not fine. i
> rear ended a car on interstate 5 about 100 yards from my exit... ugh.
>
> i jammed on brakes, so front of my car dove down, crumpled my hood et al,
> and barely touched car in front of me. i would guess it will be quite a repair
> bill but deductible only 500, so no worries. the state trooper who came was
> a great guy, and get this... out in CA they dont give u a ticket even when its
> clearly your fault. so at least i dont have that insult to injury.
>
> zatta picked me up. i watched as they towed car away, and now i will just wait
> to hear the news/damage. all in all, a pain in the ass, but could have been a
> lot worse.
>
> on week two of effexor, and i feel it. not a huge change, subtle, but giving me
> hope. best, r

Shortly after Rich sent the email about his car crash, he sent another one to
me—about Zatta:

> zatta moving out aug 7th, her new place isnt ready til then. officially its so she
> can spend more time studying. unofficially... i dont know. my heart tells me its
> over. pretty depressing. we stay at home and watch movies and thats about it.
> i look forward to effexor kicking in some more. start to get my life back. thats
> the hope anyway.

I was surprised at how well he was holding up. All this crap was building:
his psoriatic arthritis, the arthritis medications, the car crash and now his
impending breakup with Zatta. That was just the stuff I knew about, yet his
emails came across as pretty levelheaded. I figured the Effexor was helping, and
he was leaving his mood swings behind.
Shortly after Rich told me about Zatta, he forwarded Mom, Dad and me the
email he sent to his friend Warren.

> From: Richard Courtemanche
> Sent: Tuesday, July 01, 2003
> To: Ted Courtemanche; Mom; Dad
> Subject:
>
> I wrote the following to Warren, and I realize I owe the same to all of you. I
> wrote originally to Warren alone because he is helping me find a Church out

here, and I... well, I want to explain to you the same things I try (albeit in a confusing fashion) to explain to him. Please know that Zatta is taking care of me. She is helping me the best she can, but I know I need more. I believe something in me longs for the belief in God as well. The email will be difficult to read, although I would imagine, not totally unexpected. The effexor is still kicking in, and it does help, but I dont think it will be able to solve the ultimate issue.

I love all of you deeply, as deeply as I believe is possible, and yet, yet these thoughts you read are real. I have had them before, probably every 3 years or so since I was 15. And it gets worse every time. This episode is worse than when I moved to London, which in turn was worse than when I started MIT, etc etc. I will talk to you all soon, email seems a more comforting form of communication for me lately. I am trying, trying so fuckin hard. Please know that.

Here it is. Love, Richard

Dear Warren,

This email will no doubt be somewhat disturbing to you, yet it is something I owe you. It is an explanation, well, I suppose as much of one as I am capable of understanding, and I suppose a confession as well. It will be random, as my thoughts are usually random.

Warren, I suffer. Everyone does. I know this. Do I suffer more than most? I am not sure, but I do know that rarely a day passes that the thought of suicide doesnt cross my mind. Well, what does that mean, cross my mind? It means that I consider it an option, and yet, I am not sure as an option for what. Bear with me here... an option to end my life, of course, that is what suicide does. And yet, when pressed (by myself) to give an answer about why I would end my life... well, it gets hazy. I fear. Fear what?... I am not sure, but I am sometimes terrified to the point that only the numbness of alcohol or pain pills can alleviate it. I once described it like a tumor that is slowly covering my head. I hurt. Sometimes its physical pain, sometimes (more often) its a mental torture (and I do mean torture) that I am seemingly unable to stop. Unable... I write that and realize how wrong that is. I am not unable to do anything... yet its THERE, its in my head, and its real. ITS SO FUCKIN REAL. I apologize, but thats how it comes out when I type. But what is real? There is no tumor, there is no tragedy in my life. Trading is going poorly but I know if I lost everything, my family would still take care of me. But the fear, oh dear God, the fear is there. And I dont know what it is.

Zatta believes its an emptiness, an emptiness I have always had. I have filled it with material possessions, booze, some drugs, but nothing satisfies it. So I am turning to Church. You believe this will work for me. I know you do because I have seen the power it has had over you. I am asking you to pray for me Warren. Please pray for me. I live in a fear that I believe only God can help me overcome... I do believe this. And yet it still has this grip on me. I pray. I am not a Church goer in the past, but I am going to try it. But I just need you to help me. To pray. Because to be honest, every single moment I live, suicide becomes a more viable option to me. I know that may be hard to read, and I dont want you to think it is something I am going to do now. I have already decided that if I were to take my life, I would tell others about it to have one last conversation, so they could understand. You would be on that short list of people I would talk to.

I sometimes feel that I would prefer to be tortured and killed rather than lead the life I do. When I was young, I used to read about Vietnam and cry that I wasnt able to die there. I have scars on my body where I have run a knife, just some physical pain to take away the mental pain. I dont believe a therapist can help me. I believe God can. Please, Warren, help that happen for me.

Your friend,
Richard

Most of the psychiatric care provided by doctors in the United States happens in a primary-care setting. Patients spend about two or three minutes talking before the doctor makes a decision on what needs to be done. Visits with a psychiatrist take longer, but they can still feel rushed. A friend told me that the first time he went to a psychiatrist, the doctor said that he talked so much, there was hardly time to figure out what medications he should take. When Rich was prescribed Effexor, he hadn't yet been diagnosed with bipolar disorder. For people with bipolar disorder, the problem with antidepressant medications like SSRIs is that they can actually trigger a manic episode. According to the NIMH, "Research has shown that people with bipolar disorder are at risk of switching into mania or hypomania, or of developing rapid cycling, during treatment with antidepressant medication." The generally accepted practice is to prescribe a mood stabilizer like lithium or Depakote at the same time.

Is it possible that because Rich wasn't on a mood stabilizer while taking Effexor, he wrote the letter to Warren? I doubt it. He'd been down this mental path before. But it's a reasonable bet Effexor helped push Rich toward an episode that took place about a week later.

Pull-Ups, Feelings and New Year's

Back when Rich and I were in elementary school, part of gym class involved competing for President's Awards. Once a year, Rich, myself and all our grade-schools pals had to do push-ups, sit-ups, pull-ups, the shuttle run and the 600-yard dash. There were two groups of winners. One group got a Top 15 award (the best), and the other got a Top 50 award.

I could never get the Top 15 award. One of the challenges that I struggled with was the 600-yard dash. In grade school, we just ran in our regular clothes. The Pine Hill Elementary School students would meet at home plate on the Little League field and run around the backstop behind the softball field, 300 yards away, and then back. I can still see the softball backstop and feel the cramp knotting in my stomach as I tried to get my legs to go faster.

If we failed any of the challenges, we could redo them. On the second try, I could usually get my 600-yard-dash time into the Top 15 category. My nemesis was pull-ups. I practiced doing them with my friend Kevin Watson in sixth grade—the last grade we could compete for President's Awards. I figured out a "kick" strategy. Kicking kind of like a dolphin, I was able to do eight pull-ups at Kevin's house. With my one session of practice, I felt confident—this was going to be the year I established myself as a top pull-up kid. Once the competition got going, I waited in line for my turn at the Pine Hill outdoor swing set, where there was a pull-up bar. When I got to the front, I jumped up and grabbed the bar as Mr. Thacker, the gym teacher, prepared to record my pull-ups. I readied myself and then started kicking.

"Teddy, you've got to steady your legs; you can't kick like that," Mr. Thacker said.

I tried a subtler kick and got the same warning. I held on and pulled with all my might. When I was done, I'd managed to complete two pull-ups. I needed six for the Top 15 award. Both Mr. Thacker and I knew I wasn't going to get six pull-ups when I tried the pull-up challenge for the second time. I needed three pull-ups for the Top 50 award. Minus the effort spent on the kick approach, I squeezed out an extra pull-up on the second try. Mr. Thacker said, "Well, Teddy, you're in the Top 50 category." He tried to make it sound exciting, but just like we both knew I wasn't getting six pull-ups, we both knew the Top 50 didn't cut it. When I got the patch for the Top 50 award, I put it in my pocket so I wouldn't catch hell from the kids who got the Top 15 award. Rich never had a problem with pull-ups. He'd bang them right out. He struggled like I did with the 600-yard dash, but I'm almost positive that he got the Top 15 award every year.

Robert Pirsig wrote in *Zen and the Art of Motorcycle Maintenance*, "No one is fanatically shouting that the sun is going to rise tomorrow." That the sun will rise each morning is about as certain a fact as we have here on Earth. We use our cerebral cortex to process it, and that's where the fact stays, out in the logical realm of our brains. What is a person with bipolar disorder trying to escape? What do any of us seek shelter from when we're overcome by despair or anxiety? Rich said it was fear. Whatever we're fleeing, it's not facts. It's not the sterile realization that we didn't win the Top 15 award. It's not ideas without emotional roots.

Carl Jung wrote that individual consciousness is best viewed as a flower springing from a "perennial rhizome beneath the earth." It doesn't spring separately, floating like a balloon above the ground—it grows. Observing facts without feeling emotions is like watching a guitar being played without hearing the notes. There's nothing to it. For most, it's not the strumming that drives pleasure or pain. Pleasure or pain results from the way the sound from the strumming resonates in us. It's the feeling triggered by the sound that we like. The feeling is not observed; it's *experienced* by us.

In Chapter Six, we explored beliefs and how they're generated by our minds, our working brains. We also investigated time, in particular Time-Earth, whose understanding, and very existence, is made possible by our minds. Let's now turn our attention to emotions and feelings, which are likewise generated by our working brains and our nervous systems. We're "in here" with our feelings. "I feel sad" or "I feel tortured" or "I feel fear" are resonations to the people experiencing them. The whole reason I wanted the Top 15 award was because I thought Top 15 winners were special. I wanted to be admired by the other kids at Pine Hill. The prize was not their admiration; it was not the simple fact that I might get respect from my classmates. The prize was the way the Top 15 award would make me *feel*—a sensation that I was sure would be extraordinarily pleasing.

In his book *Emotions, Stress, and Health,* emotions and stress resilience expert Alex Zautra wrote, "[Emotions] provide the basic motivational templates from which we find purpose and meaning." Rich experienced his fear; it became his primary resonation. Facts processed by Rich were processed while he resonated with fear. That's the way it is for people when they're depressed. They're stuck in a dreadful resonation.

Standard economic theory holds that people are completely rational and make optimal choices at every opportunity. Reading an economic textbook, you'd walk away with the sense that our cerebral cortex rules everything we do. The problem is that each day, standard economic theory gets demolished. Every day, people drink when they shouldn't, buy things they can't afford or get caught up in the passions of the moment. Standard economic theory discounts the impact of feelings on our behavior—particularly our loudest feelings that tend to be *now* focused. There's a fledgling branch of economics called "neuroeconomics" whose purpose is to factor feelings and urges back into the economic model.

Mental health care is loosely divided into two sectors in the United States: One is the traditional medical sector with hospitals and doctors; the other is outside what health insurance typically pays for. It includes things like social service agencies, self-help groups and religious institutions. According to the United States Surgeon General, one-third of the aggregate mental health care in the U.S. is provided by the "other" category (though based on my research, that figure seems low). Studies have demonstrated that the "other" category works. For example, attendance at religious services helps people with mental disorder. And it doesn't matter which denomination the service is: The benefit isn't in the particular creed or god.

Just as researchers don't know why depression medications help or why lithium and Depakote help with bipolar disorder, no one knows why religious services help. Like a good self-help group, they can facilitate bonding and a sense of community. They can also help people to rise above the power of their short-term emotions. The effect isn't always positive. Rich asked Warren to find him a church. It never worked out. The church Rich went to made him feel guilty about having thoughts of suicide.

The crown jewel of guilt is original sin. It's been interpreted many different ways, but I'll focus on three. In the first sense, it is literally a sin passed along by

Adam to all people. In eating the fruit, Adam disobeyed God and in doing so, damned all humanity to the burden of original sin. Certain Christians, including St. Augustine, have maintained that a person could personally commit no sins and still be damned to eternal hell for Adam's transgression. In the Christian tradition, Christ was sent to Earth to save mankind from original sin.

A second and more metaphorical interpretation of original sin is that it's a separation from God. That longing we feel in our lives is none other than a longing for God. We may call it original sin, but it's not anything to feel guilty about. The fact is, here in our bodies on Earth, we're separated from God (if you choose to believe in God).

And lastly, there's a neurological version of original sin. Original sin is actually humankind's predisposition to certain animal urges. We're affected by feelings like desire. In this sense, original sin is again part of who we are, but it's not something linked to a literal fruit consumption in the Garden of Eden. We are creatures with urges, wants, moods, ingrained neurochemical and neurophysiological constitutions, which themselves represent a metaphorical original sin.

How do we overrule our biological predispositions? Just because we may want to blindly follow our short-term passions doesn't mean we'll impulsively charge forward. David Hume wrote, "Reason is and ought only to be the slave of the passions." For Hume, reason couldn't be separated from emotions or feelings. It's inextricably interwoven. From Hume's perspective, when we opt not to react angrily but with calm, when we step back and reflect on the best course of action even though one feeling is screaming, "Take the money," that's reason in action. A feeling that, in the absence of reason, would not be heard is provided a voice. We can choose to slow down, to bite our tongues, to avoid doing things that we might regret in the heat of the moment because our more sensible emotions can be championed through the employment of reason. Our passions, in a sense, use reason to choose the better option.

Why do we raise a toast? Did the first person who discovered the wheel raise his or her glass (if inclined to do so) because of the object itself? Or might it have been because no one else had ever discovered it, and the invention brought with it certain feelings of happiness and satisfaction? Resonating with these feelings, the discoverer of the wheel decided to raise a toast. Facts without feelings do not generate movement—this is the subtler point of Hume. To think that we can separate reason from passion is misguided. Passion is always there: A purely coldhearted, unemotional decision is, if inspected closely, a bowing to some other long-term effect, one that will bring with it certain feelings.

Weighing consequences outside the immediate short-term and opting for one that works best for us in the overall scheme of things—short, middle and long-term—is an example of Hume's observation. It's quieter passions being heard because of reason. Our brains are made up of three basic parts: the inner stem, the middle limbic system and the outer cerebral cortex. Experts believe that the limbic system is most directly responsible for triggering emotions. Zautra wrote, "The cerebral cortex may have evolved for just that purpose: to regulate our emotional responses." Bipolar disorder is a condition in which the loud or short-term emotions originating from the limbic system dominate the analytic system, and, worse, the information sent by the limbic system can be erroneous. The analytic system has no chance; any counsel it attempts to provide might be thwarted immediately.

There's a holiday that appears, on first glance, to favor the limbic system exclusively: New Year's Eve. With all the revelry, there doesn't seem to be much support for the analytic side. Behind the scenes, though, New Year's Eve offers a solid venue for rationality. New Year's resolutions are, in a way, an attempt to put the cerebral cortex back in charge or, more accurately, to allow our quieter passions access to reason.

One of the best New Year's I ever had was with Rich when we were living at Mom's. We went out on New Year's Eve with Kelley (his girlfriend at the time) and a few of her friends. We sat around at her apartment, had one or two beers and then came back to Mom's. We were asleep before 11:30 pm. That wasn't the good part. The good part started when I got back from the gym the next morning, and Rich was watching the 11:00 am college football game. I sat down on the couch next to him and started watching, too. Rich and I managed to see a portion of every televised game that day. We'd sit for an hour and say nothing except "Ouch" at a big hit or "Mmm" at a great catch or run. We were in a football watching zone. You don't need to talk when it happens. You just enjoy.

As I was writing this book, I jotted down notes to try to clarify my thoughts. On a piece of paper, I drew a stick figure and around the stick figure, I wrote a list of things that impact behavior at any point in time. Here are some of them: moods, emotions, known beliefs, unconscious beliefs, instincts, personality traits, learning ability, culture and current environment. There's also the physical composition of our brain and nervous system and their capacity to operate effectively—a capacity that includes things like conducting electricity, having an adequate supply of neurochemicals and enough receptors for the chemicals to be received and processed. In short, there are things outside of us and things inside of us that affect our behavior. But like Jung's flowering consciousness, the fruits of our behavior are feelings. Circulating through an endless knot, feelings both drive and are driven by behavior. It's the "driven by" quality of feelings with which I'd like to end this section.

As I sit here remembering the college football New Year's Day with Rich, I'm relaxing in the *same* resonation I felt that very New Year's. The actual New Year's and the memory of that New Year's both drove and drive the same feelings. When I think back on it, I feel happy. At times, there might be some other feelings mixed in, maybe a sense of nostalgia. The key, though, is that the original feeling is not gone forever. It doesn't disappear with the event. The same feeling can be felt years later. The feeling—soft and pleasant as it was— was the reason I liked watching football with Rich all day in the first place.

THE JULY 2003 BREAKDOWN

After Rich forwarded the email he had sent to Warren on July 1, 2003, I called him. I knew he was depressed and wasn't expecting him to pick up the phone, but he did. We didn't delve into the email; we just let it drift away. He told me one of the things he was doing to relieve his depression was watching *Dumb and Dumber*. After we'd been talking for a while, he said, "T, I feel like a failure. I've lost $200,000 since the start of the year."

"Are you still up?" I asked.

"Yeah, I've made $600,000 since I got here last year."

"Six hundred thousand! Unbelievable, Rich," I said. "Let me give you some perspective. The $400,000 you've still got is more than the CEO of our company made last year. Four hundred thousand dollars is a ton of money. I don't know what tax bracket it puts you in, but it puts you way up there. I'm floored." I was hoping he'd put the bulk of his money into something safe—a savings account would have been just fine. The conversation ended with me telling him that I was going to Boston for the Fourth of July to see Mom and Dad.

Some choices in life offer no second chances: Once they're done, they're done. We can't go back and fix what happened; we can only go forward. Every futures trader who has been in the business for very long has experienced at least one major setback—in the trading business, it's called a "blowup." On July 8, 2003, a day or two after I got back from Boston, Rich sat before his computer after experiencing the worst trading day in his life. He had only about $150,000 left of the $600,000 he'd made since arriving in San Diego.

As he sat in front of his computer, the trading day over, he grabbed a beer from the refrigerator—the first step in numbing himself to his losses. He got another and finished that one, too. Once he was done with the beers, he got a full 750 ml bottle of Bombay Sapphire gin from on top of the refrigerator, where he stored it. He took a sip and stared at his computer. I'd bet the lights on the monitors were mesmerizing, probably kind of hallucinatory. Rich stared at his screens and took another drink, and then another. Did he gulp his gin or just sip it down? Likely a little of both. My bet is that the sun hadn't fully set when he blacked out. When he woke up the next morning, twelve beer bottles littered his floor, along with an empty bottle of gin. The alcohol could have killed him.

When I visited him in the fall of 2002, Rich made it clear to me that he always closed his trades at the end of the day; he never let them ride through the night. In futures trading, even though the price of a particular commodity closes at a certain value, the value can fluctuate before the market opens the next morning. Keeping your trades open through the night exposes you to that risk. You can be impacted by changes all over the world, and you have no way to limit your losses. You're at the mercy of the market; all you can do is hope that the price fluctuations don't ruin you by the time the market opens for trading.

Early the next morning, Rich looked at his computer screen and realized he was almost completely wiped out. Once he'd started drinking, he didn't close out his trades, and his losses had mounted overnight. He went from "had it all" to "have nothing" in the course of a few months, with the final blow coming in one apocalyptic night. Mom and Dad flew out to San Diego to see him the next day. "Hang on, Rich," I thought when Mom told me about what happened. They took him back to Boston where Mom said that for the first few days, he mainly sat around the house with a glazed look in his eyes.

A few days after the July 8 blowup, Rich went to a psychiatrist and was diagnosed with bipolar disorder.

THE JULY 2003 RECOVERY

William James wrote, "Knowledge about life is one thing; effective occupation of a place in life, with its dynamic currents passing through your being, is another."

For a week after the blowup, the situation was touch and go for Rich. I'm sure he kept getting devoured by the reality of what had happened. Eat breakfast: I lost all my money. Sit in the backyard: I lost all my money. He couldn't keep it safely stowed away. It was omnipresent; he reexperienced it all day long. He left me a voice message four days after it happened, telling me he was having a hard time hanging on. I sent the following email to him after I listened to his message:

From: Ted Courtemanche
Sent: Sunday, July 13, 2003 10:26 PM
To: Richard Courtemanche
Subject:

Rich, Got your message. I'm beat and getting ready to hit the sack. Five things:

1. "Keep breathing" (remember Cast Away). Simple words in a movie but profoundly true. Your most important job for the next little while is to keep putting one foot in front of the other.

2. It's all about the story you choose to tell yourself. Everything comes down to that. Put another way, "In the realm of experience, nothing is either this or that. There is always at least one more alternative and often an unlimited number of them." (Gary Zukav, Dancing Wuli Masters).

3. Be honest with the psychiatrist. It's the only way you'll get anything out of it.

4. Seek out nature. Try sitting in front of a tree - sounds strange but something happens; it can heal.

5. Last and definitely not least, you're welcome down here anytime. I have a spare bedroom with its own bathroom and a little garden pond out back. It's slow, yes, but very accepting. Stay as long as you like.

I'll be in Portland, OR, on business until late Tuesday night.

Peace and love,
T

I thought about Rich most of the time I was in Portland. The only saving grace of Rich's July 8 blowup was this: Time-Earth didn't make much of a difference in his business. He'd earned most of his former fortune in just about a year. For most futures traders, a few big trades drive the bulk of their earnings or losses. Some days Rich made more than $50,000. He had to make big bets to do it, but he could cover a lot of ground quickly.

The first email Rich sent to me after the breakdown was dated July 20, 2003. He sent it after he got back to San Diego. A very long email, it had three parts. The first part was a message to bring me up to speed on how he was doing. The second was an email message that he'd sent to Dad, which he wanted me to see as well. And the third was a business proposition he had for me.

In the first part of the email, Rich said he was sleeping sixteen hours a day. When he was in Boston, a psychiatrist had diagnosed him with bipolar II. Rich wrote:

i had considered the fact that i might be bipolar, but i never seemed to truly have the "manic" phases a true bipolar does. well, bipolar 2 is exactly that, the manias arent as severe, but the depression is.

Rich wrote that his friend Don in San Diego also had bipolar II. Rich called him, and he set Rich up with his psychiatrist. Rich made an appointment with another psychiatrist in San Diego as well so that he'd have a choice of doctors. Rich ended the first part of his email with a recap of what had happened, about drinking all that alcohol and blacking out. The last two sentences were:

well, the money is gone... i can write that now, i guess thats a big step. one week ago i would think the thought and want nothing more than to end my life.

The second part of the email was the note Rich had sent to Dad. He copied and pasted it into the email he sent to me. In it, he asked Dad for money so that he could—what else?—start trading again. While writing this book, I reread reams of old emails; some were familiar, and some had faded from my memory. Rereading Rich's forwarded email rang a few bells, but for the most part, it was like reading it for the first time—but with a sense of déjà vu.

Rich told Dad that as long as he wasn't drinking, he was as good as any professional futures trader he knew, that he could be one of the best. When

Rich was back in Boston, he and Dad had talked about Rich's drinking; Rich told Dad that he wasn't going to drink anymore. Dad gave him a locket with his own father's picture on it. Girard Courtemanche had been an alcoholic and died when Dad was about twenty (Dad's mom later remarried, to Mickey Flynn, a.k.a. Poppop). Girard struggled with alcohol his whole life. In the message Rich sent to Dad, he told Dad how much the locket meant to him. He also told Dad about one of his girlfriends, who had been addicted to cocaine. The girl had a trick that she said helped her to stay away from cocaine. The person she respected most in her life was her father. She said she couldn't promise she'd never use cocaine again, but if she did, she'd snort the first line off her father's picture. Rich wrote to Dad:

> i promised God something similar... i carry that locket with me everywhere now. i wont promise i wont drink again, but if i do, i will have to do it with that locket wrapped in my hand, around the glass, so i will realize what exactly i am costing myself.

The third part of the July 20 email was the one that impacted me most when I reread it. In the first sentence, Rich wrote, "well, dad agreed to loan me the money, so i am all set." That information wasn't surprising; I knew that Dad had loaned Rich money to start trading again. The section that hit me came when Rich wrote, "now the part i wanted to talk to you about is if you want to get involved." He asked me if I wanted to be an even partner with him in his trading. He'd do the trading, and I'd front $25,000. I didn't remember ever having seen that offer; it didn't ring a single bell. As I read it, a bolt of panic went through me—more than three years after the email was sent. Had I never responded to Rich? He was asking me to be an even partner. Did I never read that part of the email? *Oh, God,* I thought. *I can't respond to him now. Could this have made a difference?* For what seemed like a minute or two, anxiety incapacitated me. And then I caught myself. I went through more emails and saw that I had in fact responded to his offer. In an email that I sent on July 21, I wrote:

> Rich, good to hear from you. Welcome home. Let's talk about trading over the weekend if you have a minute. You've just been through a huge ordeal. Let yourself keep relaxing.

My anxiety faded away when I remembered that we'd agreed to hold off on the partnership.

For the next six weeks after his July 20 email, Rich and I traded emails almost every day. He said he wasn't going to drink ever again: "i know i cant handle alcohol, i simply cant." In one email, he told me he had written suicide notes to Mom, Dad and me when he was back at Mom's. In another, he wrote that the day after his collapse, he saw that he had played one song on his computer 276 times in a row: "apparently i just liked clicking that nite. it was jimi hendrix, 'manic depression.' struck me as funny. dont know why."

When he met with the psychiatrist he selected in San Diego, Rich said that the doctor told him two things would get him through: his intelligence and his honesty with the psychiatrist.

i swear T, i told him everything. every single thing i have done that i have been ashamed off, every manic thing i do, and now i finally believe i can get on the proper meds i need.

Was it possible for Rich to have told his doc "every manic thing" he did? In Chapter Two of this book, I wrote about regrouting a shower in my townhouse. Are any of us consciously aware when we've slipped into a regrouting episode? Still, Rich was doing all the right things—graphing his moods, on his psychiatrist's advice; talking with his doctor about starting cognitive therapy to supplement the medication; joining an Alcoholics Anonymous group; and journaling.

Part of an email he wrote to me was about an insight he got from a journaling session.

i realized something that struck me as curious. when depressed, i get to the point where i can barely move off the couch, getting a beer and sitting back down is about all i can muster. now i might drink a 12 pack on those days, which sadly, isnt that much for me. i mean i am liquored up, but still functioning fine.

its the euphoric stages, and it doesnt matter if i am at a bar with friends ordering shots or at home by myself that i get into trouble. i found that very interesting. with my bipolar, its when an upswing starts, and my internal motor (lets call it) starts to rev, that drinking is like throwing alcohol on a fire.

Rich had been addicted to caffeine, too. Before starting on Depakote for the bipolar disorder, Rich drank fifteen to twenty big cups of coffee a day. He said he had his third pot brewing by 8:30 am. He was eliminating that as well. Since starting the medication, he was only drinking one or two cups a day.

It wasn't all up for Rich during his recovery—not at all. He had downs, too, but the downs seemed to have bottoms. The fact that Rich was aware of his symptoms and of his condition in general was a big deal. Fuller Torrey and Michael Knable noted in their book *Surviving Manic Depression* that about one-third of the untreated bipolar disorder population has "significantly impaired" awareness of their bipolar symptoms. Awareness of the disease, the authors wrote, is "one of the most significant determinants of long-term prognosis—if not the most significant."

Rich said that afternoons were worst for his depressions. Weekends were bad, too. He could manage to structure his weekday mornings, even without trading, but afternoons and weekends weren't as easy for him to organize. He could be overwhelmed by depression. In one of his down emails, he wrote:

> i just dont know if i will ever get there. i mean, if i have bipolar, then how the
> fuck do i know what normal is for my mind? i know thats going too far, but thats
> how i feel sometimes.

But then he'd bounce back up. His dogs were part of his therapy—he said they were the "best therapy." He walked them a couple of times each day, especially in the afternoons once he realized that afternoons were bad times for him.

The medications didn't stop him from being Rich. One morning, he emailed:

> i think my neighbors might declare me clinically insane after yday. i ran
> sprints on my street and when i came home, noticed the picture of Girard
> Courtemanche had fallen out. i didnt panic, but rather calmly walked the street,
> found it, and took it to a jeweler so it wont fall out again. but when i came
> home, i decided it was alcohol's way of testing me... so i took one of the beers
> i keep in bed of truck (it's not like i would ever drink one, they have baked to
> about 120 degrees in the sun) and i placed it on tailgate and smashed it.

Rich started seeing Ashley for therapy shortly after he started his medication. In Chapter Two, I referred to Ashley as a "New Age" therapist. In Chapter Three, I said that I didn't think Ashley had any specific counseling degrees. If I had to compare Ashley to an inorganic object, I'd say that she was like a full can of paint, minus the can—her therapy knew no boundaries. She told Rich that one of the keys for him was identifying irrational thoughts when he got depressed. That's a hard thing for someone who is depressed, but it's key to neutralizing the negative power of mood swings. She taught Rich breathing exercises that he could use when he began feeling anxious. When Rich found himself overwhelmed by negative thoughts, she said that his job was to identify rational counterarguments to them—rational counterarguments that she said would always exist.

At the same time, Ashley also told Rich that most people only have one-third of their soul here on Earth and that when we die, we're reunited with the rest of it. She said that every once in a while, someone like Jesus comes along who has nine-tenths of a soul, but they're extraordinarily rare. She believed that everyone's soul has a definite time to enter the world and that if Rich hadn't been born via Mom and Dad, he would have been born through other parents. Rich liked her idea of "soul groups," groups of souls that look out for other souls, or parts of souls, in bodies here on Earth. As to his cutting, she told Rich that in a past life, he was a warrior, the kind who would take the blade of his sword and cut his chest before battle.

What Ashley did that other therapists and doctors couldn't was make Rich feel like he was okay: She made it clear that his behavior and the way he felt weren't his fault. He wasn't the material Rich; he was one-third of a perfect soul, dropped into a body with bipolar disorder. The way he felt was a consequence of the body he was in. Of Ashley, Rich said:

she always provides insights that are very helpful and i have gotten to the point where i trust her completely, which of course is the only way i will really be able to help myself.

When Rich sent emails telling me something he felt badly about, I'd analyze what he said and then try to send him back a message that might help. Emailing with him made me think things over. We wrote about relationships, cutting, religion and philosophy. We tossed our ideas out to each other and knew we'd get a reply. We slowly had epiphanies, but the real joy was in the dialogue. In Rich, I saw myself, or parts of myself. I saw familiar challenges in his struggles. Our emails unlocked doors for me that otherwise would have remained closed. The six weeks after the July 8 breakdown were a single shared connection.

In one email, Rich wrote:

From: Richard Courtemanche
Sent: Wednesday, August 6, 2003 02:46 PM
To: T Home
Subject:

i havent looked at the market in almost a month. unheard of for me. the thing that is getting me lately... well... i have all these prescriptions, i am almost 34. everyone says "dont ever go off bipolar meds" - same for the arthritis. and i know thats the truth. but they make it so... well, it becomes an "is it worth it" game?

i told my therapist that a month ago if i were dead, it would be with swollen, tear filled eyes. today if i were found dead (by my own means i am saying) it would be because i simply decided it wasnt worth it. some people i know lose limbs and live incredible lives, why cant i be like that? why cant i simply accept my fate?

man, u have a fucked up brother T... but i am trying, i am still trying. best. r

I wrote back:

On the "is it worth it" piece - tough question. Plenty of philosophers, Schopenhauer is one example, have argued that this life is just a melting pot of suffering. No redeeming qualities whatsoever. I don't know. Voltaire wrote the following at age 73: "As for myself, weak as I am, I carry on the war to the last moment... I see near my door Geneva on fire with quarrels over nothing, and I laugh again; and thank God, I can look upon the world as a farce even when it becomes as tragic as it sometimes does. All comes out even at the end of the day, and all comes out still more even when all the days are over."

I do think life really is a lot of suffering - and it is generated by the very feelings that make us human in the first place. One of my favorite sayings is, "The secret to happiness is to admire without desiring."

161

From my perspective, I think the seemingly little things hold some as yet not entirely understood keys - enjoying a sunset or watching waves, laughing at a funny movie, taking pause to feel the wind blowing on your face. These are important things! They serve to stop time - in that instant, you really are one with the universe. They are available to a millionaire and a person living in a shack.

Keep breathing,
T

In our email conversations, we'd climb to a summit and from there fall backward or forward. There were so many emails—pages and pages of them. Toward the end of August, Rich sent one of his updates.

From: Richard Courtemanche
Sent: Monday, August 18, 2003
To: T Home; Mom; Dad
Subject:

hi all. figured i would give an update on things out here...

san diego continues to be hot and humid, i love it. but of course, i dont have to work in it so my opinion may not be the majority. a friend got a ping pong table and we have been playing a lot. the dogs have now 90% destroyed the lawn with their pee. picture the old west with tumbleweeds blowing and u can envision the backyard. zack loves to lie in the dirt and then sleeps in the bed with me. no wonder zatta moved out!

on more serious side... got my second remicade infusion today, it went fine. havent felt a difference yet but that takes some time. my back has been bothering me lately, poor zack. he loves to sleep with me. one nite i felt like the bed was too soft, so i moved to floor (bed is on floor already). zack must have woken up on bed, saw that i had moved, and decided to join his dad... only he stepped off the bed onto my back. ugh. its getting better though so no worries.

the afternoon depressions have lessoned dramatically. i am still on same effexor dose, although last friday the doc suggested i go up 75 to 375 (i told him how depressed i had been previous 10 days). i was planning on upping the dose but i started feeling better and the weekend was pleasant so i decided not to. i can always increase, but since we are getting toward top of prescribing range (about 450 mg) i figured best not to go up until i absolutely need it. i am fairly heavily medicated by the depakote as well. i feel it. an odd, almost surreal feeling sometimes. i know my chemistry is changing, i can feel it. and even on my bad days i had a friend tell me he notices a huge difference in my attitude which was nice to hear. doc also said i am making great progress for only 3 weeks on depakote.

all in all, i am pleased with how the week has started. i wired money to my account so i can trade when i want to. no set start date but i dont think i will have one. i think (and this will be truly amazing) that i will have the ability to trade when i want and not trade when i dont want. thats how i feel, that... calm i guess. this opposed to my old life, where i can honestly say and not with any great pride that i rarely missed more than a few minutes of any trading day. i came to hate vacations and time away from the market.

i obviously have to watch for those feelings to return, but one good thing the doc and i agree on is to first and foremost watch for any addictive behavior to return... ie, trading obsession, or wishing for alcohol or caffeine. that will be the CLEAR sign to stop, adjust medication if necessary, but mainly slow down.

other than that, i probably wont see my car until mid september. what can i do... not a thing, not a thing.

zatta is well and always sends her best. zack and daisy are now spoiled beyond belief. not only do they come to gym every day with me and sit outside where people fawn all over them... but they get leftover ribs, chicken, even steak gets cut up for them... reminds me of being young watching dad feed the dogs. alas, its not a bad thing, and we all comfort each other out here. best, r

I agreed with Rich's friend—Rich did better when he was on the medications. He could get outside himself, and the depressions weren't as devastating. If he kept working at it, maybe he could keep this disorder under control. Around the first of September, Rich sent us the news that he had started trading again. His doctor increased his Depakote dose, and Ashley gave him strategies for dealing with the inevitable stress from trading. Rich said alcohol still had no pull on him, and he wasn't even finishing his single morning cup of coffee from Starbucks.

I had mixed feelings about his return to trading. I knew how much Rich liked it and wished I could feel in my work the type of passion he felt in his, but his trading just seemed to be an out-and-out addiction. What I settled on was that he was on the right medications, seeing a therapist and really working to control his bipolar disorder—that the positives would outweigh the negatives. And this time, Rich would approach trading differently.

INTENTION, MORTAL SIN AND SUICIDE

Emile Durkheim developed a definition of suicide at the turn of the century still used by mental health professionals today: "The term suicide is applied to every case of death which results directly or indirectly from a positive or negative act, carried out by the victim himself, knowing that it will produce this result."

Through the centuries, self-killings have been more likely to be accepted by societies if they are completed in the act of saving someone or something else. Thus, the soldier who falls on a grenade is seen as a hero. In medieval times, the suicide rate among nobles was low. It's not that nobles were any less prone to wanting to end their own lives; it's just that they had easier access to alternatives in which they did not die directly of their own hands (and thus weren't considered to have completed suicide). Nobles who wanted to take their own lives might engage others in duels and perish at the gun or sword of another. Or they might join an army and go off into battle, with the full intention of having their lives ended (much of the suicide information from the medieval period tends to be male focused).

Under Durkheim's definition, though, such acts are suicide. They result from a positive action on the victim's part that he or she knows will produce a fatal result. In modern times, would-be suicide completers might engage in violent behavior, drive their cars into trees or countless other less direct ways of ending their own lives.

In the United States, about 33,000 people complete suicide each year. John Hewett wrote in *After Suicide*, "Experts claim the actual total is closer to three times that, with suicide attempts approaching eight to ten times the completed rates . . . as many as one million people attempt suicide in one year."

One of the shortcomings of Durkheim's definition of suicide is that while it acknowledges suicide as a voluntary self-killing, there isn't a timeframe applied to it. For example: "Suicide is a voluntary self-killing that is completed within Z number of hours." The suicide rate in this country tends to include only those people who directly take positive or negative action to end their lives *and* that action results in a rapid outcome. I'm going to keep the term "rapid" vague because it is vague, to a point. If some unfortunate person jumps off a bridge, death tends to be rapid—and my assumption is that most people would agree with the *rapid* characterization in this case.

The water starts to get murkier, though, when we look at other behaviors. How about smoking? Except for a few industry executives, few people would deny that smoking leads to numerous health problems which themselves can lead to death. How about risky sexual behavior? The link between AIDS and death is established and clear. How about poor nutrition, overloading on fatty foods? Like smoking, obesity can lead to heart disease and numerous other health problems. None of these activities—smoking, risky sexual behavior or eating fatty foods—will lead to a rapid death as "rapid" is loosely understood in Durkheim's definition of suicide. But chances are good each will directly lead to health problems that can cause death.

Is *rapidity* really the differentiator for deaths initiated by harmful personal behaviors? Consider the case of someone who ends his or her life through the ongoing ingestion of low levels of arsenic. The effects of arsenic are cumulative. If someone takes small doses of arsenic day after day or month after month, one of those doses will eventually be the one that causes arsenic levels in that person's body to cross the lethal line. While death itself will be rapid once the threshold is crossed, the whole process might not be rapid. It could take years, just like smoking, yet that whole process is really part of a voluntary self-killing. I think it's safe to say that most people would consider a slow death via arsenic to be suicide. Thus, it's not entirely accurate to say that the "rapidity" of the process is important. What is of paramount importance, instead, is *intention.*

The concept of intention is not included in Durkheim's definition. He knowingly excluded it. His goal in defining suicide was to study it from a sociological perspective. He wrote, "Intention is too intimate a thing to be understood from the outside other than by gross approximation. . . . We are constantly explaining actions deriving from petty feelings or blind routine as being due to noble passions or lofty considerations." Including intention in the definition of suicide would, for Durkheim, hopelessly cloud the waters.

In terms of his definition, though, if a smoker acknowledges that smoking can cause diseases that themselves cause death, each cigarette smoked becomes an indirect suicide attempt. The smoker is taking positive action that he or she knows could lead to fatal diseases. For practical purposes, *intention* is the only thing that keeps a death initiated by smoking from being included in the suicide statistics quoted earlier in this section. Alfred Kinsley wrote, "The world is not divided into sheep and goats . . . nature rarely deals with discrete categories." A smoker's intention might fall into a number of categories: fitting in for teenagers, pleasure, nicotine fix or habit for the established smoker. While the act of smoking has a good chance of leading to health problems that will lead to death, smokers are generally not smoking with the immediate intention of killing themselves.

Tort laws in the United States rely heavily on the concept of intention. All that is required to establish intention is to show that a person was "substantially certain" their actions would lead to a certain outcome, nothing more. In the U.S., determining the cause of death is a local judgment call. One way to determine that a car accident was a suicide is to verify that a suicide note was left. Thus, outside the confines of Durkheim's definition, intention plays an integral role in labeling a death as "suicide." If a person's aim through their positive or negative action is to end their life, that person's cause of death may be labeled as a suicide—regardless of rapidity or the vehicle employed. At this point, we might want to reconsider the example of soldiers who cover grenades. Is their intention really to end their lives, or is it something else?

As was discussed in Chapter Two, early Christians did not always condemn suicide; some were quite supportive of it—especially those who left this world in hopes of finding a better life in the next one. Augustine launched a change of opinion, which, after enough time, was accepted without evaluation—suicide is a sin. It got the label not because Christians thought suicide was bad but because one influential man linked suicide to sin.

I'm onto a potential third rail, but my whole reason for discussing suicide in this and other sections is to get a handle on its labeling as a mortal sin. Georges Minois wrote, "Was Christ's death a suicide? Put as bluntly as this, the question seems shocking, but John quotes Jesus as saying, 'For these sheep, I will give my life' and 'No one takes it from me, I lay it down freely myself' (John 10:15 and 10:18)." Minois said, "Medieval theologians found the passages in John an embarrassment. Origen, for example, declares, 'If we are not afraid of words and pay attention to things, we might say, finding no other expression that fits the facts, that divinely (in a manner of speaking) Jesus killed himself.'"

As presented in the Bible, Jesus knew that in going to Jerusalem, He was moving toward His death. It seems clear from the miracles Jesus performed that He could have saved His life but instead chose to "lay it down freely." If we back away from the potential ambiguity of local cause-of-death certificates and return to Durkheim's definition, Jesus took positive action (going to Jerusalem) that He knew would lead to a fatal result. Intention, however, in the story of Jesus' death would appear to be everything. Christians believe that Christ died for all humankind's sins—that by dying on the cross, His intention was to save the world. His act was the ultimate covering of a grenade.

Sticking with the topic of intention, what are some actions where intentions might belie outcomes? Is it a good act if someone donates to charity strictly for tax purposes? How about if someone performs a public service simply because they've been ordered to do so by the court—is their action good or is it really just an example of fulfilling an obligation? How about if someone kicks a suitcase off a crowded train, making the suitcase's owner miserable but most of the train passengers happy in the process? We're into the realm of ethics. Consideration of intention is par for the course here.

What was Rich's intention in the greenbelt? What is the intention of anyone who is backed to a wall by the resonations in his or her own head? Hewett wrote, "The best explanation of suicide about which I know deals with the question of escape. . . . The suicidal person feels trapped in a corner by this overwhelming and unbearable mental pain." Yes, Rich knew his action would almost certainly end his life, but was that the ultimate goal? Life was not something to be taken lightly for Rich. He felt life so passionately, was so intimately entwined, that he could only consider options from the frenetic reverberations of his emotions. Had there been another lasting solution he could have recognized from his state, a solution that would have spared him his suffering, I think he would have embraced it. Rich felt out of options.

For many who complete suicide, it appears to be the only lasting alternative that can free them from their pain. If, as most ethicists and theologians hold, it's intention that truly matters, the whole notion of suicide becomes a lot more complicated. Few people voluntarily go to their deaths for the purpose of dying. Like a smoker, they have something else in mind. The end they are hoping to achieve is *freedom*, not death.

While intention may or may not be factored into the labeling of a death as suicide for statistical purposes, intention would seem to *the* defining element of any act designated a mortal sin.

FLYING TO AUSTIN

The Saturday morning after I learned that Rich had shot himself—that he was in a hospital in Austin—I got up earlier than usual and made the morning coffee. I used the same coffee that Deana and I had brought back from Maui after our honeymoon. Waiting for the coffee to brew, I checked on flights to Austin, not sure when I should fly down. Around 10:00 am, I called the hospital to confirm that Rich was there. Unlike the night before, the hospital employee now said that Rich was a patient.

I asked to speak to someone in the intensive care unit, where he was. When I was put through, the person who answered said that Michele, his current nurse (the nurses change according to the shift), was with another patient and that I should try back in ten minutes. When I called back, I was put through to Michele.

"Hi, this is Ted Courtemanche. I'm calling to see how my brother Rich is doing."

"Hi, Ted. I'm sorry, but for patient confidentiality reasons, I'm not allowed to release patient information over the phone," she said.

"I'm in the process of trying to figure out if I should fly down today or wait until next weekend," I said.

"I'm sorry, I really can't tell you anything." I didn't know what to say. I knew all about patient confidentiality from my job; it was kind of an unmovable bypass, and I was about to say goodbye. "I know your mother's going to be here in about two hours," Michele continued, "and once I talk with her, she'll be able to let you know how Rich is."

"All right," I responded, and then didn't say anything.

She broke the silence by saying, "You can go ahead and ask me questions, and I'll answer them if I can."

"Okay," I said. Then my mouth just started talking. I asked, "Well, is Rich conscious? Does he know what's going on?"

"Yes, he follows you with his left eye when you go in the room."

A chill went through me. He's conscious, I thought, but the bullet probably shattered the area around his right eye. He's going to need plastic surgery. Michele and I finished our conversation, and I told myself I would get plane tickets for the next weekend and go down then.

The weekend before all the chaos broke out, I'd started prepping the living room in our house in Greensboro for repainting. I sanded the walls and put tape on the baseboards. After I got off the phone with Michele, I started painting. Manual labor always helps to quiet my brain. I painted away, satisfied to be lost. A few hours later, at about 2:00 pm, Mom called from the hospital.

"Hi, Mom," I said, walking out the front door and sitting on the steps. "How's he doing?"

"Your brother had a stroke while they were doing surgery last night. They think he'll pass within the next twenty-four hours."

I curled over on myself. The situation had transitioned so many times. There was the phone call from Rich and the suicide email I read at work. Next, the news that he had checked into a hospital in Ohio. After that, Dad had called telling me that Rich had passed, but he was actually in the middle of a creek in Austin, surrounded by a SWAT team and hostage negotiators. Then, I got the news that Rich had been shot, and shot himself. Rich went from critical condition with survivable wounds to following nurses around with his left eye to dying within twenty-four hours. I shook; I felt part of my heart and stomach break away. I couldn't move. Rich was going to die in twenty-four hours. Around me, grass grew imperceptibly, the sun shined, insects sang, leaves fluttered, tree branches stilled and birds carried on with the day.

When I hung up, I told Mom I wasn't sure whether I could come down or not—I'd have to check if any flights were still available. Deana and I immediately started racing around. Two tickets were still available on an American flight out of Raleigh, a direct flight that would get us into Austin at 8:00 pm. We found a kennel that could take the dogs (most were closed after 12:00 pm on Saturday). As Deana and I ran around, taking care of everything we needed to take care of to catch the flight, I felt like I was floating outside my body. Things seemed to be happening in slow motion. I was remembering times with Rich. In just the past week, Deana and I had picked out our wedding pictures. Rich looked so good in them.

When Mom had arrived at the hospital in Austin, she was first directed to a plastic surgeon who told her about the multiple operations Rich would need to repair his jaw. After this fifteen-minute discussion, another physician met with her and told her that Rich had about twenty-four hours left to live. Why they felt the need to have her talk to the plastic surgeon is beyond me.

Rich had suffered a stroke during the operation to repair his carotid artery, which had been pierced by his gunshot. The doctor said that 85 percent of the population is able to support blood flow necessary for the brain to continue functioning normally with only one carotid artery. Rich was in the 15 percent of the population that couldn't.

I pictured Rich in the greenbelt, having been shot by a SWAT team member, going to his rage place and then shooting himself. At the same time I checked plane flights earlier in the morning, I'd also looked on the Web to see if there might be anything there about Rich. An Austin paper, the *American-Statesman*, had a picture of the scene. The first line in the article stated, "An Austin police officer shot a man who then apparently turned a shotgun on himself." That was Rich. There was a picture of the riverbank, with a yellow "Do Not Cross" tape line and investigators going over the scene. One picture showed the Austin police chief holding a shell, which he said came from Rich's gun.

Once our suitcase was packed, Deana and I got in the car and dropped the dogs off at the vet. During the drive from Greensboro to Raleigh, the sun was beginning to set. It was soothing to see the blur of the trees, mixing with the setting sun, as we traveled at a constant eighty-five miles per hour. We arrived at the airport in plenty of time to catch the flight. There's always been something oddly calming about taking off in a plane for me. When I used to get really anxious, air travel was always an oasis—I was being transported away from everything. I thought I might be able to read on the flight, but I couldn't concentrate. I kept seeing Rich and kept being reminded that I'd never see Rich again. I cried most of the flight. The only things that helped were Deana rubbing my back and looking out the window.

When we got off the plane, the airport seemed dark, like some of the fluorescent bulbs were out. All the restaurants and food kiosks were closed. Dad had taken a flight to Austin that was due to arrive ten minutes after Deana and I got in. We didn't know where his flight had connected and didn't know which flight was Dad's. We waited at the bottom of an escalator that passengers from arriving flights traveled down in order to exit the airport. As Dad was waiting for us on the top level, we were on the bottom. Dad remained on the top level for an hour. After watching multiple groups of people from multiple flights going down the escalator, we decided we must have missed him and caught a taxi to the hospital.

In the taxi, we passed broken-down bars with bright red and yellow Christmas lights out front, lights with big bulbs. I saw auto shops and body shops and vacated tin buildings. It looked like the underbelly of any major city. This was part of where Rich had lived. Even if he'd never seen it, this area represented, to me, a slice of his life. I knew almost nothing about his time in Austin. In the last six months, Rich had moved so many times from Austin to San Diego and back; I'd lost track of exactly where Rich lived. He'd moved back to Austin just five days before he shot himself.

The hospital was in the middle of the city, a big public hospital. As the cab approached it, people were waiting to get into a music club a few blocks away. Some had beards, unchanged clothes and jeans with holes in them—people who had seen a lot of life. There were also students and young professionals in tailored shirts. All were mingling around the same area. Rich had said Austin was a place where he fit in. It kept hitting me that at some other time, this trip would have been a lot of fun—flying down to visit Rich for a weekend in Austin.

The taxi driver dropped Deana and I off at the emergency room. We took our suitcase and backpacks from the taxi and walked in. It was a normal city ER. It was packed; some people would wait for at least five hours to be seen by a doctor. Many looked indigent, getting health care the only way they could. A man with a cloth around his hand, bright red seeping through, sat in a chair. Children in braids slept on their mothers' laps. An older man, unshaven, was chewing his gums and rubbing his head. One couple, the husband or boyfriend in a wheelchair, was waiting against a wall, seemingly distancing themselves from the scene.

I told a man at the front desk that we were looking for the intensive care unit. Maybe he guessed from our suitcases or our expressions that the situation was tough. He said, "The ICU? You walk down that hallway, and you see the 'Exit' sign?" And then he said, "Never mind, I'll walk you over there."

THANKSGIVING AND RESONATION

The Thanksgiving I'm remembering was years and years ago; Rich and I must have been about five and seven at the time. Each Thanksgiving until Rich was about eleven, we went to Granny and Gramps's house in Feasterville, Pennsylvania, about six and a half hours away. Six and a half hours—this was long before the introduction of portable movie devices; it was before CDs. Rich and I didn't have battery-powered tape players, and we didn't have access to the car radio. The only luxury we were afforded was an empty peanut butter jar that we could use in case we had to pee.

We needed entertainment. That's where our German shepherd, Olie, came in. Olie was the third oldest member of the Courtemanche family, beating me by about a year. Shortly after Mom and Dad got him, Olie jumped out the window of their moving car when he saw a squirrel. Dad didn't know what was going on until Olie had squeezed his whole torso out the back window, cracked specifically for Olie's comfort. Mom yelled when she saw what was happening; Dad hit the brakes, and Olie flew out of the car. He tumbled on the pavement, righted himself and ran off after the squirrel. As other cars on the two-way street stopped, Dad pulled the car to the side of the road, and first Mom, then Dad, jumped out to catch Olie. They finally got him a few minutes later under a tree the squirrel had run up.

Olie hadn't mellowed much since Mom and Dad first got him. About an hour before we finished packing Bessie, the family station wagon, Dad and Mom tried to give Olie a tranquilizer to keep him settled down for the long drive. Each Courtemanche car trip over four hours started about the same way.

"Betty," Dad called out to Mom on this particular trip, "could you come here? Olie's doing it again. He's not taking his pill."

"Did you put the cream cheese around it?"

"[Whisper] That goddam cream cheese. [Full volume] Yes, I put the cream cheese around it; he keeps spitting the pill out."

Dad tried the cream cheese method four or five times. No matter how deeply he buried the pill in the cream cheese, Olie found it and spit it out. From there, Mom and Dad moved on to the "tag team" approach. Dad grabbed Olie and put him in a headlock. Using both legs and his free arm, Dad tried to brace Olie's moving parts. It was hard to get all four of Olie's legs braced, so he'd scratch, claw and hop during the process. Once Mom and Dad agreed that Olie was restrained enough, Mom went to work putting the pill into Olie's mouth.

The logistical problem was this: Opening Olie's mouth was a two-handed job, but Mom needed one hand to hold the pill. To get around it, Mom improvised: She pried open Olie's mouth using both hands, then used her index finger and thumb (from the hand holding the top of Olie's snout) to pop the pill as far back in his mouth as she could get it. Then she quickly used both hands to close Olie's mouth, tilting his head up so that the pill might slide to the back of his throat—where instinctive swallowing action could take over.

We always had a moment of hesitation once Mom did her part: Did Olie swallow the pill or not? As soon as Dad released him, Olie used his tongue to search for the pill. It took a few seconds, but when he found it, he launched the pill across the kitchen floor in a loud cough. Olie won a lot of willpower battles with Mom and Dad, but the tranquilizer pill was a fight he could never win. Eventually, with enough swearing and enough wrestling moves, Dad and Mom got Olie to swallow the pill. Somewhere in his dog brain, though, Olie probably realized that the pill swallowing was just the first step in a much longer struggle—a struggle he'd inevitably win.

Pharmaceuticals affect different people differently. Benedryl, for example, makes some people anxious and energized but makes others tired. People with depression usually need to try multiple experiments with medications to find one or a combination of several that works effectively. Whether the tranquilizers simply weren't strong enough (even at the maximum dosage) or actually had the opposite effect on him, Olie usually became hyper after taking them.

With Bessie fully packed and the house double-checked against plugged in electrical appliances, open windows and unlocked doors, we prepared to leave. Rich and I sat in the backseat while Olie was cornered in the rear cargo area, behind the suitcases. Shortly after we backed out of the driveway, Dad said, "Olie, I'm not going to say it again, quiet down." Within a mile of the house, Olie managed to squeeze himself between the suitcases and into the backseat with Rich and me, barking and screeching as he did.

With his tail wagging and eyes beaming, he raced from one side of the backseat to the other, covering Rich and me with dog hairs and slobber. "Bark, bark . . . yelp, yelp . . . bark, bark, bark . . . yelp." Having listened to him for about five minutes, Dad stopped the car at the top of the hill near the Murphys' house. "Dammit, Olie, get in the back of the car!"

Either Rich or I opened the door (depending on whose side Olie was on), and Dad grabbed Olie. If he was really irate, Dad might paddle Olie on his rear. Dad was irate that day. A good smack or two just upped the ante on Olie's behavior. He was through the suitcases and into the backseat again before we hit twenty-five miles per hour.

Most dramas reach a point when the characters have to buck up and overcome adversity. The trip from Sherborn to Feasterville went through Connecticut, New York and New Jersey. New Jersey was the Courtemanche buck-up point. By New Jersey, the transformation of the cream cheese in Olie's stomach from solid to gas was complete, with him releasing it in short, invisible bursts. Rich and I couldn't tell if the noxious smell was the New Jersey oil refineries or Olie, but it didn't matter: We couldn't escape either. If we closed the window, we got more Olie; if we opened it, we got more New Jersey refineries.

If Olie had worn himself out at all in Connecticut or New York, the traffic jam in New Jersey gave him new life. "Bark, bark, yelp, yelp . . ." he started again. Dog hairs flew everywhere.

All the people traveling on I-95 on the day before Thanksgiving seemed to converge in New Jersey. The trucks were the worst. "This truck just keeps boxing me in," Dad said about some eighteen-wheeler right next to us, its tires eye level with the car windows. Dad followed up the comment with one for the wild animal in the cargo area: "Olie, for Christ's sake, quiet down!" Then returned his attention to driving: "Goddammit, I can't get into the other lane thanks to this goddam truck."

"Bob, the boys are in the backseat," Mom said.

"I know, Betty. I know."

Dad was silent for a little bit, but then the constant pounding of Olie's barking weakened his restraint, and he cursed another truck. If things got really out of hand—say we were approaching an exit and needed to get over and Olie was screeching and we couldn't get over and dog hairs got in everyone's mouth. Say all that was going on, and Dad was close to his breaking point even before it started; what would happen next was what happened on this trip. Dad rolled down his window and flung his hand out. He put it up high so Rich and I couldn't see what signal he made. Then we got a honk from a truck. Dad answered with more arm gyrations.

When the driver-side window first opened, Rich and I slid to the floor mats, where it was a little calmer. We stood a good chance of finding something interesting down there. It might be an old Bazooka gum wrapper, a pen or just a pebble or two for us to toss back and forth. This time, we tapped on the peanut butter jar, playing it like a miniature drum. When we finally got out of New Jersey, Dad noticed the noise. "Boys, *please*," he said, and we left the fort and returned to our seats.

All the houses on Granny and Gramps's street in Feasterville were three-bedroom ranches. Granny, Gramps and Uncle Ed could see everything that happened on the street from the bay window in their family room. By the time Bessie was parked in the driveway, they were standing outside the front door. Mommom and Poppop were there, too. When we got out of the car, everyone hugged each other, and the grandparents told Rich and me how much we'd grown.

As soon as that was done, the two of us went into the single-car garage. That garage always smelled good and was filled with interesting things: a push lawnmower, wooden fruit boxes, old-fashioned yard tools and worn-in baseball gloves. Above where the car parked were wood beams. During past explorations, Rich and I had found good stuff up there—old toys in boxes. We eyeballed the wood beams from the ground to see if more boxes might have been added on top of them. It didn't look like it, so we ran into the cellar, which had one large room holding a Ping-Pong table as well as two smaller rooms. One contained shelves of canned goods (we could usually find a few favorites—maybe Spaghettios), and the other had a workbench, offering a good opportunity to nail together a few stray pieces of wood.

By the time we ran back upstairs to the kitchen, Granny had mixed a pitcher of manhattans. We followed her as she carried the pitcher onto the covered porch where Gramps had lit a fire in the wood-burning stove. Once the adults finished a few manhattans, Rich and I had the rest of the house to ourselves. We climbed on top of the washing machine that was directly underneath the pull-down ladder to the attic, which we brought down so we could sneak into the attic and investigate. Granny and Gramps's house was magical. It seemed like if we searched enough, we'd find something really good—maybe a motorized go-cart Uncle Ed had forgotten about.

We rummaged around in the attic until Mom heard us up there and told us to come down. We sat on the porch, listening to the adults talking for a while, and then went to the garage and got a football out of the sporting goods box. We ran to the front yard and began a two-man football game, with the goal line marked by a flagpole and a tree.

After an hour, my pants are covered with grass stains, especially at the knees. I feel the wetness from the nighttime dew against my skin. A streetlight shines from the other side of the driveway, and stars fill the sky. We hear laughter and occasional dog barks from inside the house. It's fourth and one. I'm on offense, and Rich is playing defense. I approach the line of scrimmage and say, "Down, set, hut, hut . . . hike!" I score because I'm at the stage where I'm still bigger than Rich and can run with him holding on to me. Mom calls us in for dinner. Before going in, Rich and I toss the football a few more times under the streetlight.

No one paid much attention to what Rich and I ate at dinner, so we didn't eat a single vegetable. When it was time for us to go to bed—a deadline that was highly negotiable on nights when manhattans were consumed—Rich and I brushed our teeth in the only bathroom in the house. It was just the right size for the two of us. We used some of the mouthwash in the cupboard and got Uncle Ed's bucket of toiletries from under the sink, spraying his shaving cream into his shampoo container.

Each set of grandparents had space for only one extra bed, so Rich and I shared it. I found something comforting in knowing Rich was right there. After we were in bed for a while, I'd whisper, "Hey, Richard." If he didn't answer, I'd put my hand under his nose to make sure he was still breathing. Satisfied that he was, I could fall asleep.

Our family protocol was to arrive at Granny and Gramps's house on the day before Thanksgiving. Thanksgiving Day meant more football, more searching through the house and more attention from the grandparents. Granny and Gramps didn't have a formal dining room, so we ate dinner in the kitchen. The dinner table was right in the middle of the kitchen. Granny couldn't cook and have people around the table at the same time because the chairs would be in her way.

At dinner, Gramps sat at one end of the table and Dad sat at the other. Before the meal started, everyone bowed their heads. The Courtemanches

173

weren't a religious family in the traditional sense, but at Granny and Gramps's, we said a pre-Thanksgiving dinner prayer.

"Heavenly Father," Granny started, "thank you for bringing everyone together and for the bounty we are about to share. May Your blessing be on everyone at this table today and every day so that we may serve Your will. Please also bless Uncle Jimmy and Aunt Alice, who couldn't be here today. Thank you, dear Lord. Amen."

Once the prayer was done, dishes were passed, utensils rattled and everyone dug in. When we thought no one was looking, Rich and I ate pieces of the chocolate turkeys Granny set out on the table as decorations. It always felt complete sitting at Granny's table, with all the generations resonating in unison.

On Sunday, we went home to Sherborn along with all the other traveling families. Olie was a little calmer on the ride home, or Dad just didn't pay as much attention. For lunch, we ate turkey sandwiches packed by Granny.

Investigating the Mind Conference

Two months after Rich's July trading blowup, both Rich and I were back in Boston for a conference called *Investigating the Mind*. The Dalai Lama was going to be participating in the two-day event, which took place on September 13 and 14, 2003, at MIT. It was billed as a forum for learning about how the ideas of Buddhism meshed with Western psychiatry. Dad had bought two tickets for him and me and then another after he talked with Rich, and Rich wanted to go. Dad went all out for the conference. If it had been a sporting event, we'd have been in the luxury boxes.

On the first day, Rich guided us through the streets of Cambridge to find parking. Rich hadn't been back to MIT since he graduated. There weren't many cars at 7:30 am on a Saturday morning to compete with for spaces. We parked a short distance from the auditorium where the conference was being held. Rich, Dad and I walked in a clumsy threesome on the sidewalk, which we had to ourselves. Dew was still heavy on the grass that grew in neat squares on the campus, and the sun was shining through a morning haze.

Once we got to the auditorium, we weaved through the crowd and to our seats, which were in the middle section, about thirty rows back. The room probably held about a thousand people. The stage was set up like a debate with chairs on either side, facing each other. On one side, a group of Western physicians and researchers were talking among themselves. They looked excited in a kind of pure, childlike way.

On the other side were the Buddhist monks and scholars. Any discussion on that side was quiet and soft. Most sat peacefully with their hands folded in their laps. I was struck by their calm. It was a calm that gently radiated out—I'd never witnessed a group so perfectly at ease.

The crowd was decidedly pro-Buddhist. One of the physicians tried to snare the Dalai Lama in a logic trap about an hour into the conference. I forget the exact circumstance, but he employed a method whereby you get someone answering yes to a series of questions that ultimately undermines their side: "Okay, so you actually like ice cream! I thought you said you didn't care for dairy products?" The Dalai Lama peacefully went along with him without undermining his own perspective. The crowd jeered the physician, clapping loudly when Buddhist scholar Alan Wallace savaged the physician's tactics with the equivalent of a logical sledgehammer. The physician politely recanted on his approach in the afternoon session, and the crowd let out a forgiving applause.

Richard Gere and Goldie Hawn each attended the conference, and we ate in the same dining room as they did. Rich, Dad and I were also part of a group that got to shake hands with the Dalai Lama. I didn't get to shake. As the Dalai Lama entered the hand-shaking area, a crowd of about thirty jockeyed for position, little of the goodwill being promoted by the conference evident among the group. After her husband aggressively secured her a first-row position, a woman asked the Dalai Lama to bless a scarf that looked like a giant squirrel's tail filled with static electricity.

The ultimate question being considered by the participants of the conference was the degree to which people can control their own minds, by controlling that which they pay attention to. If you've never tried it before, try to think about nothing. Just shut down your mind, and let it go blank. If you tried, how did it work out? Were you able to stop your thoughts or did they just keep cascading, one after another? Though our minds are sometimes equated with who we are, they don't seem to be entirely under our control, often bouncing around from one thought or idea to another.

Have you ever noticed that the thought that typically catches your attention is the one that carries an emotional charge? Consider a shower first thing in the morning. There you are, lathering a bar of soap, when out of nowhere, a thought hits: "Tonight, I'm going to bed an hour earlier." After that, you'll have another, "Hmm, I wonder if it's too cold for a short-sleeve shirt today?" And finally, the anchor, the thought with a solid emotional tie . . . "That's right, I almost forgot; that son-of-a-bitch Henderson pissed me off in the meeting yesterday. Dammit, why did he do that? He's a jerk, that's why!" More than likely, Henderson consumes the bulk of your thoughts during the shower.

Getting better control over the mind's attention takes years of practice, but like weightlifting, you can see the results building on themselves right away. When we're stressed, our mind races in a fight-or-flight reaction. Our emotion system is on high-alert. It's providing feedback to our body that something needs to be done, but if we're in the office or the highway or a lot of other places, the stress simply builds up. There's no fight and no flight, only inertia. Meditation is a way to control the mind's response to stress. A common meditation technique is to pay attention to your breathing. By doing so, you can focus your mind, freeing yourself from the chaos of the fight-or-flight response.

About a week before the conference, Rich helped me out with my own disaster at Synchronic. There was a wholesale group of promotions—people getting raises and new titles, and I wasn't included. When I read about the promotions in a company-wide email, I was livid. I was ready to walk out, to quit on the spot. I sent Rich an email, telling him about the situation. He sent me the following back:

From: Richard Courtemanche
Sent: Wednesday, September 03, 2003
To: Ted Courtemanche
Subject: Re:

ok. dont quit at end of the day. just give yourself a night to think about it. i know how it feels to want so bad to walk out the door and all but the fact is it wont matter, it will only limit your options.

take a xanax if you have em at work. just try to get the anxiety under control. take 2 or whatever it takes. dont let your body get into knots so bad that it starts crushing you. if you can (i know i never can... but) take a walk, drive whatever... give me a call later if you can. or whenever you want. we will talk about it. hang in there. call when you can. R

Nietzsche wrote, "Some cannot loosen their own chains and can nevertheless redeem their friends." Rich's email defused my state. It didn't solve it, but it took away some of its power.

At the conference, attention was defined as "the capacity to selectively process information available to the mind." Sometimes when we're conscious of our attention, we can do the selecting. Other times, when we're thinking about a Henderson or overcome by our emotions, the selection is done for us.

After the conference was over on Sunday, Rich, Dad and I walked as fast as we could back to the car. We were focused on getting back to Dad's house for the 4:00 pm Patriots game. We got caught up in traffic on Massachusetts Avenue. Rich and I beat up Dad for his poor driving skills. We told him he needed to be quicker getting into the moving lanes. We said he needed to really narrow his attention. "You're a driving laser beam," we told him. He laughed and gave up his spot behind the wheel. Rich took over, and then we fired away at Rich. We got back to Dad's house about halfway through the first quarter, and we watched the Pats thrash the Philadelphia Eagles for the next three hours.

A few days after the conference, Rich emailed Mom, Dad and me separately—each email had the same message.

From: Richard Courtemanche
Sent: Thursday, September 18, 2003 11:22 AM
To: Ted Courtemanche
Subject:

its the 18th of september. since being back [in San Diego] i have lost money. and... well, i am sorry guys, but i am about to give up. i suppose if i do give up i will add to this. but let me explain some stuff.

176

the conference this weekend was wonderful... truly wonderful. and yet, i come back home and nothing has changed. my need for money, why?? where does this come from? what drives it? material objects? maybe. but outside of my car, what do i really care about materially? a sign of worth? i dont know. i just dont know. but it is there. without a doubt it is there.

i am not crying now. not even... well, i am sort of in shock. but not collapsing as i used too. why? the medicine? Absolutely... but am i a little closer to accepting death? maybe. i sit with a shotgun barrel in my mouth... why? what do i derive from that?

its no ones fault. i know that. definitely no one around me is to blame. and i dont blame myself either. that is very important. i dont blame myself. i dont hate myself. i am no longer violent towards myself. the cutting is not about punishment, its about release. i guess thats why a shotgun is so appealing (apologies to those reading this, it must be difficult to read that last line, but bear with me). a shotgun blast will be (will it? would it?) the ultimate release. no single cut from a knife but an ending with finality.

getting much closer... i think? am i? but i wont do it here. no way. i will go somewhere by myself. peaceful. call my loved ones. and then call 911. it is all surprisingly crisp to me. why? zatta will take the pups to Arizona [where the breeder lived]. i ask 2 things. please cremate my body and please put my locket with my remains. keep them or spread them. either is fine. just keep the locket with me. please

I didn't know what to say. I just wrote what came to mind.

From: Ted Courtemanche
Sent: Thursday, September 18, 2003 11:59 AM
To: Richard Courtemanche
Subject: Re:

Okay... Okay... Okay. Oh, Rich, I feel the same way sometimes. Then, the clouds clear and it all seems to be worthwhile. I do know this - that whether to move on or not is a choice. By laying out what you've laid out, you're paving the way for the time when it will happen. You're taking baby steps towards the event. In a sense, justifying it. I wish I could take you from San Diego, take you from the pain, take you from the trading, take you to some mountain where we could sit together, just you and me, and consider the senselessness of it all. Where we could see that the pain that we feel is isolated to a point in time, to a situation in time and that there are birds, trees, winds and waters that move about, doing their thing, despite it all. We could see together that they know the secret, and they do it every day. That we are of value just because we're here. Call me if the pain gets unbearable, call me. Love, T

A few hours later, Rich sent an email telling Mom, Dad and me that he'd had a horrible two days of trading and that he was stopping. He said he was collapsing from it. He ended his email with the following paragraph:

please dont feel the need to respond. one thing that troubles me is i feel people get sick of hearing the same old complaints from me. again and again and again. thats why i always loved alcohol. it offers relief and doesnt ask a fuckin thing in return. of course it does take something in return. i know that. but... well, i am rambling. alas, waiting for drugs to kick in that can help this fuckin mind of mine to JUST FUCKING STOP!!!

your son and brother. R

I didn't know anything about "kindling," about ongoing stress permanently debilitating someone with bipolar disorder. I just knew his moods swung with the fortunes of his trading. It was a relief that he was stopping—even if just briefly.

The night of September 18, Rich called me. The phone rang at about 10:00 pm, and I had a feeling it was him. I picked up the call. He wasn't drunk. He had a question he needed to ask.

"T, could you loan me $25,000? I can't go to Dad for it. Not now."

My financial situation had changed some in the last year. Synchronic had been purchased in late 2002, making my stock options liquid. Before I even thought about my response, I said, "Yes, I can loan you the money." I wasn't aware of being aware. I was in the moment. The words came out of my mouth without filter. Rich told me my loan would be secured by his M5.

A little over a month later, Rich sent out another update.

From: Richard Courtemanche
Sent: Tuesday, October 28, 2003
To: T Home; Mom; Dad
Subject:

hi all. i know its been a while since i updated you, been a tough time recently. as far as the bipolar goes, my doctor and i are now trying a new mix of drugs. the depakote, even at its maximum dosage, has started to fail me. by fail me, i guess i mean that mood swings have been greater and alcohol is next to impossible for me to resist. the effexor doesnt seem to be having much of an impact either. my doctor continues to be amazed at how quickly i metabolize the drugs i am given. we monitor drug levels in the blood through weekly blood tests. depression is my big problem, so now i am on a new mood stabilizer called lamictal. i am in some ways as confused and bewildered as ever with this, but am hoping the new drugs help out some.

as for my knees [which tended to ache from the psoriatic arthritis], well, they are still ok, but the psoriasis has come back on my skin. i have to see my doctor again about that as its not a good sign.

other than that, things are ok. the dogs are wonderful, daisy has finally learned how to swim. she swam in the ocean. she loves it now and poor zack feels a bit left out. maybe someday he will take the plunge.
only other note is i am selling my car. its the prudent thing to do. i was having

trouble with the decision but my doctor helped me see it as a sign of strength that i can make that decision. i guess he is right, but still tough.

i will try to be better at updating. problem is i like to send you hopeful messages. lately i just havent been feeling that way.

dont ever feel sorry for me, though. i dont think u do, but i have to deal with the cards i am dealt just like everybody else.

love r

Treatment for bipolar disorder is centered on medications, but it can't end there. It's got to be more all-encompassing—medications are only one part. So many other things have an impact on mental health: relationships, day-to-day circumstances, routines and careers—all the things we spend the bulk of our time engaged in. If those other things are harmful, if they initiate the very states of mind that the drugs are intended to prevent, they can overpower the rest of the treatment plan. Even with all the fire engines in town on the scene, some fires burn on, especially if they're being stoked by the fuel that gave them life in the first place. Three days after his October update, Rich told everyone he was stopping his medications because of the side effects. He said he would "rather just suffer the ups and downs without them."

The low point in his emails came two weeks later. He wrote, "i am a fucking loser at everything i do. I am an embarrassment to everyone." His message was laced with expletives. He ended it with:

it doesnt matter if i am medicated or not. trading or not. i slice my body with a knife in a desperate attempt to stop my mental pain. but it never fucking stops. no medicine, no alcohol, nothing stops it. and i let it beat me. every single day i let it beat me.

i am going to go to sleep and pray to whoever fucking God is to grant me sanity. but i know it will never come. i will write you later. i am so fucking tortured

After all the emailing Rich and I had done, all the emotional effort we'd expended, Rich's latest email didn't move me, the same way sirens stop affecting longtime city dwellers. It just seemed like more of the same. Two days later, Rich talked to me about my work situation again. As always, his advice was right on. Life moved forward. One of Rich's favorite song lines was from "Jungleland" by Bruce Springsteen: "And the poets down here don't write nothing at all, they just sit back and let it all be." About a year after the *Investigating the Mind* conference, Rich was considering buying a house for almost $1 million along the Colorado River in Austin.

❧ CHAPTER EIGHT ❧

Mystic shadow, bending near me,
Who art thou?
Whence come ye?
And—tell me—is it fair
Or is the truth bitter as eaten fire?
—Stephen Crane

RANGELEY

In 1974, I started kindergarten at Pine Hill School in Sherborn. My teacher was Mrs. Matkins. This was the year I got my first bicycle and I learned how to ride it. That year for vacation we went to Rangeley, Maine. It was nice there but the water was very cold.
Richard Courtemanche
School Writing Assignment, September 20, 1982

Rangeley? That's going pretty far back. Rich and I were about four and six at the time. I can't remember Rich's first bicycle. Was it the red one? Or did he get a hand-me-down bike from me, the brown one with the banana seat that I once flew through the handle bars on? The present moment is gone before we can say, "That's the present moment." The present moment—the one we're supposed to spend all our time in—is a ghost. We can't catch it, can't put our arms around it, can't do anything with it, except experience it.

All our memories are made from past-present moments. We may keep the memories intact, but we can misplace the true chronology of any particular memory. Without the aid of Rich's 1982 writing assignment, I wouldn't have had any idea when he started riding a bike. I could have put bike scenes at the wrong moment in Time-Earth. The scene would stay the same, but it wouldn't be in the right order.

We can't remember the vast majority of our past-present moments. Most come and go, never to be seen or heard from again. This life we pine for—that we hope will last eternally—is largely a series of forgotten past-present moments. From my own grab bag of memories, I can see the following scene from our 1974 family vacation to Rangeley:

Rich and I are running down a long, wooden walkway to the cabin. The walkway and the cabin are stained deep reddish-brown. I lose my balance. After banging my knee on something sticking out of a board, I take a few more tumbles and fall off the walkway, onto the ground a foot or two below. There are pine needles everywhere, and sunlight is cascading through the trees and the clouds. Rich helps me get up. Enough sun has hit the walkway that it's hot, singeing my bare legs as I sit on it. I use my hands to close the cut on my knee, and I can see water on the lake shimmering through the trees. The scene fades out. I've still got a scar on my kneecap from the fall.

Aside from the image of the wipeout and the scar, the other lasting memento from Rangeley is a little pine tree. Rich and I loved trees. In the Rangeley woods, we found one we just couldn't bear to leave, so Dad agreed to dig it up. It looked like a little Christmas tree.

We decided to plant it near the side of the house in Sherborn, along the route that Rich and I walked each morning to get to the school bus. It made a perfect end-zone marker for the two-man football games Rich and I used to play. The tree was resilient. We'd crash into it, get cut up, and the tree would bounce back. As Rich and I got older, we stopped playing our two-man football games, and the pine tree was left to grow in peace.

Eventually, Mom and Dad sold the house. I don't know if the tree is still there or not. If it is, I'm sure it's grown. I'd be able to recognize it based on its placement in the yard, but if someone dug it up and moved it, I wouldn't be able to recognize it. Even now, in my memory, its location among the images of the Sherborn yard is my primary means of identification. No matter, it still serves as a reference point for the trip we took to Rangeley back when Rich started kindergarten. The little tree, or its image, is a link to my childhood and Rich.

House Hunting and Oneness

Rich and I were emailing about the Red Sox. They'd just rallied from three games down against the Yankees to bring the 2004 American League Championship Series to three games to two. Rich and Sharon had gone to Austin at the same time.

From: Rich Courtemanche
Sent: Tuesday, October 19, 2004 7:24 AM
To: Ted Courtemanche
Subject:

hey T. best sign i saw on tv was sox fan with "every time i think i am out they drag me back in." exactly how i feel. but at least they made it competitive... amazing.

austin was really nice. very refined downtown, people were unbelievably friendly. and every person we met said austin was only place in texas they would live. housing is certainly cheaper than san diego, which is nice. the colorado river runs right through the city, and we found a property that would be interesting. unfortunately, its expensive. but its on the river, boat dock and everything. its got these giant... i mean 14 feet around trees on property. i felt so peaceful standing there by the bank of river. we might toss a bid in... not sure. it goes for 975k, and house needs to be completely done over. but it has pool, and its the location. it is really amazing. if we got it (might start a bid at 750K), then we would remodel of course over years. it would be expensive. but its the opportunity to own a dream home (its not big, 2600 sq ft) in 5 years after all fixed up. interesting anyway.

austin will be hot in summer, no doubt. but river gives nice breeze which helps. anyway, if u want the link to see house i will send it. i hope u guys had a great weekend. r

I asked for the link, and Rich sent it along. He also sent links for a few other houses he was looking at in Austin. I emailed back.

From: Ted Courtemanche
Sent: Tuesday, October 19, 2004 10:13 AM
To: Rich Courtemanche
Subject: Re: Lake Fronts

Rich, these houses look really nice! I'm assuming that trading is going pretty well? T

A few hours later, Rich sent a reply.

From: Rich Courtemanche
Sent: Tuesday, October 19, 2004 1:24 PM
To: Ted Courtemanche
Subject: Re: Lake Fronts you saw

funny. sometimes i dont know how i survived last year. but i did. and by the way. i never would have without u and ur support. but last year i lost 450k. this year i am on track to have best year ever. over 800k so far. crazy business. i started w/23k in my account this year. got some lucky breaks, but as buffett would say, rather be lucky than good. i am anxious to buy a house to put some capital into something tangible. i will keep u posted, but i think u would love visiting austin. trails and hiking galore. the colorado river makes the whole city lush green. its amazing.

sharon changing a lot too. last fall i used to spend hours with a shotgun barrel in my mouth. sad... but i did, and its part of me. with her help, we recently turned the gun into the police and threw away the shotgun rounds. it actually scared me. like it took away an option, but at the same time, i guess it let myself know that i would make it.

I'd heard only tidbits about how Rich's trading was going since I'd loaned him $25,000 in September 2003—nothing to indicate he was up close to a million bucks. In one fell swoop, it seemed like Rich was back on top of the trading world. I was relieved to hear that he'd gotten rid of his shotgun; as always, it made me think he was leaving his depressions behind.

Five months before Rich told me about the house hunting in Austin, he moved in with Sharon in San Diego—in the middle of May 2004. He'd only been dating her for about three months. I heard the news through Mom, and when I did, I assumed his trading wasn't going well, that moving in with Sharon was really just a way to save money. I tended to assume most of Rich's actions were manifestations of his trading. Then he told me about his new Harley-Davidson motorcycle in an email. He said he liked riding it more than driving the M5—I figured things couldn't be going too badly if he could afford a Harley.

Two weeks after he moved in with Sharon, Rich sent me one of his off-the-wall emails.

From: Rich Courtemanche
Sent: Monday, May 24, 2004
To: Ted Courtemanche
Subject:

hey T... please answer with all honesty. i can accept whatever. if i choose to leave s.d., could the dogs and i stay with you temporarily? i would only bring my pc and some clothes and the dogs. i would pay rent and bills.

i may never mention this again. i may ask to stay with you next week. i dont know. i just wanted to ask. thanks. r

I sent an email back telling him that he could move in if he needed to. A couple of hours later, Rich told me about a recurring dream he used to have:

random thought... about two years ago, trading was going real well. i started to have a recurring dream. maybe one or two times a week. i would be on the ground, watching a plane take off. the plane would start to climb too quickly and then stall. a stall for a plane is very hard to recover from, the engines still work but the "lift" under the wings is gone. u may know what i am talking about. anyway, i would watch as the plane fell out of the sky and crashed. then i would wake up. i had this dream over 50 times. i sometimes wonder if somehow i knew in my dream that i was watching myself... taking off too high, only to crash with trading. interesting. anyway, i havent had that dream since my collapse last july. who knows... funny how the mind works.

The year—2004—had been filled with the usual ups and downs. On January 1, 2004, I found a small box sitting by the front door of my townhouse. It was addressed from San Diego. I opened it, and Rich's Rolex was inside. He included a note that said, "This watch used to mean the world to me. I haven't worn it in months." I put the watch in a drawer in my bedside dresser and told Rich it would be there for him if he ever wanted it back.

The same day he sent the watch, he told me that his health insurance company had canceled his policy. Rich hadn't told them about the psoriatic arthritis when he applied for his policy, and now they were treating it as a preexisting condition. What surely happened is that someone at the company saw his Remicade expenses at $2,000 a pop and looked into it. I thought I might be able to find an out in the paperwork he signed that would allow him to maintain his coverage. I couldn't. After he lost his health insurance, Rich negotiated payments for Remicade directly with his physician. He bought most of his other medications online.

In the middle of January, Rich started drinking again. He wrote to me, "i dont believe there is a better remedy for heartache than your favorite drink (mine, sapphire and tonic) and hank williams jr, despite his monday nite football atrocities." From that point forward, I never heard mention of the locket with Girard's picture again.

Rich was still working on his bipolar disorder. He tried going to a bipolar disorder support group. Part of a group email he sent to Mom, Dad and me in February described his experience:

> i have been going (well, only twice) to a weekly bipolar support group. its been interesting. its very highly recommended, but i just dont feel its right for me. its great if you feel like crap and want some support, but at other times... well, a lot of it centers on the fact that you arent alone, others suffer too. well, i get that. second, the people seem to focus only on drug remedies. they seemed almost alarmed when i told them i was trying to find ways (meditation, exercise) to get through this without drugs. but even more amazing, we stop for smoke breaks and they serve krispy kreme donuts! i know first hand that when i eat like crap i feel way worse. so in some ways i applaud them for looking for help, but i just dont know if its the right path (drug only) esp for me. last nite there was a skinny 18 year old kid who wanted to find new drugs to calm him down and everyone mentioned their favorites. i thought, "geez... go run around or something..." lord knows its hard to do when you feel like crap, but i am feeling a lot better now off the drugs then on. simple as that. i still have my down days, but so do we all.

The group setting wasn't working for Rich. It didn't surprise me. He was never comfortable in it—even if the group had been made up of all Riches, he probably wouldn't have liked it; he'd rather be off on his own. That he still wasn't taking any bipolar disorder medications hit me as more of an afterthought. The main sense I got from the email was that Rich was doing better. It reinforced in me a belief in his ability to cure himself.

By July of 2004, Rich made the last payment on the $25,000 I'd loaned to him. He'd been paying it off in $5,000 chunks. Two months after he paid off the loan, he told me he was starting to look at rings for Sharon. I hadn't known he was that serious. Yes, he was living with Sharon, but he'd lived with Zatta, too. The ring shopping wasn't sitting well with him. He was having nightmares about being married. At the beginning of October, with the ring shopping going in earnest, Rich asked if I'd mind sending the Rolex back to him. He was going to pawn it for a ring for Sharon—making the fact that he was considering bidding $750,000 on a house perplexing.

The day after Rich told me he'd earned over $800,000 in 2004, he sent another update.

From: Rich Courtemanche
Sent: Wednesday, October 20, 2004 8:11 AM
To: Ted Courtemanche
Subject:

i find it somewhat ironic that yesterday i told u how i had made so much... well, last nite i had huge position go against me. lost 300k.

still been a good year. but i didnt handle it well. i broke my hand putting it through the tv. luckily sharon has some nurse friend who helped me out as i dont have insurance... its not a bad break, tv is gone though. i know there is a lesson in here somewhere. i will make it though. i know i will get through this.

When should you tell someone to stop what they're doing? And how do you do it? My stomach dropped when he told me that he'd lost $300,000. I sent the following email back to Rich.

From: Ted Courtemanche
Sent: Wednesday, October 20, 2004 9:44 AM
To: Rich Courtemanche
Subject: Re:

I'm really sorry to hear that. I don't know, maybe there was a reason I asked how the trading was going yesterday.

I just want to give you some of my own observations - no problem if you find no sense in them at all. I included in the email yesterday but removed the following: the pattern seems to be you go up big, take a big hit, go up bigger than you were before and take a big hit.

That is, back in London, you were up about 125K, then 9/11 came and it was a pretty big hit - not crushing but pretty big from what I remember. You built it back up to over 600k and then took a series of hits culminating in the really bad one back in 2003. Then you built it back up well beyond where you were before and took a hit last night.

There's no question you're extremely talented at this. It seems like the key is taking the setbacks (which are inevitable) and not feeling like you've got to get it back too quickly. You will get it back.

What amazes me is how many times you've taken <30K and built it to a lot of money! It's almost as if you're really comfortable with the prospect of building up <30K. You've done it enough times that it's your sweet spot - you just know you can do it.

You will get this latest one back. The only question is how you go about it and what kind of pressure you put on yourself in terms of time to get it back.

From what I've observed, you could drop the 500K you have into savings, start with 20K now and get that up some time next year to above the 800K mark. I'm not sure if this helps or not. I hope it does. Even if it doesn't, you'll be sitting on a big pot of money again some time in the future - no question.

Peace,
T

In response, Rich said I was right and that he appreciated hearing it. He also told me to enjoy the Red Sox game that night. Not too long after Rich went through the 2004 Austin setback, he wrote an all-family email:

From: Richard Courtemanche
Sent: Tuesday, November 02, 2004
To: Betty Courtemanche; Bob Courtemanche; Ted Courtemanche
Subject:

sharon today, after hearing me throw my chair against the wall once again, simply came to me and told me she was tired. tired of everything i put her through. we talked. i am still hopeful it will work out. but she has been through much. 9 days ago i asked her to take my life. she has seen me cut myself, put my fist through walls, doors, my tv. She has seen me come home drunk as can be, barely able to stand, yet i had been driving. in short, she has witnessed many of the same things you all have been forced to deal with. and so let me say to you what i said to her. i am sorry. i know you all realize i dont do these things to hurt you. but i know they do. i know my emails, like this one, will sadden you. and i am sorry. i know you realize as bad as you suffer, my suffering is probably worse. i am seeing a hypnotist today. perhaps he can help. i am not giving up yet. not yet.

love, richard

About three weeks later on the day before Thanksgiving, Rich sent an email asking me if he could borrow $25,000. It hit me like a punch in the gut. I didn't know what to do. When I'd loaned him the money after the 2003 blowup, I hadn't asked for payback at any certain date. The thing that chafed me, though, was that during the same time, he'd purchased a $20,000 Harley-Davidson. I never told him that bothered me.

With the request for more money, I didn't say, "Rich, the last time I did this, you bought a Harley before you repaid me everything." I didn't say, "Rich, this is too much, time to cool out for a while." Instead, I waffled for five days without talking to him once. Should I loan him the money? Should I not? I went back and forth.

I should do it because he's my brother. . . . If Rich treated it like a business, he wouldn't be in this situation—I shouldn't do it. . . . I should do it because I'm the one who pumped him up after his latest downturn. . . . He's willing to risk it all every time, that's just too risky—I shouldn't do it.

On the Monday after Thanksgiving, I sent my reply.

From: Ted Courtemanche
Sent: Monday, November 29, 2004 10:40 AM
To: Richard Courtemanche
Subject: Re:

Hey Rich, it's been a busy morning - sorry for not getting back to you earlier. Hope the Thanksgiving was good. Heard from Mom that you've got an apartment in Austin, sounds exciting.

This isn't the greatest time for me from an available cash perspective. I've just about picked out a ring for Deana, and I'll be fronting the tab for the wedding. Plus, we're starting to look at houses - basically, we've outgrown my townhouse. If you can get by or can figure out another option, it would be better for me.

Let me know,
T

William Least Heatmoon wrote in *Blue Highways*, "Caring breaks before the man if he can only wait it out." I've always taken comfort from that quote. In the case of bipolar disorder, though, each stress, each trade gone bad and each relationship turned sour is a permanent cut. It's another infusion of arsenic. The effects are cumulative—that's what kindling is all about. I wish now I'd had some way to rip Rich away from his trading. I wish I'd been able to communicate to him that he was of value to me and everyone else—most importantly, to Rich himself—because he was Rich, communicated it in a way that he could hear.

Maybe Rich himself couldn't have gone any other career path. Maybe any other path he'd have chosen would involve the kind of risk that can tear a person apart. In *The Americas: The Democratic Experience*, Daniel Boorstin wrote about the Old West. He described the people who settled it as "go-getters." They were risk takers. Boorstin quoted one of them, Charles Goodnight, who said, "Most of the time we were solitary adventurers in a great land as fresh and new as a spring morning, and we were free and full of the zest of darers." They sought their fortunes in cattle, land, gold and oil. They could lose it all, build it back up and lose it again. In that vast, open space, they could bay at the moon and start over. There's a balancing act any go-getter needs to walk if he or she is to avoid burning up.

This is how Rich responded when I told him it would be better for me if he looked for another option.

From: Richard Courtemanche
Sent: Monday, November 29, 2004 1:56 PM
To: Ted Courtemanche
Subject: Re:

no worries at all T. i will be fine. congrats on the big plans. thats fantastic. keep me posted and glad u guys had a nice thanksgiving. r

The next time Rich and I spoke was around Christmas—when Rich heard from Mom that Deana and I were engaged. I'd meant to call him right after I proposed to Deana but got caught up in other things. A couple hours after I told Mom and Dad, Rich called to tell me congratulations. It wasn't until the middle of January 2005—when I told him Deana and I had bought a house— that we emailed again. He sent a quick note to let me know he was happy for us. We sent a few emails back and forth over the next couple months, mainly sports stuff, before Rich sent the all-family email in March telling us that he was going to ask Sharon to move out of their apartment in Austin.

From: Richard Courtemanche
Sent: Wednesday, March 16, 2005
To: Mom; Dad; Ted Courtemanche
Subject:

hi all. as soon as she gets home (at gym now) i will be asking sharon to leave. i will explain it to you later if u want. but i guess my simple (albeit extremely selfish) explanation is that i am sick of hurting her. i cut myself quite often. sometimes badly. i can no longer endure her seeing it. i am hopeful she will hate me. at least that way she might forget she knew me sooner rather than later. we have both been in quite a bit of pain in this relationship. not all my fault, not all hers. but pain nonetheless. i wish i could try harder for her. but i am reminded of a quote from al pacino in "scent of a woman." in a speech he gives he says, "i have always known the right path to take. without exception, i knew. but i never took it. because it was too damn hard." well, i know the right path is to try harder. to work on my anger, to accept myself for who i am. to be gentle on myself. but you know what... it is too damn hard to do that. its so much easier to blame myself. to hate myself. so i cut myself and i drink and i push away sharon.

cest la vie i suppose. with love. r

Two days later, Rich let us know that Sharon was staying but that he told her he could no longer promise that he wouldn't take his life. If he'd sent those two March 2005 emails back in July 2003 after his trading crash, I'm sure I would have spent hours crafting responses. I sent only one response to his latest flurry—and only in response to the email in which he told us he was asking Sharon to leave.

I emailed, "Rich, hope things went okay. Good luck. T."

For the rest of 2005, Rich lived his life in Austin and San Diego, and I lived mine in Greensboro. We drifted. We'd drifted before. Deana and I were planning the wedding; work was hectic: It was a busy time. The good news was that outside of the March emails, life seemed to be going okay for Rich. In May, he asked if I wanted a bachelor party. The day before he asked, I ruptured my Achilles tendon playing softball. I told Rich we'd play the bachelor party by ear, "maybe something small." We never had one.

A few weeks before Deana and I got married, I got the real scoop on how his trading was going. Rich asked if I'd mind if he didn't send a gift—he'd lost money ten out of the last eleven months. I emailed back to him, "Don't worry about a wedding present! Just looking forward to seeing you."

When he arrived for the rehearsal party the day before the wedding, I forgot all about his trading issues, all about his bipolar disorder, all about his psoriatic arthritis—there were no signs of them. As soon as I saw him, an awareness resonated in me: Rich was here with me for my big day. My friends gawked at how big he was; they hadn't seen him since he'd gotten out of the marines more than ten years before. He was as vibrant, as full of life, as I'd ever seen him. I was thrilled he was in Greensboro, seeing where I'd been living all these years.

Toward the end of the rehearsal party, Rich and I sat at the bar, next to each other. As we did, we shared a bourbon together—did I mention that? And did I say that as we sat next to each other, I wasn't aware of anything but the flowing oneness of it all?

MAGIC SHOW, PRAYER AND DESCARTES

Rich and I once tried to put on a magic show. This was in the same general time period as the Halloween when Rich was the Easter Bunny. I wore my Dracula cape, and Rich wore his rabbit costume (indicative of what I was going to pull from the baseball hat sitting on the coffee table). I didn't know how magicians pulled rabbits from hats, but I knew they typically said, "Abracadabra." As Mom and Dad, the two-person audience, sat on the sofa, I got ready to do the trick.

"Abracadabra," I said, and not one rabbit appeared in the hat. I said it again, this time with arm waving, nothing. Rich repeated it (though this shouldn't have carried the same weight, as he was in a rabbit costume and I had the magician's cape), still nothing.

"Oh, you pulled a rabbit, and there he is," Mom said, clapping and pointing at Rich.

I wasn't just upset that a real rabbit hadn't appeared; I was offended. Come on! I said the magic words. I did what magicians are supposed to do—and still no rabbit appeared. As emotional as I got, it made no difference. In his costume,

Rich was the closest thing to a rabbit in the room. The reality, of course, is that pulling a rabbit from a hat is a logical trick. There's a rabbit sitting around somewhere; there's a false bottom somewhere, and when you do all the things you're supposed to do, each in the right order, you can complete the trick known as "pulling a rabbit from a hat."

❖ ❖ ❖

I expected Rich's bipolar disorder to go away. I expected the ups and downs he faced, ups and downs that got progressively worse over time, to magically settle down. In the last chapter, I wrote about Thanksgiving dinners at Granny and Gramps's—how we used to say a prayer before the meal. One of the primary forms of prayer is petitionary prayer. It's asking God for help in the expectation that God will reach into our lives and intervene directly. It's a hope for magic. When I was in Little League, I regularly sought God for help when I was at bat. Most of the time, He didn't deliver. Physicist Chet Raymo wrote in his book *Natural Prayers*, "We were taught that God hears and answers prayers; a careful examination of the evidence reveals no compelling measure of response."

In our culture, objects are routinely mistaken as sources of happiness and satisfaction. "I want the corner office." Why? "Because in addition to money and the hope that other people will admire me, it will make me feel good about myself." If worried about long enough, the corner office comes to be mistaken as the primary vehicle for the feeling. Without the corner office, the desirer might feel less complete, unworthy, possibly slipping into a depression. The corner office was always just that: a corner office—*an object*. The desirer attached to it emotional significance, building it up and building it up until it became a kind of living thing. It never was. There were all kinds of vehicles for the feeling he or she was after, but the desirer blocked them out for the one prize. The corner office, through a logical but mostly unconscious process, became the instrument for the person's own self-approval.

The irony with petitionary prayer is that the object being prayed for is not the real prize. This point gets entirely lost. Thinking the object is the prize is why I used to rail silently at God for not providing me what I asked for (the railing would be followed by guilt and worries of eternal damnation). The challenge is to identify the reason that object is being prayed for—what's the true goal? In considering why he or she is asking for something, the person praying seeks to get beyond the object, whatever it is, and to the meaning the object provides for him or her. It's in transcending the object that the person has an opportunity to experience a connection to the eternal. That's the real goal. It's an opportunity to experience the Divine.

Petitionary prayer isn't the only kind of prayer. Praying techniques are as varied as the religions that teach them. One of the most sacred prayers within the Catholic Church is the Rosary. By ritualistically repeating *Our Father, Hail Mary* and *Glory Be* prayers, the Catholic faithful are, like a Buddhist monk, focusing their thoughts. They're blocking out all the other noise flying around in their heads. The focus is intended to open them to communion with God. Within Eastern Orthodox Christianity, the second largest Christian order in the world (second only to Catholicism), the faithful practice forms of *hesychasm*—a technique strikingly like meditation. Hesychasts rely on prayers, chants, breathing techniques and bodily postures to escape the control of their senses. The goal is to transcend earthly concerns and actually invoke Jesus Christ.

Joseph Campbell described religious orders as spokes on a wheel. On the outer rim, the spokes appear individualized; there's one spoke and then another and then another. On the inside, though, each spoke comes to the same center. At the *Investigating the Mind* conference Rich, Dad and I attended, the participants talked about "judgment." Each day, we unconsciously pass value judgments on the world around us. It's through this practice that we mistakenly start to ascribe things the power to make us happy or sad. For Buddhists, the remedy starts with awareness. A Buddhist's beginning awareness is not unlike what a person offering a petitionary prayer feels when struck suddenly by the deeper meaning of his or her request. For Buddhists, this awareness is the first step in pulling back the mind from all the objects it has managed to attach itself to. Awareness is not about ignoring the attachments; it's seeing them for what they are and then letting them go—those objects are just vehicles for certain states of mind. The concept of "releasing attachment" is not unique to Buddhism. Theologian William Adams Brown wrote, "Prayer, to be effective, requires detachment."

One of the ways to cultivate awareness and release attachment in the Buddhist tradition is through meditation. As with prayer, meditation techniques run the gamut. Some believers prescribe certain ways of crossing your legs, holding your hands, positioning your arms, breathing, keeping your eyes open or closed. The "spokes on a wheel" analogy applies equally to meditation techniques. All of them are driving toward one core goal. Sogyal Rinpoche describes it as "bringing the mind home." A Buddhist monk meditating is working to shed thought, to go to the place between thoughts. Evagrius Pontus, a fourth-century Christian monk, similarly believed, "prayer means the shedding of thought." Prayer and meditation, on closer inspection, start to sound like two words describing similar, if not identical, processes.

Where a person in prayer is seeking communion with God, a meditator is seeking what has been called "pure awareness." It's a state that's said to transcend both life and death. People who pray regularly and those who meditate (and those who practice both) describe feelings of calmness, acceptance and energy during and after their practice. One of the problems with being on the outer rim of the wheel is that the spokes can actually look different. Is there one best way to get to God or pure awareness? William James once rhetorically asked, "Is the existence of so many religious types and sects and creeds regrettable?" His answer was no. For James, we couldn't possibly expect one path only to salvation: "No two of us have identical difficulties, nor should we be expected to work out identical solutions."

When we were living with Mom in Natick, Rich and I used to listen to motivational tapes. We had one of Brian Tracy's (our preferred motivational speaker at the time) earliest tapes: We called it "BT Raw." Some of his tapes sounded to us a little overrehearsed, like he was speaking canned words into a microphone with his hair perfectly combed. In BT Raw, it sounded like you were sitting next to him having an unscripted conversation. One of his mantras was: "Tell yourself that you like yourself." Say, "I like myself, I like myself, I like myself." Neurologically, saying "I like myself" over and over is like repeating the Rosary. It's a construction of new neural pathways that the repeater can go to without thinking—a new emotional response for the person, a kind of habit.

From a religious service perspective, we saw in Chapter Seven that the critical element for mental health is not the creed or type of service or denomination. It doesn't matter if it's Christian, Islamic or Judaic—the saving grace is not in the name or in the particular rituals. Not surprisingly, the benefits of prayer and meditation are not tied to which God or Higher Power is prayed toward or if one is invoked at all. William James quoted Frederic W. H. Meyers, who said, "*Prayer* is the general name for that attitude of open and earnest expectancy. If we then ask to *whom* to pray, the answer (strangely enough) must be that *that* does not much matter."

Meyers also observed that no one knew enough about how prayer worked to say why it worked. His observation is as true today as when he made it at the beginning of the twentieth century. It's the same with medication, counseling, physical activity, twelve-step programs or social support services. We can surmise why they work but can't say for sure. Ten years from now, the mechanism might be totally understood, but right now, it's a kind of magic. The effect is not in the dogma but in the effort. It's not prayer based but can be initiated through prayer; it's not meditation based but can be initiated through meditation. It can be generated through the intentioned repetition of a meaningful phrase, a phrase meaningful to the individual only. It's a conscious decision to redirect the mind.

Another way to cultivate awareness from a Buddhist perspective is to simply pay attention to what you're doing. If you're washing your hands, pay attention to how the water feels as it touches your skin, how the soap feels as you lather it between your hands and the sensation you get when you dry your hands on a towel. At the *Investigating the Mind* conference, one panelist described a monk who was said to have discerned the seventeen distinct movements that comprise the snapping sound made by a person's thumb and finger. The goal is not tedium; it's awareness. Through it, we're open not only to particulars but to more of life. As Brown says of prayer, "It can open our eyes to the beauty and wonder of the world in which we live."

From a neurological perspective, meditation, prayer and intentioned repetition can help us to transcend the power of the limbic system, where our emotions originate. Jung suggested that human consciousness in which we are "aware of being aware" came about as a means of opposing our own instincts.

The cerebral cortex is in this sense—as Alex Zautra remarked earlier—a means of controlling or understanding our emotions. Paul Ekman has written that our emotions are part of an "automatic appraisal" process; messengers supplying the "you" in you with information about your current state.

Emotions are the ultimate double-edged sword. The "Pull-Ups, Feelings and New Year's" section in Chapter Seven described how they can both drive and be driven by behavior. Emotions are the reason we want the things we want, and, at the same time, can also be the reason we don't want other things. The problem is not that thoughts appear to fly randomly through our heads; the problem is that they get drawn toward emotions. The *corner office* is, for the thinker, an intellectual concept or thought to which certain emotions are attached. Once an emotion is triggered, more thoughts are generated in support of that emotion—the gravitational pull of the emotion gets stronger. One little thought can trigger an avalanche.

Exactly how many emotions we have is a subject of debate. Carroll Izard, one of the most influential researchers in the field, wrote that we have ten that mix together to form our expansive range of feelings. Of the ten emotions, two are positive (interest and joy), one is neutral (surprise) and seven are negative (anger, contempt, disgust, distress, fear, guilt and shame).

We're wired to notice the negative. Doesn't it make sense? Isn't that what kept us alive out on the savanna—our ability to recognize danger early? Many experts believe that certain emotional responses, such as fear of snakes or spiders, are hardwired into our systems. Ekman wrote, "Our emotion system was built to keep triggers in, not get them out, mobilizing our emotional responses without thought." Would it be helpful to our survival if we forgot certain emotional triggers after we'd learned them? These days, the problems aren't spiders and snakes. The problems are wishes for corner offices, perceived slights, the car that cut us off, the belief that our material possessions are less than they should be or the self-inflicted observation that we just don't stack up.

When Buddhist or Christian monks talk of watching your thoughts rather than getting attached to them, in a way they're saying that we should consciously observe our thoughts through the lens of the cerebral cortex—we should use it to tame our emotions so that we're not drawn into an emotional sinkhole, experiencing our thoughts among the roar of their emotional entourage.

In the section titled "Suicide and Augustine" in Chapter Two, I said the real trick Augustine employed was creating an "us-versus-them" paradigm. The way we as a species survived, however, was by being acutely aware of us and them. "Them" could mean impending death. It's been twisted, though ("bastardized" might be a better word). Objects and things have been granted powers they should never have in the first place. It's not the object we want; we're after the state of mind that object will bring. The idolatry we commit is endowing that thing with the power—or more, the absolute power—to trigger a state of mind.

It's a trap set by society and culture—by our ancestors, by us and by all our shared beliefs—in which we manage to ensnare ourselves every day.

Viewing the world as us-versus-them necessarily involves comparison—and proliferating the cycle, comparison reinforces us-versus-them. Stigma is a natural offshoot. In the field of mental health, René Descartes has tended to be held in dubious esteem. In a 1999 report on the state of mental health, the Surgeon General suggested, "Explanations for stigma [against mental disorder] stem, in part, from the misguided split between mind and body first proposed by Descartes."

Ironically, Descartes recognized in his own research how the ideas of philosophers who had come before him were interpreted in ways that the original authors had never intended. In his *Discourse on Method,* he asked, or in his word, "begged," his readers "never to believe what I am reported to have said unless I have stated it myself." Even though the concept had been around for ages before Descartes picked it up, the separation of mind and body, or *dualism,* has popularly been ascribed to him. It's been interpreted to mean that events in our minds are independent of events occurring to or in our bodies. Some have interpreted it to mean that emotions as well are independent of our bodies. Here's what Descartes actually wrote on the issue in his *Sixth Meditation:* "I am not just lodged in my body like a pilot in his ship, but . . . I am intimately united with it, and so confused and intermingled with it that I and my body compose, as it were, a single whole."

In Chapter Six, we investigated beliefs—how they come to be and how they influence our lives. Bad beliefs, we observed, can drive real suffering. In this section, we've looked at prayer, meditation and intentioned repetition as tools for redirecting our mind's attention, as tools for building new neural pathways—so that we can defuse painful emotions. Descartes offered a technique that went beyond redirecting our mind's attention; he went to the heart of the bad belief. He observed that he had certain beliefs—opinions about how the world is, how he is, how others are—that he'd never evaluated. He simply accepted them as true. Descartes' philosophy sprang from a kind of rational introspection. He was using his cerebral cortex to identify which of his beliefs were solid.

In his quest, Descartes threw out all of his beliefs; none of them was afforded unfettered freedom. His intention was not at the outset to say that mind and body are two separate and distinct things. That is, he didn't have an axe to grind, at least not on the subjects of mind and body. Descartes was interested in discovering which of his opinions were valid, and central to his pursuit was determining what he really knew. For Descartes, beliefs should be grounded in a solid foundation—"knowledge" was that foundation for him. As he considered what he knew, it occurred to him that before he could know anything, he had to know something about himself. The most basic thing he could know about himself was that he *actually* existed. If he didn't exist, nothing else was solid.

He concluded that he was aware of the fact that he was thinking and because there must be a thinker to have a thought, he existed: *I think, therefore I am.*

Bertrand Russell observed that "I think, therefore I am" simply shows that a thought exists, not that you as an individual actually exist. Others have observed that it means that you exist in the second or millisecond in which you have the thought but says nothing of the past or the future.

Notwithstanding, it's not the conclusion but the process that Descartes spent the most energies describing in the *Discourse on Method* (the book in which he introduced his famous quotation). He embarked on his whole philosophical voyage precisely to get better control over what he believed to be the interplay between his mind and body, releasing attachments that caused him undue suffering. Descartes didn't want to accept things just because he was told so or because they were part of public opinion. Instead, he wanted to step back from the fray, ask questions and seek truth as he understood it. Today, the questions would be ones like: Is money the goal? Should I base my opinion of myself on what others tell me? Descartes was concerned with beliefs that drive a person's outlook and course in life.

Consider one of today's generally accepted beliefs: A new car is a good thing. As a society, we're not averse to going into debt to afford a car that reflects well on ourselves. We're encouraged to do so by advertisers, car manufacturers, fellow humans, and, most insidiously, by ourselves and our own need for validation. It's not the car itself that we're after; it's the feeling the car generates in us. Let's follow Descartes' advice and evaluate the truth of this statement: "An expensive new car will make me feel good."

Because it's a feeling we're after, it's worth inquiring into the feeling we'll get. To do so, maybe we can start with a thought experiment. Imagine yourself in your new car:

You're sitting in a leather interior, the sunroof is open, the sound system is playing and sunlight is reflecting off the shiny exterior. What is the feeling? It's actually hard to put your finger on any one feeling, isn't it? There are a few: excitement, expectation of driving it and the looks you'll get as you drive; there's a sense of accomplishment, there's happiness—maybe it's pride, but it seems like happiness.

The next question is: Will any of these feelings last? As anyone who's owned a new car knows, the car eventually morphs into obscurity. The new car smell wears off. After reflecting on the longevity of the feelings, more questions might spring to mind. Will we shortly need something else to sustain the feelings? In the long run, might the new car cause us worry in the form of payments, upkeep and scratches? Might there have been a better way of getting at the feelings we wanted? After we've exhausted all of our questions, there might be room for one more: Are these really feelings we wanted in the first place?

This is the exercise Descartes was involved in. He wasn't saying emotions don't impact the mind. He knew they can smother all other thoughts so that nothing else matters. Descartes offered the *Discourse on Method* as a vehicle that worked for him—it helped him to feel better. He wasn't a fundamentalist. He didn't say his way was the *only* way, just that it had worked for him.

Meditation, prayer and intentioned repetition are cognitive tools that can settle, redirect and open the mind. They're tools that can provide us shelter from hurtful mental states. No single technique works for everyone. Mired in a depression, an individual will be challenged to access the freedom of meditation unless it's a neural path that's been progressively strengthened over time. A route trod only occasionally won't ever become a viable path. It needs to be walked regularly.

Descartes' rational introspection affords the practitioner a way to defuse existing beliefs before they can trigger emotions—to settle disagreeable mental resonations by employing the cerebral cortex in the construction of consciously grounded beliefs. He's not the only one to forward rational introspection. It's a standard psychological technique anyone can use to determine the validity of his or her own beliefs. It's best done with a pencil and paper or computer and keyboard, typing out beliefs and the underlying assumptions those beliefs are based upon—to nail down the beliefs rather than letting them wistfully surface and then dive. It doesn't have to be exclusively a written process, though; the key is identifying influential beliefs and ensuring they're moored on solid, rational ground. Doing so helps us avoid habitual emotional landmines we step on without even realizing we're doing it.

We left petitionary prayer to consider other prayer techniques and then wound our way to Descartes. It's worth returning to petitionary prayer again, to consider it more closely. We're a culture that ascribes power to things. In this kind of culture, petitionary prayer improperly practiced can reinforce the very *things* its practice is meant to transcend. The danger in petitionary prayer is in believing the benefit of the practice is to entrench our position on the outer spoke of the wheel. Some believers in petitionary prayer hold that the reason particular prayers aren't answered is that whoever was praying just didn't pray the right way. In this view, Sudanese refugees are where they are through some fault of their own. God saves one child and not another because the parents of the child who died didn't pray correctly. Miracles and magic happen only if you do the trick exactly right.

Raymo writes, "All my life has been a relearning to pray—a letting go of incantational magic, petition, and the vain repetition 'Me, Lord, me,' instead watching attentively for the light that burns at the center of every star, every cell, every living creature, every human heart." Petitionary prayer, if not carefully practiced, cultivates comparison, stigma and us-versus-them. It also can foster an expectation of fairness: I should have Y because Smith has Y. My situation should be like Smith's because it wouldn't be fair otherwise.

One of my foundational expectations has always been that life *should* be fair. Even if I said to myself, "I understand that life isn't fair," my limbic system would tell me otherwise. *Fairness* is a dangerous and potentially life-threatening concept for anyone who has lost a loved one or friend to a condition or event that smacks of unfairness. Holding on to a belief in fairness eventually imprisons whoever expects it. The philosopher Heraclitis said, "Nothing ever is, everything is becoming." To be attached to anything is to hold on to something that is going to change. There's not any question about it.

What is fairness? More to the point, why would I expect it? Who among us remembers being consulted before being dropped here on Earth, to see if you were okay with the whole situation? Does anyone recall being asked, "Okay, we're going to put you into the following set of circumstances: Your eyesight will fail, you'll tend toward obesity, and math will never make sense to you. Sound good? Terrific, off you go." We woke up in this thing. Before we could say, "I realize I'm here," we were here, alive in our earthly form—no justification provided.

One of the maxims Descartes followed was "always to attempt the mastery over myself rather than over fortune, to try to alter my desires rather than the course of the world." He believed the practice of *nonattachment* by the ancient stoic philosophers enabled them to rise above "the influence of fortune, and, amid suffering and poverty, enjoy a happiness which their gods might have envied." It doesn't always work out exactly right. When it comes to running a marathon, few people can just tie up their sneakers and go. Most are like me, the guy who makes jogging look painful at every step. Mental training is no different. It can be exceedingly difficult. But as with weightlifting for Rich and me, subtle changes, simple freedoms and temporarily blissful states of mind nurture the path.

It used to be that scientists believed we were just observers, watching the world happen around us. The concept was popular in Isaac Newton's time. The discovery of quantum mechanics changed that. It ushered in the realization that we are part of the world, in here with everything. Anything that we do impacts something else. Liberties have been taken in interpreting the ramifications of quantum mechanics, liberties that lead to the notion that we can use our minds to more or less telepathically influence the future. That's a loaded notion. It's like petitionary prayer generating material things: There are too many instances that don't substantiate it. Roger Jones wrote in his book *Physics for the Rest of Us*, "In quantum theory, Heisenberg's uncertainty principle tells us that an observer has a random and irreducible effect on any observation." The key in the Jones quotation is that the effect the observer has is *random*. Even if the randomness happens within a range—say, between "okay" and "perfect"—we can't know with certainty where in the range the randomness will ultimately land. The actual outcome is, as far as we know, the realm of magic.

The only way we can control magic is if we know the logic behind it. But as Descartes suggested, our goal is to free ourselves from attachment to the vicissitudes of fortune. The path to Descartes' freedom is not magic; it's a conscious weakening of the bars on our self-imposed prisons, a process that inevitably lingers as a kind of unanswerable question, always influenced by nature and nurture—sometimes irreversibly. And for all who embark on it, it's forever a work in progress.

THE INTENSIVE CARE UNIT

The taxi dropped Deana and me off at the Austin hospital where Rich was in the intensive care unit. When a man at the front desk in the emergency room said that he'd lead us to the ICU, we followed him down a series of hallways. As we walked, doctors and nurses breezed by. Some were looking at clipboards, others straight ahead; some were serious, some drab; and none acknowledged our leader or Deana or me as we walked. When we saw the sign for the ICU, we thanked the man, and he went back to his post at the ER.

The ICU had a waiting room. It wasn't as full as the ER's but still looked busy. Families were in there, wondering about sons just stabbed, fathers who'd had heart attacks and grandparents after strokes. I stepped out of the waiting room and into the hallway, near the Coke machine, and dialed the number I'd called earlier in the morning when I was in Greensboro. Someone in the ICU picked up.

"Hi, this is Ted Courtemanche. I'm here to see my brother. I think my mother should be in there."

"Yes, hi. Go to the doors outside the waiting room, and I'll buzz you in," someone in the ICU said. Deana and I waited by the doors; it felt sterile, and the lighting was fluorescent bright. Once we were buzzed through the first set of doors, we were buzzed through a second set. Directly in front of us, lying in a bed in a small ICU room, was a man with no family by his side. Machines monitoring his vital organs quietly illuminated the walls.

We walked by, and Mom and Sharon were in the next room. Rich was lying in a bed. Like the man in the other room, machines all around him were quietly flashing, lines going up then down, up then down. If I didn't know Rich had been shot, I'd have thought he was taking a nap. Mom was rubbing his leg on the other side of the bed. I kissed him on his shoulder.

Rich had stubble on his face; he'd been growing a beard, and he was tan. A white towel covered the area of his jaw that had been damaged from the shooting. It seemed like just a small piece of his jaw was missing, the very end tip under his ear. The towel could have been just a towel he'd left on his face, maybe after wiping sweat from exercising. But it wasn't; it was a towel that covered his wound. His right arm was wrapped where the police had shot him.

I dropped off our bags in the corner of the room. Maura, one of the nurses, explained to me what the doctors had already told Mom. The stroke had cut off the blood supply to Rich's brain. The right side of his brain was dead and in the process of folding into the stem. The left side would do the same. He no longer had the ability to talk or communicate, she told me. He was not officially brain dead yet. That would happen when the left side of his brain folded into the stem.

I wasn't ready for that much information and was quickly overwhelmed. Rich had spoken at the wedding just two months before. Before me, he lay in a bed, probably twelve hours left in his life. My dear baby brother was dying in the bed before me. I won't ever forget that sight. I sat in a chair in the corner and sobbed. Mom tried to tell me that it was no one's fault. I couldn't stand to hear it. I just wanted to cry. *Death doesn't care; neither does life. Both just do what they do,* I thought. I cried until I couldn't breathe through my nose.

I'd brought the *Tibetan Book of Living and Dying*. I had good memories of the book. I used to read it when I lived in the townhouse in Greensboro. Usually, I'd read it at night as I sat on my back deck. Around me, insects would chirp and black birds would rustle in the bamboo trees behind the house. Sometimes when I read it, I'd look through the tree limbs that crisscrossed the now-dry ravine behind my townhouse. On the other side of the ravine are bungalows built in the 1960s. Usually, there'd be lights shining through the windows, warming the scene. I'd look up through the trees and see the stars or the moon, or I might see an airplane flying across the sky, lights blinking as it went.

I never finished the book but knew the crux of it: It said the most important thing you can do in life is to prepare for death. I knew there was a section in the book that had instructions on what to do when you were with someone who was dying. That's the reason I'd brought the book; in my state, I figured the book would help me guide Rich from this world to the next. I'm sure it would have looked strange to a bystander as I frantically flipped through the pages, beset by the notion that I had to find the right section—now is when my brother needed me most.

Once I found the section I was looking for, I said, "Rich, I'm going to read to you." Mom nodded as I did. I read aloud about the stages some Buddhists believe we go through when we die, about "space dissolving into luminosity," about "a flowing vibrant world of sound, light and color" and about "the ordinary features of our familiar environment [melting] into an all-pervasive landscape of light." As I read, the exercise became rhythmic, the effect of speaking the words, meditative. I felt comfortably connected to Rich. After about five minutes, I stopped and looked at Rich. He was peaceful in the bed. A calming energy filled the room. Mom kept rubbing her hand slowly on his leg.

When I'd started to read, I was sprinting—I needed something to do; I needed to bring a semblance of control to the situation. Now I was running out of energy. I stopped and then remembered a long-forgotten experience. When Rich and I were small, I once watched a star dancing in the sky on a night when I couldn't sleep. The two of us shared a bedroom. I stared at the star so long that it started to look like it had wings like an angel. I woke Rich and told him to look at the star. "Rich," I said back in the house in Sherborn, "there's an angel," and we both watched. By Rich's bedside in the hospital, I felt small and helpless. I felt my mortality. And I felt a warmth, strange though it sounds, the same kind of feeling I had during that night back in Sherborn.

After the short break, I read aloud again to Rich from the book, about the final stage of "spontaneous presence," where the dying person sees past, present and future lives. I got to a part that described how if the dying person isn't careful, he or she will look down, away from the visions before him or her, which are "as bright as the sun." The book said that in looking down, the person will be drawn into one of the "six realms of existence" and once that happens, the individual is destined to be reborn.

I'd never thought much about what exactly I'd want when I died, if perhaps being reborn might be something I'd like. The book was unequivocal: Being reborn is not the fate a dying person wants; he or she wants enlightenment, freedom from the delusions of the six realms of existence. That part of the book didn't resonate with me, and I got lost on the details, on exactly how a dying person can avoid the rebirth fate.

"Rich," I said, "as best I can understand it, you're going to see light. Keep looking up; keep your head up. Remain centered the whole time. If you can just remember to stay centered, you're going to be okay. Stay centered, my brother, stay centered."

As I spoke, a tiny amount of spittle went out of and back into Rich's mouth. He was so peaceful lying there. Every once in a while, his leg would twitch, and Mom would massage it. I caressed his arm. I touched my palm on his forehead. This beautiful man was being pulled from my life while I sat here watching. The reading absolved some of the hopelessness. "Stay centered, my brother," I said a few times more.

Dad eventually took a taxi from the airport. He got lost three or four times in the hospital, looking for the ICU. He looked under control when he arrived in Rich's room. He saw Rich and knelt by his side; he put his head down and prayed to him, holding Rich's bandaged and wounded arm. I'd never seen Dad like that.

Maura came into the room right after Dad. Each new person got the story of how Rich's brain was folding into itself. Maura then asked about organ transplants. Did we want to have Rich's organs donated? We looked at each other. "Of course," was our consensus. It would be beautiful if Rich could save another life. Maura talked more about the organ donation process, but no one was really listening. She asked which one of us would speak to their transplant coordinator, Rebecca. I was elected.

Rebecca was not at the hospital but called from home.

"Hi," I said into the phone outside Rich's room. "This is Ted Courtemanche."

"Hi, this is Rebecca. How can I help you?"

Weird, I thought. "Well, I was told you're going to talk with me about the organ transplant process."

She started talking but didn't seem to be saying much. I know from my business experience that when someone is talking but not making sense, either I don't know what they're talking about, they don't know what they're talking about or they're hiding something. Rebecca went on talking. "Your brother is going to save people's lives."

Just a short while into the conversation, she said something that stopped me cold: "If he does recover, he wouldn't have any function." Now, if those weren't the exact words, the exact words were close. She was trying to make me feel good about the organ donation decision, I guess.

"What do you mean?" I asked. "There's a chance he could recover?" Maybe, it occurred to me, this was all a ruse. A sense of hope went through me.

"No," she said. "No, I never said that."

"You just said that even if he did recover, he'd have no function."

"No, I never said that."

What's the best way to describe how I felt? Furious? Yes, that's partially it, but "violated" gets closer to the truth. I had no interest in getting into a he-said, she-said contest. Immediately, Rich was dying in my mind again. I went back to the concept of organ transplantation. As Rebecca started talking again, she didn't offer any kind of summary statement I could give to Mom and Dad.

"How should I explain this to my mother?" I asked.

"Well, you need to tell your mother that Rich is gone; he's brain dead. What you're seeing there is not Rich."

"What?" I said.

She repeated herself.

There was no way I was going to tell Mom that; no way I was going to allow myself to hear it. I said, "Is there going to be a psychologist or a psychiatrist who will be here to help?"

"No," she said. "I'm a trained counselor. I do this all the time. I'll be able to talk to your mother."

As Rebecca gave more details, it sounded like Rich would be kept alive while they waited to find donors. He'd be a human incubator. Part of what I'd read in the *Tibetan Book of Living and Dying* was how important it is for the body to be in a peaceful state after death. Sogyal Rinpoche, the author, wrote, "I remember in Tibet how everyone took great care to maintain a silent and peaceful atmosphere around the body . . . to avoid causing the slightest disturbance." As neuroeconomists teach, the most important thought at any moment is the one that's presently accessible. What Rebecca was describing sounded like the antithesis of what the book recommended.

For the fourth or fifth time, Rebecca launched into how much good Rich could do by being a donor, but I still felt like she was dancing around exactly how the process would work. She also explained that if we did not want Rich to be an organ donor, we could still have his retinas, skin and bone marrow donated. No sooner had she referenced this other possibility, which would not require Rich being kept alive, then she went back to pushing the full organ transplant. Like a telemarketer, Rebecca was making a hard close on Rich's organs.

She made references that bordered on calling Rich a vegetable. She might have said it; I don't remember for sure. What I did know was that Rebecca was not going to talk to Mom. I couldn't believe the hospital let her talk to anyone in the emotional state we were in. She had no respect for any beliefs we had. She didn't even ask. Here I was, I said to myself, being told matter-of-factly that lying on the bed was not Rich but something else. I don't know if Rich heard a word I said, but I wasn't about to accept the idea that he was gone.

After I explicitly asked when the organ donation process would begin, Rebecca told me that they would start at 8:00 the next morning. It was about 11:00 pm as we spoke. This is how it appeared to me: Basically, everyone would get a good night's sleep, and they'd approach Rich as the business object they clearly believed he was rather than my brother of thirty-six years, who deserved a little more goddam sensitivity and compassion.

"How long will he be kept in the state he's in?" I asked.

"Until we're able to find donors."

"No, my question was *how long will he be kept in the state he's in?* Is that clear?"

"No later than Monday morning."

It was Saturday night at the time. I couldn't get past the inference that Rich was simply a human icebox. While I was listening, a nurse hurriedly turned over another patient's chart. Her look said she suspected me of reading it. In the process of flipping it over, she managed to hang up the phone. Rebecca was gone, but only for a minute. She called right back, and I spoke to her for a minute or two more. The conversation shifted from the organ donation process to Rebecca insisting that because of her experience and training in psychology, she was fully prepared to talk with Mom.

The best I could do at the time was walk away, with Rebecca left talking to the table and whatever charts were on it. When I went back into Rich's room, I told Maura that Rebecca was still on the line, and she went out to talk.

I explained the situation to Mom and Dad. Mom wondered why they couldn't just take Rich's organs as soon as he died. She said if they could get someone in here right when he died, they could do the organ transplantation. I didn't know how to put it. "Mom, they won't take his organs until they have a recipient. He'll be kept alive for his organs."

As soon as Mom and Dad heard that, we decided not to pursue the full organ donation and asked to have the ventilator removed. Hearing our request, Maura was convinced that we just didn't understand how the process worked. She started explaining the whole thing again. She also told us Rebecca was on her way into the hospital.

"Tell her not to come," Dad said.

Mom just looked at Rich in tears. "There's too much confusion in here," she said. "Let my baby be in peace."

In response, Maura made a comment that still blows me away today. She said, "Rich is in heaven; he's not here anymore." *Are you out of your mind?!* I thought. We asked her to find a doctor who would disconnect the respirator.

Maura seemed irritated about our decision. She tried to imply that a legal bind was created when Mom signed papers earlier in the day saying Rich should be kept on a respirator. After we insisted, she then told us the person who could authorize the disconnection had gone home but that there was another doctor who could do it. He was in a different wing of the building.

"Find him," Dad said.

We quietly sat around Rich and talked after Maura left. "This is the way Rich lived his life. It wouldn't have been Rich if there wasn't confusion at the end," I said. Everyone agreed. Gradually, the tension lifted and we hugged each other and Rich.

About fifteen minutes later, there was more commotion outside the room. Deana heard Maura say, "But Rebecca is going to be here any minute."

A man said, "This is my call. Do you all understand? This is my call."

With that, a doctor entered the room. He was an older man, a no-nonsense guy. As with Maura and Rebecca, he went through the whole transplant process again. He talked about how Rich's brain would never support communication again, how it was folding into itself. He went through the story about how Rich was one of 15 percent of the population who couldn't support blood flow to the brain with a single carotid artery. Everyone sat or stood quietly as he spoke.

At the end, Dad, who'd been sitting with his back to the doctor and the scene, said, "I don't know why we're talking about this; we've made our decision. We want the ventilator removed." He turned his neck so that his face was in the direction of the doctor as he spoke. The conversation stopped.

"I will authorize the removal right now," the doctor said. He respected our decision. Things again settled down in the room. There's a calm that comes when the inevitable is accepted. Rich was going to pass. Maura told us he'd probably pass sometime in the morning. Maura and one other nurse said he'd taken twelve breaths when the respirator had been removed temporarily earlier in the day. Mom, who'd been there most of the day, did not see it happen, but Maura assured us he had.

The doctor and the nurses left the room. Mom, Dad, Deana, Sharon and I looked at each other and breathed. Just as the last nurse left, we heard another commotion outside. I can't put my finger on the combination of disgust and rage that came over me when Rebecca came through the curtains. My stomach curled. I wanted to scream at her.

In his book *How We Die*, Sherwin Nuland wrote of the lack of compassion exhibited by medical personnel for those who end their lives by suicide. I would never have believed it possible, not in a million years. But here it was, happening in the ICU. I can't forget the incredibly, unabashed extent to which I saw the very phenomenon Nuland wrote about happen before my eyes. I know people can get hardened, that hardening is part of the survival process, but I cannot understand what happened with Rebecca that night. Part of me still hopes it's not possible.

"Mom, how we doing?" Rebecca said to Mom, like she was making sure Mom's case of poison ivy was clearing up. Rebecca wanted to talk organ donation. It's hard, remembering this, not to think she was on some kind of a ghoulish, utterly incomprehensible commission plan.

"Leave," Mom said. "Just leave." Rebecca tried to squeeze in a few more sentences. She wanted to confirm that Rich's skin, bone marrow and retinas would still be donated. "Yes," Mom said.

After that, Dad said, "Look, will you just *leave?* Get out of this room."

Finally, Rebecca left. The turmoil was over. It shouldn't have been the way that it was—but it was. I know other families who have had exceptionally caring and healing experiences with the organ donation process, but we did not.

We started quietly talking about Rich once Rebecca left. We talked about vacations in Camden, Maine. We talked about the rock, "Big Ledge," that jutted into the lake and about how the nights would be cool and about the warmth of the cabin. I told Mom and Dad how Rich and I would fish with spools of thread and hooks, how we'd play in the water and explore the woods. We talked about how each year in Camden, we'd have a lobster feast. Rich loved lobster. He was an expert at squeezing every last piece of meat from his lobsters. He'd eat the claws, the tail and the legs. Wherever there was meat, he'd get it. I can still see him standing on his chair at the wooden table in the cabin where we had the feast, his little lobster bib flipping around as he reached for more lobster.

The mood got light and peaceful. The lights were low. We sent good thoughts to each other and to Rich. After a while, the only sound in the room was the respirator breathing for Rich. About half an hour later, the respiratory therapist came in. I recognized her from earlier in the night; she'd been in the room adjusting something with the respirator when I first arrived. She went to the corner of the bed and disconnected the respirator. Other nurses disconnected other lines from Rich.

I walked to the side of the bed closest to the door. A machine there recorded how much oxygen Rich had in his bloodstream. It steadily dropped. I asked Maura what it meant.

"He's losing oxygen in his bloodstream," she said.

Rich never took another breath after the oxygen machine was turned off. When I realized what was happening, I went to the other side of the bed, the one closest to the wall. I put my hands on Rich. Mom was on the other side with her hands on Rich as well. Dad stood peacefully next to Mom. I kept saying, "Move on, my brother, you can move on." The mantra kept me calm as Rich's vital signs shut down.

With my hands on Rich, I continued chanting, softly but deliberately. He passed. We covered his body with a sheet. Mom didn't want to leave. Though I told her we had to go, in that instant, we held on to the same desperate idea: Maybe if we stayed, we could hold on to Rich forever. This beautiful man, I would never interact with him ever again.

When I left the room and went to the hall, a fury ripped through me. I wanted to punch holes in the walls—I raised my fist, then stopped. I clenched my jaw and screamed low in my throat, muffling all but a low reverberation. It released a part of me. I agreed with Schopenhauer and all the other philosophers who wrote that this life is just a cruel, dark *wasteland*—nothing redeeming in this kind of anguish.

Maura came out into the hallway with tears in her eyes. I didn't want to hug her but couldn't stop when she put her arms out. Maybe she'd seen that it wasn't just a body lying on the bed. Maybe she saw instead that it was my brother, Rich, with whom I'd enjoyed a life.

When he was thirteen years old, Rich had to write about his earliest memory for school. This is what he wrote:

> *I was about three years old. I was in my back yard in the summer when it was very hot. My grandparents and my brother were there. My brother and I were playing in our little pool. We were jumping and splashing, and we were throwing water at our grandparents. Then we went playing in sand and we got all dirty.*

I hope that what Rich took with him just before he left was the feeling of all of us around him, sending him love. I said a prayer at his service that went like this:

Thank you God, thank you Universe and most of all, thank you Rich for the time you gave me while you were on Earth. You are no less real to me today than you were before. I will always be honored to say you are my brother. And my brother, you will always be here, in my heart, with me. You will continue to help me here and now. I know you made peace with your Maker and that you are in His or Her safety. For now, I'm happy knowing you're at peace with Granny and Gramps and Mommom and Poppop and all the other souls no longer with us in physical form whose lives you touched. When I look at a sunset, I will know a small glimpse of the bliss you now feel. God, continue to spread Your compassion, and Rich, continue to spread the joy that you alone could spread to all of us still here in this bodily form. Someday, Rich, we will embrace again. Amen.

Until then, peace, Rich. I was lucky to have you as my brother.

"HOW DO YOU DEFINE YOURSELF?" EMAIL

Mom has always liked to peek beneath the surface, trying to see what was really going on with Rich and me. Usually, Rich remained private, as do I. Two decades after the mandatory family trips were done, Mom sent out an email with the following question: "How do you define yourself?" She'd been asked the question by one of her friends and thought it was interesting.

I never fully responded but Rich did. He forwarded his answer to Dad, Zatta and me with the following preface: "hi all, mom asked this question. i just figured i would send my response to all of you. if for no other reason then to let you know i am doing well out here and am truly happy. r."

From: Richard Courtemanche
Date: Friday, March 22, 2002
To: Betty Courtemanche
Subject: Re: How do you define yourself?

hi mom. interesting question. my answer is... well, i am a visitor here, someone who is here, living life, but wont be forever. i am completely comfortable with that. i am not sure what will happen in my life as time continues. when i someday pass on, is that it? nothing else. maybe, but i dont think so.

when i say i am a visitor, i guess its because sometimes i almost feel that life is surreal, that i am just an observer. and i can be overwhelmed by it. the beauty, the wonder. those are my good days, when i feel as if i am at one with everything, not living my life per say, but rather just living. experiencing it all. of course, there are times i get wrapped up in the meaningless tribulations that we all do, but they are getting fewer in my life. i think quitting work [and starting futures trading on my own] was the best decision i have ever made. i wasnt experiencing life, i was just going through the motions. keep in mind, when i say this, it doesnt mean a physical change so much as a mental change. i feel much more free, but its not like i wasnt free at work. just that i felt my mind was limited.

so who am i. well, i am someone taking a trip, a wonderful ride, sometimes the ride gets rough, and sometimes it feels like your car breaks down! but other times, it feels like i am flying down the road, no distractions, just pure bliss. and i dont know where i am going. but when i get there, i think i will be comforted by the trip i have taken. memories, some good, some, well, not painful, but thought provoking, and most of all, i will have experienced life, met people, and in the end, accepted myself as someone who although not perfect, tried to improve, and hopefully, made things a little better for some others as well.

by the way, one of my favorite things to do out here [in San Diego], is when i am walking, i look up at the sun, it shines so bright. and i stretch out my arms, look up at the sky, and just feel completely at peace.

love ya. rdc

❧ Chapter Nine ❧

Wider and wider they spread, expanding and always expanding,
Outward and outward and forever outward. . . .
There is no stoppage, and never can be stoppage.
—Walt Whitman

Viewing Death Differently

As far as humans know, we're the only creatures who are aware we're going to die. And we're aware that we can ponder our own awareness of this inevitable fact. We live each minute knowing the end is out there. When Rich passed, the hardest part, for me, was the finality of it. He was here, and then he wasn't. The purpose of Chapter Nine is to help us defuse some of death's finality. As we explore, perhaps we'll come away with a different way of looking at death; perhaps a number of different ways.

In Chapter Eight, Rich described the large trees, fourteen feet in diameter, on the property he considered bidding on in Austin. He always liked trees—as do I. Maybe reviewing the life and death of a tree is a good place to begin. The tree starts as a seed, possibly carried from one place to another in the dung of a bird or the fur of an animal. The seed germinates—keep in mind, not all seeds will germinate; this particular seed necessarily germinates at the expense of other seeds. Slowly a tree begins to appear. Young leaves turn into branches from which new leaves grow, creating more branches. Wherever a branch appears, a kind of decision is made and that branch can't grow somewhere else. Each fall, the leaves drop to the ground and are replaced in spring by new leaves, which tend to be indistinguishable from the old leaves. The process repeats itself. The tree continues to grow. Old branches sprout new branches that grow in ways that might seem chaotic to the tree were it conscious but that look structured when the tree is viewed as a whole.

During its life, the tree is part of a community: Birds, bugs, squirrels and other creatures live in and among it. Other trees protect it from wind and the elements, and it protects other trees. Branches fall to the ground and other branches take their place. Parts of the tree die, and parts of it are reborn. It's never the same tree from one moment to the next. One day, it stops growing and from there, it begins to die. Once dead, it gradually decays. Soil that would have nourished the tree nourishes something else. Sunlight that would have been used by the tree for photosynthesis is used by some other plant. The tree itself becomes home to other animals and plants as it weakens and falls apart. Eventually, all of its parts nourish other beings. If we go far enough into the future, we won't even see a tree where the tree once stood; it will have been reabsorbed back into the earth. The tree's death brings life just as the tree's life brought death; the tree was here, then was gone, but the cycle of creation and dissolution remains.

The first thing for us to keep in mind about death is that it's part of a cycle—as necessary for life as life is for death.

CHRISTMAS AND LIFE AFTER DEATH

Christmas was an important holiday when Rich and I were growing up; I'd be hard-pressed to overstate its importance. I was somewhere around eleven at the time of the "Desk Christmas," a day that has become Courtemanche family folklore.

As I sat cross-legged beneath the tree on Christmas morning, I considered what had just taken place in the last fifteen minutes. Somehow, the gift I'd been looking forward to ever since Thanksgiving turned out to be a desk— and Rich got a race car set. I felt a tear welling up in my eye. Where's the justice? I wanted to know. I thought maybe if I nudged the race set into my gift section, I could take ownership; no way. Rich understood well the bounty he now commanded and was not going to be deprived of a single thing—and definitely not the race set.

Yes, Rich had gotten a little nervous when I opened a small box, and it instructed me to go into the cellar and look under a bedsheet. He was right behind me, step for step, as I ran. He stopped short of pulling off the sheet, but he probably wanted to. "Is this it?!" Rich might have thought. "Will this send Theodore over the top? All he's had so far is a toy bow and arrow, but might this be the bike he's been asking for?" Rich was good at math when he was small. I'll bet he started doing some calculations in his head: fun value of bike, fun value of the gifts he'd gotten. I'll bet it was close. It probably tipped things in my favor. Then he waited for the sheet removal. The entire Christmas hinged on what was under there.

When he saw the desk, I'm sure things settled down in his head. There was no need to worry. He was the clear winner this Christmas; his options for fun were legion: He had the race set, an Evel Knievel windup motorcycle and a toy bulldozer with operating crawlers. Rich wandered back to the tree where his stuff was. After I sat at the desk for a few seconds on Christmas morning, I ran back to the tree, too—maybe I'd missed my real gift. My reaction probably hit Mom hard. I'd seen her staining the same desk in the garage months before. I wouldn't have imagined that the desk was an impending present, even though she told me not to go in there while she was working, which was unusual.

Once I realized I had no more gifts to open, I went outside to play with the bow and arrow. It was a white Christmas, and the snow on the ground was virgin white. Each footprint I made was a new one, made visible by the sunlight shining through tree branches. I pulled back on the string; it was the same kind you'd use to fly a kite, only thinner. I pulled hard because I wanted the arrow to *go.* The bow was a just a regular piece of wood, about an inch wide and a quarter inch thick. Rich came outside, too. He was playing with his bulldozer. If Rich had read up on engineering, he could have explained to me that the force I was exerting on the string was too much for the bow. If he was a little older, he could have said, "T, it's just a toy bow and arrow." If I was a bit more mature, I would have understood the same thing.

As Rich was plowing a little road near the driveway, I let out a loud "Waah!" from the woods. The bow had broken. Rich came over to see what was the matter. I was making enough of a stink that Mom came outside, too. She said that the next day we'd go to the store where she bought the bow and arrow to get a replacement. Hearing that, I pulled myself together. Rich and I went inside and started playing with the race car set. Rich and I usually got each other dinky gifts when we were small. One time I got a watch for my birthday, and I tried to pawn it off on Rich as a Christmas present three months later. After that, we regularly gave the watch as a gift back and forth to each other. The year I got a desk for Christmas, though, Rich designated a car from his race car set that was mine to use "whenever you want to play with it, Theodore."

I get old Christmases mixed up. Sometime after the Desk Christmas, we went through a three-year streak when our bull mastiff, Chester, peed on the Christmas gifts. The first year was a total surprise. Rich went to put on a sweatshirt, and it was wet. As I was putting on a similarly wet sweatshirt, Rich smelled his and said, "Gross! It's pee." The next year, we weren't as surprised when we learned that for the second Christmas in a row, Chester had piddled on the gifts. (Chester must have thought that being under a tree, they were fair game.) The following year, we closed the two doors that led into the family room where the Christmas tree was standing. We made sure that they stayed closed when we weren't in there. That's the year that we recognized Chester had a talent. Somehow, he managed to get in the room, and once again, he peed on the presents.

There's the Christmas that we got an air hockey table. The sun has set. Rich and I have been playing outside with the neighborhood kids. We're walking back home, coming down the hill from the Andrews' house. Just before we start walking along the trail we use to get to the school bus, I survey the scene. The snow is crunching under my feet. There's a luminosity from the moon reflecting off the snow. I know that in just a few minutes, we'll be inside where it's warm. It makes the cold bearable—not just bearable, I savor the sting. All this goes on inside my head, and I have a good feeling as Rich and I walk through the frozen snow.

When we were really small, Rich and I got up at about 4:00 or 5:00 am on Christmas morning. Mom and Dad would send us back to bed unless Dad had gotten us presents he was excited about, too, and then we'd get to stay up.

One Christmas Eve when Rich and I were probably five and seven, something startled us, and we woke in the middle of the night. Rich was the first one attended to by Mom. Mom took him into the guest bedroom down the hall. As I waited in our bedroom, I heard a kind of low exhalation outside the door. I stayed perfectly still. I heard the sound again. It's not accurate to call it a moan, but it wasn't a sound of joy from what I could tell either. Have you ever heard Johnny Cash? Imagine Johnny Cash whispering something unintelligible in his lowest voice. I didn't care to learn if the sound outside the bedroom door was real or just in my head, so I ran down the hall to where the rest of the family was. My heart was beating so loud I could hear it when I crawled into bed with Rich.

Mom and Dad settled us into the guest bedroom, and then Dad checked for the source of the sound down the hall. Reporting back to us that all was clear, he shut the lights off. I kept my eyes wide open. *Thank God I was in bed with Rich.* As we lay there, I heard a can rolling underneath the bed. Here we go, I thought. As soon as the can hit what seemed like the back wall underneath the bed, I saw a flash of static electricity in the doorway leading to the hall. I stayed absolutely motionless. It happened again. The can rolled, hit the wall and electricity flashed in the hall. I forget how many times the process—can rolls, hits wall, electricity flashes—repeated itself. It didn't seem ominous to me. It simply seemed to be the way it was that night, so I fell asleep. I told myself before I did that I'd look under the bed the next morning. I forgot to look under the bed until a few days later. When I did, nothing unusual was under there—no can and nothing that could roll.

Quoting the psychiatrist Alfred Binet, Carl Jung wrote, "The unconscious sensibility of an hysterical patient is at certain moments *fifty times* more acute than that of a normal person." The study of paranormal experiences was one of the leading factors that drove Jung into psychiatry. Can I ever prove that there was, in fact, a can crashing and electric flashes in the hallway as Rich and I slept so many years ago? No, I cannot. The only investigation I did at the time revealed that there wasn't a can, and I confirmed with Mom that she hadn't cleaned out anything from under the bed. What I think I observed cannot be proven. It goes beyond the realm of reason. Some things in life are just destined to remain mysteries.

Rich liked brain teasers. He'd say to me, "T, look at the sun setting on the horizon. See how big it is?"

"Yes," I'd answer.

"Next time it's up in the sky, pay attention to how big it is. It won't look as big as it does right now. But you know what? It's the same size. No one knows for sure why it looks so big on the horizon and so small up in the sky."

Science helps to clear up some mysteries, but more answers lead to more questions. Why are we here? Debate rages on that one. Isn't it the most important question of all? As we've seen in this book, no one was asked if they even wanted to be here in the first place. Reason isn't always that helpful for the big questions; sometimes the best we can do is patch together answers as we go along.

One of the most important questions from Jung's perspective was: "What is the myth I'm living?" Answer it, or seek to answer it, and *remember the question* when times get tough, and it will help. The question's value rests in its potential to change our perspective. It reminds us to consider how any particular problem plays into the myth of our lives, prompting us to take a longer-term view.

Joseph Campbell, himself heavily influenced by Jung, wrote in *The Hero with a Thousand Faces*, "We have not even to risk the adventure alone; for the heroes of all time have gone before us, the labyrinth is thoroughly known." Campbell believed that if we studied mythology, if we familiarized ourselves with the myths of the world, we'd find direction. There are real dragons out there; they just don't have tails and big teeth, and they don't breathe fire. If we see a problem—or any particular challenge—as a ferocious dragon, we're in trouble. If we see it instead as a vehicle for greater awareness, as a source of learning and growth, the dragon ceases to be a dragon.

The religions of the world are intended to offer similar direction. At their best, religion provides guidance that individuals can use to navigate their way through life's ups and downs. When Rich asked his friend Warren about religion, he was hoping to find guidance—and maybe salvation. What is religion at its worst? Physicist Stephen Weinberg wrote, "With or without religion, good people can behave well and bad people can do evil; but for good people to do evil—that takes religion." At its worst, religion employs dogma created by individuals to promote us-versus-them thinking. Certain religious beliefs can cause the family and friends of people who complete suicide to suffer well beyond the loss of their loved one.

I just said that Rich was looking for guidance in religion. Victor Frankl, who survived the Nazi concentration camps and wrote *Man's Search for Meaning*, was fond of quoting Nietzsche: "He who has a why to live can bear with almost any how." Rich was looking not for a "how" but a "why." With all his pain, why should he continue on? Jung believed that the major challenge of the second half of life was identifying a *why*. One such why, in his opinion, was the prospect of an afterlife. Jung wrote, "The ancient . . . medicine of immortality is more profound and meaningful than we supposed." An afterlife offers the possibility that this life is preparation for the next, and whether true or not, can give hope—a why—to those of us here on Earth.

This brings us to the question that drove me so much angst as a kid: What happens to us when we die? Where is Richard now? As with the "Why are we here?" question, there's no definitive answer, is there?

By trade, I'm what you might call a quasi-statistician. Statisticians resolve themselves to a world without absolutes. Whether they outwardly realize it or not, that's what they do. Statisticians live in the world of probabilities—one of likelihoods. When you flip a coin, will it be heads or tails? The statistician decisively says, "I don't know." Then says, "I can tell you that the probability is overwhelming that it will be either heads or tails; there's also a remote chance it will land on its side, but so remote I wouldn't worry about it unless you're playing on a surface with slots. Are you playing on a surface with slots? If so, then we'll need to do some more calculations."

How about probabilities and an afterlife? The world's religions, though differing on the particulars, are almost uniformly in support of the notion of an afterlife. The most notable abstainer is Judaism, but Judaism doesn't say there isn't an afterlife—in fact, some sects hold that there is. In general, the Jewish position is exemplified by scholar Robert Goldenberg: "Because no evidence is available according to which [life after death] can be decided, those who consider these questions must acknowledge that we cannot ever answer them with certainty."

As to other religions, both Christians and Muslims agree that there is an afterlife. Each has some quirks like Purgatory in Christianity or the Interworld in Islam, but the individual moves on. What happens when you get there is open to debate. When I was a kid, I envisioned people sitting on clouds, playing harps. The more theoretical afterlife interpretations hold that the individual arrives at a kind of pure consciousness, where he or she is one with God's love. How about Hinduism or Buddhism? Here, believers assert that the individual is reincarnated. While the goal is to escape the constant cycle of death and rebirth—to achieve Buddhahood or nirvana—the death of the physical body is not the end but simply a way station in the journey, as with Christianity and Islam.

Religious scholar Judith Berling wrote that for Chinese religions, "the boundaries between life and death [are] relatively porous. That is to say, 'existence' on the two sides of this line [is] not always as radically different as we might expect. There may be 'deathlike' experiences in life, and 'lifelike' experiences in death." While not as central to Chinese religions as Christianity or Islam, there is a belief in an "eternal salvation."

For the religious person, then, chances are good that whatever religion is practiced, life does not end with the death of the physical body. The individual continues on—even though we can never really be sure.

I wrote about the desk that Mom and Dad gave to me for Christmas. That desk turned out to be one of the best gifts I ever got as a kid. I sat at it for hours scribbling ideas, drawing pictures and wondering. When I outgrew it, we gave it to our next-door neighbor's son. I don't know what happened to the desk once he took ownership, but it certainly enjoyed some kind of a rebirth.

SITTING IN RICH'S CLOSET

Two days after Rich passed, I sat in the bedroom closet at his apartment in Austin and cried. That was the best I could do. On Saturday night when he died, I got almost no sleep. On Sunday night, I was exhausted but still couldn't get a full night's sleep. On Monday afternoon, as I sat in his closet, the sun was shining, and the apartment reminded me of Rich's place in San Diego. I curled up in the corner and tears emptied down my face. Rich wasn't in the other room; he was gone. One of his two boxers, Zack, saw me. Deana and I had just taken Zack and Daisy for a walk. He came over to me as I sat among Rich's clothes and lay by my side.

On Sunday morning, I'd cried uncontrollably at breakfast, twenty minutes of tears. Deana, Mom, Dad, Sharon and I ate breakfast at the Marriot in Austin, where we stayed. Sunday morning was a beautiful morning; the sky was blue, and the temperature was going to be eighty. It just didn't seem possible that Rich wasn't going to join us. He was going to march up the stairs to the outdoor patio, smile and walk right over to us. That's the kind of thinking that will really devastate you. At least, it devastated me that morning.

From the closet on Monday afternoon, I looked over at the bathroom sink; fifty syringes were neatly stacked next to it. One of the police reports said that officers had confiscated steroids from Rich's apartment. The finding made sense. Rich was ripped (very muscular) at the wedding. When he used steroids, he told me that the pain from the psoriatic arthritis went away—the steroids, he said, lubricated his joints.

No one bothered me as I sat with Zack. Deana, Mom and Sharon were in the kitchen with Heidi, the girl who'd been watching Zack and Daisy. Sharon was trying to find out about Heidi's relationship with Rich. At one point, Rich had lived in Austin by himself, for about six months, while Sharon lived in San Diego. Heidi told Deana in private, away from Sharon, that no one in the complex knew Rich was engaged. He hadn't told anyone. Heidi worked at a bar Rich liked, and no one there knew Rich was engaged either.

One of the times Rich moved back to San Diego after living in Austin, he told his friends in Austin that he was going to an Indian reservation where he'd work with spiritual healers to remedy his bipolar disorder. To some friends, he said the reservation was in Arizona. To others, he said the reservation was in Maine. He told the same friends that he was going to see Dad in Boston as well, because Dad was dying from cancer (he wasn't).

Rich had flipped off a metaphorical cliff during his time in Austin. I was struck by the reservation story. When I visited Rich in the fall of 2002, the drive I'd taken on I-8 from San Diego to southern Arizona was spiritual. It calmed me; I could sense the vastness of the desert, and my problems melted into it. Deana and I had considered spending a year on a reservation. I'd told Rich about it. Deana would get a job as a pharmacist on the reservation (there are quite a few openings for pharmacists), and I'd take a year off and write.

Some Sioux Indians call money the "green frog skin." In a book written by Richard Erdoes called *Lame Deer: Seeker of Visions*, Lame Deer, a Sioux medicine man, said, "The world in which you paint a picture in your mind, a picture which shows things different from what your eyes see, that is the world from which I get my visions." He said the vision world is where he lives—"I tell you this is the real world, not the Green Frog Skin World. That's only a bad dream, a streamlined, smog-filled nightmare."

For Lame Deer, the green frog skin would ultimately lead to the end of Western culture. Once the addiction to buying ended, Lame Deer said the world of money would have no more use for people. According to Lame Deer, Americans "have become frogs themselves. Some cruel child has stuffed a cigar into their mouths, and they have to keep puffing and puffing until they explode. Fat-taking is a bad thing, even for the taker."

There is no one reason someone takes his or her life. There's no one reason anything happens. The present moment is a synthesis of beliefs, emotions, moods, choices, actions—it's a meeting of past perspectives and future expectations that generates a memory subject to the same forces. Rich didn't take his life because of materialism. He had so much going on when his physical body passed. He'd slipped over a line where he went to mystical retreats, maybe retreats he knew never happened or ones he conjured up as real in his head. The talk about suicide, though, had been going on since he was a teenager.

Mom, Dad, Deana, Sharon and I had gone to pick up Richard's truck on Monday morning from the private lot where it was impounded. Normally, the daily fee at the lot was $50. The sergeant who handled Rich's case with the Austin police told me to call the man who owned the lot; he said be sure to catch him personally. The man used to be on the Austin police force and was a friend of his. I called the lot owner on Monday morning, and he told me there would be no charge for keeping Rich's truck. It was a strange twist—the Austin police we dealt with cared, the kind of caring I would have expected in the hospital.

The lot itself was off the main highway. It was surrounded by a chain-link fence with barbed wire on top, and there were metal bars on the window where Mom and I went to find out about Rich's truck. I had to slip the receipt the sergeant had given us into a revolving drawer under the window. The woman on the other side of the window, seeing the receipt with the sergeant's notes on it, left her desk and came around to the front. She walked us across the street to where Rich's truck was, and then left us to continue forward on our own.

While Deana, Dad and Sharon stayed in the rented minivan, Mom and I walked across the sandy, dirt lot in private. I could feel something inside the truck when I first went in—my skin tingled. I was acutely aware that there was no more physical Rich to drive it anymore. The cab was warmed from the sun. In the holding area between the two front seats was a twelve-pack of Heineken; all the beers were unopened except one that was halfway empty. In the backseat were clothes, mostly shirts. Rich hadn't bothered to unload them.

Books about suicide say that when a normally depressed and suicidal person gets calm, that's the time to worry. After the service, Miguel, one of Rich's friends from San Diego, told Mom that Rich had been unusually relaxed as he watched football with him the Sunday before. Normally, Rich would get all tense, especially when the Patriots were playing. That last Sunday (before he moved back to Austin), Rich stayed calm, stretching his arms across the top of Miguel's couch.

Miguel worked in commercial real estate, and he told Mom how Rich would help him solve problems he was having at the office—strategic problems like what way interest rates were going. Rich liked to meet Miguel and his friends after work for beers. They'd show up in coats and ties, and Rich in flip-flops, jeans and a T-shirt.

On October 31, 2005, the Monday that Rich arrived in Austin, he rented an apartment at the same complex where he'd lived before. As he was moving in a few things, he saw Heidi (with whom he'd been friends before). Heidi said he smiled and said, "Hey, neighbor, how's it going?" He was completely at ease and remained so most of the week. When Heidi asked Rich what he was doing on that last Friday, November 4, he said he was about to drive to the greenbelt to shoot himself. She pleaded with him to stop, but he shut the door to his truck, rolled down the window and kept driving. Once Rich drove off, Heidi called the police.

When Rich got to the park, he met a girl while he was walking to his spot in the creek. After they spoke for a while, she asked him what he was doing: He was carrying something under a blanket the whole time they talked. Rich said it was a shotgun, and he was going to shoot himself. What could the girl say? She, too, called the police. She happened to have bipolar disorder as well. After Rich's service, she sent an email to Rich's tribute page in the online edition of the *Boston Globe*. She said she'd always remember Rich.

After he took his position in the riverbed, Rich called 911 so that the police would know where to find his body. According to the police report, Rich told the girl who answered the call that she was the last person who would ever hear his voice. That hit me when I read it: that poor girl—all three girls that day—each brought into the circle of suffering.

Once Mom and I got into Rich's truck in the impoundment lot, I drove it out. Dust kicked up as I steered past the chain-link fence, before parking next to the rented minivan. Rocks made popping sounds under the tires as I brought the truck to a stop. The drive lasted about fifteen seconds. Mom got out of the passenger seat while I sat on the driver's side for a minute or two more. I kept thinking that this was the last vehicle Rich had driven on his last day. It was as if the truck was repeating the thought to me. Rich knew when he got into the truck that he'd never ride in another vehicle again. He must have drank his half beer as he rode out to the greenbelt, I thought, or maybe he drank it at the park.

A common Buddhist practice is to imagine yourself on your own deathbed. See yourself and more importantly feel yourself there: You aren't in the present moment but are actually preparing to breathe your last breath. The power of the exercise is twofold. It forces you to acknowledge what's important and what's not important in your life, lifting you out of the "ho-hum" of day-to-day existence. Practiced enough, it also desensitizes you to the moment that's waiting for all of us. I tried to put myself into Rich's shoes when he got to the park.

I imagine turning off the ignition in the truck. I see myself as Rich, grabbing the gun sitting in the passenger seat beside me. I cover the gun with a blanket and exit the truck, noticing the air hitting me as I do. The sky looks different; it's sharper. The colors are brighter, resplendent. I walk in slow motion. After talking with a girl who is walking there, too, the trip to my spot in the creek is its own little eternity.

What was Rich thinking about as he went? Was he at peace? He was going to move on, and, more, he knew he was going to move on. Nothing mattered anymore; nothing ever mattered. There would be no more bipolar disorder for him, no more psoriatic arthritis, no more back pain, no more trading, no more aggravation and no more laughter. His debts: They were meaningless. On his last day, the walls, once unscalable, tumbled down—dissolving into the sands they always were.

It got so crazy once he took up his position in the riverbed—the shouting, the police, the SWAT team, the reporters: all the swirling mayhem. The walk, though . . . I hope that walk gave him the serenity he'd been searching for.

The philosopher Benedict de Spinoza predicted the day he would die from consumption (a kind of lung disease). He felt his death in his bones and approached his last day like any other. Death had no hold over him because he chose not to fear it and not to anguish over it. That kind of approach to death didn't just happen because Spinoza wanted it to happen. He *lived* his philosophy every day. It was, for him, an ingrained habit. On his last day, he knew that he was going to die, but there was nothing he could do about it, so he approached it like any other day. That's how he'd trained his underlying emotions to work.

In Roman times, the philosopher Seneca was sentenced to death by the emperor Nero, his former pupil. Seneca had done nothing wrong. He was sentenced to die simply because Nero had gone insane and came to believe through his paranoid delusions that Seneca was involved in a plot to kill him. In his book *The Consolations of Philosophy*, Alain de Botton wrote of Seneca, "He had from the first conceived of philosophy as a discipline to assist human beings in overcoming conflicts between their wishes and reality." Seneca's friends wept when Nero's men came to kill him. When he saw them weeping, Seneca asked, "Where [has your] philosophy gone? . . . Surely no one was unaware that Nero was cruel."

De Botton wrote that a single theme runs throughout Seneca's work: "that we best endure those frustrations which we have prepared ourselves for and understand and are hurt most by those we least expected and cannot fathom." In other words, all we can control is how we train ourselves. We can't change fortune as Descartes said, but we can change how we respond to it.

As I sat in Rich's closet on that Monday afternoon in Austin, I thought about visiting Rich. I thought how the apartment and the bathroom seemed like Rich's other apartments. I thought if not for a single moment in a single day, I could have been in there while Rich was out in the other room. Rich's physical body was gone. I think Mom and Dad said it best after the service. The idea hit me in the closet, but I didn't realize it until I heard the words: "I'm no longer afraid of death," they both agreed, "because I know I'll see Rich when it happens." Said once, it's a saying. Said a few times, it's more of a bent. Practiced enough, it's a habit; it's a philosophy, and, yes, it becomes an escape. And no one in the world can prove it one way or the other.

Zeno, Time and Infinity

I'm not sure I ever saw Rich wear the same sunglasses for more than six months at a time. He always seemed to have a new pair. By the time I got around to buying sunglasses similar to what Rich had last worn, they were dated. I'd boldly wear my new shades—say, if we were vacationing in Cancun (which I'll describe in the next chapter)—and then Rich would put on an entirely different pair, making the ones I was wearing look obsolete. Sunglasses change the way we see the world. They might make things look darker or maybe sharper, but the world looks different than it would look otherwise.

So far in this chapter, I've written about the concept of afterlives and how to employ philosophy to defuse some of death's sting. I'm going to start mixing in ideas from physics and a few from math, too. Death is a complicated topic, and to explore it, we'll need to explore some complicated ideas as well. Bear in mind as you read that the purpose of our inquiry is to develop new or different ways of thinking about death, a process which has helped me come to terms with Rich's death.

Perhaps the way to start this section is with a couple of pointed questions. First, Is it possible that we're all wearing the same kind of metaphorical sunglasses as we move through life? And second, Maybe without our shades, some of the things that we simply accept without question—things like time's coldhearted forward march, even things like *the finality of death*—would also look different?

An ancient philosopher, Zeno, constructed the paradox of Achilles and the tortoise. The essence of the paradox is this: If you are going to walk from where you're reading this book to the front door, you will need to traverse some finite distance. That distance, however, can be divided infinitely. Consider the distance between 1 and 2 feet. It can be divided by 2, to 6 inches, and by 2 again, to 3 inches, and again and again. There's no limit—no matter how small the distance, it can always be divided in two. Thus, to travel from wherever you are to the front door, you have to cover a space that can be divided infinitely many times. That seems to require that you must cross an infinity, which is impossible—yet, as long as no physical constraint limits you, you can go to the front door.

Zeno's point is that both perspectives are supported. You can both argue that you should never be able to get to the front door *and* successfully prove that it can be done. For our purposes, the real key to Zeno's paradox is that it implies that *even with all the time that's ever been, we won't get to the front door because we'd have to cross an infinity to do so.* If that were actually the case, it would have some powerful ramifications on death. We'd have to do the impossible: We'd have to cross an infinity to get to wherever we were going to die.

But hold on—if each time we go someplace, we have to cross an infinity to do so, how would we ever get anywhere? It sounds so ridiculously counterintuitive. Maybe we should just trust the world we're seeing through our sunglasses and disregard the notion from the start? Before we do, let's consider an argument that's been used to zap Zeno's paradox of its strength, an argument that relies on mathematics—I'll call it the "math refutation."

The reason we can cross a finite space composed of infinite divisions, say those who employ the math refutation, has to do with certain mathematical observations—specifically, each time we divide the distance between the front door and us by 2, we have to divide the time it takes to get there by 2. The mathematical assertion is that in considering the distance to the front door, we must also consider the time it takes to get there. Thus, when we talk about crossing an infinity, we're not just dividing distance in isolation—we're also dividing the time it takes to cross that distance. Once we get down to $1/1,000,000$ of a unit of distance, it will similarly take only $1/1,000,000$ of a unit of time to cross that distance. Infinitesimally small distances take infinitesimally small amounts of time to cross.

The math refutation eliminates the infinity problem by subtly introducing another reference point: *time*, thus treating time as if it has an existence of its own. The problem with this treatment of time is that most experts believe it's not accurate: Time only makes sense in combination with something else. Einstein, for example, held that time has no independent existence; it is part of space-time. We saw in the "Watches" section of Chapter Six that the time watches keep, Time-Earth, is relevant to the movements of the Earth as it spins on its axis and orbits the Sun.

Even if we acquiesce and allow an independent existence of time (for argument's sake), there is another weakness present in the math refutation of Zeno's paradox. It has to do with the type of time the math refutation proponents couple with distance—specifically, they assume that there's only one kind of time. What if we stepped up and said, "We'd like to introduce an alternative reference point to Time-Earth—it's called *Time-Infinity*." After quietly discussing our position among ourselves, we'd inform those employing the math refutation that we're taking advantage of the fact that clocks placed in strong gravitational fields go slower than clocks under the influence of Earth's gravitational pull. "Time-Infinity," we'd say, "is measured relative to the gravity within a black hole, where nothing can escape, not even light, because the gravitational force is so strong."

In his book *A Brief History of Time*, renowned theoretical physicist Stephen Hawking described a thought experiment in which an "intrepid astronaut" is on the surface of a star as it collapses into a black hole. Hawking asked his readers to suppose that each second, the astronaut sends a signal to colleagues on a spaceship orbiting the star. Further suppose that at 11:00, the star will collapse into a black hole. During the star's implosion, all the signals being sent by the astronaut and received by the colleagues appear to be sent at a rate of one every second. It seems like business as usual. Finally, we get to the last second. What happens to the signal sent to the spaceship between 10:59:59 and 11:00? The answer is that the astronaut's colleagues will "wait forever." The reason?

Hawking wrote, "The light waves emitted from the surface of the star between 10:59:59 and 11:00, by the astronaut's watch, would be spread out over an infinite period of time, as seen from the spaceship."

Hawking, of course, cautioned that anything on the surface of a star collapsing to a black hole would itself be crushed. However, as interested spectators, we can use the time within a black hole—Time-Infinity—as the reference time for the walk to the front door. In this case, we'll never get to the front door. Any distance, even one trillionth of a trillionth of an inch, is an *infinity* away. Even though no one's actually experienced Time-Infinity, if we employ it, Zeno's paradox is back to its old devastating self. The math refutation of Zeno's paradox, thus, depends on the kind of time being referenced.

Swimming in a mathematical river can be discombobulating. The river can have rapids that are recognizable only once we're in them. It's easy to get confused and perplexed and turned upside down. In the case of Zeno's paradox, the math refutation simply takes advantage of a unique set of gravitational circumstances here on Earth. It's says, "Out of all the possible times, I'm going to select just one." It's like announcing, "The reason I can walk to the front door is that I can walk to the front door." As far as we can tell through our sunglasses, that's true, but it doesn't change the fact that the distance you or I travel to get there can always be divided by 2 one more time.

Zeno's paradox can also be applied to human beings when we consider what we're ultimately made from. At first glance, we sure seem solid. Considered more closely, though, we can break ourselves down into systems (cardiovascular system, central nervous system), organs (heart, liver, kidney) and cells (nerve cells, brain cells, blood cells). It doesn't stop at the cellular level; we can keep going deeper. Cells in humans have a nucleus, ribosomes, mitochondria, centrioles and chromosomes. Chromosomes contain DNA and other proteins. Going further and smaller, DNA is made up of nucleotide monomers. Eventually, we'll get to atoms. The ancient Greeks thought an atom was as small as you could practically go. However, we know that you can get smaller still. There are quarks—what physicists presently believe to be fundamental building blocks of the universe, as small as matter can get.

The issue with matter like quarks is that they don't seem to have the kinds of properties you might expect in solid, fundamental building blocks. The best physicists can deduce, with the tools presently available to investigate quarks, is that they have no size and occupy no space. If we were building something like a tree fort, our first choice probably wouldn't be boards made from matter that has no size and occupies no space. Based on their description, it sounds like quarks would be hard to see. In fact, they've never actually been seen. Their existence is inferred from scientific experiments involving particle accelerators, sophisticated detection equipment and reams of data analysis.

If you've ever read a book about American Indian folklore, you may have heard about *shape-shifting*, a magical process whereby people can change into birds or wolves and then back to humans again. Well, shape-shifting is not just folklore for matter—matter actually shape-shifts. Some types of matter can change to antimatter (particles with the opposite electrical charges of their matter counterparts) and then back. In Chapter Four, we talked about some of the foibles of brains—for example, causing us to see mirages on highways. Mirages are nothing compared to the idiosyncrasies of the matter that we're supposedly made from.

As if what we've learned so far about matter isn't confusing enough, the concept of matter has, itself, undergone an even more fundamental change. It used to be that matter was considered primary to space. You couldn't have space without matter. The new thinking is different: Space is the necessary precursor to matter. In his unpublished paper "Universe, Life, Consciousness," physicist Andrei Linde wrote, "In this picture, instead of using space for describing the only real thing, matter, we use the notion of matter in order to simplify description of superspace." So what? we might ask. The change in perspective is, in Linde's words, "one of the most profound (and least known) consequences of modern physics." In this sense, matter is more like an *idea*, a helpful way of making sense of space.

In terms of applying Zeno's paradox to what we're ultimately made from, our fundamental building blocks are sizeless, spaceless bits of matter that have never been seen, can shape-shift and are really just useful tools, or ideas, for making sense of space. Which idea is more disconcerting: that we can never get to the front door or that we're made from ideas?

If all this is a little much to digest, let's step back and consider light. What is light? Some experiments demonstrate that light is a continuous wave. Other experiments show equally convincingly that light is made up of noncontinuous particles. Light, as it turns out, is both a wave *and* a particle. For physicist Niels Bohr, the wavelike and particle-like properties of light demonstrated a principle in nature called "complementarity." Light behaves like a particle or like a wave depending on how we observe it. Neither position is wrong, and neither, according to Bohr, is the whole picture—for that, you need both views. What light is to *us*, in other words, depends on our perspective.

The purpose of Chapter Nine is to help us diffuse some of death's finality. In order for death to be final, Time-Earth must move in only one direction— forward. If we could reverse it, we could go back to visit our departed relatives and loved ones again. Time-Earth, as we've seen, isn't the only kind of time. In this section on Zeno's paradox, we investigated a theoretical Infinity-Time. In Chapter Six, we also explored Time-Memory, by which we can instantaneously pull up, in our memory, events that happened years ago.

Philosophers like Zeno have long debated what exactly we can *know*. It's easy to get caught thinking we know something, when, in fact, it's simply a consequence of our perspective. Sometimes things aren't as straightforward as they first appear. It seems like we can walk to the front door, but there are convincing arguments that we shouldn't be able to. Our bodies seem substantive, but a closer examination reveals no substance in the sense that we typically understand it—stable objects having size and occupying space.

Maybe if we consider Time-Earth more closely, we'll find some more paradoxes. Perhaps, the finality of death *hinges on our perspective*, and as we putter around our world, we're stuck in the only one we can recognize. Through our shades, I wonder if we're presently seeing light as a wave or a particle?

GAZING AT THE BONFIRE

Deana and I were sitting in the Austin airport as clouds hid the sun outside. I stared out a window at the runway. The weekend was over, its own little eternity, twenty years in the making. Country music was playing, and people walked around the airport like it was a regular day. The world moved forward, less one person. One of the cruelest things life can do is to continue on without any regard to tragedy, and maybe that's the best it can do.

When we boarded the plane bound for Greensboro, I was drained. Once we got home (and after picking up the dogs), I focused on writing Rich's obituary. Immersed in words, a little bit of my brain had time to adjust ever so slightly to life without physical Rich.

The day after we got home, Deana had to travel for business. When she left, I went into the backyard and raked leaves. Fallen branches were everywhere. When Deana's around, we strictly adhere to town regulations concerning fire in the backyard. With Deana traveling, I went into the garage and got some of the oil we use in the citronella candles on the deck. I poured the oil over a clump of tree branches and lit a fire. For most of the afternoon, I added branches to it and watched them burn. Our dog Jack likes a good fire, so he joined me. Rocky, our other dog, stayed up on the deck. He's a little bit more cautious about things like fire and prefers to keep his distance. Eventually, he came off the deck and joined Jack and me. The flames danced in front of us.

A fire depends on three things: an ignition source, fuel to burn and gas to sustain the combustion. The flames in a fire need the right circumstances to happen, and there in the backyard, they had it, so I sat and watched them.

To me, a flame looks alive, a kind of unique living being. It's not; it's a burning gas, but it seems alive—as if sustained by a kind of life force. In one form or another, the concept of a life force has existed from civilization to civilization. There's qi, mana, bioenergy and orgone to name just a few. Qi is the force some believe is being redirected when people get acupuncture. The life force, as adherents hold, rolls through our bodies, giving the inorganic chemicals, of which our bodies are made, life. The life force has tended to be an eternal concept. It survives the death of the physical body like a soul. It's not quite energy, not quite anything we can put our fingers on, but it's everywhere.

When I think of Rich's death, only a tiny percentage of cells in him changed, but because blood was cut off from his brain for long enough, parts of it died. His body, of which his brain was a part, could have been kept alive longer. The hospital could have kept running current through him until other organs such as his heart eventually shut down. But the ability for Rich to connect with the world the way that he had a few moments before was lost because of a brief cessation of the blood flowing to his brain. Even if the life force was still rolling through him, his ability to communicate depended on the proper functioning of his brain. The whole system is fragile. It's so very fragile. Rich, like a lot of people, died on a technicality—in Rich's case, his carotid artery just couldn't pump enough blood. That makes me consider now that we're wonderfully complicated machines, capable of enjoying the arts, nature and everything else because our brains allow us to do so.

A battery-powered robot converts the energy in batteries to an electrical current, which in turn powers the robot. Some walk; some can do household chores; they can do all the things their mechanical engineers designed them to do. Descartes likened the human body to a machine. The philosopher Thomas Hobbes did, too. Through the process of breathing, humans are able to access the energy in food, converting that food to the currents we need to power us. We combust food in the presence of oxygen. If there is no food or no air, we soon have no "being alive." Likewise, with a battery-powered robot: no batteries, no power source, and there is no movement—no "robot operating properly," which I loosely link to "no robot being alive." How different is our state of being alive from the robot's state of operating properly?

Bill Bryson asked in *A Short History of Nearly Everything* whether our living might not be as miraculous as it first appears. The fact that we have all the chemicals we need to *live* may be the simple result of our developing within the confines of what was, and is, available to us. We breathe O_2 because O_2 is what's here. In some other world, we might breathe O_3 because that's what's available there. We evolved to breathe O_2. Whatever nutrients and chemicals were available to us were used. God, or the universe, or the combination of random luck and skill, created us with the ingredients that were available at the time. We were improvised. We evolved simply because that's what happened. Not only wasn't it miraculous, but it was also inevitable.

In this sense, we're walking, breathing chemical reactions. Human reasoning and self-awareness are the simple results of the parts and reactions in our brains. We think and feel emotions because of neurons and brain synapses and electricity and chemicals. From a robotic perspective, it's not the life force that generates consciousness; it's the way our bodies, including our brains, are put together. In the presence of food and oxygen, we're able to experience a particular form of *aliveness* in which we're conscious. There's nothing especially divine about it at all; no life force needed.

Mystics, on the other hand, talk of experiencing the oneness of it all, moments when they're aware of being part of something more. They're not individual, sophisticated robots but part of a whole, part of the dance of life. As Native Americans were being forced onto reservations in the late 1800s, they began a ceremony known as the Ghost Dance. In *Black Elk Speaks,* Sioux holy man Black Elk described a "great happiness" that overcame him when he heard about the Ghost Dances. He interpreted the happiness as a reminder "to get to work at once" and help his people live in "a sacred manner pleasing to the Powers of the Universe that are One Power." In *Myths to Live By*, Joseph Campbell described an Eskimo shaman's description of his version of the life force: "Sila [is a power] that cannot be explained in so many words: a very strong spirit, the upholder of the universe, of the weather, in fact of all life on earth." For Black Elk and the Eskimo shaman, life is a function of a single force—a belief that sounds uncannily like the modern physics notion that we touched on in the last section: the notion that space is the precursor to matter.

Seneca cautioned us to prepare for possible eventualities so that we're not devastated by them. What if Rich and everyone else are simply walking, talking, sophisticated chemical reactions—and the life force or souls or God has nothing to do with it? Should I worry?—it won't do me any good. I can't change it. If I am a chemical reaction, it won't matter when I die because my death will be the end. No more joy, no more sorrow, no more humanness. Does that mean no life after death? Even if I am simply a chemical reaction, am I precluded from living on in some form?

The physicist David Bohm wrote in *Wholeness and the Implicate Order*, "Life itself has to be regarded as belonging in some sense to a totality." As with a tree whose life depends on many things outside the tree itself, as with a flame that needs ignition, fuel and gas so that it can burn, nothing stands in isolation. If we are just chemical reactions, we are, at the very least, interdependent chemical reactions. When Rich died, he left the myth of his life, in all its forms. He left the stories I'm writing about, the perspectives he brought to the world. Those stories and perspectives can bring new stories and perspectives. The chain continues on despite the absence of Rich's physical self.

Archaeologists dig in dirt, sand and rocks. They uncover artifacts created thousands of years ago but are seeing them for the first time today. Are archaeological discoveries just old relics or are they literally new? What the archaeologists see is new to them—the observers. In *The Book*, Alan Watts wrote, "The death of the individual is not disconnection but simply withdrawal. The corpse is like a footprint of an echo—the dissolving tract of something which the Self has ceased to do."

Whether there is a life force or not, whether we are simply chemical reactions or have souls that live on, the living can develop new relationships with those who have died. We can become archaeologists. It's still possible to have epiphanies and surprises. It takes more effort on our part. We have to dig a little. But in the digging, we can transcend questions about an afterlife. The "Self," as Watts described it, is still available for connection.

CARTOONS AND HUME

I crawled up on top of the washing machine and pulled down the cereal. Rich got the milk. We plucked bowls out of the dishwasher and spoons from the drawer. Rich and I were somewhere around eight and ten years old, enjoying a typical Saturday morning. The cereal today was Lucky Charms, our favorite. We liked Frosted Flakes, too, but if we let those flakes sit too long, we'd have mush. Lucky Charms was designed for the repose of a Saturday morning. The little marshmallows got better when they were bulging with milk.

On most Saturdays, we got up at about 7:30 am, filled our bowls with sugar cereal and milk, and went into the family room to watch cartoons. Mom and Dad would wake up around the same time. One of them would turn on the oven and put honey buns in, and the other made coffee. By the time the honey buns were ready, Rich and I would have about two bowls of sugar cereal coursing through our little systems. You might think it would be a prime time for fights, but it wasn't. We were two happy, wired kids on Saturday morning, agreed on what the day's schedule would look like. Neither one of us cared much for *Scooby-Doo*, but he was a good transition to the cartoons we wanted to see. During *Scooby-Doo*, we played with LEGO bricks. Once Foghorn Leghorn (the big rooster) came on, we stopped with the LEGOs and focused our attention on the television.

"Boy, I say booooy, what are you doing down thar, boy?" Foghorn Leghorn would say to the little chicken hawk, as the hawk was doing something like trying to carry Foghorn off by his toe. Then he'd whisper to the TV screen, "The boy's about as sharp as a bowlin' ball." When he did, Rich and I cracked up. What entertainment!

On one of the cartoons, Bugs Bunny (it could have been another character, but Bugs is a good bet) drew his own cartoon. He created a bunch of pictures of a dog. When he was done drawing, he flipped through the pictures, and the dog looked like it was running. "So that's how they do it," Rich and I concluded. And that's how they actually do it. An animated cartoon is created through a series of individual pictures. The illusion of animation results from three things. First, you have to arrange the individual pictures in the right order. Then you film each picture in its proper sequence; in a typical cartoon, there are twenty-four picture frames shown every second. Finally, you allow the mind to fill in the blanks. A sequence that shows a cartoon dog running does not need a picture for each millisecond movement of the dog. Our minds take care of that.

❖ ❖ ❖

Within this book, we've seen that not only are we made from scraps, but we're also physically changing in terms of cell composition from one moment to the next. Our bodies, which appear to have substance, aren't so solid at the sub-atomic level. In terms of nailing down what we actually are, it's not clear-cut, given that we're constantly changing. Like the rest of our bodies, our brains change, too. In Chapter Five, we defined a working brain as a *mind*. To make things even more convoluted, we found that our minds rely on external objects in the process of thinking—objects like sticky notes, calendars and notebooks. I've been trying to figure out what we miss when someone dies, but I don't seem to be getting anywhere.

In the section on the *Investigating the Mind* conference in Chapter Seven, we saw that even though our minds are sometimes equated to us, we don't always have control over them. Maybe exploring another aspect of what our minds *do* will yield fruit in our search for what in us is invariable over time.

In addition to allowing us to enjoy entertainment like cartoons, our minds also generate thoughts. That's perhaps the central duty of our minds, the one that separates us from all the other animals. Our minds generate lofty thoughts like "I think, therefore I am" and not so lofty thoughts like "How could my big present for Christmas be a desk?" In Chapter Six, we explored beliefs and how they influence our lives. Our thoughts, including our beliefs, tend to define who we are to other people: for example, thoughts concerning ethics, religion and politics. And our thoughts define who we are to ourselves—such as thoughts about our value as individuals.

Is it possible that we are our *thoughts*? Before we consider that question, let's first get a handle on what a thought is. Is a thought substantive, like a body seems to be, or ephemeral? According to most experts, thoughts are a combination of neural pathways, chemicals and electricity. That is, a thought is a community of neurons, activated when electricity drives the release of neurochemicals, which then find their way into the right neuron receptors. Thoughts are pathways in use. They're announcements made over the audio-visual systems of our minds. As with everything else, though, our thoughts are interdependent—they're influenced by biology, circumstances, moods, past thoughts and other things.

If you've just been cut off in traffic, you'll be prone to a different set of thoughts than if you're comfortably sitting on your back porch, having just been awarded a raise at work. As to whether we *are* our thoughts—which thoughts? Are we all our thoughts, all the thoughts we've ever had? Don't people change their thoughts over time? Have you ever said to yourself, "I'm all turned around on this subject; I now think that such-and-such is right or so-and-so is wrong"? Or, "Last week I liked my career, but this week, I don't"? As far as equating ourselves to our thoughts, the moment we identified all the thoughts that seemed to represent us, another one would come along and muddle the picture.

As we've seen throughout this book, minds are also emotion generators. Perhaps we are our *emotions*? What are emotions? Experts hold that they're not unlike thoughts: They're neural pathways activated by chemicals and electricity. They're pathways brought to life by awareness, even if we, as individual minds, appear to play very little or no role in the "awareness" part. But as with thoughts, emotions change. We can become emotional about subjects that previously drove no emotional response and unemotional about subjects that used to drive emotion.

When he was small, Rich loved bulldozers. If a bulldozer was going and Rich saw it, you'd have to stop if you were with him. Mom used to pack him a lunch in the summertime when he was about six years old. He'd march up to a construction site (there was no shortage in our neighborhood) and sit nearby to watch. The workers would see a little kid sitting all alone near the site, eating his sandwich and watching their every move. By the end of the day, Rich would be sitting in the bulldozer and helping the driver plow a pile of dirt. Rich loved bulldozers. As he got older, the strength of Rich's emotional connection to bulldozers waned.

Emotions may be part of us, but they're not invariable. One minute we can be happy, and the next, sad. As has been the case throughout this book, we seem to have hit another wall in our search for what we miss when we miss someone. There doesn't seem to be a single thing we can nail down as an unchanging us that can be missed.

David Hume spent a great deal of energy exploring the kind of topic we're presently investigating: What in us is *invariable*—what persists through the changes in our bodies and minds over the course of our lifetimes? In his book *A Treatise of Human Nature*, Hume wrote that when he searched for the "self" in himself, he got lost. The self is supposed to be constant and invariable—we don't look in the mirror and conclude that the impression we're seeing today is similar to but not exactly the same as the one we saw yesterday: The person in the mirror is *me*. The self in us has staying power over time. Hume asked what this staying power, this invariability, actually is. What in us is the same as it was yesterday or last year?

After he analyzed the idea of an unchanging self, doggedly evaluating potential candidates that might fit the bill, Hume found himself at a loss. He wrote, "There is no impression constant and invariable." That is, everything we think and everything we feel comes and goes—"Pain and pleasure, grief and joy, passions and sensations succeed each other, and never all exist at the same time." Hume then concluded something perhaps more baffling than what we learned about matter in the section on Zeno's paradox. He wrote, "It cannot, therefore, be from any of these impressions, or from any other, that the idea of self is derived; and *consequently there is no such idea*" (italics added).

For Hume, humans are just "a bundle or collection of different perceptions, which succeed each other with an inconceivable rapidity and are in a perpetual flux and movement." To be clear, Hume held that our yearning for an unchanging self is in vain—it doesn't exist.

Before we go on, perhaps we should verify Hume's credentials? In his book *The Philosophy of David Hume*, Vere Chappell wrote, "David Hume was probably the greatest philosopher to write in English." Of the criticism of Hume's work, Bertrand Russell wrote, "For my part, I find none of their refutations convincing."

What if we were to change direction a bit here and make a case to Hume that our minds are the core of our unchanging identity? What if we said, "Maybe there is no unchanging self, and maybe all the things our minds *do* are subject to change. But our identity is not linked to any of that. It's linked to our minds, and they, themselves, are unchanging!"? Hume might smile (he was known for a cheerful disposition) and say, "I'm glad you asked." He likened the mind to a theater, "where several perceptions successively make their appearance, pass, re-pass, glide away, and mingle in an infinite variety of postures and situations." He warned his readers that the comparison to a theater must not mislead them into thinking that a mind persists over time. The mind is just a term that's applied to our awareness of the successive perceptions. He wrote, "The identity which we ascribe to the mind of man is only a fictitious one."

The criticism of Descartes' proof of his own existence is that it simply proves the existence of an individual thought. Hume's philosophy doesn't hide from the fleeting nature of existence but rather *embraces* it. All we can ever be is what we are right now. As Foghorn once said, "Well, paint me green and call me a pickle."

Before we walk away with the impression that Hume's conclusions are just philosophical gobbledygook, consider the findings of neuroscience researchers Gerald Edelman and Giulio Tononi. In their book *A Universe of Consciousness*, they wrote that within any live conscious scene, human beings can report at most four to seven independent pieces. That is, when we look out over a meadow, for example, we think we're seeing many different things—different kinds of grass, rocks, trees, maybe fences and horses, and leaves ruffling in the wind. The whole scene looks like a continuous whole. However, within that whole, we're only capable of holding on to four to seven independent pieces— perhaps one of the horses and a few items around that horse. Edelman and Tonini wrote, "The seeming richness of detail of many conscious scenes is more apparent than real." Just as Hume concluded that our sense of ourselves as unchanging personal identities is fictitious—so, too, it appears, is the detail we seem to see in conscious scenes. Most of that seeming detail is a product of our mind's ability to endow what we observe with *wholeness.*

Hemineglect is a neurological syndrome in which people lose the ability to focus awareness on one side of their body. Edelman and Tononi described the case of a man who suffered a stroke that resulted in his developing hemineglect. He shaved only the right side of his face, saw only the right sides of pictures and read only the right sides of words. He ignored any sense information, including touch and sight, presented to his left side. The power of the mind's ability to create a unified whole is underscored by the fact that the man denied anything was wrong with him: He thought he was seeing the whole picture. This kind of response is the norm for people with hemineglect. Their minds seal the gap and present the new half scenes as full scenes—scenes those with heminglect firmly believe to be whole.

As we saw in the section on Zeno's paradox, sometimes things aren't as straightforward as they first appear. Our inability to isolate multiple objects in any conscious scene is one of the reasons we can enjoy cartoons. When we watch a cartoon, we're actually observing twenty-four pictures per second, but because our minds can't isolate them and retain them individually, they look continuous. If we could perceive the pictures faster and hold on to those perceptions, we'd see the cartoon as individual pictures.

Back when Rich and I used to watch Saturday morning cartoons, the cartoon pictures were stored on a reel of film. That film was then fed into a projector in which light was shined on the individual pictures as they passed by, creating the illusion of animation, making the pictures look like they were going forward in time. When we last spoke about Time-Earth, we considered that perhaps it goes forward simply because of the sunglasses we wear. In the case of the cartoons that Rich and I used to watch, the projector served a sunglasses-like function. The pictures appeared to move forward in time because of the way they were projected and then observed by Rich and me. The cartoons themselves were simply individual pictures stored on a reel of film, always available for viewing as long as a projector and an observer were available.

With our background on Hume and cartoons, there's one more piece of information we need to consider before tying the various elements of this section together: a paradox concerning time. In an article for *Scientific American*, theoretical physicist Paul Davies wrote, "Physicists prefer to think of time as laid out in its entirety . . . with all past and future events located there together." In the same issue, *Scientific American* editor George Musser described "the problem of frozen time" that happens when physicists use a procedure called "canonical quantization" to translate Einstein's general theory of relativity into a theory compatible with quantum mechanics. It results in a formula called the Wheeler-DeWitt equation, which has no time variable. Musser wrote, "Taken literally, the equation indicates that the universe should be frozen in time, never changing." This is to say, when the universe is viewed as a complex mathematical model, there is no need for time. It is simply a useful means of describing what we observe through the lens of our brain, a kind of frosting on a cake which, in actuality, has no need for frosting.

The paradox for Time-Earth, then, is not that we can somehow alter its forward movement or stop its wheels from spinning and make it go backward: *The paradox is that Time-Earth is simply an illusion*, not unlike Hume's conclusion on our personal identity or the seeming richness of detail we perceive in conscious scenes. If time is actually *frozen*, if past, present and future events all exist right now, then the metaphorical sunglasses we talked about in the section on Zeno's paradox take on a more literal quality.

If time is frozen, it wouldn't just be cartoons that are stored on reels of film; our lives, too, would actually be stored on the metaphorical equivalent of a reel of film. They'd be like sophisticated cartoons, individual pictures wrapped together in a kind of film reel, projected through our brains and nervous systems, and observed by us. If this is too weird to contemplate, think about how DVDs work. A DVD is really just data burned onto a polycarbonate disc. Just like the old-time film reels, the data must be read by a projector—a DVD player (another kind of sunglasses)—in order for its contents to be revealed as a cartoon or movie and observed on a TV screen. In actuality, all the richness of detail on a DVD is simply the product of data and special sunglasses.

As far as human lives are concerned, if there is no time, then we take on the role of both projector and observer—displaying our lives on what Hume would say is the theater of our minds. In this way, it's not that Time-Earth really moves forward; it's just that it appears to move forward because that's how we, as dual projectors and observers, both project and observe it.

This notion of what I'll call a "cartoon universe" seems so bizarre that we might be tempted to ignore it as hocus-pocus. Before we do, consider the work of physicist David Deutsch. In his book *The Fabric of Reality*, he wrote that when we sense the passage of time, we interpret it "as evidence that our consciousness, or the present, or something, moves through time." That interpretation is incorrect, according to Deutsch. Temporal change—the flow of time—is an illusion. "Nothing can move from one moment to another," Deutsch wrote. *"To exist at all at a particular moment means to exist there forever"* (italics added).

In a cartoon universe, time seems to flow forward, and we appear to have pasts and futures, simply because that's the effect generated by our working brains. In such a universe, the lives of Rich and of you and of me are metaphorical cartoons, patterns of cosmological data, so to speak. They're always available for activation, a process that gives the observers of those cartoons sensations of personal ownership—ownership that, in the case of humans, is just an artifact of human sunglasses. In a cartoon universe, the films of our lives are always resting out there somewhere on a metaphorical shelf, waiting to be replayed.

This isn't science fiction; it's realistic scientific possibility. It might seem weird because we have brains that are conditioned to see things in familiar ways. Any death awareness in a cartoon universe would simply be a function of the way we, as dual projectors and observers, interpret the frames in the cartoon that we're viewing. We have the sensation that our lives are playing out in front of us this *one* time, but they're actually always available for viewing. This is really just a small step from Descartes and Hume, and one, as with the brain-in-a-vat paradox, that is supported by logic. It's scientifically and logically possible that our lives are simply pictures within metaphorical film reels. As far as lessening death's sting is concerned, we wouldn't even need to bother if we could recognize our world as part of a cartoon universe. Death is no more existent than time in a cartoon universe.

Scientists and philosophers frequently make reference to a principle called Occam's Razor. Essentially, Occam's Razor maintains that in explaining any phenomenon, the least complicated explanation is to be preferred. If something adds only complexity, it should be dropped. Which is less complex: a perspective that holds we must be present every millisecond of every day—the standard perspective, or one that requires our presence only about twenty-four times per second (or what our minds perceive to be a second)—and offers the same sense of continuity as the standard one?

In one of Rich's and my favorite Foghorn Leghorn cartoons, he plays hide-and-seek with a little chicken that wears glasses and has a hat with a propeller on it. Foghorn hides in a woodbin and then watches as the little chicken scribbles a few calculations and then starts walking across the yard, away from him. Foghorn laughs because the chicken is going the wrong way. In the next scene, the chicken starts digging in the yard with a shovel. After a few shovelfuls of dirt, he digs up Foghorn. Flabbergasted, Foghorn asks the viewers how he ended up where he did. The episode ends with Foghorn walking back over to woodbin where he was hiding. He gets ready to open it and just before he does, stops, saying, "Nope, I aint gonna look . . . I might just be IN there."

THE ISLAND TUNNEL

A month after Rich passed, I had a dream. In the dream, I'd flown out to California for the weekend. When I got there, two lines of people were waiting to go to an island just offshore. The first line was on land, on a dock. People in that line were being taken to the island by ferry. There was another line that was in the water. People there were being taken to the island via smaller motorboats. After I saw the lines of people, I considered whether to go home to North Carolina or not. I thought about the fact that I'd spent $1,000 on a plane ticket to fly to the West Coast. I decided it wouldn't make sense to fly all the way out and then turn around and fly all the way back.

As soon as I made my decision to stay, I was then with Rich. We were swimming together from the mainland to the island. Rich was leading me there; he knew the way because he'd been to it before. Everything felt right. I was *actually* with Rich. As we were approaching the island, I saw a mountain rising out of the water. When I looked closer, I saw the mountain *was* the island. It was evening, and as we neared the shore, I saw rocks beneath the surface of the water. I told Rich to be careful, but he didn't need the warning because he was skilled in navigating around the rocks. When we got on to the island, I had a sense that there was an entryway to some other area but couldn't see it.

Rich and I decided we'd go out on the island later that night. As we did, I remembered renting a car on the mainland and started worrying about it being towed. Rich showed me a shortcut from the island to the mainland, and my car was right there. I hadn't remembered parking it, but as soon as I saw it, I did. I said to Rich, more exclaimed, that we'd swam all this way to the island, and there was a shortcut right to where I'd been! When I saw the car, I also saw the hotel in which I was supposed to be staying. It was within easy walking distance of the island. Everything was falling into place. It felt so *fulfilling* to be there with Rich.

All of a sudden, we were on the island again. We were walking through a tunnel. Inside it, I was spontaneously aware that Rich had shot himself a few days before, and we were in the final month of his life—the wound would take him in a month. I then realized I had a chance to talk to him about the whole experience. I started to ask him if he'd been able to hear me talking to him in the hospital when he was in the coma. But before Rich could say anything, I was out of the tunnel. Just as I'd been whisked away, he indicated that only he could go on. I was next flying over the line of people in the water. With my ability to fly, I flew back to the mainland.

The scene changed again, and I found myself floating above an intersection with trees around it, a circle intersection where cars can enter and exit at multiple places. I was no longer in California but suddenly remembered that I would be flying out to the West Coast again in a week. I had a feeling that I might see Rich again on my next trip.

PARALLEL UNIVERSES

At the beginning of this chapter, I said that we were looking for ways to diffuse some of death's finality. The first thing we observed is that death is as necessary for life as life is for death.

We next saw that religions almost uniformly support life after death, the kind where the individual continues on, aware of being aware. Within our inquiry, we considered the possibility that we're just chemical reactions, like battery-powered robots. Even if that is the case, we found that we can still live on. We may or may not be aware of it, but our living relatives—if they're willing to take on the role of an archaeologist—can develop an entirely new relationship with us, complete with epiphanies and surprises, just like when we maintained our physical form. We've also seen that some people hold that we're all part of a greater whole, believing a life force, or something like it, gives us life. Here on Earth, we seem separate, like individual waves, but when we die, we live on, returning to the greater whole of which we were always a part.

Part of our investigation has included philosophy. Seneca's advice was to prepare for eventualities so that we're not caught by surprise by life's painful turns—advice not unlike Descartes' maxim to change our own desires rather than trying to change fortune. The philosophy also took us down some unexpected routes. Hume offered a unique way of thinking about life and death: that we don't actually have a personal identity to cling to; it's illusory. Buddhists, Hindus and Eastern mystics support his view. The theaters of our minds create the sense that there's any continuity, any identity to cling to. We last saw that it's possible—weird but possible nevertheless—that the life we long to maintain after death is itself simply a kind of cosmological cartoon. Our moments of suffering, joy, doubt, conviction, surprise, expectation and all the other perceptual experiences are always there, waiting for activation.

❖ ❖ ❖

As we end this chapter, let's investigate one more scenario—one which, for me, is perhaps the most reassuring. William James wrote, "The whole drift of my education goes to persuade me that the world of our present consciousness is only one out of many worlds of consciousness that exist." In his book *The Elegant Universe*, Brian Greene described a twenty-first-century version of James's intuition: "Imagine that what we call the universe is actually only one tiny part of a vastly larger cosmological expanse, one of an enormous number of island universes scattered across a grand cosmological archipelago." The focus of this section is on those universes within that grand cosmological archipelago that are the same—so called *parallel universes.*

The genesis for a scientific theory on parallel universes started when Hugh Everett III wrote his PhD thesis on "relative state" formulation in 1956. It was later picked up under the rubric "many-worlds interpretation." Everett left the field of physics and pursued a career in defense consulting after his theory was met by a resounding thud within the physics community. Over the years, the idea of parallel universes has gone from science fiction to mainstream topic of scientific study, with Everett (who died in 1982) eventually returning to the field given its resurgence. Today, the question about parallel universes is no longer one of possibility. It has become: What kinds of parallel universes are out there?

We've been talking about infinity in this chapter, a special kind of infinity that exists between two finite numbers. Have you ever considered the size of the universe? What would be on the outside? In his paper "Parallel Universes," cosmologist Max Tegmark asked, "What would lie beyond the sign saying 'SPACE ENDS HERE—MIND THE GAP?'" In the simplest parallel universe, there's another copy of you out there in a place just like Earth. Tegmark estimates that the closest copy is about $10^{10^{29}}$ meters away (much too far away to afford any possibility for contact). You might be making different choices in that other world, but it's *you* making them.

A second kind of parallel universe also allows for multiple versions of you in multiple universes, but they aren't neatly spaced out. Each universe is created by prior universes in a continuously expanding and contracting cosmological collection of universes. Lee Smolin, hailed as the new Einstein, has forwarded a theory that new universes are "spawned" through black holes—that natural selection favors universes that produce the most black holes. One way to imagine this is to think of bubbles: One bubble sprouts another bubble, which sprouts another bubble, and so on. As in the first kind of parallel universe, you wouldn't be able to contact the other yous—unless we figured out how to travel through black holes without being squashed.

Before we consider a third type of parallel universe, let's go back to the shape-shifting concept we considered in the section on Zeno. We know that matter can change to antimatter and back. Is it possible for the same object to go beyond shape-shifting—and actually be in two different places at one time? Scientists have in fact observed conclusive evidence of small particles being in two places at once. There's a famous physics experiment called the *two-slit experiment.* In it, physicists fire a beam of electrons against a shield that can register their presence. Before the electrons strike the shield, they must first pass through two small holes, spaced closely together, on a dividing plate. Intuition tells us (or me) that the electrons will create two points on the shield. Instead, they create a pattern. The significance of the pattern is that it demonstrates that the individual electrons go through *both* holes at the same time. The electrons act like waves as they pass through the holes, thereby producing a pattern, rather than two individual points, on the shield.

The two-slit experiment can actually be conducted—and repeated—so that only one electron passes through the dividing plate at a time. The outcome is consistently the same: Instead of producing a single point on the shield, that single electron creates a pattern, confirming its wavelike properties. While scientists can't actually observe the electron going through the holes in the plate, they can do a proxy. If one hole in the plate is blocked, thus allowing the scientists to determine which hole the electron went through, the pattern disappears—what they see instead is a dot indicative of an individual electron passing through an individual hole. That is, if the electron is forced to go through *one* hole, it acts like a particle and creates a single point on the shield. If, on the other hand, it is allowed to go through both holes, *it does*, and creates a wavelike pattern on the shield! The relevance for our discussion on parallel universes is that even in the world that we observe, it's possible for one thing to be in two places at one time.

Richard Feynman won a Noble Prize for his work with quantum electrodynamics. He was famous for his Feynman Diagrams—stick-figure sketches illustrating complex scientific ideas. Aided by his diagrams, he recognized that when scientists observe changes in quantum states (like electrons hitting a shield), what they really observe are *outcomes*. They can't tell what happened from one outcome to the next, how one quantum state changed to another. Feynman did some more sketches, used calculus to verify his theory and concluded something so utterly fantastic that it hardly seems plausible: that on quantum scales, all possible routes from one outcome to the next are always taken. As it turns out, it's not just fantasy. Paul Halpern summarized Feynman's conclusion in his book *The Pursuit of Destiny: A History of Prediction*: "Somehow, in every physical interaction, all the alternative scenes are played out at once—with only the final results discernible to onlookers." That all the scenes are played out at once on quantum scales is an accepted scientific fact, at least in the theoretical physicists' community.

All this talk about objects being multiple places at one time has been confined, so far, to very small objects—objects on quantum scales. Why is it always small objects? Why can't dogs or cats or mice or humans be in two places at once? The answer has to do with an effect known as *decoherence*, whereby an object's ability to be two places at once is eliminated once it interacts with its environment—that is, once it is observed. There are few things in the universe that can register really small objects like electrons. As long as small objects like electrons remain unobserved, whether by humans or anything else (the observation can be through an interaction with another particle), they can take on superpositions in which they're in two places at once. As far as we know, they can be almost infinitely many places at once. In John Brockton's book *The Third Culture: Beyond the Scientific Revolution*, astrophysicist Martin Rees commented, "One of the embarrassing features of our current perception of the universe is that 90 percent of what it's made of is unaccounted for."

Getting back to parallel universes, a third kind allows that maybe big objects can be two places at once—they just can't be aware of being two places at once.

233

This is the kind of parallel universe Everett was getting at with his "relative state" formulation. To think about this, Tegmark suggests we consider frog and bird perspectives.

A frog hops along from one point to the next. For practical purposes, it's on the ground. The frog is aware only of the individual choices it has made. It was going straight and then decided to hop left. Its perspective can be likened to a single path. The bird perspective, on the other hand, is broader than the frog perspective (think of the bird perspective in terms of a mythical, "all seeing" bird). When the frog made the decision to hop left, the bird saw the same frog simultaneously hop right. However, each version of the frog was only aware of the direction it—the current-version—hopped. In this case, the frog is capable of superpositioning, but once it hopped one way or the other, both versions of the same frog continued hopping along, neither one of them aware of the other. That is, one frog jumped both ways but in doing so, could only be aware of the leap that *it*—the frog that jumped right or left—took.

The bird, meanwhile, saw both versions of the frog, each hopping along different paths. If you think this might present some strange consequences, you're right. If the frog really did jump both left and right, the implication is that when we're faced with a choice in life, all options are ultimately taken. Feynman's observation—that all options from one quantum state to another are always taken—is therefore extended beyond the quantum world. Humans and everything else do it all! However, one of the limitations of human brains (or our sunglasses) is that we're in the frog perspective. We can only be aware of one choice. If we're at Frost's fork in the road, we take both the traveled and less traveled paths, but—and critically *but*—we are only aware of one choice. In other words, at the fork, two conscious versions of us move forward, unaware that one version of us went one way and another went the other way.

As is par for the course in Chapter Nine, we're investigating really weird territory. Shouldn't we somehow be able to feel it if we're simultaneously going right *and* left at a fork? Everett was once asked the same question in a letter exchange with the physicist Bryce DeWitt (whose Wheeler-DeWitt equation, formulated with John Wheeler, leads to the notion of "frozen time"). Everett famously replied, "Do you feel the Earth move?" DeWitt went on to be one of the leading advocates of Everett's theory.

In considering the third kind of parallel universe, also remember that physicists view time as being frozen. If all possible routes are taken every time, and all past choices have been made—then all future choices have necessarily been made as well (talk of past and future being useful metaphors only). Not only is there another you out there in a parallel universe, every possible version of you is out there. One of the quirks within a cartoon universe is that there is only one reel of our lives available for viewing. In the third kind of parallel universe, there are countless reels. Every possible life choice, every possible decision, they've all been made. As with the brain-in-a-vat and the cartoon universe scenarios, the third kind of parallel universe is logically and, more, scientifically possible. It's as real as any other perspective.

I said at the beginning of this section that parallel universes are perhaps the most reassuring topic I investigated in coming to terms with Rich's death—I was actually referring to the third kind of parallel universe. What does it mean for Rich? To me, it means that somewhere far away or maybe right next to me (I'm just not aware of him there), Rich made a different decision. Maybe he's not a futures trader. Maybe he tried it and decided it wasn't for him. Maybe he never had big trading setbacks or maybe they don't affect him. Maybe he's controlled his bipolar disorder in a gigantic group of universes; maybe he doesn't even have it in others. The possibilities are limitless. He's out there, having survived the gunshot wound in some, not having pulled the trigger in others and not even considering owning a gun in still more. In an uncountable number of universes, Rich lives on—telling stories, being happy, being sad, feeling all the possible emotions and living life. And in those universes, I'm there, too, enjoying his company.

ໜ CHAPTER TEN ໜ

But when their chains are cast aside,
See the glad scene unfolding wide,
Clap the glad wing, and tower away
And mingle with the blaze of day.
—Thomas Parnell

SITTING ON THE BEACH

I sat on a folding chair on the beach, kicked off my sandals and dug my toes into the sand. This was the kind of night Rich would have liked, mild and clear, just right for relaxing and enjoying the sounds of the surf. The constant blowing of the trade winds kept the bugs away.

Deana and I had used our airline miles to fly to St. Thomas in February 2006. We put a lot of research into the vacation. We pored through information on tropical destinations and paid careful attention to the feedback on the Internet travel sites. We liked what we read about St. Thomas and especially the condo complex where we decided to rent.

Of course, we weren't told that there would be mice in the unit and that one would run over Deana's foot on the first night. She shrieked the kind of shriek that meant rodent, roach or unspeakable filth. Fortunately, I'd faced a mouse problem at my old townhouse and knew how to set a mousetrap. The mouse problem was largely cleared up in the first two days.

The complex was basically a retirement community. Most afternoons, residents and guests engaged in competitive shuffleboard matches. In addition to the shuffleboard courts, the property also had walking trails, dinosaur-sized iguanas, palm trees and a barbecue grill for each condominium.

The first night, the guy in the unit one down from ours told me, "The rule of the grills is that you can use anyone else's if the coals are still hot." He said it to me the moment after I'd lit a quarter bag of charcoal in the grill in front of our unit. I'd noticed his grill before I lit mine; it was full of still-burning, usable charcoal. I'd actually wondered whether I should wait before lighting my grill so that I could take advantage of precisely what he'd just suggested.

After his comment, I smiled, not sure what to do, and said, "Is that right? Well, I'm just getting going here but will remember that for next time . . . blah, blah, blah." I went on for what seemed like a couple of minutes. He seemed to enjoy my awkwardness.

I asked him what he was cooking because it smelled good. He answered, "Charcoal." When I got back inside our unit, I swore to Deana that I would never use the leftover charcoal in that guy's grill because of his catty remark. It turned out that he was just a guy who was uneasy in social situations and had a really dry sense of humor. He probably had a good chuckle when he went into his unit.

The night I wrote about in the first paragraph was our last on St. Thomas. As I sat in the chair, a full moon danced on the small, rippling waves that stretched out to St. John, itself just across the bay. Overhead, thick, cotton-ball clouds whisked across the night sky.

There are times I get a strong sense of Rich, that he's present with me, literally by my side. The ancient Celts believed in "thin places," where the divide between this world and the next is thin. In the days and weeks after Rich's death, I thought about and conversed with him more regularly than possibly ever before. Even a year after his death, I'll look up, or in, and start talking. One of our family's friends lost his wife to cancer about fifteen years ago; he told Mom that he talks with her every day. The beach in St. Thomas that night was a thin place. I pictured Rich sitting there next to me; if I concentrated, I could see him clearly. Had he been there, sitting next to me, we wouldn't have done much more than I was doing: hanging out silently, taking everything in.

In August of 2000, Rich and I took a vacation to Cancun. We had talked every so often about taking a vacation together but never followed through. Discussing it was like a martini conversation that made both of us feel good, minus any commitment. At the time of our Cancun trip, I hadn't seen Rich in about two years. Our only communication was via telephone and email.

The genesis for the trip was that I'd just broken up with my girlfriend. As we talked about the breakup, Rich suggested we go for a week to Cancun. He got excited about the idea, and the same day that he made the suggestion, he reserved a room for seven nights. He told me he definitely was going, even if just by himself. Because I was teetering mentally from the breakup, I wasn't sure if I could stay for an entire week. Given my mental state and that I knew it was possible that Rich could sink into a depression that could throw the whole vacation, I set up my stay for only four nights.

Chaos greeted me at the Cancun airport when I landed in the early afternoon. About a thousand people and I waited to go through security. At the time, the Cancun airport had a system by which you pressed a buzzer to exit the baggage claim area. Everyone going through stood in single-file lines, pushing or pulling their luggage as the lines slowly moved forward. The person at the front of a line hit a black button. If the buzzer went off, the person had to move to the side, where security agents would pull apart their luggage. Rich was en route from London. When we talked about it later, we both liked the fact that by pressing the button yourself, the security agents were absolved of any responsibility—your fate rested in a little mechanical contraption.

Once I was through security (without the buzzer having gone off), a crush of taxi drivers grabbed at suitcases. In the frenzy, I couldn't see any sign of the free transportation to the resort that had been promised by the booking agent, so I took a cab.

When I first looked out at the beach as the cab driver and I rolled onto the resort property, it seemed like quite a few women were wearing skin-colored tops. In Europe, toplessness is no big deal. For an average, single American male, it was a surprise of the very best kind. I put my bags in the room that Rich and I would be sharing, took a tour of the grounds and then went back to the room to hang out. The room didn't offer much: two single beds, one or two chairs, a giant shower and one small desk. I sat at the desk, turned on my laptop and did a little journaling, trying to make sense of my most recent breakup.

Rich arrived in the early evening. With my obsessive compulsiveness in full swing, I'd already arranged books that I had brought on a shelf that ran the width of the room, above the two single beds. The look on Rich's face when he walked through the door to our room told me that coming on the vacation was the right idea. He had a way of smiling, of extending his presence, that could fill your entire body. We shook hands, hugged and Rich soon hit the sack, exhausted by the fifteen-or-so-hour trip from his home in London.

The next morning, while I was working out, I told another guy at the gym that I was originally from Boston. He asked me if I knew a guy named Rich. He'd ridden in a taxi with a "great guy" named Rich who had lived in Boston but now lived in London.

When I got back to the room, Rich was just waking up. Once he was up, we got lunch at the main restaurant and then went to the pool, where a resort employee was yelling into a microphone, speaking English with a French accent. He was hyping some event that was starting in a few minutes. Someone came over to us as we were sitting in lounge chairs and suggested that we toss the guy with the French accent into the pool. It turned out to be one of the three guys Rich had met on his taxi ride from the airport.

I enjoyed an instant bonding with the whole group. They were from California, and Rich got the lowdown from them on what it was like to live in San Diego. One of the guys was a doctor; he also liked philosophy and was thinking about writing a book. After he suggested that we toss the resort guy into the pool, we all decided that going for a swim in the pool was a good idea. We jumped in and started playing water basketball. The resort had two small hoops set up on both sides of the shallow end of the pool. Water basketball became our game of choice for the whole vacation.

Rich could bench press about 350 pounds when we went to Cancun, and he was in his element in the pool. As a kid, Rich loved pools. We liked visiting Mommom and Poppop in the summer because their apartment complex had a pool. At the resort, people thought Rich was a pro football player. When he made a basket in pool basketball, he usually did a little dance. No one could trash talk like Rich. He'd stick out his tongue (à la Michael Jordon) and then launch a sideways spinning shot that made its way into the basket only because he was confident that it would.

We usually ate dinner with the guys from California. Every time I sat down to a meal, with or without Rich, people knew of me because they'd met Rich, and he'd told them about me. He made me feel important—he could always do that. He validated me, which was exactly what I needed after the breakup. We signed up for an all-inclusive meal package at the resort. The meals were cafeteria style. Rich would visit the buffet at least three times each meal. There he is, right in my memory, bringing back a plate of food, with dessert balanced on top.

In the mornings, we went to the beach, swam out to the edge of the swimming zone (marked off by a rope and small buoys) and treaded water. We didn't talk all that much during our morning swims. We looked at the clouds or at a boat in the distance or just enjoyed the warmth of the water. Every so often, one of us slowly released the breath from his lungs and sank to the bottom, about ten feet down. The object was to stay there for a while, until it started to feel uncomfortable, and then dart to the surface where we'd take a huge breath— which felt all the more life-giving when we took it.

Sima Halevy and her colleagues wrote an article in 2001 for the *Israel Medical Association Journal* about the effect of Dead Sea salts on people with psoriasis. The essence of the article is that it's possible for lithium to be absorbed through the skin by people with psoriasis. The authors wrote, "Although the exact components of the Dead Sea bath salt, which are responsible for its therapeutic effects, are still obscure, the present study implies that elution of lithium from the salt may enhance its therapeutic properties." According to the same article, sunbathing served to enhance the therapeutic effects of the Dead Sea salts. No matter the reason, Rich and I always felt calmed whenever we went swimming in the ocean.

In the evenings in Cancun, Rich and I sat on a stone wall that overlooked the beach and talked. One of the guys from California might join in, or it might be just Rich and I. We told stories, laughed and drank a couple of beers. In Cancun, everything seemed new: The sights were new, and the daily routine was new. Psychiatrist Kevin Turnquist wrote that future treatments for depression "might include travel and activities aimed at increasing exposure to novel experiences and new challenges for the memory apparatus." If you've ever been depressed, you know it's possible to forget about your state, if just for a second or two, when your brain becomes occupied with something else.

After dinner, Rich and I would head to the outdoor bar, where we sat in cushioned chairs, chatting with the guys from California or people we ate meals with or girls we'd met on the beach. The property had a dance club that opened later at night. Normally, I'm not a dance club fan, but this one was right on a little peninsula. We could walk there from the outdoor bar. From the dance club, it was another short walk, about a hundred yards, to the end of the peninsula. You could sit either at a picnic table or on rocks and watch the moon and the ocean. From my vantage point on the rocks where I usually sat, the moon seemed to float on the ocean. The moonlight created a shimmering pathway over the water, which, with a little imagination, I could walk to the moon itself.

Sometimes during the day, I went to a different beach, away from the popular one. What it lacked in topless sunbathers, it made up for in simplicity. I could just sit there and watch the waves rolling in, one after another, the only distraction being the birds running around on the beach looking for food.

Paul Ekman, author of *Emotions Revealed*, described the sense we get when we're immersed in nature as a kind of emotion, a form of pleasure.

As I sat on the secluded beach, Rich might come visit. One day, he told me about his recent trading. He said he'd noticed that, for some reason, the market as a whole was moving in unison with Microsoft. It lasted only a week or two, but it was a profitable week or two for Rich. He made more than $1.5 million, that I know about, in the three years he traded full time, losing just a little bit more in the end. During a standard trading day, his winnings and losses could vacillate wildly. On a minute to minute basis, I'd guess his winnings and losses were easily a hundred times greater than what ultimately settled in his account at the end of the day. As we spoke on the isolated beach, waves kept washing over the rocks, one breaking after another.

Within a day of my arrival in Cancun, I decided to extend my vacation to six nights, but not seven nights, like Rich. In my mind, I wasn't missing out on one last night but instead was saving money by staying only six nights. I'd be able to use the savings for something else.

On my sixth and last night, Rich didn't come back to the room until about 4:30 in the morning. When he came in, he told me he'd been looking at the turtles coming ashore on the beach. His jeans were soaked. In the early dawn light, I could tell that he'd been crying. I learned a few hours later, from one of the girls we met on the trip, that he'd been really emotional sitting on the beach—he'd watched the turtles with her. That's the way Rich was. The switch would flip; it always flipped eventually, and when it did, chances were good that the results would be devastating.

From what I heard, the next night, Rich's last, was worse. It's also the night he met Zatta. She helped him through his breakdown that last night in Cancun. The Cancun vacation cycled from "top of the world" to "crash" in a day. That's the way it went for Rich.

From a Time-Earth perspective, I'm now more than six years past the trip to Cancun. During that trip, I tapped the best feelings I could. As I've rolled it over in my mind, I'm tapping the same feelings. I feel the same ease when I think about sitting on the isolated beach or at the end of the peninsula or on the stone wall with Rich during sunsets. I realize I got what I wanted most on that trip—I was close to Rich, and he was up. When he was up, nothing could stop him. It never happened again, that kind of extended, in-person experience with Rich, but I have it now—and with a little imagination, I'll tap it again.

MEMORY AND KANT

I've been exploring, in various places in this book, exactly what Rich was. When I pointed at Rich, what was I really pointing at? All I can tell you for certain is what my working brain, my mind, allows me to write. Brains, as we've seen, are prone to making mistakes. All any brain can do is process, analyze (at times) and direct information. Nothing that happens to you, that you observe, can happen without being run through the filters of your brain. What's more, nothing happens "live"—nothing. There's an infinitesimal delay in everything we take in by either sight, sound, touch, feel or taste.

The light I observed reflecting off of Rich during his life, which I took to be Rich's body, was not actually Rich's body; it was the light reflecting from his body, a pattern. I'd grown used to the pattern and could recognize it as Rich, but it was not his body: It was an image my mind displayed on my own personal, mental movie screen.

I spent a good portion of the last chapter exploring where Rich might be right now. Religion says that the same Rich I knew lives on. From a physics perspective, multiple Riches are living right now, somewhere else. It's also possible that we're living in a cartoon universe, in which there is no time and the episodes of all our lives are always available for activation. Earlier in this book, I said we have to know what we're missing to miss it. We're not our physical bodies, we're not our thoughts or our emotions or any of the things our minds use our brains to *do*. At best, our minds appear to be us for a frame at a time—and never the same from frame to frame. We're not any one thing. It becomes a vexing problem. What do I miss when I miss Rich? With all the exploration I've done, I still don't know what Rich was.

An ancient Greek philosopher named Protagoras said, "Man is the measure of all things." It's worth repeating—"Man is the measure of all things." Could that be the missing link? If Protagoras is right, the answer to my question would simply be this: *You* are a sensory experience to me, and I to you. That's all. We considered the same notion within the context of Plato's cave allegory back in Chapter Six. This is not to say the only reality is what's in our heads—in fact, we've seen that our minds must utilize things outside us in the process of thinking. But if Protagoras's statement is accurate, it would mean that Rich was always an interpretation made by my mind, which took information sent from Rich and processed it, with that *processed information* representing—or more accurately, being—Rich, for me.

The fundamental issue here is whether we can conceive of the outside world without the use of our senses. If we can't, then Protagoras is right, and the implications for Rich's life and death are profound. One hugely influential philosopher, some consider the greatest, considered rigorously the notion of accessing the external world without the use of our senses. His name was Immanuel Kant. In his book *A Critique of Pure Reason*, Kant wrote, "I call a conception problematical which contains in itself no contradiction, and which is connected with other cognitions as a limitation of given conceptions, but whose objective reality cannot be cognized in any manner." From the quotation, you probably can tell that Kant wasn't easy to follow. Accessing the world of things outside us without our perceptions is exactly the kind of conception Kant found "problematical."

In terms of what there *is*, Kant divided the world of things into two categories: the "noumenal" and the "phenomenal." Noumenal things can be thought of as being outside the limitations of our perception. Noumena are things as they *are*, not as we perceive them to be. They're the person as that person really is, not as he or she is to us. This definition creates a problem. It means that noumena are simply things we can't perceive. It's defining things in terms of what they aren't—good is the absence of bad, and bad is the absence of good. Defining things in terms of what they aren't is what's known as *negative* definition.

There is also a *positive* definition to noumena. Kant wrote:

> If we understand by [the term "noumena"] an object of a non-sensuous intuition, we in this case assume a peculiar mode of intuition, an intellectual intuition, to wit, which does not, however, belong to us, of the very possibility of which we have no notion.

In other words, it might be possible to get at noumena without the use of senses, but humans can't do it. For all intents and purposes, this definition of noumena is a sleight of hand, but one that is necessary because for Kant, "[We] are not entitled to maintain that sensibility is the only possible mode of intuition."

Thus, Kant allowed for the possibility of sensation outside our senses, but there's a catch: We can't *know* anything about it. If we can't know anything about noumena, we can never appreciate noumena for what they truly are because we can't go beyond the sphere of our own perceptions. For this reason, noumena—things outside us *as they really are*—can never usefully be defined in anything more than a negative sense. What's the conclusion? Kant summed it up as follows: "Our knowledge of the existence of things reaches as far as our perceptions"—all we can ever know about the world of things is what we perceive.

The perspective I espoused in the last chapter was fundamentally Rich's. That is, I was concerned with where *Rich* is now. I've been trying to sneak outside myself and into Rich to ask if he is in an afterlife or in another world. I'm going to turn the perspective back to you and to myself. In deference to Kant, I'll turn it back to *me* alone. Here goes: What was Rich to me? A sense perception is not the real object; it's not the noumena. It represents the mind's interpretation of some outside or inside thing. When I go back over Rich's life, or when I envision a future with Rich, I'm seeing an image of Rich. All I ever saw of Rich was an image. I didn't see the real thing. It wasn't possible for me to see the real thing.

Consider next what happens when we recognize someone. Don't we need to see a person at least twice to be able to recognize him or her? The first time we see a person, we create an image of that person in our memory (if we're paying attention). The next time we see them, we link the present-moment image to the past image, consciously or unconsciously evaluating the similarities, and determine whether or not we recognize them. The more we see someone, the more memories we have to compare against, and the better the chances we will recognize the person. When we recognize anyone, we're connecting memories. Once we have enough stored memories of a given person, we're able to think about them, to recognize them, without them being physically present.

As far as my recognition of Rich was concerned, not only did it rely on stored memories, but Rich in fact lived for me *primarily* in my memory. The external inputs I got through present-moment perceptions of Rich's physical self were a teeny, tiny fraction of what's needed to say "That's Rich." Another way to think about it is from a deck-of-cards perspective: The present moment is a single card in an immeasurable, universal deck. It took memory to experience the cards that represented Rich. That I could recognize his moods or laugh with him about shared experiences was a result of the stockpile of Rich cards—or memories—in my brain. *This last point is critical.* The Rich standing before me or talking to me on the phone made sense to me, or more accurately, initiated in me a sense of recognition, precisely because of stored memories.

For a person with advanced Alzheimer's disease, no one is recognizable anymore. The afflicted person has a new series of perceptions with no connection to anything but the present one. The capacity for storing and retrieving memories is gone.

According to Hume, *memory* is the reason we think that there is a constant and invariable self in us. He wrote, "As memory alone acquaints us with the continuance and extent of this succession of perceptions, it is to be considered, upon that account chiefly, as the source of personal identity." Our sense that we have invariability over time is an illusion generated by our capacity to store and retrieve memories. We're tricked by memory into thinking that something in us persists over time. In a way, our memory says, "Well, the you that was there yesterday is close enough to the you that's here today. For the sake of simplicity, let's just say it's the same."

What *is* a memory? It used to be that researchers thought it was like unchanging computer code stored in the hard drives of our brains. That's no longer the case. Daniel Schacter, considered to be one of the leading authorities on the subject, wrote in his book *Searching for Memory,* "We now know enough about how memories are stored and retrieved to demolish another long-standing myth: that memories are passive or literal recordings of reality." Today, the perspective on memory is a lot like that on thoughts or emotions. Schacter wrote, "Neuroscientists believe that the brain records an event by strengthening the connections between groups of neurons that participate in the experience." Memories, in this way, are activated neural connections.

We have to be careful in our discussion of memory, though. When we remember an event, we're activating connections, but those connections won't all be the same ones each time we remember it. In Schacter's words, "When we remember, we complete a pattern with the best match available in memory; we do not shine a spotlight on a stored picture." We use whatever neurons are available at that moment. The next time we remember the same event, it won't be with the same exact neurons connected in the same way. A memory can change over time. At best, researchers maintain that we hold on to the essence of past events, but not each and every detail.

Once created, memories are not free of context. They're affected by our present situation. Kevin Turnquist noted that a person in a depression will have a different recollection of his or her childhood than the same person once the depression has lifted. A memory is our brain's interpretation of an event, subject to augmentation by new events, circumstances, feelings or moods. Old memories affect new ones, and new memories affect old. Everything that happens to us happens in the presence of everything else.

It's time to start pulling pieces from this section together. Through Kant, we found that the material world can never be anything more than a sense perception to us. Next, we observed that each time we recognize someone, we employ the resources of memory. When Rich's physical form moved on, I used my perceptions and my memory to interpret that he had died.

We also know that memories are dynamic. In reality, the memories I relied upon to recognize Rich changed each time I remembered them. They weren't "locked down" and couldn't ever be "locked down." But hold on. If memories are, indeed, dynamic, then isn't it more accurate to say that we're *perceiving* them? That is, when we recall what seems to be a static memory, we're actually perceiving a new version—the present version—of that memory. Memory, in this sense, starts to sound a lot like perception. In fact, neuroscientists Gerald Edelman and Giulio Tononi wrote, "Conscious perception and memory should be considered two aspects of one and the same processes." Memories are, in actuality, *ever-changing* perceptions. As Hume would say, *Rich was never the same Rich.*

Now our investigation in this section starts to get relevant in terms of this central question: What do we miss when someone dies? We've not been able to pin ourselves down as being any one thing. Cells change and thoughts change; we're stable for a moment and then we're new. We're like a vibrating pattern subject to the context in which we vibrate, and as it turns out, our memories are the same thing. What's more, what we are to anyone and what anyone is to us depends entirely on our memory. When I saw the physical Rich, I was perceiving him; when I remembered him minus the presence of physical Rich, I again was perceiving him.

Chapter Five discussed memory triggers. To me—and it's important to stress that it is to *me*—the physical Rich I perceived was simply a trigger for new and existing oscillations of memories. In missing the physical Rich, I'm mourning the loss of a trigger, a trigger that, like me, was changing and evolving—a tremendously influential trigger, but a trigger nonetheless. The fact that Rich's physical form—the noumena that drove my phenomena—is no longer here does not diminish the fact that I have all these memories of Rich, memories that can still begin to swirl, to dance.

Rich was and is a spontaneous interaction of past and present sense perceptions—"present" being in actuality ever so slightly past. He didn't depend on any single perception but instead on the interaction of the ones I remembered or perceived at any given time. Rich was not the trigger; he was the *interaction.* He was the wave I happened to perceive at a given time, a wave that was constantly changing, both for him and for me, a wave further linked to past waves by memories. What Rich actually was to Rich or what I am to myself or what you are to you *doesn't matter* to those who live on once your physical form passes. As Kant demonstrated, I can never get to you in the first place. What you are to you is your business and can't be anything other than your business. What matters to the survivors is what their loved ones were to them.

I said that if Protagoras was right—and he was—it would have profound implications for Rich's life and death. If, as I am suggesting, Rich was actually an interaction, what then? If he was an interaction of sense perceptions, then he's as real to me today as he was when his physical form was here. For me, Rich was and is a sensory experience. I can still perceive him in my memories. That's all I could ever do: *perceive him in my memories.* His passing negates none of his previous impact and does not prevent me from having present and, further, *future* sensory experiences. These future sensory experiences will be dynamic. While Rich was here in his physical form, I was building new memories of him, with the old ones dying, in a sense, each time I pulled up a new version. Even though his physical form is gone, the same thing is still happening. Rich remains a living, and dying, dynamic—less a memory trigger. How does any of this help with the terror I face at missing Rich's physical presence? It helps in this way: I know the physical presence was not really Rich; it was a symbol of Rich. Rich, you see, is not gone.

In our society, we look at death as an end. Where did this idea come from? Could it be rooted in us-versus-them thinking? We're so attached to material things, to physical things, that it makes sense to us that when the physical body no longer exists, that's all there is: It's over. My challenge is to ignore the parts of Western culture that preach Rich and everything else takes the form of physical, material objects. "Horse feathers," in the words of Colonel Sherman Potter (Rich and I liked the television series *M*A*S*H*). That's all I have to say: "Horse feathers." I must disregard the advertisers, I must disregard Hollywood and I must disregard all the mumbo jumbo that makes me think that things are the be-all and end-all.

Each time I remember Rich, I interact with him as I did when his physical form was here. For me, the Rich I knew was always in my head—*always!* He's permanently part of my memory (at least until that particular capacity leaves me). What I perceived when I perceived Rich was *my* interpretation of Rich. Rich literally was *new* every time I saw him. He's new as I remember him now. He will grow old with me.

That's my answer to missing Rich's physical body. Yes, a trigger is gone, but Rich was so much more than a trigger; he is a series of interactions and connections I'm actively experiencing today. I'm missing a symbol. The real thing is still in here with me.

BUILDING A LADDER

When I go back through Rich's life and back over his death, I see smiles, I see laughter, I see pain and I see anguish. If I look too long at the death of his physical body, I can get swallowed in angst. There were treatments that went untried—perhaps electroshock therapy would have helped. Someday, bipolar disorder may be like polio, requiring the futuristic equivalent of a vaccine to hold it at bay.

When I think about the fact that I'll never see Richard's physical form again, it can be paralyzing. If I think in terms of objects and get fooled into thinking that this life is about what I can hold and feel, material things—as every advertiser would have me believe—I don't know if I could go on. I'd be digested in a black hole of frenzied terror.

Not a day goes by that I don't think of Rich, that I don't see Rich right in the middle of my mind. I can get caught wanting his physical form back. I have an image, of Rich and me, stored away in the back of my head. Every so often, it'll get triggered, usually by something totally unexpected, and flash in my mind. The scene in the image is years from now; Rich's depressions have lifted. We're laughing the way we used to laugh. We're on a porch in the summertime as the sun is setting, and we're looking out over the ocean. We're two old geezers in rocking chairs, sharing some beers, laughing and talking about life. It's such a beautiful sight; it can hit me in a funny way. My heart can drop.

When I get like that—when I start pining for Rich's physical form—I have to remember what's really happening, that the pining is not about Rich. When I'm being honest with myself, I understand this: The pining is actually about me. What I'm saying when I pine for Rich's physical form is that I didn't get enough of it, that I need more; I need more than the overflowing library of memories I already have. It's deeper than that, though—beyond saying I need more Rich. I'm proclaiming to myself, "I don't want to change my vision of the future that always included physical Rich." In doing so, I hold on to a future that never was promised to me, never actually existed. It was a future in my head only.

How do I escape? How do I avoid the anguish this unpromised future unleashes when I snap out of my daydream and realize it will never happen? The same way as any other anxiety or any other feeling: *I must let it go.* In his book *The Concept of Time in Psychology*, Jon Roeckelein wrote, "The universal division of time into past, present and future is expressed in Hebrew (as in other Semitic languages) by a spatial metaphor. Contrary to Western usage, the past is what lies ahead and is therefore known; the future is unknown and is behind." I have to let the future flow up from behind and expand in front of me.

String theory holds the promise, according to some physicists, of tying together Newtonian physics and quantum physics. Newtonian physics applies to big things, quantum physics to very small ones, and neither is a good predictor of things best predicted by the other. String theory is as yet unproven, but its equations are accurate predictors of outcomes both large and small. String theory is a belief that the universe is made up of tiny, oscillating strings. These strings are less than a billionth of the size of an electron, itself almost impossibly small. The oscillating strings produce all the things that we observe in the universe—light, music, organic beings, inorganic objects, electromagnetic forces and gravity. The universe, from this perspective, is a giant collection of oscillating strings.

Buddhists hold that compassion is the single most important quality we can bring to the world. Likewise, Christ said, "Do to others as you would have them do to you" (Matthew 7:12). Viewing others as extensions of myself helps me to maintain some semblance of compassion. We all are merely oscillating strings, the same events oscillating some of our strings in harmony, and others not.

Mental perspectives such as thinking about the universe in terms of oscillating strings don't spring into being all at once. I can't just say, "I'm now going to recognize the world as a mental construct in my head." My mind wants to believe that what I see is not just an interpretation made by my brain. It wants to think that concepts such as fame, wealth and material things have meaning outside my head. Why is that? One explanation is that the human species would not have survived for long if we questioned everything our senses presented to us. Our ancestors would not have enjoyed much longevity had they said things like, "My eyes are telling me there's a lion in the distance, approaching pretty fast. Hmm, what is the noumena behind the lion's phenomena?" We have survived to this point precisely because we've relied on our senses to provide us with reliable information.

Alex Zautra wrote in his book *Emotions, Stress and Health* that our cerebral cortex may have evolved as a means of regulating our limbic system. In this way, the cerebral cortex is an override tool, employed to help us select the right emotion to listen to, regardless of which one is screaming the loudest. It's an evolutionary recognition that emotional responses left to their own devices can result in poor outcomes for humans, outcomes like prolonged anxiety and despair.

In Chapter Six, I quoted economic historian Fritz Heichelheim who wrote that the need for material distinction was important for humans as far back as 30,000 years ago. The annals of history are replete with examples of inventions and ideas that once served an important purpose but needed to be modified, or became obsolete, over time. A long time ago, the human appendix was possibly involved in the digestion of leaves, but now it's generally considered to be an appendage that no longer serves much purpose. Most experts believe it can be removed with no ill effect. Perhaps the intensity of the human preoccupation with material things will someday realize the same fate.

In the first six months after Rich's passing, I would wake up in a panic once every week or two. I'd shoot up in bed and remember physical Rich had died, that I'd never talk with him again. That experience was like waking up from my worst nightmare and realizing that I'd like to go back to sleep, to get back to the nightmare. In the early morning, when my guard was down, when my emotions were free-flowing on their own, the realization of Rich's physical absence strangled me. The first part of the recovery, then as now, is for me to step back mentally. I'm no match for the reality that Rich's physical body isn't here anymore. I have to consciously remember that everything in this "being alive" state is a mental construct. I need to take deep breaths, go through my good memories of Rich and gather hold of my emotions, stabilize.

Once I'm able to escape the panic, I consciously switch over to building what I call my "ladder." I use the ladder to crawl out of panics. It's a mental strategy. With a good ladder, the next time the panic hits, I'll be able to escape a little more quickly. Biologist Mary Clark wrote in her book *In Search of Human Nature*, "Stories . . . are part of the behavioral guidance system needed for human survival." They don't just make us feel good. Clark wrote, "Our enormous ability to 'learn from experience,' and hence adapt to widely diverse environments, could not properly be orchestrated. We need context, a story, a frame for thinking." In building a ladder, I'm creating a new story or multiple stories. I want as many escape routes from emotional suffering as I can get. The *Philosophy of Rich* represents the most reliable ladder I've built to date.

When I first wrote and read through the stories about the last two months of Rich's life, I was almost always overwhelmed with painful emotions. After being overwhelmed, I'd usually go outside and walk or just sit quietly and meditate, embracing the painful emotions as best I could. Next, I might read through some of the philosophy sections—Descartes' rational introspection, Seneca's advice to mentally prepare for painful eventualities, Hume's insights on personal identity or Kant's logic regarding perceptions. From there, I might do some research on bipolar disorder and depression, or investigate ideas from physics like parallel universes. The practice came down to this: feel the hurtful emotion, deal with it, develop new ways of approaching the triggers of that same hurtful emotion—strengthen the ladder, so to speak—and move on, repeating the practice as often as necessary.

A ladder is only helpful to the degree that it's used. It's easy to fall into familiar habitual reactions—like panicking at the thought of Rich's physical absence—unless I actively employ my ladder. In Chapter Eight, I said that Descartes was not a fundamentalist. This is what he wrote in the *Discourse on Method:* "My present design, then, is not to teach the method which each ought to follow for the right conduct of his [or her] reason, but solely to describe the way in which I have endeavored to conduct my own." In deference to Descartes, I acknowledge that while the notion of building a ladder is a strategy that has worked for me, I'm one observation, a single data point among billions. As fervently as I'd like to believe it could help anyone else, my opinions are simply that: my opinions. I've floated them out there within this book, and now I have to let my attachments—my expectations as to how I think my opinions might impact others—go.

The metaphor I used in Chapter Nine was sunglasses, how they can change what we see. As we end this section, let's enlarge the metaphor just a little, from sunglasses to windows. Windows come in all shapes and sizes: Some have multiple panes and some just one; some have shutters and others do not. Windows can be made from different kinds of glass, different kinds of materials. Though windows serve many purposes, I'd like to focus on one: how windows allow people on the inside of a structure—be it a building, car, boat or other—to see outside.

What if someone offered you right now an opportunity to look through a window? What if they didn't tell you anything about what you might see? The view could be phenomenal or awful; it could provide sensations of elation or despair, each to a degree beyond your wildest imagination. The window might be in perfect shape, or it could be falling apart; it may start out in perfect shape and then fall apart or vice versa. What if the only information the person provided you with certainty was as follows: The window is not permanent; it could last days or over a century, but as long as it lasts, *it would be yours to look through.* How about if instead of consulting you first, the person just stuck you in front of a random window?

In a way, the only thing we're given on Earth is a window through which we can view the world. Looking at ourselves as windows says nothing about whether the situation is good or bad, fair or unfair. We know we're going to die; we know others are going to die. What we do with the temporary window we've been provided is up to us.

WHAT'S THE QUESTION?

I've presented rationale that the concept of suicide as mortal sin is a tragic misunderstanding. I've compared it to a lie that's been perpetuated often enough, from generation to generation, that it became true. The suffering wrought on survivors of suicide by the "mortal sin" label is brutal. I've presented evidence that the line between a death fundamentally triggered by cigarette smoking and one caused by a more obvious suicide is murky at best. I haven't said, however, whether I think suicide is right or wrong. In asking the question, we're again into ethics.

It's worth considering the end game before you or I try to answer the question: "Do you believe suicide is right or wrong?" Why are we asking it? Are we seeking knowledge or truth or something else? Is it potentially one more vehicle for us-versus-them thinking? As I've thought about it, as I've kicked around the question and its value, I've concluded that for my purposes in this book, the question holds no value.

There are better questions. "Do you believe suicide is right or wrong?" is a divisive question. It's a way to create a partition that stops forward progress; it can lead you or me to associate the other's position with *that* person. We can lose sight of each other and instead see a single opinion, which we then use to pigeonhole the other. Chances are, either you believe suicide is right or you believe it's wrong. Perhaps you've never had occasion to think much about it. Once your mind is made up, though, it could take an epiphany to change it.

Logic won't do it, nor will talk about God's will. If you and I disagree, we'll dig ourselves a hole as we argue back and forth, neither one of us doing anything more than throwing stones against armor that can't be dented by stones.

Rich's physical form is gone. It happened. Death has happened before, and it will happen again. What am I to do? That's a better question. Saying that suicide is good or bad doesn't help those of us dealing with the aftermath. What are you going to do? That's the question you need to answer. Kipling wrote:

> If you can fill the unforgiving minute
> With sixty seconds' worth of distance run—
> Yours is the Earth and everything that's in it.

What am I to do? For me, the answer is the same as it would be for any other loss or any other gain: I must keep filling the "unforgiving minute." My task is to live, knowing at some level that each breath brings me closer to the death of my current physical form. At times, my task seems like a blessing, at times a curse; most of the time, the reality of my task doesn't even occur to me.

Why do I fill the unforgiving minute? What is the myth I'm living, and is there a meaning to it? Bertrand Russell asked, "Is man what he seems to the astronomer, a tiny lump of impure carbon and water impotently crawling on a small and unimportant planet? Or is he what he appears to Hamlet? Is he perhaps both at once?"

Isn't your answer or my answer one of perspective? If someone believes we're just tiny lumps of impure carbon, is he or she wrong? We *are* tiny lumps of impure carbon. As to whether Earth is a cold, dark place or our only opportunity to marvel at sunsets, our only opportunity to experience *ourselves* in the community of others like us—isn't that our choice?

Each day, people fill the unforgiving minute. Joseph Campbell said, "Follow your bliss." You're free to see the meaning of your personal myth revealed to you over the course of your life. You're free to search for the Holy Grail, for the Philosopher's Stone. It's a journey whose end won't ever be fully realized, an end that's ephemeral but whose pursuit is the reward.

My task of living and my pursuit of bliss can be consistent with your task and your pursuit, no matter what you and I believe at the level of details. We can disagree on an almost infinite level of particulars—that there should or should not be a designated hitter, that there's life after death or not, that Christianity or Islam or Judaism is the chosen religion, that the Bible is literal fact or a metaphorical collection of ethical codes and stories, that suicide is right or wrong. We can disagree on all of that and still appreciate the fact that each day, our task is to get out of bed in the morning and carry on. We can appreciate that some things bring you rapture and some things bring me rapture and that despite our differences, there are many important things we can agree on.

Where is Rich now? He may be in an afterlife; he may be in a countless number of parallel universes; maybe, like a cartoon, he's in the current mental frame I'm accessing. Maybe all of us are constantly shifting from frame to frame, and there is no such thing as time, instead just a shifting among frames that are already there. Rich simply may be in the presently safe domain of my memory—the same place he was for the vast majority of the time his physical presence was here on Earth. Maybe Rich is in all those places.

For me, at this instant, Rich is in my memory. Should I be troubled by the fact that I can say no more than that Rich is in my memory at this instant? What about the philosophical ideas that we can't say for certain that we're not just brains in vats or that all of this is an illusion—that we can't say for certain that we ever had a past or that one second from now we'll occupy the same history we did the second before? These are troubling questions, aren't they?

In *East of Eden,* John Steinbeck explored the Hebrew word *Timshel.* It means *thou mayest.* The path is open—we can choose; we have options, even if those options are limited to how we process a memory. *Timshel* is, in Steinbeck's words, "a ladder to climb to the stars. You can never lose that."

As for you and me in our quests, we can have faith. I can have faith that there is some permanence, that Rich existed outside my memory and that all of this matters. I can have faith that I have the choice *to have faith.* Thou mayest. I have an almost infinite number of choices. As to my pursuit, I can choose to seek rapture or not. I may not think Rich was right when he took his life, but that won't change a thing. I may think Rich was completely justified, and still, here I am, sitting at the computer, with an emptiness in my life that was not there before.

No matter my answer on the details, or yours, we can agree on particular facts. One fact is that some people can't even ponder the question of whether suicide is right or wrong. There have been, there are now and there always will be people at a point at which they just don't care. Their present world is one of anguish. Some live with bipolar disorder or major depression, with a brain that sends them messages they can't trust. In their lows, they can't see that there's a way out. Anguish becomes their eternity. Intellectually, Rich understood his depression, but he was unable to escape it.

Experts agree that a sense of community can help those in anguish. That's another fact, maybe not a full-fledged fact like 2 + 2 = 4 but, at the least, a universally held belief. If you are willing to comfort a person in anguish, to provide him or her with a semblance of community, that's something both of you can appreciate. Despite all our differences once we start talking fair balls and foul balls, religious codes of conduct, God or no God—in short, details— before we get to all that, I can observe you providing comfort and community, and I can still feel a connection that cuts across it all.

Gordon Lightfoot asked in his song "The Wreck of the Edmund Fitzgerald" if anyone knows what happens to the love of God "when the waves turn the minutes to hours?" I can ask the same thing about reason or whatever else buoys my ethics, hope or pursuit. When the waves turn the minutes to hours, details like whether suicide is good or bad don't mean a thing.

T. S. ELIOT AND CANDLES

When T. S. Eliot was awarded the Nobel Prize in Literature in 1948, he said in his banquet speech, "I stand before you, not on my own merits, but as a symbol, for a time, of the significance of poetry."

We are all symbols, for a time, of the creative power of the universe, or God, or random chance and skill. The life force, if you will, rolls through us and out, not with any malicious intent at all, just because that's what it does. We are free to see everyone else as symbols or individuals, as enemies or partners in this experience, no different than we are, created equally for our creator's employ.

Rich wasn't the candle or the match but the flame that burned. In so burning, the match was discarded and the candle devoured. He burned not of his own accord, but because he was lit and the air made it impossible not to burn. Now the candle is gone, as was inevitable, and we are left with the imprint of Rich's flame. Around us, flames burn, matches are discarded and candles are devoured every day.

The process is neither good nor bad—it is what it is. No amount of suffering on our part will change it. And acceptance of this inevitable truth is, paradoxically, our passage to freedom.

We're all in this together, not because we chose to be, but because we *are*. We can hide from destiny in our work and our cars and our clothes, in our battle of us-versus-them, in our fatally flawed and illusory self-images. We can hide from destiny in our details and all the other distractions we create and that are created for us every day. But wherever we hide, destiny will find us. That's what destiny does. There's no escape. So, very well: As I live here behind my temporary window, as I burn, I have the imprint of Rich's flame and the dancing of all the other flames, both imprinted and burning, to keep me company.

What more do I need? I dance with eternity each time I melt in a sunset, enjoy waves crashing on a shore or soak in the imprint of Rich's presence. I dance with eternity, I have danced with eternity and I will dance with eternity. In that much, I believe. Burn brightly.

❧ ACKNOWLEDGMENTS ❧

A book is not an individual endeavor, though it may appear that way. So many people contributed to *The Philosophy of Rich* whether they realize it or not—everyone who provided input for the stories in the book, be it through commentary or participating in the events themselves. I would like to thank all who attended Rich's funeral service; your emotional response formed the genesis of this book. Thanks to everyone who read early versions of the book and provided me with feedback and support: Paula Polk, Quenton Washington, Matt Trelegan, Alex Zautra, Roberta Hayes-Bautista and Kevin Turnquist. Thank you to A. J. Sobczak, whose editing support helped me to see the book from a different angle, and Carrie Andrews, whose proofreading helped clean the book up. Thank you to Doris Bruey for her tireless graphic design efforts. Thanks to all Rich's friends who shared their stories. Thank you to my parents, Betty and Bob Courtemanche. Mom and Dad, your bravery and selflessness allowed this book to stand on its own. Thank you to my wife, Deana. Deana, there is no way this book would have turned out as it did without your love and support. And thank you to my brother, Richard Douglas Courtemanche. My brother, the book wouldn't have happened without you.

❧ BIBLIOGRAPHY ❧

PHILOSOPHY

Baggot, Jim. A Beginner's Guide to Reality. New York: Pegasus Books, 2006.

Bostrom, Nick. "Are You Living In a Computer Simulation?" Philosophical Quarterly Vol. 53, No. 211 (2003): 243-255.

de Botton, Alain. Status Anxiety. New York: Vintage Books, 2004.

de Botton, Alain. The Consolations of Philosophy. New York: Pantheon Books, 2000.

Clark, Andy and David Chalmers. "The Extended Mind." Analysis Vol. 58 (1998): 10-23.

Dennett, Daniel C. Kinds of Minds: Toward an Understanding of Consciousness. 1st ed. New York: Basic Books, 1996.

Dennett, Daniel C. Darwin's Dangerous Idea. New York: Touchstone, 1995.

Descartes, Rene. Descartes' Discourse on Method, and Other Writings. Trans. Arthur Wollaston. Baltimore, MD: Penguin Books, 1960.

Descartes, Rene. Discourse on The Method of Rightly Conducting the Reason and Seeking Truth in the Sciences. Project Gutenberg, 1993 [Etext# 59]. <http://www.gutenberg.org>.

Flanagan, Owen. The Problem of the Soul. New York: Basic Books, 2003.

Hume, David. The Philosophy of David Hume. Ed. V. C. Chappell. New York: Modern Library, 1963.

Hume, David. A Treastise on Human Nature. Project Gutenberg, 2003 [Etext #4705]. <http://www.gutenberg.org>.

Hume, David. "On Suicide." Philosophy Department St. Anselm College. 1996. St. Anselm College. <http://www.anselm.edu/homepage/dbanach/suicide.htm#A1>.

Kant, Immanuel. The Critique of Pure Reason: The Critique of Practical Reason and Other Ethical Treatises: The Critique of Judgment. Ed. Robert Maynard Hutchins. Chicago: Encyclopaedia Britannica, 1952.

Kant, Immanuel. The Critique of Pure Reason. Translated by J. M. D. Meiklejohn. Project Gutenberg, 2003 [Etext# 4280]. <http://www.gutenberg.org>.

Nietzsche, Friedrich. Thus Spoke Zarathustra. New York: The Modern Library, 1995.

Pirsig, Robert. Zen and the Art of Motorcyle Maintenance. New York: William and Morrow Company, 1974.

Plato. The Republic. Translated by Benjamin Jowett. Project Gutenberg, 1994 [Etext #150]. <http://www.gutenberg.org>.

Russell, Bertrand. History of Western Philosophy. London: Routledge, 2004.

Spinoza, Benedict De. Improvement of the Understanding: Ethics and Correspondence of Benedict de Spinoza. Trans. R. H. M. Elwes. New York: M.W. Dunne, 1901.

Spinoza, Benedict De. The Ethics of Benedict de Spinoza: Demonstrated after the Method of Geometers, and Divided into Five Parts, in Which Are Treated Separately: I. of God. II. of the Soul. III. of the Affections or Passions. IV. of Man's Slavery, or the Force of the Passions. V. of Man's Freedom. Vol. 1. New York: D. Van Nostrand, 1876.

Watts, Alan. The Book. New York: Vintage Books, 1989.

PSYCHOLOGY

Ekman, Paul. Emotions Revealed. New York: Henry Holt and Company, 2004.

Frankl, Victor E. Man's Search for Meaning. New York: Touchstone, 1984.

Freud, Sigmond. The Interpretation of Dreams. New York: Random House, 1950.

Healy, David. "The Latest Mania: Selling Bipolar Disorder." PLoS Med 3(4): e185 <http://medicine.plosjournals.org/perlserv/?request=get-document&doi=10.1371/journal.pmed.0030185>

Izard, C. E. The face of emotion. New York: Appleton-Century-Crofts, 1971.

Janowsky, D.S., M. Leff and R.S. Epstein. "Playing the Manic Game." Arch Gen Psychiatry Vol. 22 (1970): 252-6.

Jenkins, Janis H. "Chapter 3 Cross-Cultural Studies of Depression." Psychosocial Aspects of Depression. Ed. Joseph Becker and Arthur Kleinman. Hillsdale, NJ: Lawrence Erlbaum Associates, 1991. 67-91.

Jung, Carl Gustav. The Portable Jung. Edited by Joseph Campbell. New York: Penguin Books, 1971.

Menninger, Karl. Man Against Himself. New York: Harcourt, Brace & World, 1938.

Mondimore, Francis. Bipolar Disorder, A Guide for Patients and Families. Baltimore, MD: The Johns Hopkins University Press, 1999.

Papolos, Demitri and Janice Papolos. The Bipolar Child. New York: Broadway Books, 1999.

Pope, H.G., G.H. Cohane, G. Kanayama, A.J. Siegel and J.I. Hudson. "Testosterone gel supplementation for men with refractory depression: a randomized, placebo-controlled trial." American Journal of Psychiatry. Vol. 160, Issue 1(2003):105-11.

Pope, H.G., and D. L. Katz. "Affective and psychotic symptoms associated with anabolic steroid use." American Journal of Psychiatry Vol. 145, Issue 4 (1988): 487-490.

Roeckelein, Jon E. The Concept of Time in Psychology: A Resource Book and Annotated Bibliography. Westport, CT: Greenwood Press, 2000.

Sapolsky, Robert. "Taming Stress." Scientific American September 2003: 87-95.

Silverman, Julian. "Shamans and Acute Schizophrenia." American Anthropologist New Series, Vol. 69, No. 1 (1967): 21-31

Strong, Marilee. A Bright Red Scream. New York: Penguin Books, 1999.

Sturt, Mary. The Psychology of Time. London: Kegan Paul Trench, Trubner & Co., Ltd., 1925.

Torrey, E. Fuller and Michael B. Knable. Surviving Manic Depression. New York: Basic Books, 2005.

Turnquist, Kevin. "Are We Becoming a Nation of Depressives?" The Humanist Sept.-Oct. 2002: 27+.

Waltz, Mimi. Bipolar Disorders, A Guide to Helping Children and Adolescents. Sebastopol, CA: O'Reilly Media, 2000.

Warner, Richard. Recovery from Schizophrenia: Psychiatry and Political Economy. New York: Brunner-Routledge, 2004.

Zautra, Alex J. Emotions, Stress, and Health. New York: Oxford University Press, 2003.

SCIENCE

Bohm, David. Wholeness and the Implicate Order. New York: Routledge, 2002.

Clark, Mary E. In Search of Human Nature. London: Routledge, 2002.

Davies, Paul. "That Mysterious Flow." Scientific American September 2002: 40-47.

Deutsch, David. The Fabric of Reality: The Science of Parallel Universes and Its Implications. New York: Penguin, 1998.

Duke, Richard C., David M. Ojcius and John Ding-E Young. "Cell Suicide in Health and Disease." Scientific American December 1996: 80-87.

Edelman, Gerald M. and Giulio Tononi. A Universe of Consciousness: How Matter Becomes Imagination. 1st ed. New York: Basic Books, 2000.

Feynman, Richard. Surely You're Joking, Mr. Feynman. New York: Bantom Books, 1986.

Greene, Brian. The Elegant Universe. New York: Vintage Books, 2003.

Halevy, Sima, Hani Giryes, Michael Friger, Nili Grossman, Zeev Karpas, Batia Sarov and Shaul Sukenik. "The Role of Trace Elements in Psoriatic Patients Undergoing Balneotherapy with Dead Sea Bath Salt." IMAJ Vol. 3 (2001): 828-832.

Halpern, Paul. The Pursuit of Destiny: A History of Prediction. Cambridge, MA: Perseus Publishing, 2000.

Hawking, Stephen W. A Brief History of Time. New York: Bantom Books, 1988.

Jones, Roger S. Physics for the Rest of Us. Chicago: Contemporary Books, 1992.

Linde, Andrei. "Universe, Life, Consciousness." Andrei Linde Website. 2002. Stanford University Department of Physics. <http://www.stanford.edu/~alinde/SpirQuest.doc>

Musser, George. "A Hole at the Heart of Physics." Scientific American September 2002: 48-49.

Pickrell, John H. "Chimps Belong on Human Branch of Family Tree, Study Says." National Geographic News. May 20, 2003. National Geographic.com. <http://news.nationalgeographic.com/news/2003/05/0520_030520_chimpanzees.html>.

Raymo, Chet. Natural Prayers. Saint Paul, MN: Ruminator Books, 1999.

Rees, Martin. "The Multiverse." Whole Earth Winter 1997: 69+.

Schacter, Daniel L. Searching for Memory: The Brain, the Mind, and the Past. 1st ed. New York: Basic Books, 1996.

Spalding, Kirsty L., Ratan D. Bhardwaj, Bruce A. Buchholz, Henrik Druid and Jonas Frisén. "Retrospective Birth Dating of Cells in Humans." Cell Vol. 122 (2005): 133–143.

Tegmark, Max. "Parallel Universes." Astrophysics. February 2003. lanl.arXiv.org. <http://arxiv.org/abs/astro-ph/0302131>.

Tegmark, Max. "100 Years of the Quantum." Astrophysics. Jan 2001. lanl.arXiv.org. <http://xxx.lanl.gov/abs/quant-ph/0101077>.

Weinberg, Steven. "A Designer Universe?" Physics & Astronomy Online. 1999. PhysLink.com. 13 September 2006 <http://www.physlink.com/Education/essay_weinberg.cfm>.

Zukav, Gary. The Dancing Wu Li Masters. New York: Perennial Classics, 2001.

"Preventing Cells from Committing Suicide." USA Today (Society for the Advancement of Education) June 1998: 4+.

Sociology

Boorstin, Daniel J. The Americas: The Democratic Experience. New York: Vintage Books, 1974.

Bryson, Bill. A Short History of Nearly Everything. New York: Broadway Books, 2003.

Campbell, Joseph. Myths to Live By. New York: Penguin Compass, 1972.

Campbell, Joseph. The Hero With a Thousand Faces. Princeton, NJ: Princeton University Press, 1968.

Durkheim, Emile. Readings from Emile Durkheim. Edited by Kenneth Thompson. New York, Routledge, 1985.

Erdoes, Richard and John (Fire) Lame Deer. Lame Deer Seeker of Visions. New York: Touchstone, 1972.

Frazer, Sir James George. The Golden Bough. New York: The Macmillan Company, 1951.

Heat-Moon, William Least. Blue Highways. New York: Little, Brown and Company, 1999.

Heichelheim, Fritz M. An Ancient Economic History: From the Palaeolithic Age to the Migrations of the Germanic, Slavic and Arabic Nations. Trans. Joyce Stevens. Revised ed. Vol. 1. Leiden, The Netherlands: A.W. Sijthoff, 1957.

Hewett, John H. After Suicide. Louisville, KY: The Westminster Press, 1980.

Hine, Thomas. I Want That! New York: Perennial, 2003.

Hooff, Anton J. L.Van. From Autothanasia to Suicide: Self-Killing in Classical Antiquity. London: Routledge, 1990.

Kinsey, Alfred Charles, Wardell B. Pomeroy and Clyde E. Martin. Sexual Behavior in the Human Male. Philadelphia: W B Saunders Co, 1948.

Lambert, Craig. "The Marketplace of Perceptions." Harvard Magazine March-April 2006: 50+.

Minois, Georges. History of Suicide. Baltimore, MD: The Johns Hopkins University Press, 1999.

Neihardt, John G. Black Elk Speaks. Lincoln, NE: University of Nebraska Press, 1988.

Nuland, Sherwin B. How We Die. New York: Alfred A. Knopf, 1994.

Robinson, Rita. Survivors of Suicide. New Jersey: New Page Books, 2001.

Shakespeare, William. Hamlet, Prince of Denmark (Collins edition). Project Gutenberg, 1998 [Etext #1524]. <http://www.gutenberg.org>.

Steinbeck, John. East of Eden. New York: Penguin Books, 2002.

Twitchell, James B. Lead Us into Temptation: The Triumph of American Materialism. New York: Columbia University Press, 1999.

STATISTICS

WHO. "Disability adjusted life years (DALY) [xls 884kb]: Estimates of DALYs by sex, cause and WHO Region for 2002." Revised Global Burden of Disease (GBD) 2002 Estimates. 2005. The World Health Organization. <http://www.who.int/healthinfo/ statistics/gbdwhoregiondaly2002.xls>.

WHO. "DALYs by WHO Region [xls 1.54Mb]: Projected DALYs for 2005, 2015 and 2030 by WHO Region under the baseline scenario." Projections of mortality and burden of disease to 2030. 2006. The World Health Organization. <http://www.who.int/ healthinfo/statistics/bod_dalybywhoregion.xls>.

NOTE: The two WHO spreadsheets above were used for the disability rankings described in Chapter One in the section "A Primer on Bipolar Disorder." Both spreadsheets share the same format. The disability rankings were determined for 2002 and 2030 as follows: (1) the Cause utilized was the third level of detail or column E, and (2) the number of Disability-Adjusted Life Years (or "disability") utilized was in the first Total column or column G—which aggregated all ages groups for both males and females.

THEOLOGY

Aquinas, Thomas. Translated by Fathers of the English Dominican Province. Summa Theologica, Part II-II (Secunda Secundae). Project Gutenberg, 2006 [EBook #18755]. <http://www.gutenberg.org>.

Armstrong, Karen. A History of God. New York: Ballentine Books, 1993.

St. Augustine. St. Augustine's City of God and Christian Doctrine. New York: The Christian Literature Publishing Co., 1890.

St. Augustine. The City of God. New York: The Modern Library, 2000.

Bachelor, Stephen. Buddhism Without Beliefs. New York: Riverhead Books, 1997.

Berling, Judith A. "Chapter 13 Death and Afterlife in Chinese Religions." Death and Afterlife: Perspectives of World Religions. Ed. Hiroshi Obayashi. New York: Praeger, 1992. 181-189.

The Bible, King James version, Book 5: Deuteronomy. Project Gutenberg, 2005 [EBook #8005]. <http://www.gutenberg.org>.

The Bible, King James version, Book 2: Exodus. Project Gutenberg, 2005 [EBook #8002]. <http://www.gutenberg.org>.

The Bible, King James version, Book 40: Matthew. Project Gutenberg, 2005 [EBook #8040]. <http://www.gutenberg.org>.

The Holy Bible, New International Version. Grand Rapids, MI: Zondervan Publishing House, 1997.

Bond, George C. "Chapter 1 Living with Spirits: Death and Afterlife in African Religions." Death and Afterlife: Perspectives of World Religions. Ed. Hiroshi Obayashi. New York: Praeger, 1992. 3-16.

Brown, William Adams. The Life of Prayer in a World of Science. New York: C. Scribner's Sons, 1928.

Goldenberg, Robert. "Chapter 7 Bound Up in the Bond of Life: Death and Afterlife in the Jewish Tradition." Death and Afterlife: Perspectives of World Religions. Ed. Hiroshi Obayashi. New York: Praeger, 1992. 97-105.

James, William. Varieties of Religious Experience. Project Gutenberg, 1996 [Etext #621]. <http://www.gutenberg.org>.

Obayashi, Hiroshi, ed. Death and Afterlife: Perspectives of World Religions. New York: Praeger, 1992.

Rinpoche, Sogyal. The Tibetan Book of Living and Dying. New York: HarperCollins, 2002.

To order additional copies of *The Philosophy of Rich*, please visit
www.thephilosophyofrich.com